Notes from the Balkans

PRINCETON MODERN GREEK STUDIES

This series is sponsored by the Princeton University Program in Hellenic Studies under the auspices of the Stanley J. Seeger Hellenic Fund.

Firewalking and Religious Healing: The Anastenaria of Greece and the American Firewalking Movement *by Loring M. Danforth*

Dance and the Body Politic in Northern Greece *by Jane K. Cowan*

Yannis Ritsos: Repetitions, Testimonies, Parentheses *edited and translated by Edmund Keeley*

Contested Identities: Gender and Kinship in Modern Greece *edited by Peter Loizos and Evthymios Papataxiarchis*

A Place in History: Social and Monumental Time in a Cretan Town *by Michael Herzfeld*

Demons and the Devil: Moral Imagination in Modern Greek Culture *by Charles Stewart*

The Enlightenment as Social Criticism: Iosipos Moisiodax and Greek Culture in the Eighteenth Century *by Paschalis M. Kitromilides*

C. P. Cavafy: Collected Poems *translated by Edmund Keeley and Philip Sherrard; edited by George Savidis*

The Fourth Dimension *by Yannis Ritsos. Peter Green and Beverly Bardsley, translators*

George Seferis: Collected Poems, Revised Edition *translated, edited, and introduced by Edmund Keeley and Philip Sherrard*

In a Different Place: Pilgrimage, Gender, and Politics at a Greek Island Shrine *by Jill Dubisch*

Cavafy's Alexandria, Revised Edition *by Edmund Keeley*

The Films of Theo Angelopoulos: A Cinema of Contemplation *by Andrew Horton*

The Muslim Bonaparte: Diplomacy and Orientalism in Ali Pasha's Greece *by Katherine E. Fleming*

Venom in Verse: Aristophanes in Modern Greece *by Gonda A. H. Van Steen*

A Shared World: Christians and Muslims in the Early Modern Mediterranean *by Molly Greene*

After the War Was Over: Reconstructing the Family, Nation, and State in Greece, 1943–1960 *edited by Mark Mazower*

Notes from the Balkans: Locating Marginality and Ambiguity on the Greek-Albanian Border *by Sarah F. Green*

Notes from the Balkans

LOCATING MARGINALITY AND AMBIGUITY
ON THE GREEK-ALBANIAN BORDER

Sarah F. Green

PRINCETON UNIVERSITY PRESS

PRINCETON AND OXFORD

Library of Congress Cataloging-in-Publication Data

Green, Sarah F., 1961–
Notes from the Balkans : locating marginality and ambiguity on
Greek-Albanian border / Sarah F. Green
p. cm. — (Princeton modern Greek studies)
Includes bibliographical references and index.
ISBN 0-691-12198-2 (cl : alk. paper) — ISBN 0-691-12199-0 (pbk. : alk. paper)
1. Marginality, Social—Greece—Pågåni Region. 2. Pågåni (Greece : Region)—
Social conditions. 3. Hybridity (Social sciences)—Epirus (Greece and Albania)
4. Epirus (Greece and Albania)—Ethnic relations. 5. Greeks—Epirus (Greece
and Albania)—History—20th century. 6. Greece—Boundaries. 7. Albania—
Boundaries. I. Title. II. Series.
HN650.5.Z9M264 2005
305.5′6′094953—dc22

                                                                2004058686

British Library Cataloging-in-Publication Data is available

This book has been composed in Sabon

Printed on acid-free paper. ∞

pup.princeton.edu

Printed in the United States of America

10 9 8 7 6 5 4 3 2 1

*To all the people of Pogoni, who taught me
to see differently*

Contents

Maps and Figures

Tables

All the tables are located in the appendix, page 249.

Acknowledgments

I OWE DEBTS AND THANKS to hundreds of people as a result of having spent more than ten years carrying out the research for, and writing, this book. They contributed hugely to any insights it contains and, as important, to the passion the topic evoked in me. I wish I could name all these people, for their contributions weave through this text. Of course, omissions and misunderstandings are entirely my responsibility.

All the people I met around the Kasidiaris mountain almost invariably treated me with generosity, kindness, and compassion for my ignorance. I owe particular thanks to the people of Mavropoulo, Zavroho, Katarraktis, Doliana, Ktismata, Delvinaki, Despotiko, Dolo, Pogoniani, and Pontikates. Also, the numerous civil servants in Ioannina and elsewhere whom I kept pestering were extremely generous with their time, especially those at the Ioannina offices of the Department of Agriculture, the Office of the Statistical Service of Greece, the Department of Land Improvements, the Forestry Commission, and the Union of Municipalities and Communes of Ioannina Prefecture. I am also very grateful for the help provided by staff at Epirous S.A.

My introduction to Epirus more than twenty years ago was made possible by Geoff Bailey, who allowed me to participate in his Paleolithic rock shelter excavation at Klithi way back in the summer of 1983, after I simply turned up without notice as a second-year undergraduate. That sparked my fascination with the area, for it was nothing like my previous experience of Greece (growing up on the island of Lesbos and later living in Athens), and I began to wonder about the difference. Nine years later and shortly after I had completed a doctorate in social anthropology, Geoff gave me the opportunity to pursue my interest when he invited me to carry out a brief ethnographic project in Epirus in 1992. That was supposed to last three weeks, but in the event it marked the beginning of many years of research; I asked for more time because in three weeks all I learned was that I understood nothing at all. The extended research was made possible by Sander van der Leeuw, the coordinator of the various research projects that funded my time in Epirus over the years. Sander was unstintingly supportive and generous with his time, and he allowed me free rein to research more or less what I liked, a real rarity in large research programs these days. Without his support, and the financial support from a range of sources, this book would not have been possible. I owe special thanks for financial support over many years to DGXII of the European Commission, the University of Manchester, and Churchill College, Cambridge. Further, the Department of Social Anthropology at the University of Manchester allowed me the time to work on the manuscript and provided support in many other ways, and Churchill College granted me a six-month fellowship in 2000, which allowed me to nurture the seeds of this book.

The following people helped and supported me in Epirus both intellectually and personally in innumerable ways over the years: Eugenia Adam and Peros; the Kirgios family in Doliana, especially Ritsa Kirgiou; Maria Anagnostou and Michalis Anagnostos, as well as Dina, Pitsa, Michalis, and Yiannis; Victoria Matsia, as well as Angeliki, Fani, and Polyxeni at Ktismata; Spiros Petalas; Kostas Matsis; Kostas Zongas; Makis Chrisafis; Kostas Miriounis; Vasilis Nitsiakos and Voula Papapetrou.

I want particularly to mention Aspasia Theodosiou (Sissi) here. Sissi provided continual intellectual inspiration both in Epirus and during her time as a postgraduate student at Manchester, and has been enormously helpful in many practical ways as well, from finding me obscure references to keeping me continuously in touch with Epirus when it has been impossible for me to be there in person. She also kept reminding me that I needed to finish this book, and when academic life is so full of other distractions, that was an invaluable regular prod in the ribs.

Over the years, Geoff King has provided constant intellectual collaboration, companionship, and lengthy conversations during this research, whether in Epirus or elsewhere. That his technical and intellectual skill made the maps in this book possible has been the least of his contributions (and I apologize to him for being unable to reproduce them in color); we jointly worked out many issues to do with what on earth "place" might mean, and he provided me with innumerable ways to understand the gaps between anthropology and the geophysical sciences in that respect. It has been a rare privilege to work with him, despite (or rather because of) the habit we developed of continually challenging each other's most cherished assumptions.

There are numerous anthropologists to whom I owe a special debt. Michael Herzfeld and James Faubion read the manuscript and constructively commented upon it with enormous care, wonderful advice, and encouraging generosity just at the moment I most needed it. Furthermore, they saved me from reproducing most of the linguistic idiosyncrasies that I developed through growing up bilingual in Greek and English. Karen Sykes repeatedly came up with the right thing for me to read at the right time; my conversations with her about issues in this book have been truly invaluable, particularly for chapter 4. Marilyn Strathern has been an intellectual inspiration and challenge to me for many years; she has also been extraordinarily generous with her time and made especially helpful comments on early versions of some of the arguments in this book. Jane Cowan and Anastasia Karakasidou have been equally generous with their time and comments; Georgios Agelopoulos, Alexandra Bakalaki, and Dimitris Theodosopoulos also made very helpful comments. In addition, Beverley Skeggs's reading of a nascent introductory chapter gave me the inspiration to carry on. I repeat that any omissions, errors, and lack of understanding in the text are my responsibility.

I have gained much inspiration and food for thought from the audiences of various seminars and conferences, particularly those given at the University of Cambridge, the University of Manchester, the University of Sussex, the University of Oxford, the Center for Slavonic and South-east European Studies at London University, the Center for Byzantine, Ottoman and Modern Greek studies at Birmingham University, Goldsmiths College London, the London School of Economics, and the University of York.

Mary Murrell at Princeton University Press made the whole editorial process almost entirely painless for me, and she was a source of continual encouragement at crucial moments, even during the final period of her time at the Press, ensuring a seamless handover to Fred Appel. Hanne Winarsky and Dimitri Karetnikov have been similarly unstintingly and generously helpful; their skill, care, and willingness to help beyond the call of duty made the final production stages for both the text and the artwork much less of a nightmare than they could have been. Lauren Lepow's copyediting was truly fantastic, and I will always be grateful to her for it.

On a more personal note, I owe several people debts for their patience while I secluded myself away to complete this book. I owe special thanks to Penny Harvey, who generously put our joint projects on hold while I worked on this one, and who also provided intellectual inspiration over the years we have worked together. Thanks are also due to Nikoleta Katsakiori, Susanne Langer, Paul Hawkins, Sarah Staves, Lucy Pickering, and Anita Jones, all of whom have been immensely patient with the fact that my attention has been directed away from postgraduate supervision for more months than I care to admit. In addition, Nikoleta has been particularly helpful in finding me obscure references just at the moment I needed them. I am especially grateful to Nikoleta for putting me in touch with Asterios Koukoudis, who was also extremely generous with his time.

Finally, I would never have stopped endlessly rewriting this book without the enormous support and patience of Andrea Campbell. She has helped me find the determination I needed to see this project through, as well as the courage to realize that nothing is ever complete, not only in Epirus but also in writing books about Epirus.

The University of Manchester
June 1, 2004

Notes on Transliteration, Translation, and Pseudonyms

In transliterating Greek terms, I was principally guided by how the language sounds when spoken, rather than strictly adhering to formal textual rules. The following table provides an outline guide of the "system" that evolved out of that effort.

Single letters

Αα	a	Ββ	v	Γγ	g
Δδ	d	Εε	e	Ζζ	z
Ηη	i	Θθ	th	Ιι	i
Κκ	k	Λλ	l	Μμ	m
Νν	n	Ξξ	x *or* ks	Οο	o
Ππ	p	Ρρ	r	Σσς	s
Ττ	t	Υυ	y *or* i	Φφ	f
Χχ	h *or* ch	Ψψ	ps	Ωω	o

Digraphs

αι	ai	αυ	av	ει	ei
ου	ou	γκ	g	μπ	b
ντ	nd *or* d	ευ	ef *or* ev	οι	i *or* oi

One important exception is the word *Gréki*. This is not in fact a transliteration, as I only heard the word spoken and have not seen it written down in a Greek dictionary precisely as it was spoken (see the final section of chapter 2, "On *Gréki*").

Where I quote authors writing in English who have themselves used transliterations, I have retained their conventions.

TRANSLATION

The book contains numerous conversations that I had with people in Epirus over the years, some of which appear in the text as direct quotations, and all of which I translated from Greek into English. In many cases, I had taped the conversations; in other cases, I took detailed notes while I spoke with people. I had practiced memory skills before beginning fieldwork and occasionally tested myself for accuracy by taking notes as well as taping a conversation, and then comparing the two.

In every case I have attempted to capture what I understood to be both the tone and the meaning intended by the speakers in the context in which they were speaking. Whenever possible, I relied upon direct translation of Greek words into English ones; where I felt the meaning of a Greek word was not reflected in the literal English translation of the word, or where there was no obvious English equivalent, I used a word that I thought came as close as possible to the speaker's intended meaning.

PSEUDONYMS

I have used pseudonyms for all the people discussed in the book, with the rare exceptions of some public officials, whose genuine names have been used. All the pseudonyms are names used by people in Epirus, but no pseudonym has been selected for its similarity to a person's actual name. I use "Dimitris" and "Spiros" to refer to more than one person because these were particularly common names in Epirus.

Notes from the Balkans

CHAPTER 1

Marginal Margins

THIS IS A STORY ABOUT the marginality of both place and people, and how their marginality is continually reconstructed while somehow also staying the same. The place is in and around Epirus, a region in northwestern Greece (map 1); the story mostly concerns an area known as Pogoni, which, depending on how you look at it, either runs along or straddles the Greek-Albanian border (maps 2 and 3). And the people are those who live in, pass through, or come and go around this place, most particularly around the Kasidiaris mountain, a relatively small and not much noted landmark in the southern part of the Pogoni area. It is difficult to give any more specific details about either the place or the people just yet, precisely because of their marginality: they both are and are not something, somewhere, and someone in particular.

"Marginality" is a tricky word, a kind of poor relation to "otherness" and "difference"; it explicitly evokes a sense of unequal location as well as unequal relations: being where you are and being from somewhere always matters, even if it does not mean you stay in one place, either physically or perceptually, for any length of time (Gupta and Ferguson 1999b: 3–17; Clifford 1997: 2–3). That is one of the problems with the condition of being marginal: it is not necessarily clear exactly where you are or where you are from, and that can make you only partially visible, only partially connected.[1] Ironically, during this period of emphasis on transnationalism, transmigration, and multiculturalism, being marginal can negatively affect your ability to have a name that could be used to challenge whatever center happens to be significant at the moment.[2] As James Boon put it in describing himself as marginal, this kind of marginality sometimes involves being "interpretively homeless, devoid of passport, alienated from certainties and edges as well; even the borderlands refuse me shelter" (Boon 1999: 198).

In those terms, marginality implies a difficult and ambivalent relevance to the heart of things. Perhaps for that reason, there has been a fascination with marginality in Euro-American anthropology, a sense that shining a spotlight on the discarded, ignored, shifting, semivisible, and perhaps transgressive nooks and crannies, where many anthropologists find themselves anyway in the course of their exploration of otherness, might help to make the implicit explicit, might draw out the hidden cogs, wheels, or (cob)webs of what we know to be central, and might provide an antidote to master narratives (Seremetakis 1991: 1–7) . Marginality, too, can become part of the heart of things, precisely because of its asserted marginalization in relation to the heart of things.

Beyond anthropology, marginality has also become increasingly noted and remarked upon in recent years, partly as a result of numerous studies of what goes into making people and places marginal in the first place, in terms of both how it occurs and what the consequences of marginality might be.[3] In one particularly pertinent example for my purposes, Misha Glenny suggests that the continual interventions of the "Great Powers" into the Balkan region's conflicts—most recently in those involving former Yugoslavia and Kosovo—generated the Balkans as a very particular kind of place, as *the* margin of Europe, and also made the place a key center of attention (Glenny 1999: xxiii–xxv). After quoting John Gunther's assertion that "these wretched and unhappy little countries in the Balkan peninsula can, and do, have quarrels that cause world wars" (ibid.: xxiii), Glenny argues that this kind of perspective "reflects a solid body of Western popular opinion that regarded and still regards the Balkans as a toxin threatening the health of Europe" (ibid.: xxiv). One could hardly be more simultaneously marginal and central than that.

Marginality has, of course, also taken a central place in the ethnography of Greece, though this is not often directly related to Greece as part of the Balkans. Michael Herzfeld's work focuses on Greece as being "in the Margins of Europe" (Herzfeld 1987), somewhere at the crossroads between East and West (Herzfeld 1997: 97).[4] He explores the diverse ways (disemic, in Herzfeld's terms) in which Greeks imagine being Greek, and how this became entangled in the creation of a sense of national homogeneity in Greece out of a tense combination of Western (Hellenic) and Eastern (Byzantine) concepts. In the course of this, Herzfeld discusses, and critiques, how contemporary Greece has been marginalized both in Europe and in anthropology, partly as a result of a perceived ambivalence about how to locate Greece in modern binary divisions between East and West. He repeatedly points out that Greece is the only country in Europe which has the word "modern" placed before its name, implying that (to the modern mind), the classical version was much more at the heart of things, or perhaps even at the root of things.

Herzfeld is by no means alone in his reliance on the concept of marginality in analyzing Greek ethnography. For example, Seremetakis describes the Inner Mani, located at the southern extreme of mainland Greece, as "a detached fragment of a global modernity" in which she "explores the internal margins that organize the relation of Inner Mani to that modernity" (Seremetakis 1991: 1). Seremetakis insists that the kind of marginality she is describing (a "fragment") is not necessarily dependent upon any center: "To stand in the margin is to look through it at other margins and at the so-called center itself" (ibid.). And the significance of that, for Seremetakis, is that the women of Inner Mani whom she focuses upon constitute another example of the ability to identify "strategies of resistance that emerge and subsist in the margins" (ibid.).

A third approach can be seen in the work of Evthymios Papataxiarchis, who analyzes gambling among men in coffeehouses in a village in northern Lesbos as an aspect of "counter-hegemonic space that was historically established in conditions of the prolonged political and economic marginalization of the island" (Papataxiarchis 1999: 158). He treats gambling as a form of "constructive resistance" (ibid.: 159). Here, the marginalization in question is considered in terms of political economy: the men who gamble are "denied access to state-controlled political and economic resources" (ibid.: 160), and they come to equate money with the hierarchies and dependence generated by the state. In this, gambling "seems to be a major symbolic gesture of emancipation from economic debt, of defiance of the institutional producers of money; it is an important response to economic dependence, social displacement, and class marginalization. In this capacity, it can become an extreme demonstration of autonomy" (ibid.: 172).

Herzfeld's, Seremetakis's, and Papataxiarchis's studies are just three examples of the search for resistance, forms of empowerment, forms of critique, in and around margins and marginality—a common theme, not only in the anthropology of Greece, but in much of the rest of anthropology as well.[5] Sometimes, such studies can draw out how marginality itself can be strategically emphasized or even generated by people who are marginalized, such that marginality is turned against the center. As Anna Tsing has noted for the Meratus Dayaks of South Kilamantan in Indonesia, some "marginal" people can make their own marginality central: "The cultural difference of the margins is a sign of exclusion from the center; it is also a tool for destabilizing central authority" (Tsing 1993: 27). The value of Tsing's comment is to make the point that marginality is not so much imposed as negotiated, and that it is not necessary to forget the imbalances of power involved—the power to exclude places and people, for example—to recognize this point.

These kinds of studies often constitute challenges to (Euro-American) modernity in its self-satisfied mode: they take a poke at the certainty of modernity's omniscience and superiority, both morally and intellectually. At other times, marginality is used to explore (Euro-American) modernity in its self-pitying mode: the sense of having lost something through being modern, usually something involving authenticity, and wanting to have it back. Here, anthropologists have analyzed the search for redemption in margins. For example, Kathleen Stewart suggests that marginality within the United States generates spaces or gaps in which it is imagined a lost "authenticity" might still exist, an imagining that renders such places central because of their marginality: "There is a dream that somewhere out there—in the space of marginalia and ex-centricity—there are 'places' still caught in the ongoing density of sociality and desire. Places to which 'we' might return—in mind, if not in body—in search of redemption and renewal" (Stewart 1996: 5).

Whatever aspect of marginality is focused upon, these examples are enough to show that marginality has been repeatedly regarded as geographically, politically, socially, culturally, and/or temporally significant, and has become more so in recent decades, partly as a result of changing transnational relations (Danforth 1995), and international and supranational agencies involved in recognizing and supporting human rights, especially for those peoples defined as minorities (Cowan, Dembour, and Wilson 2001). Boon goes so far as to suggest that attacking the center (whichever center that may be) through focusing on any number of marginalities is now standard practice, both in the academy and outside of it, and has resulted in a plethora of "isms" and identities. However, for Boon, these "isms" and identities do not constitute the essence of marginality. For him, what makes something truly marginal is its *inability* to become an "ism" or to be "identitied," as he puts it (Boon 1999: 208). He uses the example of Tantric practices: "usages customarily designated Tantric, whether Hindu or Buddhist, do not necessarily mark off any corporate identity or 'ism' (even underground). They include a gamut of transgressions—a polymorphous reservoir of ex-centric ritual possibilities" (ibid.: 207). For Boon, then, to be marginal (both for himself and for "ex-centric" ritual practices) is to be in between rather than on the peripheries: it is to be neither one thing nor another, or possibly too much both one thing and another.

This more recent fascination with ambiguous marginality, a focus on its fluidity, its lack of boundaries, and the inability to pin it down, marked a turn toward an interest in the postmodern, either as a condition in the world (postmodernity; Harvey 1990) or as an intellectual approach to challenge modernity (postmodernism): having done away with the self-satisfied and self-pitying certainties of modernity, the postmodern dwells in uncertainty and a refusal of borders. Some saw considerable potential for escape from the hegemonic in that. However, rather than resistance, this approach emphasizes inventiveness, the possibility of making something new out of making things uncertain.[6] Terence Turner, for example, in his analysis of the rise of the explicit use of culture in politics, advocates "critical multiculturalism" as a means to avoid essentialist notions of culture embedded within what he calls "difference multiculturalism" (and what many others have referred to as "identity politics"). In this, Turner approvingly quotes Stam and Shohat (n.d.): critical multiculturalism, they say, "rejects a unified, essentialist concept of identity. . . . Rather, it sees the self as polycentric, multiple, unstable, historically situated, the product of ongoing differentiation and polymorphous identifications" (Turner 1993: 418).

Such a focus on the way modernity tried to hide its own lack of fixity, its underlying fluidity and instability, is not limited to anthropology or to more recent postmodernist theory, of course. Aside from Bruno Latour and other actor network theorists,[7] as well as Judith Butler and other queer theorists,[8] there are also those who have focused on the places and spaces of marginality. Walter Benjamin, for one, became fascinated by the Parisian arcades, which were derelict and abandoned when he passed through them, but had been built in the mid–nineteenth century by people who were at the heart of things, and who had believed that the arcades would shape Paris forever (Benjamin 1999; Day 2001: 110). Or Michel de Certeau, for another, who wandered around the "waste products" of cities, arguing that cities inevitably generate marginal places because city planners keep executing plans about how cities should be, thus axiomatically creating anomalies and gaps: places and people that do not fit the plan (de Certeau 1988: 94).

Whether marginality is depicted as a kind of periphery containing distinct people or places that have been ignored and/or oppressed, and/or misrepresented by the center, or as the ambiguous flotsam and jetsam of life that has been discarded or hidden in the process by which things are made to seem clear, bounded, and fixed, there is often a warm hope implied in these studies of marginality, even an assertion at times, that focusing on it will show marginality to be truly central, at the heart of the matter (Stewart 1996; Herzfeld 1987); and that it will demonstrate the incoherence of what we think we are sure about (Steedly 1993; Tsing 1993), and therefore that it will highlight the ultimate pointlessness of trying to pin things down, showing that master narratives never have the last word (Seremetakis 1991), and that this goes as much for anthropological narratives as for any others (Riles 2000; Herzfeld 1987). Even Boon's perspective, which describes marginality as something that cannot cohere into an identity or "ism," as a condition that generates an inability to engage in the "self-other," "center-periphery," "identity politics," and "cultural fundamentalism" (Stolcke 1995; 1999) projects that are generated in the current version of modernity (or postmodernity, call it what you will)[9]—even Boon is hopeful that there might be ways to challenge the normative through marginality:

Not quite invisible, opaque polymorphoses refract forces of regimental surveillance, evade bureaucratic stratification, and dodge centralized control. Some "Tantric practices" may be better at "deviating" from enforced conformity than are sect-ualities or sexualities when "identi-tied", incorporated, or made into a dogmatic *cause*. (Boon 1999: 208, emphasis original)[10]

Initially, I shared that hope when I began fieldwork in northwestern Greece. As I became familiar with the peoples and the place (Pogoni), I also became increasingly aware that they were being regularly described as not only marginal but marginal within the marginal. I had evidently chosen to be in a place and among people that few thought were worth paying attention to, which appeared to have something to do with their lack of distinction. While both people and place were identifiable in some senses, by the same folkloric[11] markers as identified others in the region (people could point to Pogoni traditional dress, easily identify Pogoni music, and know more or less where Pogoni is), they also seemed some-how nondescript or relatively undistinguished, compared to other places and peoples in Epirus. This comparison included a hierarchy of distinc-tiveness of geomorphology and vistas. For example, the Zagori, made famous in anthropology by John Campbell's study of the Sarakatsani (Campbell 1964), has also come to prominence more generally in recent years as the main tourist attraction of the region, containing as it does the biggest national park of the area, one of the more starkly attractive and climbable mountains (the Gamilla/Timfi; map 3), deep forests, fast-flow-ing, clear-water rivers, mountain gorges and valleys, and villages that have been "conserved" through regulations preventing the use of anything ex-cept local and "traditional" building materials, and by various recon-structions of "traditional settlements." All of this contrasted starkly with the predominantly fairly low, shrubby, and scrubby landscape that charac-terized Pogoni, the absence of a national park there, and little in the way of conservation or preservation of villages. And a distinctly uncomfort-able issue—that is, an issue whose implications were usually avoided—was that "traditional" Pogoni, the Pogoni used to evoke folklore and cultural heritage, stretched beyond the Greek state boundary into south-ern Albania, a region known in Greece as Northern Epirus. This had been a repeatedly contested border, one that often involved states other than Greece and Albania (particularly Russia, Britain, Italy, and Germany in the years before the Cold War, the former USSR and China during the Cold War, and the European Union and NATO thereafter). The location of the border—which, despite the battles over the years, has shifted only slightly from the location designated when it was initially established as a state border in 1913 following the end of the Ottoman era—formally divided the peoples associated with the Pogoni area between two states.[12] It remains contested, at least in map form: there is a continual drawing and redrawing of borders across maps of this area, both in accounts about the history of the region and in more polemical texts about where the borders *should* be located—a habit that is shared with Macedonia, the region to the east of Epirus (Cowan and Brown 2000: 8).[13]

I will not pursue that issue much further yet, except to note two things. First, for many people associated with Pogoni, the process of locating the border (how it ended up there, ways in which it was negotiated and fought over), as well as its closure and reopening, did not appear to have a great deal to do with *them*, even though that ongoing process obviously affected their everyday lives.[14] And second, ever since the border was partially reopened (made permeable; some would say "leaky") following the political changes in Albania after 1991 (from socialist to "postsocialist"), there have been many events and debates that have increased, rather than decreased, the sense that people associated with this place are neither one thing nor another, or alternatively altogether too much both one thing and another, and somehow still not particularly noted or notable.

At times, it was difficult to avoid the easy conclusion that these peoples had been neither wealthy nor politically powerful, and this made their marginality (neither one thing nor the other, sometimes in an edgy way, sometimes not) of little consequence for others.[15] In any event, one of the strongest views expressed by the majority of people around this place was that it had been undergoing a process of abandonment and neglect for some decades: grazing lands that used to be intensively used for sheep and goat pastoralism were now overgrown; scattered fields on the hills and small valleys that used to be cultivated were now abandoned; schools once full of children were now closed down; village squares once bustling with activity were now quiet. In village after village, with few exceptions, people would sigh and say, "Only pensioners live here now."

Already, this view of the place suggested I would have difficulty in directly applying, here, analyses of marginality as resistance or inventiveness, as useful as such analyses are in other ways. This was so despite the fact that this depiction of abandonment was not quite all it seemed: many of the villages transformed from quiet, sleepy places into lively, bustling, and loud ones between winter and summer, as people arrived from cities both in Greece and elsewhere to spend summers in villages with which they were associated; some of these people, while not living there permanently, came and went fairly regularly in other ways as well (and had done so for the entirety of the remembered past, including the period when villages were full of children); and the opening of the Greek-Albanian border had led to a considerable amount of fuss (φασαρία) in the area, which, if the newspapers were to be believed, made the region the polar opposite of quiet and sleepy. But none of that detracted from many people's sense of an underlying lack of interest in and neglect of this place, as a place, and them, as people.

I became intrigued because this story of abandonment was told in every part of mountainous Epirus that I visited, and not only in Pogoni. However, it was also clear that different peoples, and different places, were not the same in what this was taken to mean. Pogoni was regarded, both by people associated with Pogoni and by people living in neighboring areas, as being worse off than most, except for one part of the Thesprotia region, just south of Pogoni. That region, like Pogoni, also runs along (or straddles) the Greek-Albanian border, and also has relatively low mountains and a scrubby landscape in comparison with some neighboring areas. At the other end of the spectrum, parts of Zagori and the peoples associated with that region were regarded as being a lot better off: their abandonment had been converted into a national park, which emphasized the natural wilderness of the place (abandonment becomes nature); and as I have already outlined, the region is now widely represented, both in tourist brochures and in folklore studies of the area, as having significant cultural heritage (abandonment becomes tradition and authenticity). That had not happened very effectively in Pogoni: despite the fact that polyphonic singing, a musical genre particularly associated with the people of this region, has in recent years come to typify Epirot music in the rest of Greece,[16] Pogoni as a place and Pogoni peoples remained somehow nondistinct, unclear—unrecognized, to use the language of recognition politics.[17]

While this form of marginality seemed somewhat more akin to Boon's definition of Tantric practices than it did to an "identity politics" kind of marginality, it did not seem to me to constitute a marginality of inventiveness or resistance—or, come to that, of accommodation in Nugent's terms (Nugent 1999). The depiction of abandonment in Pogoni was a mark of something else; it was one transformation of a story about continually appearing, disappearing, reappearing, and disappearing again; it was about separation, division, and recombination; and it was also, for some of the people associated with Pogoni, a story about ordinariness (a point to which I will return). Abandonment was one among a number of past chapters and an infinity of possible future chapters that told and would tell that same story: of change—the place used to be full of people and now it was not—that somehow also constituted the same thing. While the events or details of each chapter differed, the story, the process (appearing and disappearing, separation, recombination, and, for some, ordinariness) remained the same. And the next chapters would tell the same story as well—the one about the opening of the border, or about the new interest in cultural and natural heritage (as opposed to the folklore studies of the past), or about the building of asphalt roads. That is what this place

Map 1. The regions of mainland Greece and northern borders (modified from Green and King 2001: 256)

meant to many people: constant change, and appearing and disappearing, while the process stayed the same, and (for some) ordinary. There was a mythical feel about the way that story was described at times, in Lévi-Strauss's terms (continual transformations of the same story; Lévi-Strauss 1963); but it was also experienced: it was not only narrated, it was also lived and dwelled in, and upon.

This book explores that issue; most of the chapters either parallel or trace the story of different moments of appearing and disappearing in differing transformations, and it considers various ways in which such appearances and disappearances were constituted: not only in stories, but also in maps and other techniques of accounting for places and change; in censuses and other statistics about places, people, animals, and activities; in EU-funded ecotourism and cultural heritage projects;

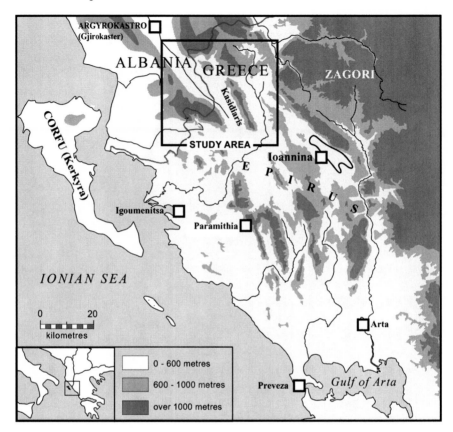

Map 2. Epirus and the Kasidiaris area (modified from Green and King 2001: 257)

and also in people's experiences of places, relations, and travels. Through this, it explores what makes some places and some peoples in "the margins" seem undistinguished or apparently a matter of indifference in political, cultural, or even topographical terms, while others in "the margins" have come to gain considerable distinction (positive, negative, or both) and interest.[18]

I argue that in this case, the way marginalization plays out has to do with a rather odd combination of ambiguity and ordinariness (or the lack thereof). First, on ambiguity: there was a quiet yet constant, even hegemonic, insistence on ambiguity in the Epirus region as a whole, but it seemed to affect Pogoni more than Zagori; a continual, though rarely entirely explicit, assertion that things cannot, and perhaps even must not, be pinned down, be fixed, be clarified. That is what made it odd: most (modern) hegemonic assertions (except perhaps psychoanalytic, aesthetic,

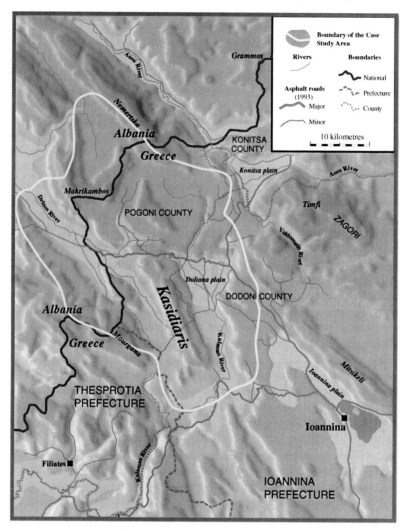

Map 3. Topography of Pogoni/Kasidiaris area with county and regional boundaries (modified from Green and King 2001: 260)

and metaphysical ones) are aimed at avoiding or concealing ambiguity, not asserting that ambiguity is the point of something (Herzfeld 1997: 93). One phrase, spoken occasionally when I expressed confusion about an event or statement during my time in Epirus, summed this up for me: "This is the Balkans, Sarah; what do you expect?" (Εδώ είναι Βαλκάνια Σάρα. Τι περιμένεις;). The statement caught me by surprise the first time I heard it: I was not really thinking in terms of the Balkans at all when I first arrived in Epirus, let alone thinking of the Balkans as the answer to a question about something that was confusing. I was being told that I should expect to be confused, because this is the Balkans; at least, I should not expect to get to the bottom of things, never mind to the heart of things: that is not what the Balkans are about.[19]

Initially during fieldwork, my attempts to clarify the ambiguity became something of a guilty obsession. I felt I had no business imagining there is such a thing as clarity, and that the search for it was probably an outcome of too much Euro-American intellectual training, which used to teach, naively and hegemonically, that it is important to pin things down and to make things explicit. Resistance to such pinning down has been the leitmotif of many recent ethnographies, including Anna Tsing's (1993) and Kathleen Stewart's (1996). Yet being on the Greek-Albanian border on and off for a few years led me to conclude that the difference between ambiguity (continual and contingent indeterminacy) and clarity (ontological knowledge) is not as enormous as the literature implied, at least in terms of what generates the sense of their being authoritative accounts. Ambiguity can be as hegemonic and subject to disciplinary regimes as clarity; confusion, lack of a means to pin things down, can be as actively generated as positive assertions and constructions of truth: "This is the Balkans, Sarah; what do you expect?" I was continually being exhorted to stay confused, to let it go.[20] Far from an apparent stability and fixity that the analyst must unpick to reveal the fluidity and indeterminacy upon which it is based, the hegemonic discourse on the Balkans insists that the region is fluidity and indeterminacy personified, right on the surface, a completely explicit fog, as it were.[21] I will return to this in detail in chapter 4. For now, I will just note that areas considered to have been divided by the Greek-Albanian border (e.g., Pogoni and parts of Thesprotia) were more affected by this assertion of muddiness, this lack of precise clarity, than some other areas of Epirus, though all were affected to some extent.

As to the second issue, ordinariness: the reputation of some Pogoni peoples of being ordinary also seemed odd, not only because in this age of multiculturalism everyone ought to have some distinctiveness (Strathern 1995; Stolcke 1995; Herzfeld 2004), but also because many others in the region were asserting some kind of distinctiveness and were occasionally explicitly using that as a means to attract both recognition and economic resources (in cultural heritage terms). As in every other part of Epirus, in Pogoni there were a range of differences marked between peoples: some were called Sarakatsani, some Vlachoi, some Gypsies, some Northern Epirots (peoples from southern Albania who were considered to be Greek), and some Albanians. But there were a significant number of people who were not called anything in particular; they were "just Greeks." The term *Gréki* was occasionally used to refer to people who were "just

Greek" in this way, and I explore that further in chapter 2, as it is a word not widely used elsewhere in Greece, and it does not evoke a sense of the binary ("disemic") division between "romios" and "hellene" discussed by Herzfeld (1987). Here, I want to note that being "just Greek" is an assertion of ordinariness, a lack of a named distinction. It is different from an assertion of being "pure Greek," which I also heard the same people saying quite often: being "pure Greek" is an assertion of distinction; it is special, even while it claims homogeneity with all other (pure) Greeks (Herzfeld 1986).

It was the "just Greek" population of Pogoni that most had in mind when they described Pogoni as lacking in distinction. Of course, there were "just Greek" people everywhere in Epirus, and particularly in cities (that is the point);[22] but in Pogoni, the asserted ordinariness (an assertion, or at least complaint, made almost as often by themselves as by others) blended in with the asserted ordinariness of the landscape and the ambiguities associated with that Balkan border. The combination generated a sense of a general lack of distinction as well as an underlying, never quite explicitly acknowledged, lack of clarity; but it did not matter all that much—it made no difference (literally)—because the place and the people were ordinary.

In that sense, even the marginality of Pogoni was ambiguous: if the people and place were marginal, it was not a marginality of otherness, of difference, or of distinction; it was more the marginality of being nothing in particular. Yet I knew that when I was asked, "What do you expect, Sarah? This is the Balkans," one of the things I did *not* expect was such an apparent lack of particularity. And although people in Pogoni complained about it, occasionally demanding to know what was so different or special about the Zagori that resulted in the Zagori's attracting tourism and funding in a way that Pogoni did not, or offering answers that evoked assertions of political machinations giving the Zagori an unfair advantage, or even pointing to a wealth of history, traditions, costumes, music, and so on that in fact made Pogoni peoples culturally distinct and special,[23] all this was hedged around with ambivalence: there remained an underlying expression, or sometimes resigned acceptance, of their ordinariness, their "just Greekness."

I argue that what *was* different about Pogoni, at least in terms of its contemporary reputation, was its relative location; it was the *where*, not the who, that mattered. By "relative location" I mean something fractal rather than linear. It was not only that Pogoni is geographically located next to, or straddles, the state border; it was not only that its topography, in contemporary aesthetic evaluations of such things, is defined as less distinctive than others—it was also that this kind of place, these kinds of spatial divisions and relations, these kinds of people, their kind of relations with others, their kind of activities and travels, and their kind of experiences, were seen as constituting transformations of many other places, people, relations, activities, travels, and experiences (there was something generic about them). While there were many differences, they were also the same—a "not quite replication," in Strathern's terms (Strathern 1991: xx).[24] That gets me back to the theme of both being and not being someone and somewhere in particular; of separations, divisions, and recombinations of places and people; and of stories that are different but the same. It was the ambiguous *sameness* that made the difference, not the differences, as it were.

Just to avoid any misunderstanding, considering the unthinking way that the Balkans have been and continue to be described both in the media and in some academic writing, I want to emphasize that I am not suggesting the people or the place is stuck in some kind of Balkan "time warp" (Cowan 2000: 2) or that they are representatives of "Balkan atavism" (Herzfeld 1997: 88), or even that they were represented that way. As I will go on to discuss in chapter 4, "the Balkans" is relatively recent as a concept and a name, and its history of appearance, disappearance, and reappearance is neither circular nor linear—nor does it involve a straightforward assertion of "backwardness"; it is, in its current hegemonic form, as fractal as what I have been describing for Pogoni, which is not coincidental. When I say that things change but somehow remain the same, my meaning is similar to Strathern's when she discusses change in relation to English kinship in the late twentieth century (Strathern 1992a). Strathern argues that although English kinship is in one sense understood to be the same as it has always already been, it is also, and at the same time, understood to be undergoing possibly profound changes, partly as a result of the introduction of new reproductive technologies. Strathern suggests it is not these technologies in themselves that enable change, but what such events are causing people to think: people have become increasingly reflexive about kinship, have made the implicit English understanding of relatedness and individuality explicit, and that changes things, while they also apparently stay the same. As she puts it, "It is, in fact, this very capacity to think one is perpetuating old ideas, simply doing again what has been done at other times and in other places before, elsewhere, that is itself a profound engine for change. . . . The sense of new values, new ideas, new epochs, comes from the conscious effort to make evident the values and ideas people already hold" (Strathern 1992a: 44). For my purposes, it is not *whether* things stay the same or change that is the main issue here (though it will be elsewhere); it is the manner in which change and sameness are constituted and understood, and the relationship between them, that is the issue; and I argue in chapter 4 that this is currently hegemonically constituted as fractal in this region.

I will give just a brief example here about the apparent ordinariness of some of the Pogoni people and the relationship of that with the "where," not the "who." I mentioned earlier that Pogoni either runs along or straddles the border, depending on how you look at it, and that the border divided Pogoni between two states. Many of the people on the Albanian side of the border were the relatives, friends, or at least neighbors of the "just Greek" Pogoni people on the Greek side. For people familiar with Pogoni, some of the area on the Albanian side was regarded as part of Pogoni; a larger part was regarded as Deropolis; either way, the people were the relatives and friends of those on the Greek side. However, unlike their "just Greek" kin, friends, and neighbors, many of those on the Albanian side had an additional name—actually, more than one: they were called Northern Epirots in Greece and either Greek Albanians or Southern Albanians in Albania. Exactly where Northern Epirus begins and ends is another one of those contested issues involving drawing lines on maps: for some it straddles the Greek-Albanian border; for others, it includes only the area in southern Albania where the population associated with it is considered to be predominantly Greek; for still others (people in Albania, mostly), it does not exist—the whole of Epirus is regarded as constituting the southern part of Albania, irrespective of the state border. In any case, the people living just inside the Albanian state border in this region, and who were considered to be Greek, were the ones called Northern Epirots in Greece—which implies, in a reversal of one of the views from Albania, that they were from an overall (Greek) geographical entity called Epirus, and the northern part happens to be in Albania. In other words, calling this region Northern Epirus effectively pushes the existing Greek-Albanian border northward in terms of "national locations," mapping them onto geographical locations; it implicitly asserts that Northern Epirus is part of Epirus, irrespective of the existence of the Greek-Albanian border, and that the people living there who are deemed to be Greek are the people who "belong" to this place, the Northern Epirots.[25]

A not-quite-replication, a half mirror image, of this situation existed in parts of Thesprotia, to the south of Pogoni, which includes an area known as Tsamouria. The Albanian government argues that in the past, a significant proportion of the population living in part of that region, on the Greek side of the border, were ethnically Albanian people called Tsamides in Greece (Cams, Tchams, or Chams in Albania); it is unclear how many of these people still live in Thesprotia (some would say none at all). In fact, the issue of Tsamides caused me more consternation than almost any other I encountered in Epirus; it was an extreme example of things appearing and disappearing almost simultaneously, and it was an explicit example of an insistence on ambiguity. I will return to that in chapter 2; the point here is this: while neither the Greek nor the Albanian government is making any territorial claims on the basis of their positions on Northern Epirus and Thesprotia, there are ongoing debates between them concerning the past treatment of the populations associated with those places. That effectively makes the border ambiguous: while it is unambiguously a state border, what it means in terms of nation is hedged around with fuzziness—and, incidentally, this is one of the reasons I am disinclined to use the forever hyphenated phrase "nation-state"; they are not the same thing.[26]

My reason for bringing all this in here is that the "just Greeks" in Pogoni and the Northern Epirots from the other side of the border often discussed how they are, or at least had been, the "same" people; but they were also different. While on the Greek side of the border they were described as undistinguished, ordinary people, on the other side of the border they were something in particular.[27] Moreover, the ambiguity about the border led to more ambiguity when Northern Epirots crossed that border: although (in Greece) they were regarded as Greeks living in a non-Greek state, and to that extent, using nationalist logic, they were "displaced" in Liisa Malkki's terms (Malkki 1992), when many of them moved across the border into Greece after its reopening, that was *also* seen by many in Greece as "displacement," for they had moved away from "their place," from Northern Epirus, to another part of Epirus. Were these people to be regarded as "coming home" (Greeks returning to Greece) or as refugees (people moving from their home, which was in another state, to Greece)? Or both? This movement evoked memories of other such movements in the past, and in particular the large-scale forced exchange of populations between Greece and Turkey in the 1920s (during which there was a dispute over whether the Tsamides of Thesprotia should be included in the exchange; the Albanian government argued not, on the grounds that Tsamides were not Turkish but ethnically Albanian). That such memories were stirred did not help matters much.[28]

This is one example of what I mean when I say that it is the *where*, not the who, that is important. In this example, the where had a lot to do with ambiguities over the relations among nation, state, and location, but there are many kinds of where. In other examples in this study, the where had to do with the manner in which people traveled or failed to travel, or the distance between Epirus and Athens, or the aesthetics of topography and landscape, or the way places were subdivided, appeared, and disappeared in administrative accounts of the region. How the where is constituted, and how that is both different and the same across a range of scales (geographical, temporal, metaphorical, disciplinary) forms a key part of this study's exploration of differing forms of marginality, their ambiguity, their appearance and disappearance, and their simultaneous similarity and difference.

That gets me back to the question of what to expect from the Balkans, a question that eventually led me to fractals—to the geometry, geography, and temporality of that which is constituted as simultaneously the same and different, of that which is fundamentally both fragmented and interrelated, and how that relates to the peculiar way in which the Balkans are currently constituted in hegemonic terms. It is here that ambiguity, distinctiveness, and ordinariness, as well as appearing, disappearing, and reappearing, seem to converge. In chapter 4, I analyze in detail the Balkans themselves, as an imagined whole that has no center or clear edges and is replicated within its many and potentially always proliferating parts (it is both singular and plural simultaneously); for the rest of this chapter, and in the next two, I explore such replications across scales concerning Epirus and Pogoni in particular.

I will start that account with how the fieldwork I carried out led me to focus my attention on things like movement and travel, places, maps, tectonics, animal numbers, and EU-funded development projects in my attempts to understand ambiguity, things being the same and different across a range of scales, and ordinariness.

Marginal Travels

Over the years I spent carrying out fieldwork in Epirus (1992, 1993–94, 1995, 1997), I wandered from place to place, sometimes in pursuit of an objective set by the European Commission–funded research projects of which I was a part, but mostly because of the persistent wandering element in how people described their diverse lives and experiences, which I ended up mimicking. Overall, though, I spent most of my time in the northern and more mountainous part of the region, and kept returning to the area around the Kasidiaris (maps 2 and 3).

Deciding what to call that place was an early experience of ambiguity. On the one hand, the Kasidiaris mountain itself is administratively divided between two Greek counties, Pogoni County and Dodoni County. Pogoni County's share of the mountain is mostly on the western and northern sides, and Dodoni's is mostly on the eastern and southern sides (map 3). On the other hand, as already mentioned, most people's sense of Pogoni as a region also goes beyond the current Greek administrative boundary, both to the west and to the east, which means that it includes areas that are formally part of Dodoni to the east, and it crosses the Greek-Albanian international border to the west. That set up an ambiguity: most people living in or around the area were aware of the administrative boundary and would often define Pogoni's current location in those terms, asserting that it is really only the people who live there who are

Pogoni people. Yet at the same time, it was also acknowledged, often by the same people, that "traditionally" (that is, both in the past and in the present, as a tradition), Pogoni did include other areas, and for that reason those areas were also in fact Pogoni; or perhaps they were Pogoni plus something else (and somewhere else) as well. This was one of my earlier encounters with how naming and renaming things, as well as the regular shifting of formal boundaries, generated an interplay of a sense of where and what things were in this region—one that resulted in no final resolution on the matter. Moreover, although it was mostly the "just Greek" population who were considered to be Pogoni people, the area identified as Pogoni was also associated in certain ways with various other peoples not considered to be "Pogoni people" (e.g., certain groups of Vlachoi and Gypsies), as well as some who had been considered Pogoni but are now considered something else (either different from or in addition to being Pogoni people)—such as those called Northern Epirots. In any case, "Pogoni" people are not only "Pogoni" people but possess a variety of other identifying (or nonidentifying) labels as well, such as being "just Greek" (chapter 2).

While this was all very intriguing, in that it led to me consider how people's understanding of the "where" made as much use of local government administrative boundaries as it did of ideas about peoples, traditions, and national boundaries, it caused me some consternation in deciding what to call the place in my fieldwork notes. As I did not have the luxury of beginning with a people and a place that had clear names, and whose assumed boundaries I could later deftly deconstruct if I needed to, I was beginning to become confused over where and whom I was referring to when I looked back at my notes. So, initially for the purely practical reason of needing to understand my own notes, I decided to use a name that nobody suggested the area was called: Kasidiaris, after the mountain that is vaguely in the middle of the area I ended up focusing upon, and which people at various times either went up, over, around, or alongside of. In the absence of an unambiguous center, I invented a center that was not the focus of anybody's attention, though most of the peoples I discuss had to deal with the Kasidiaris in one way or another, even if this mostly involved ignoring it in more recent years. Chapter 2 takes this invention further, focusing on the varieties of peoples associated with the Kasidiaris as a place in the company of others, but I do this to explore the lack of centrality, the appearance and disappearance of marginality, and the way location came into this across a range of scales.

One of the more persistent distinctions made within the Greek part of the area was a perceived division between the places located to the west and those located to the east of the Kasidiaris mountain, even though the mountain itself was not the focus of attention when this distinction was made, and even though the distinction did not generally affect people's perceptions of where Pogoni was located. As can be seen in maps 2 and 3, the west is a stretch of land currently sandwiched between the international border and the mountain, whereas the east has a fairly substantial plain, contains most of the recently developed and expanding villages in the area and the highest population of younger people, and provides easy road access through the main route to the capital city, Ioannina.[29] The eastern side therefore constituted a literal as well as metaphorical kind of crossroads within the Greek side of the area, whereas the western side constituted a kind of crossroads between the Greek and Albanian sides of the area. Because of this frequently evoked distinction, I often refer to Western and Eastern Kasidiaris in this book. In practice, the bulk of my fieldwork during the earlier years focused on Western Kasidiaris, with occasional visits elsewhere, whereas most of my fieldwork in the later years was spent in Eastern Kasidiaris, particularly in a village called Doliana, where I lived for four months in 1997 (map 4).

This also marks a division among the different things to which I paid attention. In the earlier years, one key focus was the differing ways people used and moved around the landscape, past and present, how they discussed these travels and activities, and combined them with other things (chapter 2). A second focus was attitudes toward land degradation and soil erosion—the topic of research that had brought me to Epirus in the first place, and which I will discuss a little more later and in chapter 3.[30] A third focus was the Greek-Albanian border, the various movements across it, and its closure and reopening (chapters 2, 4, and 7). In the later years, the focus shifted to EU-funded development projects that were mushrooming around Epirus, in the dual contexts of EU policies aimed at kick-starting economic regeneration of "marginal" places through agrotourism and of ongoing tensions across the border, particularly involving people moving from Albania into Greece (chapter 7). In connection with this aspect of the research, I also spent a good deal of time in the Zagori, and particularly a village called Aristi (map 4), in part to explore the ongoing promotion of images of cultural and natural heritage being applied especially to this area.

In addition, I carried out a brief ethnographic study around the small towns of Filiates and Paramithia, in Thesprotia, toward the south of Epirus (map 2), for two reasons. First, this was an area through which long-distance regional travelers—transhumant pastoralists and traders—passed after going through the Kasidiaris region, or on their way to the Kasidiaris region, usually to some final destination beyond the Kasidiaris. I wanted to take that trip myself to understand something more about descriptions people had given me of the dangers that parts of the route had involved in the past (Green 1998b). Second, as I have explained, the

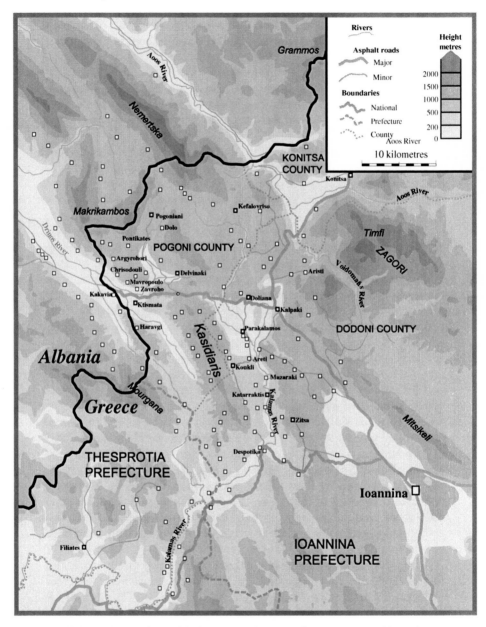

Map 4. Villages and townships of the key research area and county/regional boundaries (modified from Green and King 2001: 259)

area was considered to be as marginal as Pogoni, if not more so; that was in part because the area was associated with Tsamides, whom I mentioned earlier as causing me considerable levels of confusion. The difference was that unlike the Pogoni "just Greek" population, who were ordinary in a Balkan kind of way, Tsamides turned out to be extraordinary in a Balkan kind of way (in Epirus, at least), and that made most people even less inclined to be clear about them than they were about the Pogoni people; that is discussed further in chapter 2.

Beyond Thesprotia, Zagori, and the Kasidiaris areas, I also spent a good deal of time in the biggest urban center of Epirus, Ioannina, the region's capital. There were two reasons for this, and both of them were practical. First, getting to any given village by car was usually far less circuitous if I started from Ioannina rather than from another village, as the asphalt road system was designed to lead into and out of the city, and not between villages. Since I was not planning on being based in one particular village, it made sense to be based in Ioannina. In any case, it was difficult to find rooms to rent outside the city, despite many houses' being empty for most of the year in most of the villages; the concept of having strangers in your house, living there on their own, was an alien one, and although after a few months I could easily have persuaded someone, I chose to respect people's discomfort about this issue. The one occasion when I lived for an extended period of time elsewhere—four months in Doliana—I rented a room above a coffee shop and restaurant owned by the local agricultural cooperative and managed by a family I had come to know very well.

The second reason I spent a lot of time in Ioannina is that most statistical information about land use, animal numbers and crop production, population censuses, land improvement programs, and EU development programs, as well as detailed maps and other data, were kept in a scatter of government offices in the city. My reasons for pursuing those data changed with time. Initially, it was because I was supposed to be in Epirus to investigate people's changing relationship with their unstable landscape; I needed to know how that had been represented by the state, as well as how people living within these areas talked about it and experienced it. But later, when I began to get a sense of how things, people, and places appeared and disappeared, how they were named and renamed in a range of ways and across a range of scales—a sense I gained both by looking at these reams of data and by spending time with people around the Kasidiaris area and elsewhere—I became much more interested in the data as constituting traces of past and present negotiations and relations, as well as strange kinds of objects that were as ambiguous, ordinary, and extraordinary as anything else I had come across in this place. Moreover, they provided me with one means, among others, of looking at interrelations and representations across scales; a way of understanding how things can be different while also being the same across diverse technologies of representation and experience, and how things can be made to appear and disappear in the process. This is something I explore in chapters 5 and 6; suffice it to say here that one conclusion I drew from this exercise is that statistics do not have to be collected, used, or understood statistically. That is, the use of statistics does not necessarily imply the exclusive imposition of a formally statistical way of understanding things, of constructing reality and truth using the ideas of classification and categories, aggregates, comparison, and things' being greater than the sum of their parts. In practice, that turned out to be only one part, one fraction, of the experience, use, and understanding of statistics.

In any event, being more or less forced to spend a long time in Ioannina made the city an important part of my experience while I was in Epirus, and I regret that I have not provided much ethnographic detail about that in this book, especially since I have spent some years focusing on urban ethnography in other research.[31] Just briefly: by the 1990s, Ioannina had become the administrative, economic, and political core of the whole region, in geographical as well as conceptual terms, whereas in the past it had been one focal point among others. Nevertheless, Ioannina had its own margins, as all cities do, and during 1994 and 1995 I lived in one of them: a neighborhood on the southern edge of the city usually called "Ta Seismoplikta," a pluralized and demotic version of its official name, "Seismoplikton," which means "the earthquake-stricken"; "Ta Seismoplikta," when used to refer to this area, meant "the place of the earthquake victims" to most people.[32] I lived on a corner of the central street, which had the same name. The original houses there—small, square, flat-topped concrete structures with concrete or stone floors—had been built on scrubland by the Greek army to house the victims of an earthquake that occurred on May 1, 1967, in the Pindos Mountains just to the east of Ioannina.[33] Few people had died, but the earthquake destroyed large numbers of the mountain village houses. My landlady's father moved to Seismoplikta from Krapsi, one of the villages nearest the epicenter of the earthquake, and my neighborhood was heavily populated by Krapsi ex-residents. Maria (my landlady) had moved to Athens some years before the earthquake, but she and her husband moved to Seismoplikta in 1972. They had since built a corner shop next to their concrete house, which Maria ran, and had furthermore built two stories on top of the combined house and shop. Maria now lived on the first floor with her husband and one of her daughters (who was about to marry and move away to the Peloponnese); her other daughter lived on the second floor with her husband (she gave birth to her first daughter during my stay there). I rented the original concrete house built by the army, which I affectionately came to call The Bunker.

The building of Seismoplikta and the movement of people into the area as a result of the earthquake was not something many commented upon as a great or cataclysmic event; it was noted more as a means to explain why there was still a certain lack of infrastructure or sense of long-term "dwelling," in Ingold's terms (Ingold 1995), in Seismoplikta, and how people moving through or new to the area felt fairly comfortable there, while at the same time large portions of the resident population were closely related to one another. The area was often described as combining "transients"—students of Ioannina University, located a couple of kilometers down the road; casual workers; immigrants; and the occasional anthropologist—with a "close-knit community" that had been transported wholesale from mountain villages to the city. Listening to people talk in Maria's shop, I sometimes had the sense that this corner of the neighborhood was an extension of Krapsi and had nothing to do with Ioannina; at other times, it felt much like a bit of undistinguished urban sprawl.

What struck me about this was not so much that combination but the absence of a story about loss from the "earthquake victims": the absence of a story of disaster or an account about how they came to be there, an absence that contrasted starkly with Hirschon's account of Asia Minor refugees in Piraeus (Hirschon 1989). It seemed as if Maria's people did not have a sense of anomaly in their being relocated. In any event, the village of Krapsi had been partially rebuilt, and ex-residents from Seismoplikta regularly visited and continued to be involved in village affairs. This precisely mirrored the behavior of thousands of other residents of Ioannina who had moved there by choice (as indeed had Maria herself), and who regularly visited the mountain villages in which they grew up.

There was more to this. Maria and Michalis (Maria's husband) told me about the history of their village in terms of movement: how there had been a village in what is now Albania (or Northern Epirus) called Grapsi, and how the residents had moved to the new location, to Krapsi in the Pindos Mountains in what is now Greece, as a result of harassment by Ottoman administrators as well as irregular militias and animal rustlers. They both also talked about other kinds of movement—going to Athens for a time to live and then returning again, or even just traveling to visit relatives. Travel and movement were not anomalous activities for Maria and Michalis, even though the reasons to do it on any particular occasion may be extraordinary (such as an earthquake) or entirely mundane. Rather, movement was a key means by which events in their lives were marked, and through which they were discussed—both small and everyday (ordinary) events and large and traumatic (extraordinary) ones. Things change—you move—but they are in some senses the same: movement is what happens when things change, as well as what happens when things stay the same. It is the means by which people note that something has happened, that an event has occurred which is different from what had been happening before but is nevertheless a kind of replication, in that it involves movement; it may be a kind of movement that is the same as one that has occurred before, even if the details are somewhat different this time.

Just to be clear, the 1967 earthquake, as an event, had of course changed things fairly dramatically in both practical and emotional terms for Krapsi residents. Apart from anything else, the memory of it had generated a deep-seated sense of physical insecurity, not only for those who had experienced it, but also for others who had been told about it. A small indication of this was the panic caused among the customers in Maria's shop by a small tremor that occurred there in 1994. It was the kind of tremor that rattles your cup a little on the table, lasts five or six seconds, and might equally have been caused by a very heavy truck driving by. Such tremors occur regularly in Epirus, and I must have experienced half a dozen or so while I was there, but this was the only one that was physically felt in Seismoplikta. Discussions about it continued for days afterward, and one of Maria's daughters complained that she had been unable to sleep for two nights because she had been so worried about it. However, although the memory of the event reverberated right up to the 1990s, the extraordinariness of the 1967 earthquake did not seem to make people feel there was something extraordinary about their moving from Krapsi to Seismoplikta. It was not the movement that had caused displacement; the movement provided a means to discuss the event itself, as movement provided a means to discuss all kinds of events.

Moving People and Places

I have particularly noted this way in which movement is included in discussions of things happening for Maria's family because it was a characteristic way in which almost all the people I met in Epirus discussed their lives, their location, and their experiences. Chapter 2 explores this: different moments in people's lives were marked by one kind of movement or another; in addition, other peoples were assessed by the way in which they moved, the level of relative autonomy they had in moving, and their consequent relative status. People who moved seasonally (transhumant or semitranshumant shepherds) were different from people who moved in long-term labor migrations (as many "just Greek" Pogoni peoples had done); people who had in the past been free to wander around the Epirot region, such as traders and craftspeople (barrel makers, stonemasons, silversmiths, leather workers, bakers, charcoal makers, and loggers) as well as irregular militias and animal rustlers, were different from those who could move only by effectively leapfrogging over the region and spending long periods in cities such as Constantinople (today's Istanbul), returning only occasionally for three or four months at a time; people who emigrated as families to cities in Greece or abroad were different from those who divided their year relatively equally between cities and villages; people who apparently wandered aimlessly (e.g., Gypsies and *tsopanides*, men who offered their services as shepherds around the region) were different from those who moved up and down a mountain with the seasons; people who had cars were different from those who went on foot or used buses; and people who moved across state borders illegally were different from those who crossed with visas and passports, or who did not cross such borders at all.

The one thing that people emphasized in distinguishing between different moments in their lives, different places, and different kinds of peoples was different kinds of coming and going, and different constraints, enablements, and coercions in that movement. Those who were regarded as most free to stay put were better off than those who felt constrained or even forced to stay put (and there was a considerable gender division in that). Equally, those who were regarded as most free to move were better off than those who felt they were coerced or forced by circumstances into moving (e.g., earthquakes, enforced exchange of populations, burdensome taxes, the division of an area into two different states).

While the form in which people spoke about these differing things remained the same—discussion of movement—the kinds of movements recounted for different periods were reported as being different, and that partly shaped many people's sense of different eras. In particular, over the last century or so, many people had a sense that movement was increasingly regarded, both politically and structurally, as unacceptable: first with the creation of strongly guarded state boundaries; then with the development of often equally strongly guarded national identities; and then, ironically, with technical change. It was this last that made the mechanized, irrigated plains the only places where it was sensible to cultivate anymore, leaving the seasonally used mountain and hillside fields to grow into impenetrable prickly oak scrub thicket; and technical change also made Epirus accessible along the asphalt roads, rather than the thousands of tracks, paths, and routes over mountains, along valleys, between villages, fields, towns, and grazing areas. While the literature I was reading at the time about movement and travel was increasingly emphasizing that people have always moved around, and arguing that the world is becoming ever more mobile and interconnected—characterized by transnationalism, transmigration, globalization, and the like[34]—people in Epirus were suggesting that for them, a conceptual reversal had taken place:

whereas movement had been, in the past, the way things were and the way things happened, and the measure by which people and places were valued and judged, it was now regarded as somehow special, as something that you had to make an increasing effort to achieve and/or that involved both literal and metaphorical displacement.

What this pointed to was an increasing sense of discrepancy between Epirot people's understanding of how things are and wider political, economic, and structural conditions. If you start with coming and going, if you assume that movement is simply a part of many things, in different ways and at different times, then the axiomatic link between movement in itself and change or displacement is broken. Things that seem continually to cause change when the starting point is stasis or stability can easily lose these transformative qualities when the starting point assumes movement.[35] Further, if the starting point assumes movement, then one can imagine that *not* moving, becoming fixed in place, could be one of the greatest perceived causes of change.

This gets me back to what is and is not constituted as ordinary or extraordinary, and how the initial purpose in my going to Epirus, to look into people's relationships with their unstable environment, eventually led me to consider all these other kinds of movement and their interrelations and separations. Those new asphalt roads that replaced the thousands of tracks and paths rather neatly embodied the problem I was confronting. Asphalt is supposed to stay put and not move around, yet the asphalt in Epirus does not stay put: it had considerable trouble coping with the chronic surface movements of much of Epirus, as the all-too-common cracking, folding, gullying, and landslides regularly turn road surfaces into something that looks not unlike a crumpled gray blanket (fig. 1). Sometimes, so much of the road is lost down a gully that it becomes impassable until someone comes to fix it in the summer. Still, these days, cars and trucks are much easier than mules, horses, or walking. An elderly man from Aristi was bemused to hear that a horse trail for tourists might be developed in the area: who in their right minds would want to use horses to travel around Epirus when there was motorized transport— even if the roads do crumple a little now and again?

I was supposed to research all that land surface movement as a small ethnographic project to complement a much larger multidisciplinary, multinational, EU-funded research program on desertification and land degradation in the Mediterranean Basin.[36] It was known that Epirus is particularly tectonically active, prone to earthquakes, landslips, and the formation of badlands.[37] I was to ask people in the area, especially older people who had lived in the hills and mountains, what they had done in the past to counteract their landscape's tendency to change its shape. The assumption of the research program was that such change is anomalous,

Figure 1. Crumpled asphalt road in Western Kasidiaris

and that people prefer places to stay put, so would have done something to try to counteract the movement. Yet my questions to people about this generated mutual confusion. The following is an example of the kind of exchange I had on this issue. In this case, I was talking with a man living very close to one of the biggest areas of eroded badlands in Epirus, called Kokkinopilos (map 6)—a region of huge bare dunes made up of deep red *terra rossa* soil, going on for acres.

"So, what about those badlands over there at Kokkinopilos, where nothing grows?"

"What about them?"

"What do you remember about them, in the past?"

"What's to remember?"

"That's what I'm asking. For example, has the land changed in your memory? Has it got worse? Did people in the past ever grow anything there? Did they do anything to try and stop the erosion?"

"Changed? No. It's always been like that there. Worse? How do you mean, worse? It's just like that, that's the way it is. And as for growing things: no, nobody ever grew anything there. Why would you?"

"Okay, well. Did anyone ever try to reinforce it—to stop the erosion, try to keep it stable, so it didn't get worse?"

"No, nobody did that. There's no stopping it, anyway. It's just like that. It never changes. It's always been like that."

In retrospect, this was not a confusing conversation at all: the man was telling me that Kokkinopilos was an area of no interest to him, so why should he, or anybody else, care whether it eroded or not? I found it confusing at the time because I had been led by the research program to expect that people would notice this kind of shifting around of the landscape and would comment upon it as anomalous. In fact, most people agreed that the land did continually crack, gully, fold, erode, and slip; they also agreed that sometimes, not only in badlands, but also in cultivated areas, people's fields would suddenly drop about a meter in a year. However, most people also added that this land never changed; it had always been like that. As a result, these processes were not recognized as "erosion" because that term (for them as for me) denotes anomalous change. Since it was not anomalous, it did not constitute change.

In any case, most people kept dropping the subject and talking about something else, such as the depopulation of the area over the last few decades; or the recent influx of peoples arriving across the newly opened Greek-Albanian border; or the abandonment and overgrowth of the fields and grazing lands; or the Ottoman Empire, the Second World War, and the Greek civil war after it; or the proliferation of EU-funded agrotourism development projects in the area, and how unlikely it was that any of them would succeed. The last thing people were interested in talking about was the shiftiness of their landscape. Yet, as I had been sent to Epirus to find out about that shiftiness, I kept dropping it into the conversation. Eventually, I accepted that people did not *care* about land degradation; they were almost entirely indifferent to it, and as a topic of conversation, it was fundamentally uninteresting. Feeling somewhat as though I was playing truant from my assigned task, I began to listen to what people did want to tell me.[38]

What emerged were stories about a range of events told in terms of coming and going, through space and through time, as well as through social and political moments; and they were about how things shifted, time and again, in the same way, even though the events were different: when regular migrations became permanent emigrations with sporadic visits back to Epirus; when mountains once used for grazing and cultivation became "natural wilderness," and when the Greek-Albanian border was closed following Albania's transition into a command socialist state; or when movement became anomalous, as happened when transhumant pastoralists were increasingly pressured to become sedentary, or more recently when Albanian citizens, having been prevented from crossing the Greek-Albanian border for almost fifty years, started to cross it in droves in the early 1990s. The kind of movement that never marked any event or process was the continual shifting around of the land surface in Epirus. There was no story to tell about it. There is more to this, which is discussed further in chapter 3. Here, the point is that not all movement is the same; in fact, movement does not mean anything in *itself*, so it is not movement as such that displaces anything.

That realization led me to explore how movement was always involved in a network of relationships with, as well as separations from, other things, places, people, and events, and how that seamlessly combined the way things seem (narratives, rhetoric, representations, images, numbers, etc.) with the way things are (the political economy of life, borders and passports, social relationships, being forced or being free to stay or move). Bringing these scales together, understanding how their interrelations as well as their fragmentations informed people's experiences, became an important part of what I have tried to explore.

As it happened, I went about that more by accident than by design, and it is here that my involvement with a large research program comes in: a multidisciplinary program whose main concerns centered on patterns of land use and land degradation across a wide range of spatial and temporal scales. I have already mentioned how the demands of that program's overall objectives led me to ferret out large quantities of statistical data (something I would certainly not have done if left to my own devices), and how that eventually led me to use those data to look at relations across scales of representation and experience. But I was also continually engaged in relations with research colleagues over matters involving maps, satellite images, and GIS (geographical information systems), and over issues to do with the physical instability of the Epirot environment. Again, I was initially somewhat perplexed about how to use all these data in my ethnographic work. In the end, though, they provided me with another means to consider the interrelations and separations of different scales, simultaneously both intellectual and structural. The fact that I was not always on my own as a researcher in Epirus becomes important here.

ON MAPS, IMAGES, AND TECTONICS

Occasionally, I was accompanied in my wanderings around Epirus by colleagues from the European research programs of which I was a part. These included Paleolithic archaeologists, paleobotanists, agronomists, geologists, geographers, and GIS specialists. One of the most regular and, for me, influential of these visitors was Geoffrey King, a specialist in tectonics and earthquakes, who continually provided me with topographic maps, aerial photographs, and satellite images of Epirus. He would stand on hills and mountains to get a good view, so as to explain to me the tendency of the place to shift around. Geoff's timescale was in tens of thousands and millions of years; within that kind of scale, the mountains and valleys bobbed up and down like yo-yos, lakes formed and disappeared down plug holes, all as a result of the tectonic plates upon which all this was sitting—plates that creaked, slipped, pushed, and pulled continuously. It was a perspective quite unlike either the one with which I had started or the various ones expressed by people I met in Epirus, and in its contrast, it caused me to rethink the issue of scale and its relationship to movement.

It was also Geoff who made me understand the potential of maps, as physical objects as well as symbols, to both generate and disturb images of what I was learning from the people associated with Epirus. The issue of maps, at least the cartographic ones based on a Cartesian geometry— a modernist grid of latitude and longitude wrapped across the globe so as to classify, objectify, visualize, know, and thus control the globe—has been a matter of debate for some years, particularly in terms of how such visions became key tools of empire (Cosgrove 1999; 1996; Ingold 2000a), and how they impose the "Western Gaze" onto space (Bender 1999).

Such analyses made me initially extremely uncomfortable about working with Geoff's maps. They did indeed appear to powerfully impose a specifically visual grid, a constraining and distinctly "Western scientific" knowledge, upon Epirus. Moreover I was acutely aware of the way other kinds of maps, ones that marked divisions of states and regions rather than geomorphological divisions, were used continually in texts about the region, making conflicting territorial assertions about how Epirus "ought" to be subdivided according to the origins, history, nationality, or other characteristics asserted to be associated with the place, a habit shared with the whole Balkan region (Peckham 2001: chap. 8, "Map Mania"; Wilkinson 1951). Furthermore, I had confronted numerous difficulties in trying (usually at Geoff's request) to get hold of certain kinds of maps, particularly detailed topographic ones of the area, which were produced by the Greek military and to which access was restricted. I was made to feel that even asking for such things, that type of knowledge, rendered me a deeply suspect character and up to no good. In short, maps were highly contested and loaded objects in Epirus, and Geoff's stacks of them and requests for more of them initially made me feel I was involving myself in an activity that was fraught with difficulty, both intellectually and politically.

Eventually, though, after some weeks of working not only with standard cartographic maps but also aerial photographs and satellite images, I came around to the idea that this tension concerning maps was something to be explored rather than avoided: the maps themselves, and also the discourses to which Geoff was giving me access, provided one means to consider the relationship between powerful accounts and representations of places and the way places were constituted. In any case, in "Western Gaze" intellectual terms, maps are apparently not what they used to be; as Cosgrove notes, maps and mapping have been subjected to the same kind of radical doubt as has social theory in recent years. Not only do they represent modernist purifications, but now they are also supposed to represent "the spatialities of connectivity, networked linkage, marginality and liminality, and the transgression of linear boundaries and hermetic categories—spatial 'flow'—which mark experience in the late 20th century world. Such spatialities render obsolete conventional geographic and topographic mapping practices while stimulating new forms of cartographic representation" (Cosgrove 1999: 4–5).

Geoff King's research centrally involves producing these "new forms of cartographic representation," and he both understood and accepted that maps and maplike images constitute powerful assertions about space and place that are especially partial in Strathern's sense (Strathern 1991). Working with him, I found that they could do much more than simply assert, in a formalistic, positivist, and stylized way, where you are located in the world, so that you can know it. They also turned out to capture differing forms of coming and going, of seeing and failing to see, and differing attempts at fixing in place, both temporal and spatial, across a range of scales. The images themselves could be used to explore those scalar shifts.

A clear example of this possibility came early on during one of Geoff King's visits. One day in the summer of 1993, we were sitting in a coffee shop in Ktismata, a village very near the Greek-Albanian border post. Geoff unfurled a large, violently colored satellite image of a section of Epirus. After explaining that this was an image, not a map or a photograph, and therefore it did not "really" represent Epirus (in the same way, I suppose, that Magritte's drawing of a pipe is not really a pipe), he was trying to train me to read it, to make me literally see a relationship between the mass of squiggles and colors on the paper and the place I had been walking and driving around for months. As yet, he was failing: my brow furrowed as I tried to "see" this relationship; all I saw were squiggles and shaded colors.

After a while, our activities caught the interest of an older man who had walked into the coffee shop. For a few minutes, he stood by the table, scrutinizing the image over my shoulder, and then he put his finger on a section of it and said, "That's where we are, isn't it?" I translated for Geoff, and he agreed that indeed, the squiggle that the man had pointed to represented where we were located at that moment. I was somewhat disconcerted and asked the man how he had worked it out. Grinning, he pointed to another section of the image, which represented, it turned out, the Kasidiaris mountain, and a squiggle, which represented, it turned out, the asphalt road leading to the village in which we were sitting.

I learned later that the man was a pastoralist, a Vlach, and one of the few who still occasionally traveled seasonally between summer and winter pastures on foot rather than by truck. The way he moved around this place gave him an overview that had somehow also been captured in this image Geoff had brought. It was the first time this man had ever seen a satellite image, as it had been for me; but he was able to read it in a way that had as yet proved impossible for me.

From such experiences as this, I began to grasp how things can be different but also the same in embodied (physically experienced) as well as discursive terms; how it is possible to read and understand things using a range of different types of knowledge and experience and yet still, on some level, come to a similar conclusion—at least, a conclusion about where one is in the world. This process recalls something of the way Helen Verran describes her sense of "disconcertment" in working with Yoruba children on learning about numbers: Yoruba children clearly did not understand number in the way that classic Euro-American mathematics teaches it, and yet both Yoruba and English speakers in Verran's study were able in the end to arrive at answers that would solve the same problems (Verran 2001). Verran argues that the mathematical principles used by English speakers and Yoruba speakers—their ways of understanding number— were different but had both developed from repeated embodied social interactions that had been forgotten during the process by which some independent, universal qualities were ascribed to numbers. Whatever had occurred in that coffee shop, the skills Geoff was using to read the image, and the way in which he was trying to teach me to read it, were clearly different from the skills the Vlach man had used to read it, and yet they both agreed on at least one aspect of what it "meant" in spatial terms. The most significant aspect of this maplike object for the Vlach man, the aspect that drew his attention to it in the first place, was that it did not explicitly show political borders and boundaries, but instead appeared to distinguish between different kinds of topography, all of which he knew well from his repeated travels and planned routes around the area with his animals. Geoff's maplike image emphasized one possible representation of the "shape" of this place that was not often seen, for the more common "shape" was one that highlighted political boundaries.

As I have already implied, the significance of political boundaries on maps could hardly be exaggerated for this area. Few people I met actually used such maps to move around or find their way; the interest in them was more about the political language of maps, the kinds of knowledge and power (technology, in Foucault's terms) they asserted. This is hardly surprising given that most local books about the region show at least one map, if not several, indicating where the author thinks the international political borders ought to be, as opposed to where they currently are; or show the variety of places the borders have been at various times in the past, which draws out clearly how contested such borders have been and therefore presumably remain.[39] Of course, the same habit is precisely replicated in books about the Balkans as a whole.[40] In both, it is not only the location of the lines indicating territorial divisions that are marked as having repeatedly changed and remaining contested; names of places have also regularly changed, and many also remain contested. Self-evidently, and as noted by many over the years (e.g., Wilkinson 1951; Peckham 2001; Irvine and Gal 2000), maps involving boundaries and names are a key part of the ongoing claims to legitimacy of the state and many of its related institutions—particularly, for this area, the Orthodox Church, the military, and the police.

As a result, maps of this sort constituted a familiar technology to people in Epirus in general, and to those living near the Greek-Albanian border in particular. They symbolized the range of interests and powers directly involved in the ascription to this place of a variety of different shapes and names, and they were also often treated as powerful objects in themselves: as I have mentioned, there were restrictions in access to certain kinds of maps, and the polemical way in which others were published embroiled maps in serious disputes, not only between individuals and groups, but also occasionally between states. The power of a map depended upon who had constructed it, how much access to it was provided, and who was willing to support its boundaries and names against other boundaries and other names. In that sense, maps could be representative of an always already partial view and could also be performative, in that they could potentially alter the shape and name of a place. It was often the lack of clarity over whether a particular map was a representation alone (an assertion with no teeth) or was also potentially able to change the shapes and names of things in its image, as it were—to literally interpellate places—that caused considerable levels of tension over maps in this area.

My first direct experience of this was the result of my attempts to pursue some of the things people had said during those endless mystifying conversations about land degradation. After some months of listening to people telling me that the land degradation in their area was not about landslips and soil erosion, but about depopulation and land abandonment, I decided to carry out a detailed survey of two village territories. Many people had described what their village territories used to look like before the abandonment and overgrowth, and I realized after a time that these were descriptions not of something that no longer existed but of something that was still there for them, partially hidden. All the continual movement and activity, the "dwelling" that was associated with the past use of these village territories, had somehow, by being abandoned, been fixed in place for some people. As I was also aware of a different perspective on these abandoned areas, one that described such places as "returning to nature" or as "natural wilderness," I thought it might help if I walked every foot of a couple of village territories, to note what the different areas had been used for and were being used for now, and how all of this related to the different perspectives I was being given about the matter.

It seemed like a simple enough idea, but I did not reckon on the complexities of the politics and performativity of maps, which was in retrospect touchingly naive of me (I had not yet grasped the significance of the imposition of fractality upon the Balkans). The first difficulty was getting hold of any kind of graphic image of village territories that outlined the area in sufficient detail to enable me to walk through it and mark what was there. This difficulty had two sources: first, organizations that possessed such "blueprints" (outlines of the boundaries of land plots, whether fields or built upon) were extremely disinclined to allow me to have copies of them, even when village presidents had given me permission to have copies of the ones detailing the village they represented; and second, it turned out that a considerable number of the villages I was studying had never had any such blueprints made.

This second point was one of those things that surprised me and had led people to respond, "What do you expect, Sarah? . . ." It meant that a good number of people did not have title deeds to their properties: title deeds must contain a textual description of the property *and* a drawing of it, giving detailed dimensions and describing adjoining properties. In Epirus, such blueprints for individual properties are most often taken from available blueprints of entire village territories; this is cheaper than commissioning a survey for yourself and usually prevents arguments with neighbors about boundaries, as the village territory blueprint represents the "official" boundaries. Village territory blueprints were gradually drawn up following the end of Ottoman rule in 1913, after which residents of some communes were granted ownership of areas that they had been using under the aegis of an Ottoman landlord or administrator. For one reason or another, though—including changes in Greek government policies on granting land ownership, the intervention of wars, exchange of populations, and the later process of mass emigration from the area— the practical business of having village territory blueprints drawn up had been far from completed by 1994. This revelation would later contribute considerably to my understanding of the ambiguous and diverse ways in which many people in Epirus related to the concept of land ownership, as I discuss in chapter 6; here, I simply want to note that maps and mapping continue to be an incomplete and tense political business in the region.

Having finally secured two village territory blueprints, one of which had been drawn up in 1933 and the other in 1965,[41] and permission from the village president to carry out the survey (as well as having informed as many people in the village as I could), I began the process of hiking methodically around the two territories, in the company of Geoff King, who had come to visit for the purpose. This took two solid weeks, during which time we repeatedly got lost; through this, and through hikes around the landscape at other times on my own or in the company of people from the area, I gained considerable experience of how people had come and gone around these places in the past and more recently, how to distinguish between paths people had used and those made by goats (which usually led to nowhere in particular, except a nibbled bush), how to deal with sheepdogs, and exactly what people had meant when they said that the prickly overgrowth of oak scrub in disused fields was impenetrable.

In these wanderings, I would occasionally come across others—villagers grazing their animals or tending to some remaining fields; illegal immigrants from Albania traveling cross-country to avoid the police and army; transhumant pastoralists on their way to somewhere else; a woman collecting hay for her animals; somebody visiting a chapel, and so on. Often, the sight of me—with my blueprint and accompanying topographical maps—covered in insect bites and scratches from attempts to get through thicket, caused considerable curiosity. One reaction, from a man who was working in his field, and whom I had met several times before in the village, gives a flavor of the kinds of comments I received:

"What are you doing over there?" (No greeting, which was rare under other circumstances.)

"Good morning. I'm trying to mark down what all these fields are used for, and what they used to be used for. Are these your fields?"

"What are you doing that for?"

"Well, I'm doing a study about people's understanding and use of the landscape around here. How it used to be, and how it is today. Kind of an environmental study, in a way."

"You know there are a lot of Albanians around, don't you?"

"Yes, I know. I saw some earlier, as a matter of fact."

"It's not safe. They'll kill you for ten drachma."

"It's okay, I'm with a friend. He's over there in the oak scrub; he'll be here in a minute."

"Oh, you have a man with you? Still, it's not safe." The man paused, watching as Geoff emerged from the bushes, and then said:

"Maps and wandering around the landscape. Some people might say you were spies, you know. Are you spies?" He grinned broadly. I grinned back.

"I only wish I were. I'd get a lot better pay than I'm getting. I'm just a researcher from a university." The man laughed, and then looked at Geoff.

"Doesn't he talk, your friend?"
"Oh yes, but not in Greek."

This required no further explanation, and the man went back to his work, ending the conversation.

"Bye, then," I said. He half-raised a hand without looking up and muttered,
"People will say you're spies, you know."

Similar conversations were repeated on several occasions, even with people I encountered whom I knew quite well from the villages. Putting things on a map anywhere near the Greek-Albanian border was automatically a suspicious thing to be doing, and it had to have political motivations and connotations, even when what I was mapping were overgrown fields.[42] One of the other common suspicions was that I was in search of British gold sovereigns. These had apparently been distributed in the area during the Greek civil war (1946–49), in an attempt to support the anticommunist forces there. In fact, there is still a market for these gold coins on the Greek stock exchange. As I came from a British university, quite a number of people assumed I had inside information about where some of them might still be hidden, information that I would obviously not wish to share with anyone else. The past and present involvement of various "Great Powers" in this area was never far from many people's minds. In any case, it was quite fortunate that I carried out this kind of intense mapping activity on only two village territories—indeed, in two villages where I was known quite well; otherwise, my reputation in the area might not have survived such naive initial attempts to clarify ambiguity.

Overall, being part of a wider multidisciplinary research program often gave me a peculiar kind of ethnographic experience. For one thing, the research stretched across a number of years, a luxury that is all too rare in ethnographic research today, and that made it possible for me to spend a good deal of time in a range of different places, doing different things and focusing on the same issues in depth from a range of angles. It also continually stretched my intellectual boundaries, challenging me at every turn to justify an anthropological approach.

Most important, the range of techniques and technologies to which I had access allowed me to explore how things are different but also the same across a range of scales for the people associated with Pogoni as well as a number of other places around Epirus. Satellite images, information about tectonic activity in the region, reams of statistics about population, animal numbers, crop production, land use, historical accounts, studies on cultural heritage, information about environmental sustainability, information about borders and boundaries, visas and passports—all were treated by many people as different kinds of accounts, some more powerful and some less so, of how things seem and how things are. Each account was generally seen as the combined outcome of somebody's rules (specialization backed up by authority) and negotiation (differing particularistic interests, one of which eventually gains the upper hand, for a time; but there will always be a next time). Crudely and in general terms, people understood this diversity of accounts of "the truth," as well as attempts to combine them, as parts of contests or disagreements, motivated by partial interests stretching across a range of scales (political, economic, disciplinary, social), much as they experienced the depiction of their place and themselves (the multiple maps and names, the ongoing involvement of Great Powers). None of these accounts stood for themselves and alone; they were always assumed to exceed what they asserted they were (i.e., all data or maps were assertions, partial representations, part of an argument, and that is what made them *look* clear). As many people kept telling me in many different ways, things continually change, but they stay the same: you can divide and subdivide, redraw the shape of the place and rename it as much as you like; it will remain the same, because there will always be other divisions and subdivisions. That gets me finally to one of the more recent versions of this reshaping in Epirus, a range of EU-funded development programs aimed at kick-starting the flagging Epirot economy, while at the same time celebrating the region's cultural heritage and conserving its natural heritage. Epirus is not a part of Greece that is noted for its classical ruins, and its northern part, where I spent most of my time, is not a beach area. Instead, there are deep forests, breathtakingly high snowcapped mountains, and a lot of wildlife; and as it is an "out-of-the-way place" (to use Anna Tsing's phrase) in the European Union's terms, it is assumed to contain many "traditional" peoples and "traditional" settlements. The area is now peppered with blue signs featuring a ring of yellow stars (the insignia of the European Union), itemizing that this or that program or project has been funded for the place where the sign is posted, and that it has a budget of X amount (figs. 2 and 12). To many people in Epirus, this is another version of the attempt to change the shape and the names of places and people here, and once again it involves transnational relations, as well as transnational accounts and representations of how things are and how things seem. The difference this time is a shift in emphasis of what was to be standardized or homogenized: whereas in the past, it might have been nations and their nationals, now it seemed there was a particular standard for evaluating the aesthetics of the diversity of culture and nature, a standard that made it possible to "package" each people and place into something distinct and unique, which could nevertheless be classified and would be of interest to tourists to visit.

Figure 2. Gamilla/Timfi mountain with European Union development funding sign

This is something that Richard Wilk calls hegemonic "structures of common difference" (Wilk 1995: 118); Herzfeld calls it the "global hierarchy of value," commenting that "even 'diversity' can become a homogenous product. So, too, can tradition and heritage: the particular is itself universalized" (Herzfeld 2004: 2). All the "packages" of culture would have to take the same standard form: for people, there would be costume, food, music, myths and legends, language or argot, festivals and traditions, and so on; for the places with which the people were now indigenously associated, there would be the traditional settlements as well as the untouched natural beauty of the flora and fauna, and, in the Epirot region, the awe-inspiring height of the mountains. What is absent in these celebrations of culture and nature is, of course, any hint of conflict or political tension, as Wilk also notes for Belize (Wilk 1995: 128). This reshaping of the "where" presented a different version of things appearing and other things disappearing. The key element that remained the same as in other reshapings was that for "packaging" to be done in this way, there had to be clarity of boundaries and belonging, and a certain kind of specialness and distinctiveness for both place and people, a distinctiveness that was about culture, nature, and heritage, and not about Balkan ambiguities. Once again, the Pogoni region found itself unable to package itself appropriately. And that gets me back to the issue of the ambiguity and ordinariness of marginality with which I started, and with which I will continue.

CHAPTER 2

Travels

ONE DAY IN APRIL 1993, I was busy driving around the Pogoni area in an old Ford Escort I had brought over from Britain, to get a feel for the place, as I had been in Epirus only a couple of weeks and needed to get my bearings. I had been familiar with the Zagori area and the Louros area to the south of Ioannina from previous visits, but my knowledge of Pogoni was sparse. Since I was initially there to explore the instability of the physical environment, I thought I ought to get some sense of that for this area before talking with people about it in any depth. My arrival in Mavropoulo, a small village halfway up a hill to the north and west of the Kasidiaris, was my last stop during an increasingly worrying day. I had become hopelessly lost in a forest (which I later learned was called Bouna) that straddled the Greek-Albanian border, as I attempted a shortcut to a village called Argyrohori, about a mile away from Mavropoulo along the same hill. A Greek soldier on a motorbike had flagged me down, told me that I was in danger of crossing the border into Albania, and further told me that I must not take any photographs and that I must turn back. I finally found my way out, only to be confronted by some sheepdogs belonging to a farm on a small plain by the edge of the forest; the dogs seemed intent on chewing my car tires off. It had not been a good day.

So as to calm my nerves, I stopped at a small *kafeneio* (coffee shop) in Mavropoulo. The people I met there were among the first I came to know in the Pogoni area. It is with them that I begin this chapter, which attempts to capture something of the way differing people described and experienced the "where" of this place. They represent just a small portion of the accounts people shared with me, and this first encounter was fleeting: a half hour spent in a *kafeneio*.[1] Others involve people I came to know very well over the years, and who spent patient hours explaining things to me. Obviously, what was said, left unsaid, shared, or exchanged, and the way in which things were said within each type of encounter or relationship would be different, and I mean to reflect that by including a diversity of encounters here; but there were also elements that remained the same, replications and not-quite-repetitions, across these distant, brief, and closer relations. Overall, the chapter provides a patchwork sense of the Pogoni region during this period in relation to other places and other times, through people and events, through accounts of the past, present, and possible futures. In particular, it draws out how different kinds of movement or being prevented from moving generated distinctions that mattered as well as ambiguities and similarities between people and between places.

FIRST ENCOUNTERS

There was a man in his fifties, Yiannis, as well as a younger man and woman, in the Mavropoulo *kafeneio* on that day in April, and there was a small child playing on a tricycle on the veranda—a large, wide veranda made of concrete and perched on the edge of the hill, giving a view of the valley below, some of which was in Greece and some in Albania. The young man was the son of the *kafeneio*'s owner; he ordinarily lived in Corinth with his wife (the young woman) and child, but was briefly visiting his parents for a few days and was helping out in the shop. I ordered a coffee from him, then sat down to write in my notebook, and I could feel Yiannis studying me curiously from his table about ten feet away. In truth, I must have looked a bit of a sight: dusty from my travels across dirt track roads with the car windows open, as well as somewhat rattled and distracted by the experiences I had just been through. Eventually he leaned over and said, in a slightly aggressive tone, "If you don't mind my asking, where are you from? *If* you don't mind." I explained about my research, and he replied, "As long as you've got papers, you'll be okay. There are a lot of Albanians around here, you know." I said I knew, deliberately ignoring the implication that Yiannis was wondering whether I might be Albanian myself. I also knew he was expecting me to show him my papers, to prove that I had a legal right to be here, dusty or not. But I had already realized that nobody from the Greek side of the border presented their papers that way; only those from the other side of the border—from "Inside" (Μέσα), as Albania was almost invariably called in Epirus—would eagerly reach into their pockets for their documents when challenged in the way Yiannis had challenged me. So by ignoring his indirect request to prove myself, I was asserting that I had nothing to prove. After a couple of minutes of this standoff, Yiannis had clearly satisfied himself that I was not Albanian, for he relaxed and began to joke and tell stories for the rest of my time in the *kafeneio*. He also went on to say that Albanians were crossing the border constantly these days, and he complained about the negative effects this was having on people's sense of security and also the way it had badly affected employment. I understood the comment as an apology.

During 1993 and much of 1994, this topic of conversation (people from Albania crossing the border into Greece in large numbers since 1991) recurred so often that I began to use it, as many others did, to gauge the political leanings of the speaker. There were widely differing opinions about the level of threat (if any) these people represented and the causes and nature of the problems (if any) that they posed (Green 1998a; 1998c). For example, in 1992, during my first short research visit to Epirus and just a few months after the border had been reopened, I was taking a hike through a gorge in the Zagori with three archaeologists and with Nikos, a man in his twenties from Aristi, who now divided his time between Aristi and Ioannina, and who was a professional photographer. We were in search of Paleolithic sites, which was another part of that summer research program in addition to my work on people's attitudes toward land slippage.[2] We came across a group of five people from Albania in the gorge—four young men and an older man. Looking tired and fed up, they asked us how to get to Trikkala and where the police and military were patrolling at the moment, so they could avoid them. Their faces dropped as Nikos told them the distance to Trikkala, which is in Thessaly on the other side of the Pindos Mountains, the highest mountains in the region. Nevertheless, Nikos tried to be as helpful as he could, describing the best routes, for which they were obviously grateful. The older man then explained, in broken Greek, that they just wanted to find work; that they had left their families behind in Albania, and after they had made a bit of money, they would return. Nikos protested that they did not need to justify or explain themselves to *him*. He gave them his water bottle, as they did not have one and it was high summer, and wished them good luck.

At the other extreme, I also took a trip through some forest and disused fields very near the border in the Pogoni area with a forest guard in May of 1993. He expressed utter distaste for and distrust of people from Albania, arguing that they were "wild people" with no respect for the law, and that for him, the law was the most important thing: "Without a fear of the law, people are lost," he said. He expressed admiration for Georgios Papadopoulos, the leader of the military junta in Greece that held power between 1967 and 1973, saying that Papadopoulos had imposed discipline and order, and that was a good thing. The forest guard was also one of the few people I encountered who stated that as far as he was concerned, there was no difference between Albanians and Northern Epirots; the Greeks in Albania, he said, had lost their "Greek cultural heritage." He meant this both in social terms (in his view, decades of being unable to cross the border had socially altered these people) and in more biologically determinist terms (he believed intermarriage between Albanians and Greeks had turned Northern Epirots into "mongrels"). He added that if he came across Albanians in the forest, he would shoot first and ask questions afterward. Somewhat alarmed, for he was carrying a gun, I asked him whether that was legal, given his previous strong statements about respect for the law. He did not respond, and I was left hoping that he was not serious. Others from the nearby village laughed when I discussed my concerns about the conversation with them; the forest guard, they said, would be incapable of shooting a fly; they insisted that he was just trying to make himself look "big" for my benefit. Still, that kind of encounter, along with various others I had over the years involving the military and police in the border area, made me acutely aware of the tensions surrounding this particular kind of movement across the region.

To return briefly to the *kafeneio* and Mavropoulo: Drosoula, a woman in her early seventies, came in after a time, and Yiannis started bantering with her. The younger woman gave Drosoula an ouzo and went to the back of the shop to make her a small plate of snacks (*mezes*) to eat with it. Yiannis told her to make a garlic dip (*skordalia*), not salad, because salad was no good for Drosoula's stomach. The young woman complained, as she had only just made herself a coffee, but she made the *skordalia* anyway. Drosoula ignored the conversation, as she sipped on her ouzo and stared at me curiously, as Yiannis had done earlier. Another man came in after a few minutes, and Yiannis initially told him that I was an Albanian, a friend of another Albanian woman whom a man in the village wanted to marry, and I had come looking for a husband as well. That was another one of Yiannis's long line of topical jokes, and I thanked him sarcastically for it; he grinned broadly in response. Yiannis then changed tack, having found that the visitor was not convinced by his Albanian bride claim, and instead told him I was a journalist from a local television station, and this time he was believed, until I eventually explained my version of who I was and what I was doing there.[3] None of the people in the shop were interested that I was doing research on soil erosion and land degradation, and any small efforts I made to bring the matter into the conversation were met with indifference. They just kept warning me not to go wandering around the landscape on my own, on the grounds that it was not safe. All of them also repeated several times that I must not stop for anyone on my drive home to Ioannina, saying that any hitchhikers were bound to be people from Albania, and even if they did me no harm, then the police would arrest me, as it was a criminal offense to give a lift to an illegal alien. Drosoula in particular kept on repeating that I had to be careful of "the Albanians," for a lot of them were "bad people." She also complained about one man from Albania whom the village had taken in "as our own": they had even taught him Greek, yet he just disappeared without a word. Very bad manners, she thought. Not long after that, I said my goodbyes and made my way back to Ioannina for the evening.

Subsequently, I came to know quite a number of the people associated with Mavropoulo, as well as Zavroho and Argyrohori, neighboring villages located along a dirt track road running lengthwise halfway up the same hill (map 4). Between Mavropoulo and Argyrohori was Chrisodouli; people said that it had in the past been a "Turkish" village, and that there was still a social distance between Chrisodouli and the surrounding villages, even though everyone in Chrisodouli was now regarded as Greek. After the "Turks" left the village (some in 1913, others during the 1920s exchange of populations between Greece and Turkey), the people who moved in had been from a range of other places, and some of them were Vlachoi; in contrast, the villagers in Zavroho and Mavropoulo were described as being either "just Greek," "pure Greek," or *Gréki*. What people meant when they said Chrisodouli had been "Turkish" was that during the Ottoman period, the villagers who lived there were mostly Albanian-speaking Muslims, which was also the case for Argyrohori. One thing to note here is that when referring to Albanian-speaking Muslims of the Ottoman period, people on the Greek side of the border described them as "Turks" (a term used to describe all Muslims of the Ottoman period, wherever they were from and whatever language they spoke); when referring to Albanian-speakers (Muslim or not) of the current period, people described them as Albanians.

In any event, all these villages were included in the area I have called Western Kasidiaris, and they were unambiguously part of Pogoni, whether in terms of the county border or the wider "traditional" Pogoni. However, in addition to the Greek-Albanian border, another boundary affected them: a perceived division between Upper and Lower Pogoni. This division resulted, as everything always seemed to do around here, in an ambiguity. Upper Pogoni was generally regarded as having had closer relations with Vlach transhumant or semitranshumant pastoralists, both in the past and in the present, because of the good grazing lands in the region, people said; whereas Lower Pogoni was considered to be composed mostly of rather poor villages located on thin and fairly poor soils, and whose villagers engaged in a variety of activities, including pastoralism and cultivation, as well as long-distance labor migrations, to make ends meet. The Lower Pogoni peoples were also thought to have much closer relations (that is, kinship relations) with the peoples across the border in Albania than the Upper Pogoni peoples. Most often, people stated that Lower Pogoni was divided from Upper Pogoni by the main road connecting Albania and Greece in this region, the northern half being Upper Pogoni and the southern half being Lower Pogoni.[4] That would make Zavroho, Mavropoulo, Chrisodouli, and Argyrohori part of Upper Pogoni; yet clearly most people felt that these villages' equally strong past relations with people on the Albanian side of the border, as well as their close relations with neighboring Lower Pogoni villages—particularly Ktismata, located on an opposite hill—effectively placed them in Lower

Pogoni. In including them in Western Kasidiaris, I have sidestepped that Upper Pogoni/Lower Pogoni ambiguity for the moment.

COMING AND GOING

One of the people from Mavropoulo who came to be a friend over time was Dimitris, a man in his seventies. I met Dimitris while he was walking along the dirt track road between Argyrohori and Mavropoulo one day, returning home from tending to some of his fields, on which he grew fruit and vegetables for his own consumption. I offered him a lift, and after accepting it, he invited me in for lunch. It turned out to be one of the best meals I had eaten for weeks: Dimitris had spent much of his life as a professional cook. The following is an all-too-brief account of the story he told me.

Dimitris was one of nine siblings. He went to school until he was thirteen, but after that, his father made him leave the house to go to find work. Dimitris explained that in those days, there was not really enough food for large families, so most of the boys were asked to go off and make their own way early on. The majority of brothers were also expected to live elsewhere when they married, and all sisters were expected to do so.[5] The same had happened during the Ottoman period, Dimitris said, when most of the men in his village would travel to Constantinople (Istanbul) or other places (particularly to what are today Romania and Bulgaria) to find work, and they continued to do so, coming back for short periods and then going again, for most of their adult lives. Things had become different since the end of the Ottoman regime and the imposition of national borders, he explained, but it was the same kind of idea, really.

Incidentally, the similarity between this past pattern of moving around and the current movement of people from Albania across the Greek-Albanian border was not lost on many people associated with the Pogoni area. Even though opinions varied about these movements, those who had a history of going away repeatedly and then coming back from time to time—especially those who had regularly crossed the border into Albania in the past and/or who had kin in Northern Epirus—recognized a pattern, a similarity between their own pasts and these more recent movements, whether or not they felt happy about the way it was occurring on this occasion. In later years when I visited Epirus, many people suggested that things had "settled down" with the border crossings, but they did not mean that people had stopped crossing the border illegally. Rather, they meant that the way in which the movement occurred had become familiar. By 1995, most could identify different kinds of moving across the border, whereas it had previously seemed like a chaotic mass of movement. Now there were those people who hopped across the border just for a few hours or days to buy supplies or see relatives; there were those who intended to emigrate permanently from Albania but kept being caught and sent back, only to return the next week, or even the next night; there were those who would cross during periods of seasonal work, such as for picking fruit in the Peloponnese, and who returned after a few months; there were those moved to Epirus and began to take up trades such as mountain pastoralism and stonemasonry, which had declined hugely on the Greek side over the decades since the border had closed; there were those who were involved in various kinds of smuggling and other kinds of illegal trade, and these included people from both sides of the border, traveling in both directions; and there were those who came across to steal things and then return—*they* were unanimously condemned. Yet some people sympathized, saying that most were driven to steal out of desperation; others suggested that the thieves were the ones who had been given amnesty and let out of Albanian prisons by the first elected president of Albania, Sali Berisha; still others said that the thieves were "naturally bad" people, lacking any morals, and that this was a characteristic of Albanians in general.

I should note here that the stealing of animals was regarded as an entirely different activity from other kinds of theft, and talk about it reminded me very much of both Campbell's and Herzfeld's work on that issue (Campbell 1964: 206–12; Herzfeld 1985). Many regarded those who crossed the border to steal goats, sheep, or cattle, which were herded back across the border into Albania, as continuing an extremely long tradition for the Epirot area, one that had all but disappeared over recent decades (though never entirely). One Vlach pastoralist from Kefalovriso, a predominantly Vlach town in Upper Pogoni, told me toward the end of 1993 how twenty-two of his cows had been stolen the previous week, so he had simply gone to Argyrokastro, the main town in Albania nearest to the Greek border, to retrieve them, which he succeeded in doing. This was the same kind of thing his grandfather used to do, he said. In sum, what people meant when they said that things were "settling down" on the matter of border crossings was that these movements had begun to take on a predictability and a familiarity, a not-quite-replication of what had occurred before for people on both sides of the border.

Returning to Dimitris's story: as a thirteen-year-old boy in the 1930s, he began his working life as a *tsopanos*, traveling around the Pogoni area and tending other people's sheep and goats, but he did not earn enough to survive, so he left after a few months and went to Ioannina. The first job he got was as a greengrocer's assistant, and he slept on the floor in the shop at night. "The greengrocer was a mean man," Dimitris recalled. "He wouldn't even let me eat the squashed tomatoes that couldn't be sold. Most days, he just gave me a small piece of bread, or a few beans. You can't live on that." After a time, during which he had campaigned for better conditions, he left and got his first job in a restaurant in Ioannina washing dishes, and there too he slept on the floor at night. The owner of the restaurant was not much better than the greengrocer, Dimitris said: "Can you imagine what it was like, cleaning plates and being given the odd crust of bread, and not even being allowed to eat the scraps that people had left on their plates?" Dimitris recalled how things improved a little after "the dictator" (Ioannis Metaxas, who ran the Greek government between 1936 and 1941) came to power: Metaxas changed the law, he said, so that workers were given a minimum wage. Moreover, the mayor of Ioannina made new regulations about the minimum workers were to be fed in jobs that included meals; meat had to be provided at least twice a week.

After a couple of years of work in Ioannina, Dimitris traveled to Athens and carried on working in restaurants, slowly beginning to learn his trade. When he was seventeen, he returned to Mavropoulo to see his family. He had no money to hand over to the household, so his father sent him away again, and he returned to Athens. For a time, he joined the police force, but when Greece was drawn into the Second World War (October 28, 1940, when Italian forces invaded Epirus from Albania), Dimitris quit so he could return to Mavropoulo, which was at the heart of the first Greek region to be invaded. Resistance groups began to form in Epirus explicitly to fight the Italians and then later the Germans, but even at this early stage, Dimitris recalled, there were political differences between the groups. Dimitris called one side of this political divide the *Ethniki* (National) resistance, and the other side the *Elliniki* (Greek) resistance. The "National" resistance was right-wing, the "Greek" resistance communist, he went on. He described how members of these groups would visit the villages in the area to recruit new members. "Well, it wasn't exactly recruitment, you didn't have much choice in the matter. If you said no, they would come back and shoot you that night. So we all learned that you had to join the first resistance group that found you. I joined Zervas's people for that reason." General Napoleon Zervas was the head of a group called EDES, which was based in Epirus; although it was semiautonomous, it allied itself with the Greek army and in the subsequent civil war fought the EAM/ELAS forces, who were supporters of the communist cause.[6] "Even before the Second World War ended," Dimitris recalled, "we would go around hitting the communists, hitting the other Greek resistance fighters who were also against the Germans, because they were communists. This is the way Greek people are," he sighed. He went on to say that he had never been much interested in politics, and after that experience, he had become disillusioned with the idea of politics altogether. Still, he mused, the socialists had done some good things in recent years; they had changed the dowry system, which had relieved the pressure on parents with daughters to provide financially crippling amounts of goods, property, and/or money to the groom's family (something that had personally affected Dimitris), and had helped people who did not have enough to eat (ditto).

This story of the manner in which people in the villages in this area were recruited to fight in both the Second World War and the civil war was repeated to me many times. One man from Kerasovo, a village on the slopes of the Kasidiaris on the northwestern side, who was visiting from his home in Athens where he had lived since the wars, recalled how "gangs of guerrilla groups" would continuously pass through Kerasovo:

> Each group would turn up and would ask whether the other group had been supported or helped by us, but we soon learned that whatever answer we gave, they would whack us. They would burn a few houses down, kill and eat some of our sheep and goats, take a few of our people as recruits, and then go off. Then the opposing group would come through, ask the same questions, and do the same thing. Eventually, we just told any new group coming in to whack us and get it over with, and not to bother with the questions. Anyway, after that went on for a while, those of us who remained decided to leave. There were no animals left, no food left. We had to go.

Although this was a common account of what had happened, not everybody I met said they felt forced to join one group or another. Spiros, one man I came to know quite well, was from a small town, Despotiko, in the southern Kasidiaris area; he emphatically said he had joined EAM, the communist faction, out of commitment. As a young man, he had made his way to Athens, and while there he had begun to read Trotsky, became converted to communism, and joined EAM as a result. He left Athens toward the end of the Second World War because he was being pursued by the police for his political commitments. In any event, he said, as he had herded sheep and goats in Epirus when he was younger, he knew the mountains extremely well, so he could be helpful to the communist side of the conflict in the region. In 1946, when the civil war started in earnest, he was "out in the mountains again, fighting." Spiros was jailed in Ioannina along with a friend of his from Doliana (in Eastern Kasidiaris) after the civil war. That had not stopped him being a communist, however; when I met him, he was still proudly displaying his membership card from the KKE, the Communist Party of Greece, on his mantelpiece.

Spiros had four brothers and a sister. Two of his brothers had also joined the EAM/ELAS; following the end of the civil war, one had fled to Albania, and the other to Romania, ending up in Russia. His sister had stayed in the village and had not fought in the war. His other two brothers had joined EDES, Zervas's group, who had fought the communists. Spiros's family was thus one of the many I met which had been divided by the resistance groups that different family members decided (or were forced) to join, and this continued to have ramifications right up to the 1990s.

One of Spiros's friends in the village, Panayiota, had a somewhat different experience. Both her parents had joined ELAS/EAM (both women and men fought in the resistance, particularly on the communist side); after the civil war ended, the whole family fled to Romania. Panayiota's father died there, so her mother decided to return to Epirus along with Panayiota and her two younger brothers. Her mother died shortly afterward, and Panayiota was left to care for her brothers on her own. After they grew up, she continued to live in the village, earning her way by chopping wood for people, digging fields, harvesting crops, and gardening. She never married.

Dimitris's reasons for coming and going—and then eventually leaving for a long period in 1950, not to return until 1983 when he retired—were somewhat different. After the Second World War ended, he married a young woman from the next village and then joined the Greek army. Unfortunately, he said, the civil war then broke out forcefully in 1946, and as a soldier he was once again engaged in "whacking the communists." That was also when the borders with Albania began to be tightly controlled for the first time, for a successful communist revolution had occurred in Albania in 1944, and Enver Hoxha, the new leader (who would remain in power until 1985, when he died), was determined to prevent Greece from realizing their ongoing claims on large chunks of southern Albanian territory, some of which Greek forces had seized and then lost again during the Second World War. Effectively, Albania "disappeared" after that, for the borders would remain tightly closed until late in 1990. Parts of Pogoni on the Greek side of the border also began to fade a little after the wars ended, because it was now necessary to have a special pass to enter the borderland area, a situation that would continue up to the mid-1970s.

For Dimitris, who had returned to Mavropoulo to fight the Second World War, the border closure posed an immediate practical problem. He had inherited some land from his father, who had died a few years previously, and had bought a little more with his earnings from Athens, for a total of twenty stremmata (about five acres). Dimitris's fields were right next to the border. He explained that during cultivation, there are certain times of year when it is crucial to be near the fields almost twenty-four hours a day, to protect them from wild boar, to deal with other pests, and to water and harvest them. The area had become a no-man's-land because of the ongoing dispute between Albania and Greece over the location of the boundary, so police and military prevented Dimitris from entering the area, particularly at night. "Maybe they thought I would sell state secrets to the Albanians," he mused. He tried to carry on for a while after the end of the civil war in 1949 but finally decided it was impossible to make a living from his no-man's-land fields, so he left in 1950 with his wife and young child, first for a short stay in Ioannina, and then to live in Athens.

When Dimitris got to Athens, he found work fairly quickly in a restaurant and continued working in restaurants after that. Sophia, his wife, initially found a job in a chlorine factory, but Dimitris said he could not stand the fact that she was constantly coming home with burns from working with chlorine, so he set up a small corner shop for her in one of the rooms of the apartment he had built for his family. By now, he had four children, three daughters and a son, and they were beginning to grow up. One of his daughters had caused him particular trouble, though not much of that was her fault, Dimitris said. He had sent her to learn to be a seamstress in a textiles school in Athens, but the (male) teacher had sexually harassed her, so Dimitris soon removed her. Then she became involved with a young Athenian man, to whom Dimitris took an immediate dislike: "He used to ask me for money to take my daughter out of an evening, and he was rude all the time. He had a really bad attitude." Eventually, his daughter became engaged to him, but Dimitris persuaded her to break it off after a serious altercation Dimitris had with the young man: "I was giving him some advice and trying to get him to behave himself a little better. He turned to me and told me he did not have to listen to me because I was just an Epirot Vlach. I was not European like he was. Well, that was it. I threw him out of the house." The young man was using the word "Vlach" in generic terms, rather than as a specific reference to the Vlach peoples. When I asked Dimitris one day whether he was a Vlach, he looked surprised and said, "Of course not. I'm just *Gréki*," meaning he was "just Greek". As a generic term, "Vlach" is generally understood to mean "uneducated peasant" or "country bumpkin." In addition, the young man's reference to Epirus as contrasted with Europe was an allusion to a widespread perception in southern parts of Greece, particularly in Athens, that Epirus is more "Balkan" than the southern mainland (what that means is something I will explore in detail in chapter 4). That perception partly stems from three sources: its geographical location (bordering Albania); the reputation Epirus has of being a predominantly pastoralist/peasant region; and the fact that most of Epirus did not become part of the Greek state until 1913 and so remained under Ottoman rule for almost a hundred years more than most of the southern mainland. I will return to this perception of Epirus's location a little later. Here, I just want to note that Dimitris's deep offense at the young man's comments was based on a multitude of hurts: first, that the young man was showing Dimitris, his future father-in-law, no respect; second, Dimitris had continually experienced such insults about being Epirot from other Athenians during his years there, and he was tired of it; and third—the factor that Dimitris emphasized most strongly—he felt he was as good a Greek as anyone else, having fought in two wars to defend the country and made his own way since with no help from anyone, and he was therefore not going to tolerate a young upstart telling him that he was not worth anything. In short, Dimitris resented being told he was not just an ordinary Greek but instead a disheveled kind of ordinary Greek.

Dimitris had a number of other ups and downs during his life in Athens but carried on working in restaurants there and supporting his children until 1983, when his wife died. Ten years later when I met him, he said he was still heartbroken over Sophia's death, and that he still missed her every day. He decided then to retire, and he returned to Mavropoulo. He now divided his time between Athens and Mavropoulo, spending from March to December in the village and the winter months in Athens. Sometimes his children visited him in Mavropoulo for part of the summer, but mostly he spent his time there on his own. In recent years, he had been able to clear about half of his fields of their overgrowth, since the Greek and Albanian governments had resolved some of their ongoing differences over the border issue, and he was allowed to cultivate them again. It was the beautifully cooked products of those fields that I ate the first day I met him.

Dimitris's story was one of dozens people shared with me from this area, and all of them involved a combination of coming and going, of leaving and then coming back again, of difficult moments represented as involving powerful forces that swept across people's lives, as well as powerful representations and ideas about how things seemed. Throughout his accounts, Dimitris emphasized that he was just an ordinary person, someone who had not been highly educated and who made his way in the world, doing whatever he needed to do to get by. Things happened—wars, not having enough food, borders closing and reopening—and he became as involved in these events as the next person, sometimes because of his own convictions, and sometimes because there did not seem to be any choice. And each time, movement was simply a part of everything. That was how he had been brought up; it was what his father had taught him from an early age to expect from life.

A sense of how Dimitris's story was different but also the same as others began to emerge over time. A conversation I had with Theo, Kalliopi, and Katerina, three pensioners living in Zavroho, provided one version of how people around here had an overall sense of what had happened, what their place was like now, and what might become of it. Theo was the president of the commune that represented Zavroho, Mavropoulo, and Chrisodouli together (it was called the Mavropoulo commune); both Kalliopi and Katerina had been born in Haravgi, a Lower Pogoni village due south of Zavroho, right next to the border, and had moved to Zavroho when they married. Theo began the conversation by saying that there were no young people left in his commune, or indeed in most of the villages in the area, and it was unlikely that young people would ever return. He corrected himself a little later, saying that there were two younger people still there, but that one lived mostly in Kalpaki (in Eastern Kasidiaris, on the plain) because his children went to school there, and the other was just hanging around hunting and finding odd jobs. This was a reference to Lakis, the vice president of the commune, a man in his early thirties whose family had moved to New York when he was very young. Unlike his three brothers, Lakis had moved back to Zavroho, he said, because he did not like New York and anyway enjoyed hunting, which was something he could do here freely.

Theo recounted, as did almost everyone from these villages, how the greatest exodus of people from this area had occurred at the end of the civil war, from 1950 onward. He himself had left in 1956 and became a baker in Ioannina, but many people had gone abroad, to the United States mostly, but also to Germany, Australia, and Canada. The reason for that, he said, was that Pogoni had been devastated by the two wars, what with the number of people killed (including several members of his own family), the destruction of animal husbandry and fields, and the closure of the border, not only cutting people off from kin and friends, but also making this area into a restricted military zone. Most people had to choose between staying and starving or leaving and surviving, he said.

Even though the reasons for the move this time were dramatic, the notion of moving as a fact of life was familiar to Theo: "My father had four, maybe five brothers. There was one at Kakavia [in today's Albania], another at Argyrohori, another somewhere else—because there were a lot of siblings, they left. When a house has five brothers, four or five brothers, the house will take two of them. The rest will leave, so the family can live. You understand what I'm saying." Theo went on to say that after the devastation of the two wars, neither the government nor any international agency (a reference to the Marshall Plan)[7] had helped them; they were still not helping them now and probably never would: "They don't care, you know. There's nothing here really, as far as they're concerned." He went on to argue that this region had always been a hard place to live, that the soils were thin and stony, and that was the reason nobody was very interested in helping them. He did not believe young people would return to the area, for a range of reasons: there was little work available, the schools had closed down, there were not enough asphalt roads, and there was not much to do in the area:

> Young people today want discos, they want the cinema and all those kinds of things. This is a hard place to live, and it always has been. But they did live here in the past, though they were held back by the Turks for a long time, you know. Today, people don't like that kind of hard life; they have a better life in cities. The other day a man came here and brought his son to see the place. But he left the next day, the son didn't like it.

Katerina interrupted Theo at this point and said, "Oh yes, I remember that. His father showed him around the village and around the fields, but the boy said he didn't want to because he was afraid of the snakes! He said the snakes would eat him!" All three of them laughed, and Theo continued:

> You see, young lady? These days, the men are afraid of snakes. Unfortunately, that's the way things are today. Unless the state—unless the state thinks and brings some population from somewhere else. But they won't do that, and nobody's coming here, unfortunately. They don't come here. And if they come, they'll come for an hour to see what it is, and then they'll leave.

As I mentioned in chapter 1, notions of abandonment and neglect were common themes around much of the Western Kasidiaris region, though at the same time, most also talked of people still coming and going. Theo had two sons and one daughter, all of whom lived in Ioannina, and they visited with their own children regularly, just as the young couple from Corinth were visiting their *kafeneio*-owning parents in Mavropoulo. Moreover, many relatives of others living in Zavroho and the other villages along the hill also visited fairly regularly, a good number of them staying for the entire summer. When I spent time in these villages in the summer, they were frequently bustling with activity, the coffee shops full of people, children playing outdoors, and regular festivals held. I found myself wondering what was different: what distinguished the coming and going of the past, when most of this area's men went off for the majority of their adult lives, from the pattern of coming and going today. Most people gave the following answers: they did not expect the regular summer visits to continue for too much longer; they did not expect that as many people would return to the villages to retire as had been the case in the past; and they did not expect that the tourist development projects that were going on in some other parts of Epirus would occur here. There was something missing in these answers, however. I had expected people to say that while men in this area had always come and gone and spent large parts of their lives away, women in the past had been based mostly in one or more villages, raising their children and caring for animals and fields, whereas now younger women were based mostly in cities, along with the men. Few people said this; rather, most said that the key thing was that the *children* had gone to cities. Women had also been travelers in various ways both in the past and more recently; the crucial factor determining a sense of a base in an area was whether children were there.

One of many examples of what this meant in practice came from my conversations with Kalliopi and Katerina. Katerina had five children, two boys and three girls; they were now grown up, and three of them lived in Chicago, while two lived in Athens. Katerina also had a total of eight grandchildren living in the United States and three in Athens. Kalliopi had four children, two living in New York,[8] one in Australia, and one in Patras, in southern Greece; all of those also had children, except for her youngest daughter, who was eighteen. Kalliopi's daughter who had moved to Patras had at first lived in Australia; there she met her husband, who was from Patras, and they eventually moved back to Greece to live in her husband's natal home. Theo interrupted at this point to say that Kalliopi's children "had been scattered like the children of a jackrabbit."

Kalliopi had, over the years, traveled repeatedly to Australia (where she stayed for two years on one occasion, between 1981 and 1983), to the United States, and to Patras, to keep in touch with her children. Katerina also regularly traveled to Chicago and Athens for the same reason. She had lived for a time in Chicago, thinking she might stay there permanently, but decided against it. I asked her why, and she wrinkled her nose and said: "Chicago was a very humid place, there was a lot of water. Every evening rain, and dirty, not like here. It was a dirty place. So, I said, why move from all this oak scrub and rain here to all that dirt and rain there? Maybe it's better here? Every day rain. So I came back." Both Kalliopi and Katerina said that their children did visit them in Zavroho as well, often for as much as two months over the summer. Equally though, they traveled to their children. Over time, I understood that when this generation was young, the majority of both boys and girls were expected to leave the house where they were born at a relatively young age (early teens or even slightly before). The boys were to leave to find work and were expected to return later to marry, to set up a house either in their natal village or in another village, and then to leave again for work. The girls were expected to leave to marry, then raise their children and maintain links with relatives in other villages (including siblings who had moved to other villages), and also, when their children grew and left, to visit them regularly as well, and be visited by their children. Kalliopi and Katerina had both married in their early teens (by arranged marriage: "There was none of that love and romance stuff then," Katerina said) and moved to Zavroho from Haravgi, just as Dimitris had left his house in his early teens to wander and find work, then returned to marry and went away again. The one important difference between the past and now was that before the end of the two wars most women and men were married into villages within the Pogoni and Northern Epirot area, and children were initially raised in that area; in more recent years, marriages were occurring much farther afield, and children were generally raised in cities elsewhere. The pattern of leaving, returning, and leaving again remained; but it was also different.[9]

It was also evident that there was a perceived hierarchy ranking the areas into which women had married in the past. Sophia, a woman in her seventies from Argyrohori, recalled how women would have much preferred to marry into the Zagori area when she was a child, on the grounds that the women in the Zagori did not generally have "black knees" from working in the fields as did the women in Pogoni. Zagori village women were imagined as living in large, fine stone houses, wearing fine clothes, and pottering around the house doing not very much, rather than traveling all over the place, working in the fields and with animals in the absence of their husbands, as the Pogoni women did. These Zagori women, it seemed, had the luxury of staying put. In fact, my visits to the Zagori area suggested that few Zagori women had experienced lives of that sort, but the important thing for women associated with the Pogoni was that *some* did.[10]

Interestingly, another woman from Limni, in Upper Pogoni, used the same phrase as the Argyrohori woman on the subject of Lower Pogoni women: "The Lower Pogoni women were black-kneed because they worked in the fields. Who would want a black-kneed wife?" The important thing for her was that Lower Pogoni has some plains that could be cultivated, and that meant Lower Pogoni peoples were "peasants." In contrast, most of Upper Pogoni (still considered relatively poor, in comparison with the Zagori) is hilly or mountainous and therefore is used as grazing lands, not cultivated much at all. That meant many of the Upper Pogoni people were shepherds and goatherds (as well as long-distance labor migrants), but that was seen as better than being "black kneed." I began to understand over time that what was better about it was that people who remained in the region were considered free (or forced) to move around more; they traveled around the whole region as well as engaging in long-distance labor migrations. So not moving around a great deal was good if you were a wealthy Zagori resident; if you were relatively poor, moving around to tend fields, but not moving much beyond the immediate area, was bad; and moving around the whole Epirot region to tend animals or find work was better than just moving around a part of the region and combining that with going much farther afield to find work. In short, accounts of where women would have preferred to marry began to give me a sense of the perceived hierarchies across different areas, hierarchies that seemed to be not-quite-replicated in recent years in Greek tourist brochures about the area. However, the brochures, constituting part of what Herzfeld describes as the burgeoning neoliberal "global hierarchy of value" (Herzfeld 2004), used the language of differing forms of "natural beauty" and "cultural heritage," rather than a language of differing forms of movement.

CROSSINGS, ROUTES, AND REGIONS

There were other stories that gave me a sense of the perceived differences in a westerly, far north, and southerly direction, as well as to the east and immediate north, and I will continue now with the west, which crosses the Greek-Albanian border. Amelia was in her early sixties when I met her, and living in Ktismata (previously called Aristion and then Arnista), a village on a hill across the way from the Mavropoulo villages and right on the Greek-Albanian border. Her story is one of many that people recounted to me about the ambiguities of relations across the border. Amelia's father, who had been a cobbler in Ktismata as well as keeping a shop by the border post (called Kakavia, after the village just inside Albania that is near it), had been married twice; his first wife was from Episkopi, which is now in Albania, and his second was from Pogoniani, which is in Upper Pogoni, just inside the Greek side of the border. Her father had nine children from the first marriage and eight from the second. Of these, only two survived into adulthood from the first marriage (seven died in a flu epidemic while young), but all from the second survived into adulthood. Amelia had been one of the children of her father's second marriage. She did not know what had happened to her half-siblings, but she had kept track of her siblings: one sister married in Northern Epirus and had stayed in Albania after the borders were closed, and she now lived in Tirana, the capital of Albania, located in the north of the country; one sister had moved to Athens and was still living there; one sister was living in Neohori, a village next to Ktismata and part of the Ktismata commune; one sister was living in Ktismata; and her brother, after a long stay in the United States, was also living in Ktismata.

Amelia's mother, she said, had "several" brothers; one of her mother's brothers lived in Pogoniani, and the rest lived for most of their lives in "Poli" (Constantinople/ Istanbul), something that most men from her mother's village had done, she added. Pogoniani, a relatively large town, was also described as having been a "Turkish" town during the Ottoman period, again meaning that many of the people living there during the

Ottoman period had been Albanian-speaking Muslims, though there were also quite a number of Orthodox households.

Amelia's father had been relatively wealthy, for this area. Aside from the cobbling business and the shop, he had use of approximately sixty stremmata (about fifteen acres) of fields and had used casual laborers to help him with his flocks as well as with cultivation. In those days (meaning both during the Ottoman period and before the Second World War), Amelia recalled, people from Ktismata regularly went to "Kastro" (Argyrokastro in Greek, Gjirokastër in Albanian) in today's Albania to shop for supplies. Before the communist revolution in Albania, she went on, that area had been a lot wealthier than the Pogoni area, and getting to Kastro was a lot easier than going to Ioannina. I asked her whether the new national border had not caused a problem for people wishing to cross into Albania after the end of the Ottoman period. She looked at me somewhat puzzled, and then said, "Well, there *was* a border, but you passed across it from wherever you liked. Then they put up boundaries, barbed wire and land mines, and you couldn't pass across anymore. But that was a lot later, after the war [World War II]." This was mostly social memory in Anna Collard's sense (Collard 1989); Amelia recounted what happened when the border was introduced in 1913 as if she remembered it herself, though she cannot have done, as she was born in 1931. When I asked older people in the village about it, most said that the border had remained irrelevant until after the Second World War; what Amelia was recalling was being a young girl in the immediate prewar years and crossing the border with her father to go shopping in Argyrokastro, in the same way as most had done until the closure of the border after 1944.

Amelia was nine years old when the Italians invaded in 1940, and she was moved for safety with other members of her family to the high mountains in the Zagori, as were many of the families from the village. She returned after the war along with many others, but not to exactly the same location: before the wars, most of the houses had been located on a small hill above the current location of the village (which was then called Arnista; its name was changed, for the third time, during the Papadopoulos regime). Many of those houses had been burned down, and there was a new military post based there now, as part of the border controls. So the village moved, as it were, down the hill. Many people used the building materials of the old houses to rebuild new ones in the new location (in fact, "Ktismata" means "buildings"). This literal shifting of villages (that is, housing settlements, rather than whole territories) up or down hills appears to have been common in Epirus for centuries; people would recount to me the various previous locations of their villages, sometimes adding explanations (something happened, and people needed to move), and sometimes not. This was another story of movement that parents and grandparents recounted to their children, along with occasional name changes of villages. Argyrohori had been moved twice during the Ottoman period, people said; Areti (previous name Grimpiani) had been moved from high up on the Kasidiaris to the plain on the eastern side of the Kasidiaris. I began to lose count of the movements of villages after a time.

To continue with Amelia's story: in 1955, when she was twenty- three, Amelia married Takis, a young man from the village. She began to help in his father's plaster-making business by collecting wood for the burning process; it was backbreaking work, she recalled. Two years later, when Amelia's son Dimitris was six months old, her husband died from a gunshot wound while out hunting. Amelia stayed on in the village for a time, being helped by her siblings to take care of the young boy, but in 1966, when her son was nine, she moved to Athens with him. Even at that age, Dimitris worked part-time helping on ships, and then for a time he worked as an elevator operator. In 1969, Amelia moved again, to New York (Astoria). The boy continued to take part-time jobs there, in a fishmonger's business, a supermarket, and then a drugstore. Amelia took a variety of jobs: she worked for many years in an electronics factory during the day, which she described as "very fiddly work," and then took cleaning jobs in the evenings, to build up savings. While in New York, she bought a plot of land in Athens, planning to build there one day. In the event, though, she returned to Ktismata in 1984, after spending fifteen years in New York. Her son also moved back, first to Athens and then to Ioannina, after his marriage had broken up.

When the borders were first reopened in 1991, Amelia explained, she was in a state of excited anticipation, for she would be able to see her sister again, whom she had not seen for almost forty-five years. After managing to get in touch with her, and after the Greek government initially welcomed into Greece all Albanian citizens deemed to be Northern Epirots, Amelia found herself visited by several of her sister's children as well as a couple of her grandchildren—nine people in all—and Amelia happily arranged to help them in any way she could. By the time I talked with her, she was feeling bitter about the whole experience: "I spent thousands on them. I bought them things, I cooked for them, I let them stay here as much as they liked. But they never thanked me, and they stole from me. I'll never forgive them for that." Amelia had trouble making sense of her experiences and wondered what had happened over all those years while Albania had been "closed." She commented at one point that of her sister's five children, two had married Northern Epirots and three "took Albanians"; perhaps that was part of it, she mused.

This was another example of an ambiguity: the difference between an "Albanian" and a "Northern Epirot" was gauged in various ways, but the two most important were surname and religion: if a person had a

Greek surname, was Orthodox, and came from the Northern Epirot area, then he or she was considered Greek. Several older people in Ktismata and nearby villages had told me that their mother (never their father) had not spoken any Greek when she married, but that did not mean she was not Greek, as she was Orthodox, rather than Catholic or Muslim (which would have made her Albanian).[11] This left me with three puzzles in working out what Amelia meant when she said some of her sister's children had married Northern Epirots, and some had married Albanians. First, all the people who had married were, Amelia assured me, Orthodox, so presumably on those grounds they all ought to be Greeks. Yet there was apparently a distinction made between Greek Orthodox and Albanian Orthodox churches in Albania; although few people in Greece made a distinction between them, perhaps Amelia was doing so, in the same way many people from Northern Epirus did so. For example, one man from the Northern Epirot region whom I met, and who now lived on the Greek side of the border but who had grown up on the Albanian side, said his mother was an "Albanian Orthodox" woman who spoke no Greek when she married his father, who was "Greek Orthodox." When I asked Amelia about this, she said, "Orthodox is Orthodox," which did not help me much. Second, in the final years of Enver Hoxha's regime (from 1968 to 1985, when Hoxha died), practicing religion of any kind had been banned, so (considering the ages of Amelia's relatives who married) there would have been little easy access to religion during their younger lives. Although many reported how they continued to practice Orthodoxy secretly despite the government rules (particularly for baptism), young Northern Epirots I met over the years said religion played little part in their own choice of spouse during the socialist period. Third, I wondered what "Northern Epirot" meant in Tirana, which is not anywhere near Northern Epirus and was where Amelia's sisters' children had married; did it mean someone from the Northern Epirot area or someone who was considered Greek? I then wondered whether Amelia judged the "Albanian-ness" and "Northern Epirot-ness" of the marriage partners by their surnames. But it was well known that many people with Greek surnames had changed their names (or had been forced to change them) to more Albanian-sounding ones during the socialist period in Albania, so that was not necessarily a good guide either. Amelia was singularly unwilling to try to clarify this matter for me, simply repeating that three of these people were Albanians and two were Northern Epirots, and that was that; I was left once again with one of those puzzles that dogged me throughout much of my time in Epirus. When I returned to Ioannina one day after visiting Amelia and asked a friend there to clarify things, she smiled and said, "This is the Balkans, Sarah. What do you expect?" I was becoming used to this response by now.

Returning to Amelia's story for a moment: over the months, Amelia also told me of a variety of disagreements she had had and was currently having with her brother who also lived in Ktismata. These disagreements mostly involved jointly owned property; Amelia complained that her brother was either doing Amelia out of what was rightfully hers, or planning to make changes to the property without consulting her. On one occasion, Amelia complained bitterly that her brother intended to add a third door to the garage adjoining the house but had not asked her, and she did not want the garage changed. She had made an appeal to the president of the commune to prevent her brother's being granted permission for the remodeling, but that had not succeeded, which infuriated her. She was not, she insisted, going to give up on this campaign. This range of disagreements meant that Amelia hardly spoke to either her brother or her brother's wife, and she was not on very good terms with her sister (the one who also lived in Ktismata) either, because she felt her sister sided with her brother.

It was in the midst of the dispute over the garage door that I met Amelia's sister and her brother's wife through other friends in Ktismata, one of the few families with four generations based in the village when I first met them. I had popped in to see Fanoula, a woman in her early sixties who lived with her husband, Tasos, a goatherd now in his late sixties, and Tasos's mother. Just down the road, Tasos and Fanoula's daughter-in-law, Pinelopi, had recently moved in with her two young children, also called Tasos and Fanoula (following the common convention that firstborn children are named after their paternal grandparents). Pinelopi's husband (Tasos and Fanoula senior's son), Dimitris, was living in Athens and working as a taxi driver, but he planned to move to Ktismata as well once he secured work in the area. Pinelopi's own parents were also from Ktismata, but they had moved, first to the island of Zakynthos shortly after the civil war, and then to Germany in the 1960s, where they still lived, though they visited Ktismata regularly; her father worked as a builder in Frankfurt. Pinelopi had been born in Zakynthos and had moved with her family to Germany, where she grew up. When she married Dimitris, they decided to move back to Greece. Initially, they went to Athens, where Dimitris started work as a taxi driver. They now wanted to move to Ktismata, since they were both from the area (as it were); Pinelopi had moved there first with the children, both to set up the family's house and to see what she could do to advance Dimitris's prospects for employment in the region. This endeavor eventually failed, as Dimitris did not secure either a taxi license or a job as a forest guard; as a result, Pinelopi and the children reluctantly left Ktismata and joined Dimitris in Athens. Pinelopi felt that the deck was stacked against young people trying to make a go of things in Pogoni villages these days, in economic, political, and social terms, "but mostly political," she said. What she meant was that she believed the granting of taxi licenses and posts such as that of forest guard were in the control of elected politicians who chose candidates according to rules of patronage. That was a sentiment echoed by most young people I met on the eastern side of the Kasidiaris.

I had spent quite a bit of time with Tasos senior (Pinelopi's father-in-law), who still kept a small flock of goats; I went out with him and his animals on several occasions, to talk with him about the area, the soils (slippage and erosion issues), the landscape, and the pastoralism of various kinds that had been and was now being practiced in the area. I also became good friends with Fanoula senior, who would never let me leave her house without a minimum of a few freshly laid eggs. The day I visited Fanoula, having had a long conversation with Amelia about the dispute with her brother over the garage door, Tasos was out with the goats and Fanoula was busy making bread, which she still baked in one of the few stone ovens left in the village (she said the bread tasted much better if baked that way). Tasos senior's mother was wondering about visiting her grandson Dimitris in Athens, but she was worried about all the traffic there; she was also worried about Tasos senior being out with the goats— what with all the "Albanians" around the place these days. Two women, Maria and Katerina, were visiting as well; Maria was Amelia's sister, and Katerina was Amelia's brother's wife. Amelia's crazy, they both said. They went on to explain that the whole family used to live together, and they claimed that Amelia picked fights with everybody; eventually relations with her mother-in-law became so bad that the two refused to speak to each other anymore. This had deeply distressed Takis, Amelia's husband, before he died. Both went on to complain that if anyone was ungrateful, it was Amelia: after Takis's death, both Maria and Katerina helped to take care of the baby (Amelia's son Dimitris) and helped Amelia to travel to Athens, for which Amelia never thanked them. Moreover, they said, it was Amelia's brother who had built the house for Amelia before she got back from New York, and they could not see why it made any difference to Amelia if the garage was altered. Fanoula listened quietly to all these complaints as she carried on making bread. Eventually, when asked her opinion about the dispute, she sighed and said, "I have nothing against any of you, you know that."

The conversation moved on then to more comfortable topics, and after around an hour, the two women left, one with some bags of goat dung from Tasos senior's goat stables (good fertilizer), and the other with some peppers from Fanoula. Fanoula invited me to stay a little longer, and she moved out into her front garden to dig a plot to plant potatoes (Fanoula was always engaged in some activity or another). She was born in Argyro-hori (her mother was Northern Epirot, her father from Argyrohori, she said) and had married Tasos when she was fourteen, by arranged marriage: "I was very pleased. Tasos was a fine, handsome, tall, and slim man, and has been a good man all his life." During the civil war, Fanoula and her family were moved from Ktismata: the *andartes* (meaning communist resistance fighters on this occasion) had targeted them because Tasos and his brothers had joined the EDES forces. One of Tasos's brothers had been killed, so they decided to leave in 1947, when a considerable number of the old Ktismata houses up the hill had been burned down. Fanoula was one of the few women I met who had not traveled a great deal during her life, having been based first around Argyrohori and then around Ktismata. She did not believe many women would lead the life she had led in the future: "Things are different now; and it's hard with the border, you know. We always used to pass across the border with no problems, and then there was the closure. When it first opened again, we thought perhaps things would return to the way they were when I was small. But really, it's caused a lot of problems, and I don't know that things can ever be the same."

Tasos senior agreed with Fanoula's opinions on this, and he believed that the current problems were due to the lack of efficient and disciplined government, both in Greece and in Albania. Things were being allowed to run amok, he felt. During that initial period of "chaos" when the borders were first opened, the same kind of opinion was expressed by many people, including Michalis, a middle-aged man who lived up the road from Tasos. Michalis explained that as far as he was concerned, the people who lived around the border area—Greeks (i.e., "ordinary" Greeks), Northern Epirots, Albanians—were basically good people; he did not have any problems with any of them. In this village, he went on, many of these peoples were related to each other anyway. Michalis was aware, as everyone was, of the growing perception in much of Greece that people from Albania somehow constituted a malignant other in the midst of the Greek population, and he was anxious to let me know he did not feel that way. The problem, he continued, concerned neither race (ράτσα/*ratsa*) nor culture (πολιτισμός/*politismos*).[12] Rather, the problem was the Greek and Albanian governments, and also "that Sevastianos." At the time, Sevastianos was the head (metropolitan) of the Orthodox Church of Drinopolis, Pogoni, and Konitsa (in the north of the Greek side of Epirus), an area that straddled the Greek-Albanian border and included large parts of Northern Epirus. Before the border had reopened, Sevastianos had regularly used a bullhorn to shout the Easter service across the border to what he considered to be his lost flock, and had also regularly made strong Greek nationalist pronouncements on radio stations he had set up near the border in the hopes that his flock in Albania would pick up the signal.[13] Michalis thought all of this had been singularly unhelpful. "If you ask me," he said, "we could do without all these priests; what do we want

Figure 3. Tasos of Ktismata and his granddaughter Fanoula

with priests? They take 200,000-drachma salaries per month, and what can I do with a priest? We need doctors here, not priests. Albania no longer has religion, and it is a lot better off for it."

Michalis was trying to shock me a little, for people rarely spoke out openly against the Orthodox Church in this area (though some did do so privately, usually with reference to particular priests, not the Church as a whole); he wanted to emphasize that in his opinion, the involvement of states and the Church had caused chaos in this region. I asked him whether there had been a period when there had *not* been chaos in the area. He considered this for a moment, and then said, "Yes! When Enver Hoxha was in charge in Albania and when Georgios Papadopoulos was in charge in Greece." "Tough government?" I asked. "Yes, tough government," he said. "We had peace and quiet here then."

Michalis went on to explain that he did not like the politics of either of these leaders (Hoxha having been a Stalinist communist, and Papadopoulos a populist and strongly nationalist army colonel, who was also very supportive of the Orthodox Church). Michalis was thoroughly in favor of democracy in theory; it just did not seem to work terribly well *here*, he said. This was partly because, in his view, elected politicians behaved no more democratically than did unelected ones, so there was not that much to choose between them; the difference was that elected politicians seemed more apt than unelected ones to let things run amok, and in this area, that caused chaos. It seemed to me that Michalis was saying life seemed less chaotic when totalitarian leaders were in charge because such leaders did not permit open disagreements: dictators imposed clarity; they covered up what people felt was a continual ambiguity and tension permeating this region, the result of ongoing conflicts about people, places, and beliefs. At least, in Michalis's view, only one side of the conflict was heard on each side of the border when there were strict controls on both sides, despite Sevastianos's attempts to broadcast his view into Albania; now there was cacophony again.

Tasos also broadly reflected this view, arguing that there was less conflict, more security, and, as important to Tasos, more investment in this region when the military junta had been in control in Greece and the border was closed because Hoxha was in charge in Albania. Tasos expressed this view despite the fact that several members of his family, including his maternal grandmother, were from Northern Epirus. It was not that Tasos had wanted the border closed; it was more that its reopening had also reopened many conflicts and painful memories, many loosely papered-over tensions that would better have remained forgotten. The sense of lack of safety that so many people expressed in the Western Kasidiaris was not only a matter of the newspapers reporting every theft, act of violence, rape, or other negative event that was ascribed to the arrival of Albanian illegal immigrants in Greece; it was also, and perhaps more important, the embodied social memories (Connerton 1989) of conflicts that people felt had torn this region apart—physically, in terms of the border closure and the destruction of so many villages; but also socially and relationally, in terms of families' being split between political factions, both in their support of different resistance groups and in terms of being physically divided by the Iron Curtain. Over the decades, it seemed as though people had just about come to terms with all this imposed fragmentation, things had settled down into a clear set of divisions, and perhaps the personal cost that many had had to pay (including, for those on the Greek side of the border, the disappearance of Albania) was the price of that imposed sense of clarity. But then the border had reopened again. One woman who was 104 when I met her in 1994 in Areti (a village near the lower eastern slopes of the Kasidiaris), and who was one of the few who still remembered the Ottoman regime, repeatedly expressed her sense of terror about the wars that had been raging in former Yugoslavia since the early 1990s: "Tell people, you must tell people," she said, taking a firm grip of my arm, "that there must be unity between all places. Tell them not to argue about who is who and where is where. It always leads to so much death. Please tell them." It was through these kinds of encounters that I began to get a sense both of the insistence on ambiguity and some people's desire for an imposed clarity (the insistence on ambiguity remaining unspoken), even at the price of dictatorship.

It was in this context that I listened to Tasos explaining to me how he felt things had been better during the military junta in Greece, and how things were now going from bad to worse. He explained this as we walked around his grazing lands with his goats, in between my attempts to get him to talk about the soil erosion we were walking through (like most other people, he was indifferent about it and said it never changed). Tasos also talked about his life more generally, and his story was one of the many that told of yet another form of coming and going around this place, and another sense of the "where" of the place, closely related to moving around the region with animals (ζώα/zóa, a term used in this context to mean pastoral animals that are, or used to be, moved from one grazing area to another with the seasons—goats, sheep, and, more recently, cattle). Tasos came from a pastoral family and had been working with animals since he was seven years old, except for a period of military service and during the two wars. "In the old days," he said, "we used to take the animals to Delvinaki for about eight months every year. We left Ktismata in April and would return in December, because there was not enough grazing land here in Ktismata, since there were so many animals. Many of us did that. Now, though, I'm too old to do that kind of thing, so I only have a few goats and I graze them around here."

Delvinaki, also located very near the border, is the other main town besides Pogoniani in Upper Pogoni; it had municipal status, handling most of the local government administration for the area, and was now also the area's center for dealing with border issues. It is located in a small circular valley surrounded by hills, and it was these hills that provided large amounts of good grazing lands. These lands had been used in the past by pastoralists such as Tasos from Lower Pogoni villages, as well as by some Sarakatsani and many Vlachoi, who either passed through with their flocks and herds on their way between southern coastlands (winter) and high mountain areas (summer) or spent a portion of the year in Delvinaki (summer) and another portion of the year in the south, in Thesprotia (winter). Many people in the area referred to these latter people, the Vlachoi who spent the summer in Delvinaki, as the "Delvinaki Vlachoi," and they were regarded as being different people (that is, different families) from the Vlachoi who used Delvinaki as a staging post between more distant destinations. None of the Sarakatsani families who passed through, some of whom had traveled in the past between high mountains in what is now Albania and the low coastlands in Thesprotia, stayed to graze in Delvinaki for any length of time, though some Sarakatsani settled there after the borders with Albania were closed. This included the family of the postman of Delvinaki (Takis), who spent a whole evening on one occasion telling me about a feud between his family and a Vlach family that had erupted over a grazing rights dispute in the 1940s, and that had led to the deaths of several members of both families. Takis still felt extremely strongly about the whole affair and used it to explain his ongoing dislike of Vlachoi in general. In any case, by the time I visited Delvinaki, most regarded it as having a "mixed" population of residents: Vlachoi, Sarakatsani, Gypsies, Northern Epirots, and some Albanians, as well as *Gréki* (people with none of those additional distinguishing names, who were "just Greek").

Over time, it became clear that Upper Pogoni contained all the major transhumant routes through the Pogoni area and also attracted a number of transhumant groups to spend a portion of the year there, whereas Lower Pogoni had none of these arteries, containing only one minor route used by a few "Delvinaki Vlachoi" who traveled to Thesprotia that way. All the people I spoke with about this, including Tasos senior, said that the reason for the difference was environmental: the high-quality grazing lands in the Upper Pogoni area, and relatively poor grazing lands in the Lower Pogoni area. This difference had several important ramifications, in both the past and the present. First, Upper Pogoni in the past was regarded as generally more wealthy than Lower Pogoni, both because of the grazing land rental income and because of the trade that passing groups provided. The fact that the two main towns in the area, Pogoniani and Delvinaki, were both located in Upper Pogoni was no coincidence. In that respect, the Limni woman's view that the predominantly pastoralist Upper Pogoni was better off than Lower Pogoni, with its mixed cultivation and small-scale pastoralism, was based on an accurate assessment of relative wealth. Second, Upper Pogoni was in the past more interconnected with other areas in the region through the transhumant and trade routes than was Lower Pogoni, and therefore was somewhat more "visible" in the region as a whole. Third, although some Lower Pogoni pastoralists such as Tasos could use the Delvinaki grazing lands for a portion of the year, most of those based in the villages lying along the western side of the Kasidiaris (and some of those on the eastern side as well) could not afford to do so. That meant that they generally traveled to the top of the Kasidiaris to graze their animals in the summer and back down again to graze them on the lower slopes during the winter, which restricted the number of animals they could have.

Overall, this meant that in terms of Epirus as a whole, most Lower Pogoni villagers were effectively restricted to their immediate area; they had few ongoing connections through trade or transhumant routes with the wider Epirot area and places beyond—except, and this is an important exception, across the border into what is today Albania. The way mixed cultivation and pastoralist peoples from Lower Pogoni described their past experience of this was in terms of a kind of leapfrogging: if they moved, they leapfrogged over the Epirot region to places such as Constantinople/Istanbul; in more recent years, they leapfrogged over it to nearby cities, such as Argyrokastro and Ioannina, and later skipped from there to bigger cities, such as Athens or New York; they did not, either in the past or in the present, traverse and use the whole region as the larger-scale pastoralists had done. The closure of the Greek-Albanian border effectively made the Lower Pogoni peoples feel even more pinned down to their immediate area; and the leapfrogging had grown more extensive in both space and time.

I began to understand how this affected differing senses of belonging in the region through the contrasting stories that other peoples told of their experiences. Sarakatsani peoples in particular often emphasized a sense of pride in the levels of autonomy they had experienced in the past, and that many felt they had continued, as an inherent part of their "traditional character," into the present.[14] There had been many limitations for the Sarakatsani in the past, especially in their securing of winter grazing lands in the low coastal areas, and in the kinds of problems they encountered with a generally hostile bureaucracy, plus discrimination against them by more sedentary populations, as well as debts (particularly with cheese merchants). Nonetheless, their capacity to come and go across the region was often focused upon as the element that made them different from, and more autonomous than, villagers such as those in the Western Kasidiaris region, and particularly the Lower Pogoni "peasant" region. It was the way that they moved, not the fact that they moved (for everybody moved), that made the difference.

One Sarakatsanos family I met in the Pogoni area expressed this view in terms that made their sense of belonging to the Zagori seem, somewhat ironically, more "rooted" than anything I had heard from Western Kasidiaris villagers. This family owned the two dogs that had tried to chew my car tires the day I emerged from the Bouna forest; the dogs were protecting the seven hundred sheep and seventy cattle that the family jointly owned (which made this by far the biggest pastoral farm in the area). Two brothers and their wives lived on the farm on that plain near the forest; a third brother was a teacher and lived in Ioannina, which is also where the two couples' children lived. Other relatives lived mostly in cities around Greece, though one cousin lived in Germany and another in Switzerland. The two brothers were the only members of their entire extended family who were still working with animals, and they had both continued to move seasonally until 1980. Until the late 1960s, they had also continued to live in "traditional Sarakatsani huts," they said. Then they moved to the Pogoni area from the Zagori, during the Papadopoulos regime, having received subsidies from the junta to buy some grazing land there (100 stremmata, about 25 acres), and also having had their debts canceled by that regime. They built their current houses and stables themselves, and now rented a further 1,900 stremmata (about 475 acres) of grazing land from absentee owners—people who were now living in Australia, Canada, and the United States, as well as some pensioners who still lived nearby but were not using their land anymore.

Even after living in the Pogoni area for more than twenty years, all the members of this family expressed a deep sense of belonging to the Zagori region, couched in terms of a strong pride in the cultural heritage of the Sarakatsani peoples, which they felt was indelibly linked to that region. The brother who now lived in Ioannina had written a book about the Sarakatsani, and one of the women urged me to read it after I explained to her something of my research (Makris 1992). "You should go to the Zagori to study if you're interested in culture," she said, "there is so much culture there. There is nothing here." This was a common opinion about the Pogoni region. When I mentioned that I was focusing my attention on the area around the Kasidiaris, the response was often general blank bafflement. Another example, from a folklorist in Ioannina: "The Kasidiaris—that's in Pogoni, isn't it? You're doing your study on Pogoni? Why? The Zagori is much more culturally interesting; so are Konitsa and Souli. There's nothing in Pogoni."

Strikingly, all the areas mentioned as culturally "interesting" also contained the highest mountains in the region; areas with plains and low hills were not mentioned. I will return to this in the next chapter, continuing for now with the views of the Sarakatsani family I met in Pogoni. This family, along with most Sarakatsani I met (that is, those who emphasized that they *were* Sarakatsani), were acutely aware of how much had been written about the Sarakatsani peoples (in contrast to writings about Pogoni peoples), and strongly represented their cultural heritage with reference to such writings. The Sarakatsani were the "original indigenous Greeks" of this region, I was repeatedly told, and the Zagori was their heartland; if anyone had "roots" in Liisa Malkki's terms (Malkki 1992) in Epirus, it was these peoples. It is worth noting here that Takis's Sarakatsanos family (now living in Delvinaki) had moved between high mountains in what is today Albania and the low coastlands of Thesprotia until the border with Albania had closed; this means Takis's family did not have associations with the Zagori. The high mountains of the Zagori might have been indelibly linked to the Sarakatsani peoples, but that did not mean all Sarakatsani peoples were indelibly linked to the Zagori; accounts of cultural heritage and ideas about indigenousness tend to simplify things.

In any case, the combined sense of distinction, indigenousness, heritage, and autonomy expressed by both this family and Takis's family was in notable contrast to the way *Gréki* of the Lower Pogoni area described their lives. People repeatedly told me, echoing much of what I had read in Campbell (1964) and other studies, that until relatively recently, Sara-katsani married only other Sarakatsani; that they kept deliberately to themselves and were visibly different from other peoples in terms of dress, habits, beliefs, practices, and attitudes. That had in the past led to consid-erable amounts of discrimination against them on the basis of their *being* Sarakatsani, on the basis of their distinctiveness (Herzfeld 1987: 33); while in more recent years, their being Sarakatsani had become some-thing of an advantage in cultural heritage terms (Green forthcoming). In contrast, Lower Pogoni peoples felt they had been discriminated against because they were in the "wrong place," both environmentally and politi-cally, and because of their lack of distinction: they were often regarded as unimportant, and at most somewhat generically peasantlike. Discrimi-nation against Lower Pogoni peoples was never connected with a particu-larity of their identity; it was described more in terms of their lack of distinction, of their being in the "wrong" place, or in terms of neglect and indifference.

The language of movement that most people used in this area seemed to encompass the contrast between the Zagori, the region with which the Sarakatsani were now indigenously associated, and Lower Pogoni, the region with which "peasant Greeks" were associated. In the former, the "Zagori" Sarakatsani had relatively easily and relatively autonomously seasonally traversed the whole region, spending long periods of the year in different parts of Epirus and beyond, then returning each year in the summer to their "homeland," the higher slopes of the Zagori mountains. In the latter, the Lower Pogoni *Gréki* either moved around in their imme-diate area (becoming black-kneed) or leapfrogged beyond the region to somewhere else, and particularly to cities. Moreover, the cities to which they had leapfrogged did not necessarily feel terribly welcoming; just as Dimitris described his negative treatment by the greengrocer and restaura-teur in Ioannina as well as his experiences in Athens, and just as Katerina described her sense of alienation in going to Chicago ("every day rain"), others also described various occasions in the more distant past when they had been "chucked out" of cities. The following is an extract from a taped conversation with a group of people in Pontikates, a village very near the Bouna forest in which I became lost when I first visited Pogoni. I had been talking with the group about the past pattern of most of their grandfathers' leaving for Constantinople and other cities:

SARAH: And they stopped with Constantinople around 1935 or some-thing like that?

NIKOS: Something like that, around then, yes. It was when they were thrown out.

SARAH: They were thrown out?

NIKOS: Yes. Bravo.

SPIROS: They threw them out of [name of city unclear] as well.

NIKOS: That was something different, something else. That was earlier.

SPIROS: The Turks were always doing that—and I forget which time is which [laughs loudly]. I'm laughing now, because they were constantly throwing us out.

Once again, how you move, where you move, whether you are made to move, and when you stop moving made all the difference.

At something of a remove from the accounts of both Sarakatsani and Lower Pogoni *Gréki* was the way Vlachoi described their experiences, and this is worth considering for a moment, as Vlachoi also traversed the whole region, as did Sarakatsani, and did not just leapfrog between cities and one particular part of the region. One initial notable difference was that while Sarakatsani typically identified themselves as such, Vlachoi were generally less inclined to say that they were Vlach when I first met them; in fact, quite a few (including the president of the Argyrohori commune) said that they were "just Greek" and that their being Vlach did not really distinguish them. When such people did mention their being Vlach, this communication was rarely accompanied by long discussions about the cultural heritage and distinctiveness of the Vlach peoples; it was most often simply stated and then left at that. It is well beyond the scope of this study to outline the wide variety of Vlach groups and their relations with others and the region; in any case, other writers have done this much more effectively than I ever could.[15] The main point I want to make here is that although both Vlachoi and Sarakatsani were known as having been transhumant pastoralist groups in the past, there was, in my experience, not nearly as strong an assertion of "indigenousness" about Vlachoi as there was about Sarakatsani peoples, nor was there nearly so strong an emphasis on their distinctiveness in comparison with the Sarakatsani. I met Vlachoi in the majority of villages I visited, some of which (such as Kefalovriso in northern Pogoni) were known as being predominantly Vlach, but in most of which (such as Delvinaki, Argyrohori, Dolo in Upper Pogoni, and Doliana in Eastern Kasidiaris) Vlachoi constituted a part of the population, usually living in particular neighborhoods. There were generally more Vlachoi in Upper Pogoni than in Lower Pogoni, which was explained in terms of the strongly pastoralist history of the area, and familiarity with it through the transhumant and trade routes. Vlachoi also seemed to have a long history (not just a more recent history, which the Sarakatsani and most others had) of being engaged in a wide range of activities in addition to transhumant pastoralism; they were heavily involved in the timber industry, in stonemasonry, in all kinds of trade, and, in more recent years, in both large-scale and small-scale animal husbandry (a Vlach owned the largest chicken-farming business in Epirus), as well as most of the white-collar professions (including anthropology). Moreover, Vlach peoples were known to range right across large sections of the Balkans; they were not associated exclusively with Epirus and "Greekness," as were the Sarakatsani. Although there were Epirot-based Vlachoi (Delvinaki Vlachoi, Konitsa Vlachoi, etc.), as peoples (a "cultural" group) they were generally represented as being associated with a much wider area than were the Sarakatsani, and as including several different linguistic groups.

In short, while Vlachoi were considered distinct, they were not considered distinctly Epirot, and many had a longer history than the Sarakatsani of being involved in activities other than transhumant pastoralism. But again, one of the differences perceived between Vlachoi and the *Gréki* of Lower Pogoni was the way in which they came and went regularly across the Epirot region and beyond with relative ease.[16] That was not related to a strong notion of indigenousness (well, not often; some books and conferences did make such a connection) as it was with the Sarakatsani; but it did give that sense of past freedom of movement, of using all areas of the region, and not *only* leapfrogging. Once again, it was the way people moved and how they used the area that made the difference.

Ease of movement around the Epirot region (as opposed to the habit of leapfrogging between one part of the Epirot region and a much more distant place) also generated a sense of difference between Western and Eastern Kasidiaris. The Eastern Kasidiaris area not only had an array of transhumant routes passing through it, it also has a large plain (the Doliana Plain) and relatively easy access to Ioannina beyond that plain (for that reason, most Eastern Kasidiaris peoples used to travel to Ioannina for supplies rather than to Argyrokastro). Moreover, almost everyone said that the quality of the soils, for both grazing and cultivation, is higher on the eastern side. The people I met in the villages located around the foothills of the Eastern Kasidiaris (many of whom were the kin and friends of those on the western side) described how their lives had been much the same as those on the western side in the past, both in terms of a sense of restriction to the area and in terms of moving up and down the Kasidiaris with their animals in winter and summer. Far fewer, however, said that members of their families went to distant cities to work for their adult lives. In fact, people described far less coming and going altogether. The "serious" coming and going in this area had begun in the 1960s, people said, when whole families emigrated. Most suggested this large-scale emigration had occurred later than in the Western Kasidiaris because the civil war had not been as devastating on the eastern side of the mountain as on the western side; but it was also because there was no national border that had suddenly closed them off from an important neighboring area, as had happened in the west.

When the emigrations did begin from the Eastern Kasidiaris area, it was mostly in the form of families' leaving together to settle in one city or another, either in Greece (Athens and Ioannina mostly) or abroad. Moreover, most people said their reason for moving was to search for a "better life" and not for survival, as many Lower Pogoni villagers had described. In more recent years, some families—especially those who had moved to Ioannina—had returned to the area, not only to retire, but also to work, for there had been considerable improvements made to the plain, such that it was now possible to make a "decent" living there (chapter 6). This was not a reference to economic possibilities alone; more mechanized, more industrialized farming was seen as less "peasantlike" than the kind of cultivation that had been done in previous years. Nevertheless, those who focused on intensive animal husbandry on the Doliana Plain (pigs, chickens, beef cattle) were regarded as less "peasantlike" than those who focused on cultivation of crops, however many tractors and combine harvesters were involved. For example, most of those living in Doliana who still engaged in farming (and it was a minority) focused on animal husbandry, whereas those living in Parakalamos, in the middle of the plain, focused mostly on crop cultivation. For that reason (among others), many Doliana residents regarded themselves as a cut above Parakalamos residents. Things changed (mechanized cultivation, more sedentary pastoralism) but remained the same (pastoralism was still considered as higher-status than cultivating crops).

In sum, while Western Kasidiaris had apparently become increasingly invisible in recent decades, Eastern Kasidiaris had become increasingly visible, not as a place of "natural beauty" or "cultural heritage," but as an economically productive area that was now well connected with asphalt roads. It had become an "ordinary" place, but it was not "ordinary" in the same way as Western Kasidiaris; this was not neglected or abandoned ordinariness, but developed ordinariness. And most of the people I met around the Eastern Kasidiaris area were much less inclined to say they were "just Greek" than were those on the western side; the more common phrase was either "pure Greek" or "ordinary Greek" (meaning not Vlach, Sarakatsani, etc.).

Even here, though, there were still underlying ambiguities about that ordinariness. One ambiguity concerned whether the area was part of Pogoni, especially for the villagers along the foothills of the eastern side of the Kasidiaris, who had many kin and friends in the villages on the western side. "Well, that's not surprising, is it?" said one man from Areti. "We all used to meet at the top of the Kasidiaris in the summer with our animals." He later added that marriages were sometimes arranged up there. The Eastern Kasidiaris peoples also used to attend the Western Kasidiaris villages' festivals, weddings, and other events; it was an easy trip, many said, popping over the mountain for an evening. These days, almost no people graze their animals on the top of the Kasidiaris, and nobody "pops over" the mountain to the other side: they drive around it. In effect, whereas the mountain had previously been regarded as a connection between east and west, it now generated a sense of division between them.

The current Pogoni County border that divides the Kasidiaris parallels that perceived division between Lower Pogoni (on the western side of the Kasidiaris) and what I have termed Eastern Kasidiaris. For many, it seemed to make sense that they were now in different counties (Pogoni County and Dodoni County); the "real" Pogoni, in both administrative and social terms, was now considered to be on the western side. At the same time, most people also felt that "traditional" Pogoni included both sides of the Kasidiaris, and that this "tradition" was sustained today in the form of continued kinship links and continued attendance at each other's summer festivals. "It's good to remember the past and how things were," said one man from Repetisti (Eastern Kasidiaris); "Traditionally, Pogoni reached as far as Kalpaki, so in a sense, it still does." This would mean that the Doliana Plain was included in "traditional" Pogoni; it would also mean that the Kasidiaris was in the middle of the Pogoni area, and that each side was flanked by a large and fertile plain. The large and fertile plain on the western side stretches northward toward Argyrokastro; the plain on the eastern side stretches southward toward Ioannina. More important, the plain on the western side (the Drinos Plain) is now mostly in Albania, with only a small section in Greece (map 4). After the border closed, this effectively meant that not only were the Lower Pogoni peoples considered to be "black-kneed peasants"; they also had hardly any good cultivating land left on which to be black-kneed. In contrast, on the eastern side, the whole plain remained in Greece and over the years was considerably developed. The two sides were thus in some senses the same, but also very different. All of this is explored in greater detail in chapters 3 and 6.

THE SOUTHERN OTHER

Thus far, I have provided a patchwork of stories and accounts of the areas to the west, east, and north of the Lower Pogoni area, giving some sense of how they were constituted as different kinds of places, with different reputations, largely through a combined trope of movement (different kinds of moving and different enablings and constraints in moving) and the quality of different types of land. To the north there were good grazing lands and many transhumant routes and destinations; to the immediate east there were good cultivating lands and easy routes southward; further to the east there were the mountains of the Zagori, some wealthy villagers, and the Sarakatsani peoples; to the west there was the closing and reopening border, Northern Epirus/Southern Albania, and another fertile plain.

Finally, there is the immediate south, Thesprotia, which I have thus far mentioned only in terms of its being a major transhumant destination for the winter months. I have left that area until last deliberately, because it is the area that all people I met on both sides of the mountain mentioned the least. When people did discuss it, it was to describe three things. First, and most commonly, the routes transhumant peoples used to take (and sometimes still take) through the Pogoni area to go south for the winter months; second, how these same routes were used to trade goods between the north and the south (predominantly olive oil and salt going north, wool and cheese going south); and third, how those routes had been extremely dangerous in the past because of high levels of animal rustling and other kinds of theft that used to occur along some of the narrower and more hilly sections of those routes (Green 1998b). "The people down there were goat thieves," one woman from Argyrohori said, "terrible people, no morals at all." This sentiment about the past dangers of Thesprotia and the people who lived there was expressed often by people all around the Kasidiaris—though once again, as with Albanians and Northern Epirots, opinions about this varied. What did not vary was people's sense that there were few past or even present close relations between Pogoni and Thesprotia, even though there had been many trade and transhumant routes between the areas. It was evidently not a place to stay for any length of time, to marry into, or to visit for festivals.

Over time, and with some difficulty, I began to understand that the particular part of Thesprotia being referred to was the borderland area, and that the "terrible people" were not all the peoples associated with Thesprotia but more specifically peoples known as Tsamides—though they were rarely explicitly named as such in the Pogoni area.[17] One of the few people who did explicitly refer to them was Spiros, the man from Despotiko in the southern Kasidiaris (next to the Thesprotia border) who had willingly fought with the communists during the civil war. He blamed widespread negative attitudes toward Tsamides on two things: first, that in the past they were perceived to be "Turks" in the same way as Albanian-speaking Muslims had been perceived to be "Turks"; and second, there had been particularly intense propaganda against them during the two wars—propaganda that had led to large numbers of Tsamides' being summarily killed by the EDES forces under General Zervas. Zervas believed they had helped the Italian and later the German forces when they invaded Greece, and thus ordered a campaign against them in retribution. Spiros went on to recall that two young men from Despotiko had rescued one endangered Tsamis boy after they came across him when they were in Thesprotia to buy oil. They had brought him back to the village with them, and Spiros had baptized him in a barrel (many Tsamides were Muslim) in the local monastery. In the end, the boy had grown up, married in the village, and stayed there.

That was the only instance I came across of an assertion by anyone in the Kasidiaris area that he or she had helped a Tsamis; most people expressed either deeply ambivalent or explicitly negative attitudes toward them, and the same kinds of attitudes were expressed toward the area in Thesprotia with which Tsamides were associated. For most *Gréki* Pogoni peoples, Tsamides and the borderland region to the south signaled both danger and otherness; it was not a place they would have gone willingly in the past unless they absolutely had to, and few people in the Kasidiaris area said they had gone there, or that they knew any Tsamides. Yet this area seemed to me to be more like Lower Pogoni than almost any other: the same kind of landscape, the same border-straddling status, and a lot of the same mixed cultivation and pastoralism. But while the people in Lower Pogoni were constituted as having been nothing in particular, the Tsamides seemed to be at the opposite extreme.

At first, I was struck by a strong similarity between the way some people talked about Tsamides and the way Albanians were sometimes negatively described since the border had reopened. Indeed, many people said that Tsamides *were* Albanians, after a fashion. But it was the "after a fashion" that was the difficulty: everyone I met, and everything I read, asserted something different, and often contradictory, about Tsamides. Nobody could even agree on the language of these people (Greek, Arvanitika,[18] Albanian, their own language, or a combination of these), their religion (Muslims or Orthodox Christians), or whether they were "originally" from Thesprotia or somewhere else. Most, though not all, suggested that in the past, they were Muslim and spoke Albanian (or some dialect of Albanian, or a language akin to Albanian); but opinions differed about whether they had been Orthodox at some point before becoming Muslim, and they also differed about whether they were "ethnic Albanians" or something else. Some texts even denied that they existed in Epirus anymore, following the end of the Second World War.[19]

In short, there was a continual production of ambiguity in Epirus about these people, and an assertion that a final conclusion about Tsamides was impossible. The few people I met in Thesprotia who agreed that they were Tsamides were singularly reluctant to discuss anything to do with differences between themselves and anyone else. One older man said, "Who told you I'm a Tsamis? I'm no different from anyone else." That was as far as the conversation went. Another man, having heard me speaking to some people in a *kafeneio* in Thesprotia on the subject, followed me out of the shop as I left, to explain to me why people would not talk about Tsamides; he did not want to speak to me about it in the hearing of others:

> They had a bad reputation, you see. They were accused of being thieves and *armatoloi*.[20] But you can see for yourself, there's not much to live on around here. If some of them did act that way, it was because they had to, to survive. But there were good people too, you know; in any population, you get good people and bad people. My grandfather and my father after him were barrel makers, they were honest men. They made barrels for oil and for *tsipouro*.[21] I'm sorry that people have not been able to help you do your work. It's just very difficult; it's a difficult subject.

This man went on to explain that his father was also involved in distilling *tsipouro*, and he proceeded to draw a still for me in my notebook, to explain the process of making this spirit. But he would not talk any more about Tsamides and certainly never referred to himself as being Tsamis.

After a time, the only thing that became relatively clear was that this insistence on ambiguity was different from the sense of ambiguity in Lower Pogoni areas. Tsamides were also closely associated with the ambiguities surrounding the Greek-Albanian border, but the difference was that whereas Lower Pogoni people were represented as Greeks living on the Greek side of the border who had close relations with Greek peoples living on the Albanian side of the border (Northern Epirots), Tsamides were perceived as Albanian-like peoples living on the Greek side of the border, and having close relations with the Albanian-like peoples on the Albanian side of the border, even though they were Greeks—or at least, all of those I met on the Greek side of the border considered themselves to be Greek. Moreover, and as I have already mentioned in discussing Spiros, what Tsamides did, and what was done to them, during various parts of "big history" (particularly the debate about them during the exchange of populations between Greece and Turkey in 1923, and the events of the Second World War) was even more hedged around with tension and ambiguity, and usually discussed outside public places and in hushed tones.

The drawing on the cover of Dimitris Mikalopoulou's book on Tsamides seemed to sum this up: it is a drawing of one man whispering into the ear of another man (Mikalopoulou 1993). Mikalopoulou's prologue to the book also gives a sense of the anxiety surrounding these peoples; it recounts how the author was awakened early one morning (in Greece) by a hostile police officer who wanted to question him about his research

(Mikalopoulou 1993: 11). He goes on to state that the topic of Tsamides is not a "mirror image" of the topic of Northern Epirots, because Tsamides were never accorded a clear "minority" status in the way that Northern Epirots had been (ibid.: 12–14); they remained an ambiguity, despite various interventions on their behalf, both by the League of Nations in the 1920s and by the Albanian government. In fact, the involvement of these bodies exacerbated the ambiguity. The League of Nations never mentioned Tsamides by name; they were included in the category "Moslems of Albanian origin" (Ladas 1932: 384), which covered a great number of the Muslims in Epirus as a whole. This criterion was important at the time, because the general definition of who should be included in the exchange of populations between Greece and Turkey was based solely on religion: Muslims living in Greece; Greek Orthodox Christians living in Turkey (Hirschon 2003: 8). That created something of a complication, since the whole point of the exchange was to establish "ethnically homogenous" populations in each (national) territory out of the previously "ethnically mixed" populations of the Ottoman territories (ibid.: 15, 19). Yet Muslims of "Albanian origin" were evidently not Turkish by those criteria so should not be included in the exchange; but they were also not Greek by those criteria either (Ladas 1932: 384–390). That left them in an officially ambiguous position.

The sense of anxiety over the more recent Second World War issue was exacerbated in the early 1990s by another intervention from the Albanian government (which claimed moral responsibility for Tsamides, asserting they are "ethnic Albanians"). Albanian officials began making demands of the Greek government for compensation to Tsamides for their loss of property and their treatment during the Second World War at the hands of EDES. The Albanian government stated that Tsamides were killed in their thousands in the summer of 1944 by EDES forces under the orders of General Napoleon Zervas (as was also reported to me by Spiros). Many Tsamides who survived this onslaught (other than those few rescued by people like Spiros) fled to Albania, leaving all their property and possessions behind. Fifty years later in 1994, the Albanian parliament went so far as to declare June 27 as a day of remembrance of the actions taken against Tsamides by EDES. The Greek government steadfastly refused to entertain even the *idea* of negotiations about compensation, declaring the whole thing a "nonissue."[22]

In contrast with the ambiguities of the Lower Pogoni peoples, this was an example of the polar opposite of indifference: indeed, the (contested) difference between Tsamides and others was important in a highly charged way for almost everyone I met. That was clearly related to the long-term, ongoing disputes concerning past and present relations between neighboring states, the kind of thing that Michalis and Tasos had described as causing "chaos." And once again, it was an issue about which I was exhorted to remain confused, to let it go; "poking around" in it was troublesome and sensitive, and liable to cause upset. Those disputes had led to repeated debates between and among people in Epirus about what did and did not happen, who did what to whom and why, and how divisions and alliances, enmities and loyalties were forged, broken, remembered, and forgotten, often deliberately. Most people did not want the memories anymore.

The ambiguity surrounding the subject of Tsamides was yet another object lesson to me in the active and deliberate practices involved in the production of incoherence, which spread to an equally incoherent image of the physical place in Thesprotia with which Tsamides were associated. A symptom of this is what I came to view as the "name game": as I have already said, most peoples and most places in Epirus had more than one name, and also, different places and different peoples occasionally had the same name, just to add to the confusion. Thesprotia was known as "Tsamouria" by those studying the history and character of Tsamides as a distinct ethnic group; Tsamouria's boundaries were not exactly the same as the administrative boundaries of today's Thesprotia, but Tsamouria did usually include most if not all of Thesprotia, and some other areas as well.

This continual ambiguity about peoples and places—a condition of shifting, occasionally blending, occasionally separating, occasionally forgetting, occasionally recalling, and occasionally ignoring how things seem and how they are—meant, in practice, that resolving the issue "once and for all" was precisely *not* the point.

As a result, a few people's attempts to help me to become less confused about Tsamides invariably ended in frustration. For example, Socrates, a man living in Thesprotia who ran a small restaurant, spent around an hour one summer afternoon trying to explain to me all the different opinions about Tsamides. I asked him to do this, for at the time I was still guiltily in pursuit of clarity. Even though he had his own preferred version, he was well versed in the others. He attempted to compare and contrast them so that only one would emerge as acceptably true, thus clarifying things for me. This endeavor led to ever more complicated delving into historical accounts, theories of language and ethnicity, religion, and "Great Power" politics. Not too long after Socrates had finished covering several scraps of paper with scribbling and flowcharts, he succinctly expressed his decision to abandon the enterprise: "Oh, to the Devil with it. How do I know? They're just people in the end, aren't they? We're all just people, in the end." For the time being, then, Socrates had given up on separating things out and decided to opt for leaving things unclear: it did not matter in the end, because everyone was "just people."

The Whereness of Being Visible and Invisible

There were many more stories and aspects to people's understanding of the "where" of this place, and the ones I have included are partial and incomplete, which is in the nature of all stories and accounts.[23] Further, I have not provided many accounts from peoples recently arrived on the Greek side of the border from Albania; I have not spoken much about the people on the eastern side of the Kasidiaris, or about the views of many younger people; I have not discussed the many Gypsies I came to know, and their rather different relations to place, and to past and current practices of moving. Some of those accounts will be included in the following chapters, here and there. What I have focused upon is some of the ways in which Lower Pogoni, as a place, and the peoples most "generically" associated with that region, were constituted as marginal across a range of scales of movements, practices, and the use of places. What emerged was a sense of the relative invisibility, relative lack of distinction, and relative lack of perceived importance of both people and place here, in comparison to other people and other places. There was also a sense that some people and places were becoming more invisible, while others became increasingly visible over time.

In the past, this might have been neither here nor there; but in the contemporary world, when visibility, the power of the image, is apparently becoming ever more important (Lury 1998), it mattered a great deal. The Sarakatsani have higher visibility; the Zagori mountains, forests, rivers, and gorges constantly appear in photographs and postcards of the region, whereas the Pogoni region was almost never photographed (indeed, I was often not even allowed to take photographs around the immediate border area): these facts were noted and discussed by almost everyone I met.

A small example: one day in Delvinaki, I met Dinos, a soft drinks distributor. After unloading several crates of drinks from his truck, he sat down in one of the *kafeneia* to join a group of six men, a Northern Epirot boy, and myself. Shortly afterward, the subject of tourism in the Zagori region came up. Dinos became rapidly enraged, yelling: "What the hell is there to see in the Zagori, anyway? I mean, you tell me: what is there to see in the Zagori? A bunch of rocks, a gap in the rocks [referring to the Vikos gorge, the most photographed part of the Zagori], and a bunch of trees."

The café owner replied that it was all about the rivers, the gorge, and the forests, the traditional villages and the cultural heritage there, and that for tourists, all these things were particularly attractive. Dinos retorted: "There's plenty of forest here [in Pogoni], and rivers, and old villages. Why don't they make postcards of *this* place and have the tourists come here?" Dinos was from the Zagori and was not well pleased with the crowds that turned up in the summers there. Several others in the group then intervened, making a series of comments to the effect that they would love it if tourists came to Pogoni, but that there was little to see or do here in comparison to the Zagori, and anyway, nobody outside Epirus had ever heard of Pogoni. One man added that Dinos should not complain, for he made a lot of income from all those irritating tourists. Dinos conceded this, but muttered, "*You* wouldn't like it; all those coaches causing traffic, all those people taking pictures of sheep, rocks, and asking your grand-mother to pose for their cameras. They have no respect, those people."

Spiros, one of the men at the table, responded: "Maybe not. But pic-tures of the Zagori and your grandmother now exist all over the world." So, while there was ambivalence about the greater visibility of the Zagori, the power of visibility itself was acknowledged by most. If the Western Kasidiaris and some of the peoples associated with the area have not been particularly visible in the past and have become less so with time, that has occurred during a period when visibility has become ever more im-portant, a period when, as Celia Lury puts it, "visibility is an imperative of contemporary life" (Lury 1998: 2). In that context, being able to make things appear, as well as being able to make them disappear (through either indifference or intention), is a powerful capacity indeed; constitut-ing places and people as ambiguous, undistinguished, and/or uninterest-ing makes a considerable difference in contemporary life.

That brings me to the final issue I want to consider in this chapter: how being "just Greek" in the way I have explored for some Lower Pogoni peoples is not particularly visible in more widespread accounts of Greekness.

ON *GRÉKI*

I have already described some of what the word *Gréki* meant for people around Epirus; here, I want to take a look at its implications in a broader context. Before I went to Epirus, I had never heard the word, although I grew up in Greece. Hearing people use it sent me running to my collection of dictionaries, as it seemed odd that people would refer to themselves as Greeks using a word that did not seem to me to be—well, Greek. The word did not appear in any of the dictionaries precisely as it was spoken to me; the closest listed was *Graikoi* (Γραικοί): the plural form of *Graikos* (Γραικός) or *Graikikos* (Γραικικός). They are not exactly the same, though, for *Gréki* is spoken in Epirus with a hard G, not a soft one, and it is spoken with a stress on the first syllable, not the second.

This might seem to be splitting hairs, but I have a reason for doing so: there are both differences and overlaps between what the dictionary terms and the word *Gréki* refer to, and it is here that issues of ambiguity, and of things appearing and disappearing, come into the matter. In brief, I concluded that *Gréki* as it was used in Epirus marked something that remains unnamed in wider Greek discourses about Greekness, that it was an example of what Irvine and Gal call sociolinguistic "erasure": the process of ignoring, dismissing, or not noticing some aspects of language that do not fit within an overall homogenizing "ideology" of what a language represents (Irvine and Gal 2000: 38).[24] Irvine and Gal suggest that linguists of the nineteenth century (and subsequently) have assumed that social groups are "naturally" monolingual, rather than seeing this monolingualism as ideologically constructed, an assumption that also constitutes such groups as "ethnic" or "national" groups. This assumption implied that any aspect of actual language use that appeared to combine different linguistic registers was a "mixture" or even "debasement" of separate pure forms (ibid.: 53–54). For example, to "map" the assumed distinct and separate languages in Senegal, linguists of the day ignored the widespread multilingualism of many Senegalese groups, along with regional variations that appeared to overlap with one another (ibid.: 54–56). More relevant for my purposes, Irvine and Gal suggest this was also the case in the late nineteenth and early twentieth centuries in the Macedonian region, where the widespread multilingualism of the populations caused linguists of the period to regard the area as "chaotic" (in a Balkan kind of way). This led to a range of competing claims about the (pure) origins of the range of languages spoken there, in addition to various attempts to "disentangle" them from one another, disregarding overlaps and mixtures (ibid.: 63–72).

The word *Gréki* as it was used in Epirus seems to me to be one of the regional variations that fall into this kind of (Balkan) "erasure": people I spoke with about it in Epirus understood it to be a multilingual word with no single "pure" origin; they most often associated it with Vlach and/or Aroumanian as well as Greek. In short, *Gréki* both is and is not a Greek word; it has overlapping associations, ones that become invisible in formal etymological descriptions of particular (separated-out) languages.

Some traces of this process of erasure can be seen in what is said about the etymology of the similar words that do appear in Greek dictionaries. All of them (*Graikoi, Graikos, Graikikos*) are glossed as meaning "Greek" and apparently could be used instead of either of the two more familiar terms, "Hellene" (Έλληνας) or *Romios* (Ρωμιός).[25] According to Babiniotis, the word *Graikos* predates *Ellinas* (Hellene); moreover, he traces it as referring to peoples in the Dodoni area of Epirus before the fourth century B.C. (Babiniotis 1998: 596). Among Greek-speaking peoples, the word slowly fell out of common use during the Byzantine and Ottoman periods, until it was briefly revived by some members of the Greek revolutionary movement during the nineteenth century. During this period, there was an attempt to imbue the word with ideals of "Greekness" that were later associated with *Romios* on the one hand, and *Ellinas* on the other. With the creation of the new Greek state in the 1820s, *Graikos* fell out of favor and was replaced by the disemic split that Herzfeld refers to between "Hellene"/Hellenism and *Romios/Romiosini*.[26] In sum, Babiniotis's account suggests that *Graikos* ceased to be used, in public debates at least, at precisely the time when the political and philosophical meanings of "Greekness" as the basis for a homogenous national/cultural identity were being most strongly asserted.

This etymological story is suggestive about the current relative unimportance of the term *Graikos*, something the word shares with *Gréki*: whereas "Hellene" and *Romios* carried highly politicized (and often opposing) meanings of Greekness, *Graikos* seemed to have fallen out of favor. That is, the word is not particularly strongly related to nationalist discourses of Greekness, which is also the case for the word *Gréki*: people in Pogoni used *Gréki* to describe the condition of not being anything in particular, of being *generically* Greek, as it were, and it did not seem to have any political overtones—at least, not in terms of nationalist discourses within Greece as a whole. *Gréki* was used, in my experience, only when people wanted to refer to the fact that they were not Vlach, Sarakatsani, Northern Epirot, and so forth, but "just Greek," without any of these specific identifying labels.

There are two important differences between *Graikos* and *Gréki*: first, that *Gréki* is used only in some parts of Greece, whereas *Graikos* is used throughout the country (as are *Ellinas* and *Romios*);[27] and second, while *Graikos* carries some self-denigrating connotations, *Gréki* was morally neutral, a way of describing what a person is not (Vlach, Sarakatsani, etc.), as opposed to what he or she is. This seems to be a literally peripheral word to denote, or assert, a lack of distinction associated with a peripheral part of Greece. Nevertheless, the word is distinctive, in that it was used specifically in this region to refer to some people specifically from this region (the ones who apparently lack distinction): there seemed to be something unnamed being named in the use of the word *Gréki*, something that does not belong to the wider nationalist discourse about Greekness.

Dimitris's confrontation with his daughter's fiancé provides some sense of the importance of relative location in this context: being "just Greek" for Dimitris had to do with a tension between wanting to be seen as being an "ordinary" Greek (who could be from anywhere) and being cast, instead, as a "disheveled" Greek who was, in a generic kind of way, no different from any Balkan "peasant" ("Just a Vlach from Epirus"). Here, it was Epirus's location relative to the south (especially Athens)—in political, social, historical, and economic terms—that was one of the key distinctions. For people unfamiliar with the region, it was Epirus as a whole that was negatively depicted, as I have outlined, as being somehow less distinguished: more Balkan and less "European" than other areas.[28]

Interestingly in this respect, the only written source I found referring to the word *Gréki* (as opposed to *Graikoi*) was Koukoudis's enormous study of the Vlachoi in Macedonia; the author mentions it in passing and also associates it with the Balkans.[29] He suggests that the term is used by the Vlach-speaking peoples he studied to refer to "Christians whose mother tongue is one of the Greek dialects that have been spoken in the Balkans down the ages" (Koukoudis 2003: 33). In national or ethnic terms, it is not terribly clear *who* is being referred to, nor is it clear whether *Grékos* was a synonym for "Hellene" or, alternatively, *Romios*. It seems it could have been either, neither, or both.

Significantly, Koukoudis associates the ambiguity of what or whom the word *Grékos* referred to with the Balkan region, a region depicted by Koukoudis as being one in which people speak a diversity of dialects and languages. In this case, the way these diverse peoples are grouped together and given a name was sometimes gauged according to the language they spoke combined with their religious affiliation. It was not determined by blood, by soil, by roots, by skin color—nor even always by language. That makes the sense of the word *Grékos* rather different from either "Hellene" or *Romios*: the word is associated with a past that has to do with the Balkans, rather than a past directly relating to the "Occident/Hellene—Orient/*Romios*" dilemma, let alone the depiction of Greece and Greeks as Mediterranean. In that sense, *Grékos* is a word that is not included in Greek nationalist discourses circulating around Hellenism/*Romiosini*. Moreover, and this is key, the Greek nationalist discourse did not include the Balkans as part of its imaginary.[30]

In sum, the key distinguishing characteristic of the word *Gréki* as it was used by people I met in Epirus and as described by Koukoudis for Vlachoi seems to be in the association of the word with Balkan "mixture," rather than the competing (nationalist) origin stories implied by "Hellene" and *Romios*; *Gréki* means "just Greek" in a nondescript, implicitly Balkan kind of way. When people used it in Epirus, it seemed to evoke this sense of a particularistic, located lack of visibility: of being Greek, but being Greek in a way that was not clearly distinct within current discourses.

In this respect, there *are* also some overlaps between the connotations of *Gréki* as it was used in Epirus and the contemporary meaning ascribed to *Romiosini*. In one sense, the indeterminacy of *Gréki* appears to contradict notions of the "purity" of Hellenism in somewhat the same way as does the notion of *Romiosini* (Faubion 1993: 58; Herzfeld 1987, esp.45–46 and 101–3). *Romiosini*, a notion of Greekness that alludes to Byzantine-Turkish associations rather than "pure" Hellenic classical ones, is often glossed as referring to a mixed bag of characteristics; similarly, Koukoudis describes *Gréki* as involving a mixed bag of people in the Balkans. Faubion describes a related concept, "Romiosity," thus: "To the more rigorous of Hellenic purists, it can often denote . . . an unsavory mélange, a bastardization of Greek by other, baser compounds, with no cultural integrity of its own. Perhaps the purists are even correct: the Romaic is indeed a mixed bag, a hodgepodge" (Faubion 1993: 58).

Both Faubion and Herzfeld, in their different ways, are interested in the *Romios* notion as a troublesome contrast to the notion of Hellenism, one that points to the "impurities" of Greekness. In that sense, *Romiosini* (or "Romiosity," in Faubion's terms) is a generalized concept, a notion of impurity and mixture that applies to all Greeks anywhere, and as such it encompasses challenges to the assertions, within the concept of Hellenism, of a direct link to Greeks' membership in (Western) Europe. For Faubion, the "Romeote" notion is the "Little Tradition" of Greekness, the one that is populist (and "mongrel") as opposed to (literally) classical (ibid.). For Herzfeld, *Romiosini* marks the continual tension between the ideal (and Occidental) purity of Hellenism and the (Oriental) impurities introduced by Byzantine and Turkish influences, which is bound up with Greek Orthodox religious cosmology:

> In the cosmology of the Edenic fall, knowledge, under the twin forms of history and social experience, results from a flaw. . . . Each subsequent event is a source of a new imperfection, and an insight into how that flaw came about; and dominating the whole confusion, confirming once and for all time the Greeks' identity as *Romii* (Byzantine and Turkish Christians) rather than as *Ellines* (idealized Hellenes of the Classical past), is the original, catastrophic collapse of 1453. Europe, the product of Classical Greece, is the antithesis of history thus conceived. (Herzfeld 1987: 41)

The "catastrophic collapse of 1453" was of course the fall of Constantinople to the Ottomans, and the beginning of Ottoman rule over the Greeks, which set in train an "antithesis" between (Western) Europe and (Eastern) Byzantium. Rather less clear from Herzfeld's account is *where* (as opposed to when) the idealized Europe that was the "product of Classical Greece" was supposed to be located. To be sure, Herzfeld never intended the notion to be spatially located, as he was discussing abstract and ambivalent conceptions of Greek history and identity as expressed by Greeks based on the idea of "Europe" as an Occidental symbolic concept, not as a place as such. However, the issue of location is important for my purposes in illuminating the relative invisibility of *Gréki* compared to *Romiosini*. Here, it is important that the geographical, not only the conceptual, boundaries of what constitutes Greece have been contested repeatedly since the establishment of a Greek state in the 1820s; it is important that Epirus contains very few classical Greek sites, and none of the most famous ones; it is important that most of Epirus was not included in the Greek state until 1913, while its southern and then western mainland neighbors (Thessaly) were included earlier;[31] it is important that most of Epirus was (nominally at least) under continual Ottoman administration until it became part of the Greek state, unlike some other areas, which were variously under Venetian, Russian, French, and British control as well at times;[32] and it is important, as it is also in the Macedonian region to the east of Epirus, that the border remains contested, whether explicitly or implicitly. These things are important because in combination, they meant that Epirots generally had the impression that their region was not *entirely* included in that idealized notion of a pure Hellenic past, and therefore not *entirely* included in the Ottoman fall from it either; it was slightly off-center from it, at the margins somewhere. In that sense, Epirus was somehow outside the central geographical region that was the focus of the wider story told about what happened to Greece as a whole. To put it another way: Epirus was marginal to the story told about how Greece became marginalized.[33]

The "hodgepodge" of *Gréki* in Epirus involved the place itself as being on the borders of other Balkan places, which was more important than the general notion of Greeks and Greece as having been part of Turkish and Byzantine empires, if by these terms something akin to Orientalism contrasted with Occidentalism is implied. If *Gréki* did not match the purity requirements of Hellenism, this was more because of the varieties of relations they had with their Balkan neighbors—a Balkan "mélange" rather than an "Oriental" one.

In fact, the most famous recent historical period for Epirus was the era of its rule by Ali Pasha (1788–1822), who was anything but a typical "Oriental" or Ottoman sultan. Ali came from an Albanian family of "brigands" who at the time of his birth had recently converted from Christianity to Islam; he spoke mostly Albanian and demotic Greek and learned only a few words of Turkish in his lifetime; and he was despised by the Ottoman authorities in Constantinople for being dangerously autonomous (Glenny 1999: 25–29; McNeill 1992: 169–70; Kalliatake, Prevelakes, and Meyer 1996; Plomer 1970 [1936]; Fleming 1999). In other words, the most famous period of recent Epirot history depicts it as having been not even "properly" a part of the Ottoman Porte, but as the center of power for an Albanian brigand who, at the height of his power, controlled the entirety of the western side of today's mainland Greece and most of what is today Albania. There are still images of Ali Pasha all over Ioannina, his story is known by most people there, and the place where he was finally shot in 1822 in Ioannina (by Ottoman Porte–supported assassins, because Ali Pasha was attempting to support the Greek revolutionaries of the period) is now part of a museum. Epirus was therefore not quite what most people had in mind when thinking of either "classical" or "ordinary/folk" Greece. K. E. Fleming, in arguing against accounts of Ali that assert he was the epitome of "the Islamic Ottoman Oriental despot," neatly summarizes his ambiguous status: "He was neither truly Muslim nor Ottoman, neither Oriental nor despotic" (Fleming 1999: 23). He was, in short, a sort of "Balkan mélange."

In this respect, it is interesting that Herzfeld often uses Campbell's ethnography of the Zagori Sarakatsani (Campbell 1964) to draw out the ways in which *Romiosini* (the "flawed" Greekness) could be analyzed. The Sarakatsani were among the many peoples within Epirus who *did* claim distinctiveness (their own kind of "purity"), and who were therefore not *Gréki*.[34] Herzfeld argues that the Sarakatsani are often represented within Greek nationalist discourse as somehow distinctive Greek "wild people," somehow "aboriginal Greeks" who need "civilizing" by the Hellenic (though never achievable) ideal, but who are nevertheless clearly Greek (Herzfeld 1987: 42–43). Whether or not this is a reasonable argument, by being distinctive, the Sarakatsani's differences from and affiliations with Hellenism can be enumerated and discussed.

In contrast, *Gréki* are not distinctive in these terms, which excludes any explicit comparisons of that sort. In discussions of Epirots who lacked such specific labels, commentaries about "aboriginality" were most often replaced by generic, rather than specific, commentaries about "uneducated Epirot peasants," as opposed to "educated" (and therefore more Hellenic and more European) Greeks. Many people in Epirus associated that kind of discussion with "snobbery" (υπεροψία) on the part of the Athenian intellectual elites that Faubion studied. However, unlike many Athenians, Epirot *Gréki* did not on the whole map that distinction onto a difference between "urban" and "rural," mostly because so many *Gréki* spent much, if not most, of their lives in cities; rather, they mapped it onto an ascribed difference between the entire region with which they were associated (Epirus) and more southern parts of mainland Greece. In any case, there were plenty of "intellectual snobs" in some of the bigger villages and small towns around Epirus itself ("rural Epirus"). When people were directly engaging in wider discourses of Greekness, there was little difference between the pronouncements of Athenians and those of people living in Epirus (including the pronouncements of those who at other times saw themselves as *Gréki*). Those who wished to associate themselves with the purity of Hellenism, with being European, and with "modernity" most often did so by asserting their own people's history of high levels of education and the deficiencies of others in this respect, much as anyone else in Greece tends to do when waxing lyrical about Hellenism. It is important to note, though, that in Epirus, even this was often done through that ubiquitous trope—making distinctions by intermingling movement, place, and people—that I have been discussing throughout this chapter. Those classed as "peasants" were those who cultivated the land while in Epirus, leapfrogged to distant cities from a small area containing few large mountains and therefore little specialist pastoralism, and did not have a history of "autonomy"; these were the people who were cast as being the least educated/accomplished (*morfomenoi*/ μορφωμένοι), and therefore the least European. And people such as the Lower Pogoni *Gréki*, who were in addition constituted as being sandwiched between more visible places and more powerful peoples, and who became even more sandwiched as the border was contested, closed, and then reopened, ended up being regarded as being at the bottom of this pile of distinction, in apparently lacking distinction almost entirely (that being their distinction).

The issue of Oriental-Occidental oppositions did not come into this. Within this Epirot place-based discourse, the Europe to which Herzfeld alluded as an abstract and nonretrievable ideal as expressed within Greek cosmology did in fact exist; it was centrally located in Athens and other places in northern and western Europe, where people asserted this ideal to claim superiority over other kinds of places, and it was also evoked by Epirots in their more "snobby" moments. This Europe was not in *Gréki* Epirus, the Epirus cast as being a peasant Balkan backwater. Dimitris's encounters in Athens are an example of how that was experienced.

Overall, then, the word *Gréki* was used in Epirus to refer to "ordinary Greeks" who were associated with a place that was considered not "ordinary" but instead somewhat generically Balkan, though unquestionably Greek (which is what allowed the area on the Greek side of the border to be uninteresting or irrelevant in nationalist terms, unlike Northern Epirus and parts of Thesprotia). The place was, to borrow Anna Tsing's phrase, an "out-of-the-way place" (Tsing 1993). Using the word *Gréki* seemed to capture this ambiguous yet apparently unimportant and, in most other parts of Greece, unnamed form of marginality.

Northern Epirots, whose name was known everywhere in Greece, were therefore not *Gréki* in the sense I have been describing because they lived on the Albanian side of the border (which in nationalist terms made them "matter out of place," to borrow a famous phrase from Mary Douglas). Their situation helps to draw out the underlying point I am trying to make: that peoples associated with different regions of what is now

Greece, and some regions beyond what is now Greece, related to the notion of Greekness in different ways, and in some instances what made the difference was rendered virtually invisible in the wider nationalist discourse. This had as much, if not more, to do with the constructed "whereness" of places as it did with the "who": Northern Epirots, whose name was highly visible, were the kin and neighbors of the people who were "just Greek" on the Greek side of the border, who had no distinct name within the wider discourse and were hardly visible at all. In that sense, *Romios*, whether it represents a populist hodgepodge or the flaws in modern "Greekness," does not capture what remains unnamed in wider nationalist discourses concerning the asserted lack of distinction of some of the people I met in Epirus. The term *Gréki* provided a name for that unnamed remainder; and that name was imbued with the language of movement and place pervasively used in the Epirot region to talk about and constitute distinctions. Unlike the wider nationalist discourses, which focus on identities and the "rootedness" of such identities within state territories, this discourse integrally interwove different kinds of traveling and interrelations with notions of place. National identity was not the direct issue addressed in this discourse, for it was self-evident that *Gréki* are Greek (whether "pure" or "impure," which varied according to the topic of conversation); rather, it was the "whereness" of places, combined with the differing kinds of movements of peoples and the relationships within a web of places that these implied, which was the issue. And one underlying element that was absent in wider discourses on Greekness (Hellenism/*Romiosini*), and which was also related to assertions or resigned acceptance of ambiguity among people I met in the Kasidiaris region, was the always already shadowy presence of the Balkans. This was the Epirot version of the "space on the side of the road" in Kathleen Stewart's terms (Stewart 1996: 205–11), or the "gap" in Marilyn Strathern's terms: a gap that is represented as containing nothing by those who focus on distinctions (what things in themselves are), but that is not at all empty in the view of those who focus on connections and interrelations (Strathern 1991: xxii–xxv). So how the Balkans come to mean a gap within wider hegemonic discourses is an important question and a matter that is explored in chapter 4. Before that, I want to take a closer look at other discourses surrounding Epirus and the Kasidiaris area in particular as physical places, to complement the discussion on Greekness with which I have ended this chapter, and to extend the exploration of the importance of "whereness" in this context.

CHAPTER 3

Moving Mountains

THUS FAR, I HAVE PROVIDED an account of place as being a key part of other things through stories from people I met around the Kasidiaris and beyond. I did this rather in the way that Keith Basso uses stories to describe Apache relationships to places (Basso 1996), and somewhat in the way Tim Ingold uses stories to describe people's experience of moving through and around places, of finding their way (Ingold 2000c). What emerged from these stories was an overall sense that people did not understand place as a landscape in the classic Euro-American sense described by Eric Hirsch—that is, as a framed and separate object which is gazed upon from a distance to be viewed properly (Hirsch 1995); nor was there anything "local" about it, if by that is implied a separation between a self-enclosed, personally experienced local and an abstract global. There was clearly no separation of that sort in these stories: although there were continual important distinctions made between "here" and somewhere else (e.g., the idea that an idealized Europe existed in Athens, but not in *Gréki* Epirus), these distinctions were not discussed in terms of a local being opposed to a global. Rather, through the underlying trope of movement, distinctions between places were discussed in terms of differences in status and power, and particularly the power to ascribe different meanings to places (including the power to ignore some places altogether), as well as the power to enable, force, or constrain movement across, through, and between places. Moreover, people in Pogoni understood that power to be as active in constituting Mavropoulo as it was in constituting Athens, Brussels, Constantinople, New York, or Chicago. The difference at any given time lay in how places as well as people were located in relation to the spatial hierarchy which resulted from the continual exercise of that power; and the difference across time lay in how that power was exercised at different moments, which resulted in shifting configurations of spatial relations (and separations), as well as a shifting in the relative visibility and invisibility of places.

The critique made by Gupta and Ferguson of the notion of local as something separate from global is particularly pertinent here. Gupta and Ferguson focus strongly on connection, on the continual historical and political contingency of the construction of place and on the interweaving of place, people, and power (Gupta and Ferguson 1999a). Their account refuses a sense of an enclosed homogeneity of peoples and "their" places; rather, it focuses on how understandings of locality are "formed and lived" in all their messiness (ibid.: 6); it further argues that both identity and place are continually contested domains, and that both are constituted through processes of exclusion and othering, of generating differences (ibid.: 13–14). For these reasons, Gupta and Ferguson's account resonated strongly with what people around the Kasidiaris had been telling me; or rather, it resonated strongly with the focus of their stories. Kasidiaris peoples' narration, the particular way they constructed their accounts of their experiences, seemed to parallel closely Gupta and Ferguson's analysis, in emphasizing interconnection, hierarchies, the importance of the activities of political powers and processes of exclusion in how things seemed and how they were.

Gupta and Ferguson are of course not alone in their critique of earlier anthropological approaches to place: it is now widely argued that the earlier habit of depicting peoples as "belonging" to certain places as if they were rooted in the soil, and focusing on the separations rather than interconnections between differing peoples/places (what Eric Wolf memorably calls treating cultures as if they were self-contained "billiard balls" [Wolf 1982: 6]), generated a range of difficulties in understanding the construction of place.[1] Most particularly, earlier approaches missed the interweaving of different scales (spatial, economic, political, temporal, social) in most people's experiences of place. It has become clear through this work that people are never alone with their places anywhere in the world; they never constitute places *as* places on their own either, something I will be exploring in this and the following chapters in some detail.

In this, I am also interested in the thematic similarities between the way Kasidiaris peoples accounted for their place(s) and the way Gupta and Ferguson and others analyze the construction of place in general, for two reasons. First, although it can be persuasively argued that all places are constituted through a combination of historically contingent, politically inflected, and continually shifting relations, not all peoples around the world account for their places in that way, as did the people around the Kasidiaris. Moreover, many commentators writing about Epirus, as well as many of the regions around Epirus (those regions constituted as Balkan) also provided accounts that focus on events and relations as centrally involving politically and historically shifting and unstable relations (and separations); indeed, that is a large part of what the Balkans have come to mean over the years, a matter I explore in chapter 4. Again, while these accounts are discursively different from the stories people told around the Kasidiaris, something remains similar across these discursive scales: the notions of political and historical instability, contest, and fluidity. While perhaps all places are constituted in this way as Gupta and Ferguson suggest, in this place people made that explicit.

The second reason for my interest in the thematic similarity between these accounts is that it contrasted starkly with the almost complete lack of similarity between Kasidiaris peoples' accounts of their place and one other kind of account of the instability and fluidity of Epirus: namely, the account provided by specialists on geomorphology who were a part of the multinational and multidisciplinary research programs of which my research was also a part. As I have mentioned several times already, for the program's aims, I was expected to bring the accounts of people in Epirus and these geomorphological accounts together, as part of the interdisciplinary effort to understand the "natural and anthropogenic causes of land degradation and desertification in the Mediterranean basin" (van der Leeuw 1998). From the very beginning, this task was not straightforward, for reasons I have also explained: most people were entirely indifferent toward land degradation, and many had no idea what I was talking about when I mentioned it. Furthermore, even when I took a more phenomenological approach, focusing on embodied relations with the surrounding environment rather than on talk alone, there did not appear to be much to go on where land degradation was concerned.[2] People tended to ignore eroded and landslip areas: when a road had been made impassable by a landslide, they used different routes until someone came along to fix it (typical response: "Well, what else is there to do?"); people out with their sheep and goats either walked around badlands and gullies or allowed their animals to play in them for a time before walking on (fig. 4; typical response: "The animals like to play there, they enjoy it"); people whose fields or grazing lands had partially collapsed into a sinkhole found another use for the sinkhole rather than repairing it (fig. 5; typical response: "Fill it in? Why?"). Their relationship with the continual process of slipping, cracking, and gullying of this place seemed to consist, both in talk and in embodied relations, of rendering these processes invisible, literally and discursively of no account.

Yet the accounts provided by geomorphology specialists, which were the first accounts of the place I had read before embarking on this research, made that response initially utterly bemusing. As I will outline below, the geomorphological accounts make it seem as though it would be impossible to ignore the continual shiftiness of the land surface. In retrospect, this disjunction between the two kinds of stories of instability was probably behind the habit I developed of taking endless photographs of land degradation: people kept rendering invisible what I was supposed to be researching, and taking photographs seemed to assuage my increasing anxiety about that. It was not until many years later, after I read Celia Lury's analysis of "prosthetic culture," that I came to regard this mild

Figure 4. Goats enjoying flysch erosion in Western Kasidiaris

obsession as an unconscious act of forcing things to appear when they kept disappearing on me (Lury 1998).

There were more difficulties. By the time I had spent several months around the Kasidiaris area, and had also begun to read other kinds of accounts of Epirus, I had even less of a sense of compatibility between the research program's focus and this place. For a start, although many scholars describe the region as part of the Mediterranean (e.g., Braudel 2001; McNeill 1992), there was little that was "typically" Mediterranean about Epirus, and people rarely mentioned the area as being Mediterranean or its peoples as "culturally" Mediterranean. Indeed, several accounts assert that the inclusion of Epirus in Greece after 1913 is part of the reason that Greece came to appear to be Balkan as well as Mediterranean. For example, Peckham, in his study of the "cartographic anxiety" involved in the formation of the Greek state, suggests that Greece's acquisition of its current northern mainland during the 1912–13 Balkan wars "had made Greece a Balkan country as much as a Mediterranean one" (Peckham 2001: 149). The idea that Epirus could be in some senses included in the Mediterranean at least on the grounds that it is contiguously attached to the rest of mainland Greece, and that the Ionian Sea becomes the Mediterranean further south (map 1), grew ever less persuasive—or rather, confused. While many on the eastern side of the Kasidiaris did direct their attention and accounts of their past southward, at least where this mainland area was concerned, those on the western side tended to

Figure 5. Landslip used as sheepfold (Kasidiaris mountain in background)

focus northward and westward, toward areas marked as more "Balkan" than Mediterranean; but nobody in the research program was talking about the Balkans as part of the "Mediterranean Basin." Furthermore, for those who leapfrogged from one part of Epirus to cities, personal experience of place and location were described in terms of, say, Lower Pogoni, Chicago, and Athens, while a neighbor talked about Lower Pogoni and Patras or Melbourne; and that was set against a range of differences in the way peoples from other areas of Epirus moved and traveled around the region. In short, the way interconnection, separation, and movement were described by many people in Epirus rendered Epirus's location (in the sense meant by Gupta and Ferguson [1997]) highly ambiguous in terms of the research program's focus.

This chapter explores some of these incompatibilities as well as the compatibilities, both as a means to account for them and to begin considering the interrelations and separations (the partial connections, in Strathern's [1991] terms) across discursive scales. I build on the insights of Gupta and Ferguson and others—people are never alone with their places and never constitute them as places entirely on their own—to demonstrate how the interweaving of different accounts will always be involved. To do that, I often take each kind of account on its own terms, as I have the accounts shared with me by people from the Kasidiaris area: it is the interrelations and separations between accounts that concern me most, and it is in that sense that I do not take these narratives as either self-contained or self-evident. Here, accounts of the physical place are the focus, and once again, three interrelated themes keep emerging across scales in different ways: instability, visibility and invisibility, and movement.

THE KASIDIARIS AND EPIRUS EMBODIED

Regarded as a physical entity, the Kasidiaris (previous name Sioutistas, meaning "hornless")[3] constitutes an imposing presence: a steep-sided, long, narrow, partially forested limestone mountain, it rises 1,329 m above sea level at its tallest. Hiking to the top takes a morning of hard physical exertion, and its presence looms over most places immediately surrounding it. Like a somewhat scrubby wall, the Kasidiaris provides a western boundary for the Doliana Plain and constitutes the eastern flank of Lower Pogoni. From this perspective, the sense of physical solidity that the Kasidiaris imposes seems hard to deny: whatever else might be thought about it, in physical terms you still have to go around, over, or along it if you want to move from one place to another in that region.[4]

On the other hand, from a geophysical perspective, the Kasidiaris is constituted as a key zone of several different kinds of highly active tectonic movement; therefore it is not physically solid, nor does it appear particularly solid on the surface. It is littered with landslips, eroding badlands, gullies, cracks, even great holes, on the western side, where a section has sunk in.[5] In these respects, the Kasidiaris is an important part of the story about land degradation in this region: it is currently one of the most highly active areas, and what happens there is interrelated with what happens in much of the rest of the region, insofar as it is located at the northern end of a fault line that passes through the entirety of the middle of Epirus (map 5).

This geomorphological perspective of the importance of the Kasidiaris contrasts with almost every other account about it. As mentioned in chapter 1, from the perspective of the aesthetics of mountains (their visual, photographable impact), it is not particularly distinguished as a mountain among others in the region, at least in terms of height and limestone cragginess. To the east, there are the mountains of the Zagori, particularly the Timfi (also called the Gamilla; fig. 2), which is some 2,500 m high; to the north in Konitsa County, there is the Grammos (1,957 m) and the Smolikas (2,637 m, not shown on map). All three of these mountains, which are fetchingly snowcapped during most of the year, constitute part of the huge Pindos range, sometimes described as the "backbone" of continental Greece, which stretches from Albania to the Gulf of Corinth in the southern mainland (McNeill 1992:26). To the northeast, there is the Nemertska, rising up some 2,200 m, and to the east is the Mourgana, around 1,800 m

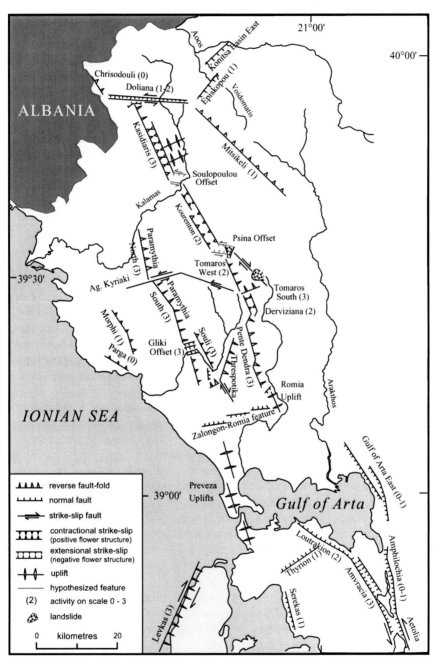

Map 5. Major active structures, Epirus (modified from King, Sturdy, and Bailey 1997: 547)

high, both of which are mostly in Albania; and the Mourgana crosses the boundary between Thesprotia and the Pogoni area, as well as the Greek-Albanian boundary. These mountains have had songs and books written about them, and some even have Web sites these days.[6] Yet, with the exception of geomorphological accounts, the Kasidiaris has not evoked the same kind of attention. Even peoples associated with the Kasidiaris area commented that there was nothing worthy of note about it: in the past, relatively poor people used to go up and down it with their animals on both sides over the seasons, and now that this hardly happens anymore, the mountain merely constitutes a barrier to get around. So, with the exception of tectonics, the Kasidiaris was mostly a matter of indifference, in the same way as were some of the people associated with it.

Beyond the Kasidiaris, at the level of Epirus as a whole, something else happens when geomorphological accounts are contrasted with other kinds of accounts of the place. For geophysicists working on the Greek side of the border, Epirus as a region is cast as an important tectonic zone of fault lines that is contiguous to other such zones throughout Greece, much as the Kasidiaris is cast as an important and contiguous part of the tectonic fault that goes through the center of Epirus. Both are essentially the same, except at the scale of magnitude: Epirot tectonic faults are smaller versions of tectonic faults through the whole Greek region, as with nested Russian dolls, where the smallest doll is the same as the largest doll, except in size. In contrast, other kinds of account of the Epirot region focus on the area more as a *politically* tectonic zone, as well as a place that environmentally contrasts considerably with other parts of Greece: it is not constituted as contiguous, as a smaller example of what occurs in the whole of Greece; rather, the focus is what makes different parts of Greece into contrasting types of places.

Yet looked at in terms of interrelations, these two forms of fault line (physical and political instability) do in fact interweave, even though their discursive constructions (contiguous as opposed to noncontiguous) are very different. This can be seen most clearly through one of the more notable aspects of the geomorphological accounts of the region: the absence of any detail concerning what happens beyond the Albanian border, on the Albanian side. Political divisions obviously also imposed epistemological separations here, broke the continuity of the geomorphological story. The absence of data on the physical characteristics of the Albanian side was due to the research's being carried out in the early 1980s, before the end of command socialist rule in Albania. At the time, the border was tightly closed, and the researchers were therefore unable to travel there. To construct the tectonic and geological maps, the team physically had to visit these places, go up and down mountains, ferret around in gorges, and walk along valleys. The maps they have produced leave a trace of this experience, going completely blank on the Albanian side of the border (maps 5 and 6). Yet a portion of that area is nevertheless included in the maps, as it is physically contiguous to the area that was studied, and it fills an otherwise empty space in the northwestern corner of the symmetrical rectangular frame that surrounds them. The fragment of Albania that is included is thus rendered a gap, but it is not an empty gap; by preference, the researchers would have filled the whole rectangular frame with tectonic activity and geology, and would have shown that area as contiguous as well.[7]

This blankness of the Albanian fragment on the maps thus visually illustrates the interweaving of scales here: sometimes, political forces become bigger than mountains, can literally erase them from view. Where state bureaucracies come into the story—where they are able to control movement and the generation of and access to data—the Greek-Albanian border becomes a seriously physical boundary. As Caren Kaplan says in her analysis of the widespread use of the tropes of travel and displacement in much postmodernist and poststructuralist theory, "To put it bluntly, few of us can live without a passport or identity card of some sort" (Kaplan 1996: 9); in this case, there was no kind of paperwork the researchers could produce that would allow movement across that border during the early 1980s. So in a different discursive form, this experience tells part of the same story as that told by Western Kasidiaris peoples on the Greek side of the border, who were equally severed from any substantial experience or knowledge of the Albanian side of the border for almost fifty years until its reopening in late 1991. It was one of the many ways in which political power made itself felt and affected what was visible in this region, even for those people telling their story of this place in terms of its tectonics and geology.[8]

For that reason, the geomorphological maps combine two very different temporal scales: the tectonic and geological data are gauged in millennia; the Albanian gap is a matter of mere decades, and specifically the Cold War decades. If, for the most part, the accounts of Western Kasidiaris peoples seemed in stark contrast to the accounts of geomorphology specialists, this was one area where they were the same, which returns me to the points that Gupta and Ferguson have made about the way power always becomes involved in the constitution of places. So, to explore that, I will go through these stories in a bit more detail, clicking between and across scales, to and fro. I will begin with the stories of discontinuities provided by various sociopolitical accounts of Epirus and its parts—ways in which the parts are separated and rendered different; and I will move on to the story of continuity that the geomorphological accounts provide, coming back in the end to some of the accounts that people around the Kasidiaris gave about the physicality of their place, their indifference to-

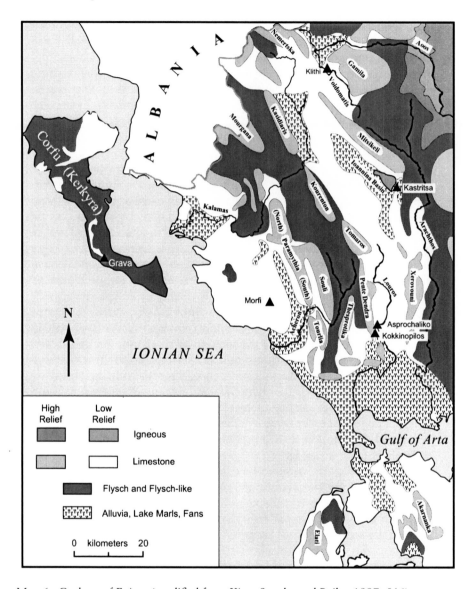

Map 6. Geology of Epirus (modified from King, Sturdy, and Bailey 1997: 546)

ward the shiftiness of the land surface, and their focus on aspects of the place that always already interweave with other things.

DISCONTINUITIES

Epirus in Greece

As I have already briefly mentioned in the previous chapter, Epirus's location in the northwestern corner of mainland Greece and on the border of Albania is frequently represented as making it distinctly different from many other areas of Greece. Within general accounts of contemporary Greece, it is predominantly cast as one of the three northern Balkan borderland regions (the other two being Macedonia and Thrace, with Macedonia receiving by far the most attention); along with those, it is also represented as having been the source of political tension for Greece throughout most of the twentieth century (Clogg 1992; Foss 1978; Hammond 1983; Sakellariou 1997; Vacalopoulou 1995). Attention is frequently drawn to the fact that Epirus (or at least the northern part of it) was not incorporated into the Greek state until 1913, during the final breakup of the Ottoman Empire. This distinction in the political history of the northern and southern territories of the mainland Greek state is also often accompanied by the assertion, or at least implication, of a cultural division between these regions, as illustrated by the quotation from Peckham above: the north is somehow more Balkan than the south. One of the more important aspects of this for the northern region as a whole is the widespread view that these borderland areas of Greece are more culturally and/or ethnically diverse than the southern areas ("Macedonian Salad"), and are therefore more "problematic" for ethnonationalist discourses.[9]

In addition to these political, historical, and asserted cultural distinctions, Epirus's geographical location is marked as being spatially distant from the centers of population and industry in Greece, which are both focused in Athens and its surrounding areas, some 470 km south of Epirus. The main center in the northern mainland is Thessaloniki, the capital of the Greek region of Macedonia, but that lies on the far side of a range of the highest mountains in the region (the Pindos range) and is therefore difficult to reach from Epirus. Furthering the impression of infrastructural disconnection, commentaries often point out that there is no railway in Epirus, and although air and road transport are improving every year, it is still a difficult place to reach, unless you have begun your journey in Athens, have enough money to fly, and take Ionnina as your final destination. Perhaps ironically, it is in practice far easier to reach many of the Greek islands, which generally have larger airports and much more frequent air and sea services owing to the tourism they attract, than it is to reach Epirus.

The way Epirus's overall historical, political, and geographical location is constituted in these accounts thus leads to the impression that it is "in the middle of nowhere," on the periphery of Greece. To this is added the generally harsher climate than exists in the south and the fairly steep topography: Epirus is one of the wettest regions in Greece, with between 900 and 1,200 mm of rain per year (table 3), and one of the coldest and snowiest regions in the winter (tables 4 and 5); as many point out, this is not a typically Mediterranean climate. Epirus is also 74 percent mountainous, compared to 42 percent mountainous for Greece as a whole (table 1). Even though Greece is generally regarded as a mountainous place, this greater density of mountains is again associated with a typically Balkan topography. In any case, this kind of classification means that a considerably higher proportion of the population in Epirus than in Greece as a whole is defined as living in mountainous areas (table 2). Moreover, as urban areas are defined as those municipalities that contain ten thousand or more residents, Epirus appears to have much higher numbers of rural residents than does Greece as a whole: 67 percent as against 30 percent (table 2). There are reasons for treating these population figures with some caution even on their own terms, as will be discussed in chapter 6; the aim here is to show the impression of Epirus generated from such figures.

These elements combine to create a stereotypical image of a ruggedly wild, remote, politically unstable, and distant (not very visible, not very known) place in Greece, and almost all commentators, travel writers, and historians talking about Epirus make a point of this, in differing ways. For example, James Pettifer, one of the more prominent English-language general commentators on modern Greece, focuses on different Greek regions to discuss aspects of recent political and social life of the country, including tourism, archaeology, language, the family, and so on. He selects Epirus to discuss the Second World War and the Greek civil war after it, and he introduces the region thus:

> Few foreign visitors go to Epirus, few Greeks for that matter. . . . After a brief period of prominence in Byron's time, when the region was the seat of despotic, glamorous Ali Pasha, the diamond of Yannina, with a huge harem and armed retinue, and who, under the Turks, ruled a vast wild domain stretching from Arta in the south to Berati in Albania, Epirus sank into primitive obscurity.[10] (Pettifer 1993:3)

This is obviously the kind of commentary that Fleming challenges in her account of Ali Pasha, mentioned in the previous chapter (Fleming 1999). It is all there: political instability and wildness that became "primitive" after Epirus's fall from grace into "obscurity." Equally, exoticism is firmly associated with the place through references to Ali Pasha and his "harem." And just in case the reader does not understand that this makes Epirus quite "other," Pettifer brings in Byron as having been present during the "wild" rather than "primitive" period. Byron was prominent among a list of nineteenth-century British poets who became as famous for their atypical, not to say transgressive, personal lives as they did for their poetry; he was also one of the earlier British philhellenes, campaigning for Greek independence from Ottoman rule (Roessel 2002). Byron did indeed live in Epirus during Ali Pasha's time, and a main avenue in Ioannina is now named after him; but evoking Byron's presence in this context emphasizes both the assertion of the exotic character of Ali Pasha's reign and the fact that there are no Byrons in Epirus *now*.

Pettifer goes on to articulate explicitly the variety of key elements that for him make Epirus "wild" and "primitive": it was one of the last places in mainland Greece to be liberated from Ottoman rule; it has ruggedly high mountains; it is a long way from Athens; it possesses only one significant classical Greek site; it is cold, so olives—one of the key symbols of membership in the Mediterranean region—grow only in southern sheltered areas; it is sparsely populated, having "empty forest roads"; and to cap it all off, Pettifer says that for Athenians, "it is the Wild North rather like the Wild West" (ibid.: 3–4). He repeats this claim in chapter 16 of the book, titled "The Hidden Patchwork: Albanians, Vlachs and Sarakatsans." In detailing the reopening of the Greek-Albanian border in December of 1990, he suggests that the influx of Albanian "refugees" contributed to "a general Wild West atmosphere around the border" (ibid.: 180).

For Pettifer, what does make Epirus a focus of attention is the region's role in both past and recent wars (one of the characteristics that makes Epirus, along with much of the Balkans, notable within hegemonic discourses). Yet even this is couched in terms that make Epirus appear peripheral. Along with numerous other commentators, he suggests that the Greek War of Independence in 1821, which had begun in the Peloponnese in the south, was crucially aided by Epirus, but not because it was at the heart of that war. Rather, it was because Ali Pasha was in open revolt against the Ottoman Porte in 1821, which the Greek revolutionaries calculated would distract the Ottoman forces' attention. Frazee, in his study of the role of the Orthodox Church in the conflict, says this explicitly: "One of the deciding factors for the Greeks in launching the revolt in the Peloponnesus had been the hope that the Ottoman army would be too occupied in Epirus to launch an all out attack against the Greek rebels" (Frazee 1969: 22). Once again, Epirus was at the periphery of the "big story."

Pettifer goes on to say that the first Italian invasion of Greece of the Second World War came through Epirus from Albania and was effectively repelled by the Greek army and resistance forces there, but only briefly (ibid.: 5); and that Epirus constituted the last stronghold of the Communist side of the Greek civil war (1946–49), which was finally routed out of the Grammos mountain through being bombed by the U.S. Air Force, in what was reportedly the United States' first use of napalm (ibid.: 5).[11] Overall, then, Pettifer leaves readers in little doubt that Epirus is quite distinct from other parts of Greece, but also constitutes it as a peripheral and fairly hostile environment in all meanings of the phrase. Within much other literature on the region, Epirus does not receive even that much prominence, not even in terms of its northern credentials as a place of Balkan conflict and instability; Macedonia is given pride of place for that (see n. 8). It is thus rendered doubly peripheral within this kind of account.

All Epirots I met, whether around the Kasidiaris or elsewhere, were well aware of this particular account of their place, as discussed in the previous chapter. Moreover, many reproduced parts of this story, when complaining about the lack of infrastructure in the place and the relative indifference shown toward Epirus by the southern centers of power, despite (or perhaps because of) the fact that the area constituted a key battle site for those centers of power on repeated occasions. At the same time, there was also a widespread rejection of the implication that this meant Epirots themselves somehow reflected the "remote wilderness" of Epirus, that they were all indigenous examples of that stereotype. With the exceptions that I discussed in the previous chapter (notably the Sarakatsani), the idea of indigenousness did not resonate with many people's sense of their relation to the place. As a result, many often resentfully commented on the views expressed by Athenians about Epirots that reflected those assumptions. The fact that increasing numbers of young Athenians were visiting Epirus as ecotourists or to experience something of authentic or traditional Greece (though restricting themselves mostly to the Zagori region) did not help matters, as illustrated by the comments in chapter 2 from the soft drinks distributor in Delvinaki. Nevertheless, how things seemed from the vantage point of Athens and that of commentators such as Pettifer and Peckham was recognized as important, even if such views were not accepted in their entirety and occasionally caused considerable irritation.

The key difference between many commentaries such as Pettifer's about Epirus and the views expressed by many people associated with the region lay in what was thought to have caused how things seemed. Pettifer made Epirus appear as a distinctly other, self-contained entity (one of Eric Wolf's billiard balls). The implication of this approach was that any asserted characteristics of Epirus—its remoteness, wildness, and otherness—were cast as being somehow natural, somehow inherent in the place itself; by extension, that would include the people of Epirus, thus rendering them indigenous. Pettifer blended the mountains and climate seamlessly with its people and its political history. In contrast, many Epirots regarded their place as a web of interconnections and separations with many other places; any remoteness, wildness, and otherness that emerged from this was generally regarded as part of a constructed hierarchy in those relations, both in terms of how things were constituted as seeming, and in the way things were made to be, in practical terms. It was the discontinuity, the separating out of Epirus from other things and other places, that was the difference between Pettifer's and many Epirots' accounts. Again, while many more recent analyses of place focus on these power-inflected interrelations and interpellations—and another pertinent example here is James Clifford's study on the subject (Clifford 1997)—in this place, that was made explicit; it was used to constitute a sense of the place.

The Kasidiaris in Epirus

Within the Greek part of Epirus itself, there are other kinds of asserted discontinuities, and here, I will focus on the way the region is divided up according to some administrative, topographical, and statistical accounts. In administrative terms, the Kasidiaris is included in the biggest region of Epirus, Ioannina Prefecture, which covers 55 percent of Epirus and constitutes the entirety of its northern half (table 1). The other three prefectures—Thesprotia, Arta, and Preveza—together constitute the southern half. While Thesprotia contains a considerable proportion of inland and mountainous regions as well as some coastline, Preveza and Arta contain higher proportions of plains areas used for commercial cultivation and have large stretches of coastline. Arta also has the distinction of having become a part of the Greek state earlier than the other three Epirot regions, during the first Greek war of independence in the 1820s. Arta is thus regarded by many, including people living in Epirus, as more of a "southern" Greek mainland area than a "northern" one. In addition, the southern coastal towns of Preveza and Parga had passed, in the eighteenth and nineteenth centuries, variously between the control of the Venetians, the French, the Russians, and the British, unlike the more northern regions, which remained continually under Ottoman control (Fleming 1999: 70–77). Once again, then, there is the replication of a north-south division, both politically and topographically. This division has implications for the generalized image of Epirus of the kind that Pettifer evoked: in that generalized image, it is the northern, mostly mountainous and forested half, not the southern half with its wide plains, earlier accession to Greece, and involvement with various European powers, that most have in mind. The more southern areas are now administratively *in* Epirus but are often not constituted as being *of* Epirus, in terms of stereotypical characteristics.

Ioannina Prefecture, which does include large areas that fit the stereotype (other than the city itself and the large plain just outside it), is administratively subdivided into four counties, of which the biggest is Dodoni County. The capital city, most of the Zagori region (which is not an administrative district in itself), and the largest plain of the northern half of Epirus, Ioannina Plain, are all located in Dodoni County. As discussed in chapter 2, the Kasidiaris itself is split between Dodoni County and Pogoni County, which renders the mountain's location somewhat ambiguous in administrative terms. The remaining two counties in Ioannina Prefecture, Konitsa and Metsovo, constitute the northern and northeastern sections of the prefecture, and Metsovo borders the region of Macedonia; these two counties are also the most steeply mountainous areas of the whole region, containing as they do large sections of the Pindos mountain range, including some of the Zagori section of those mountains.

These kinds of accounts combine topographical, administrative, political, and social boundaries that effectively render Arta and Preveza visible as productive, coastline, and more southern areas, whereas Ioannina Prefecture is rendered visible as highly mountainous, rugged, and remote and is most often taken to represent Epirus as a whole as being distinct and different from other parts of Greece. Thesprotia, once again, comes ambiguously somewhere in between those two kinds of visibility and is therefore not very visible at all, for all of this construction depends upon distinctions between regions and subregions, between mountains, plains, and valleys, inland and coastline. Things are made visible through separation and contrast, not through interconnection.

CONTINUITIES AND MOVING MOUNTAINS:
THE GEOMORPHOLOGICAL STORY

There are other ways to represent the place: as contiguous and interrelated, rather than as divided up and separated. If we ignore all the administrative boundaries and sociopolitical accounts (as geologists and tectonic specialists prefer to do), the mountain ranges, valleys, and plains in Epirus take on a self-similarity, so that even though there are differences within given areas (e.g., mountain as against valley), these differences are repeated across areas. Within this kind of account, the mountains can be represented as being roughly arranged in slanted lines running parallel to one another in a northwest-southeast direction. The Kasidiaris is at the northwestern end of the range that runs roughly through the middle of Epirus, seen partially in map 2, but most clearly in maps 5 and 6, showing the region's active tectonic structures and geology. But as mentioned already, administrative boundaries are not entirely absent. These maps indicate that the mountain ranges continue into Albania by the obviously partial illustration of the mountains that actually straddle the border: the Mourgana, Makrikambos, and Nemertska mountains appear as unfinished fragments, highlighting the fact that the discontinuity is a political one, not a topographical, geological, or tectonic one. Map 3, which was constructed by Geoff King years after maps 5 and 6, was based on a topographical map that covers both Greece and Albania; it shows the continuity that might have been included in the other maps if the geological and tectonics teams had been able to survey the area within Albania.

In any event, from a topographical perspective, one outcome of this regular and patterned arrangement of mountain ranges is a kind of corrugated effect in a north-south direction, where narrow valleys run in parallel between fairly steep mountains, occasionally interspersed with stretches of plains. The wide variation in elevation within short distances results in a range of climates within small areas, so that the tops of mountains are often frozen and snow-covered in winter and the bottoms of valleys are often burned off and extremely hot in summer. The same pattern is repeated across the region; in this account, all the mountain ranges and valleys are self-similar, not-quite-replications of one another.

There is also a repeated pattern of self-similarity in the geological account of the region (map 6). Most of Epirus is physically made up of a multilayered sandwich of limestone and flysch—a crumbly brownish-gray mixture of stones, containing mostly sandstone, but also marls, shales, and clays. The only areas where this is not the case are in the few plains, where alluvia and lake marls collect, and some areas where igneous rock exists. So in addition to variable elevations in every area, there are also variable types of geological formation in every area, but the pattern of variation is the same across the whole of the region. The core of the Kasidiaris is itself made of limestone, as are almost all the mountains in the region, but the western flank and foothills of the Kasidiaris are covered in a layer of flysch, whereas the eastern flank, foothills, and plain are covered in a layer of alluvia and lake marls. The soils on the eastern side are typically deep red and quite fine, often referred to as *terra rossa*; the soils on the western side are typically cement gray, dull brown, or a combination of those. This distinction results in very different productive potential of the land on each side. In brief, the eastern side, in addition to having a large plain, also has more fertile soils than the western side. That pattern of contrast is repeated for the flanks of most mountains in the region, so the Kasidiaris is again represented as one of a contiguous series of replications: one flank covered with one kind of material and the other flank with another kind.

For the Kasidiaris, though, the imposed invisibility of the Albanian side of these maps masks what also provides a geomorphological similarity or symmetry between the two sides, a symmetry that can be seen in map 3, which shows the topography continuing into Albania. Beyond the immediate foothills of the western Kasidiaris that contain mostly thin flysch-based soils, the rest of the plain (the Drinos Plain), which is located in Albania, also contains fertile alluvial soils, as does the Doliana Plain on the eastern side. As I mentioned in the previous chapter, before the closure of the Greek-Albanian border at the end of the Second World War, both sides of the Kasidiaris had access to a river, a fertile plain, and a mountainside. After the closure of the border, the western side was divided into two sections: in Albania, there was the river, the fertile plain, and a hostile international border; in Greece, there were the infertile foothills and mountainside, a small section of plain, a small section of river, and a hostile international border. This meant that Lower Pogoni effectively constituted a place that, in geological and topographical terms, is described as the least productive of the region. In contrast, the eastern side of the Kasidiaris remained undivided, with its river, fertile plain, and mountainside; the hostile international border was on the other side of the mountain.

Map 3 also shows the most significant rivers of the northern part of Epirus. The most important for my purposes are the Kalamas, which runs through the Doliana Plain along the eastern side of the Kasidiaris and then turns west further south into Thesprotia; and the Drinos, which runs through the middle of the Drinos Plain in Albania and then splits just past the current Greek-Albanian border. One tributary goes north and runs through Upper Pogoni, north of the Kasidiaris (this tributary continues to be called the Drinos); the other runs south along the western edge of the Kasidiaris (where the river is called Gyftopotamos, meaning "Gypsy river"). The Kalamas constituted a major conduit along which trade and transhumance traveled in previous years between northern and southern parts of Epirus: it was the river that most followed in going to and from Thesprotia with their animals, providing access to water, a route through mountains, and good surrounding grazing lands; and the Drinos was the main river along which trade and transhumance traveled in previous years between the major southern Albanian towns and mountains and Epirus, for the same reasons. All of that on the western side was literally erased from the map, rendered invisible.

That point having been made, let me briefly and crudely outline the analysis of the team researching the tectonics and geology of the Kasidiaris mountain itself, which tells a different story of movement from the one explored in the previous chapter, and one that involves a temporal scale of millennia, not decades or centuries. Geoff King and Derek Sturdy (King, Sturdy, and Bailey 1997; King, Sturdy, and Whitney 1993) suggest that the Kasidiaris is being pushed upward, tilting toward the Albanian border, and is also being skewed at either end, and folded. Map 5 illustrates this tectonic activity in the area, as well as the major faults in the rest of (Greek) Epirus. Some of the results of this push upward from the east for the Kasidiaris can be seen in map 6, illustrating the geology of the region. Again, it shows that the western flank of the Kasidiaris is mostly flysch right up to the Albanian border, but that on the eastern side, the area is mostly alluvia, lake marls, and fans. According to King and Sturdy's analysis, the flysch eroded off the western side of the Kasidiaris as it uplifted from the east, and the alluvial deposits and fans were generated as the Kasidiaris uplift slightly tilted the Doliana Plain, causing sediments eroding off slopes around the plain to collect in the plain.[12] Moreover, Sturdy and King suggest that one further result of the Kasidiaris uplift was to drain what was, during Paleolithic times, an enormous lake in the Doliana Plain, by opening up a gap in the plain in the south at Soulopoulos (map 5). What remains is the Kalamas River, which runs through the plain and through the same gap (map 3). Again according to the analysis, in recent millennia, the Kalamas River is once again cutting down, through the silted-up deposits, into its preexisting riverbed as a result of uplift caused by the Kasidiaris fault.

This particular account of the Kasidiaris and its surroundings as a continually moving and not-very-solid object has left visible traces today. On the eastern side, the Kalamas River now sports some fairly impressive waterfalls, notably near Katarraktis in the south of the plain, which is one of the villages whose territory I surveyed (chapter 6); in other areas, the river now cuts some thirty meters into the ground, an alteration that the people of Katarraktis have witnessed happening within their own lifetimes. When this is combined with the silting-up of the plain from the tilt caused by the uplift of the Kasidiaris, new deposits are submerging some areas and others have lost fields into the erosion caused by the river gorge. Elsewhere, the silting-up of the characteristically red soils that come off the limestone hillsides has generated badlands all along the eastern foothills (fig. 6), and in other places, sinkholes have appeared, where the surface has dropped down by as much as a meter or so fairly suddenly (fig. 5). All of which adds up, within this story, to a considerable amount of visible movement on the surface of this place, which is accounted for by its fundamental interconnection with a network of activity going on underneath the surface, stretching across the entirety of the region and indeed the entirety of Greece.

On the western side, this moving land surface manifests itself largely in pockets of badlands (some fairly large) consisting of dull, gravel-filled material, fine gray cement-colored dust, or gray-brown flysch deposits, numerous slopes sporting flysch landslips and rather scrubby vegetation which results from the thin and poor-quality soils that develop on flysch

Figure 6. *Terra rossa* erosion on Katarraktis territory (Eastern Kasidiaris)

(figs. 4 and 6). Again, though, much more visible on the maps of the western side is the international border, which simply cuts across the region and has generated the blank northwestern corner showing no geology or tectonics.

Furthermore, taking photographs anywhere near the border was forbidden, which generates yet another gap in contemporary terms, though two photos I did manage to take provide two partial (in both meanings of the word) visual images of this place during my fieldwork. Figure 7 was taken on a dark and rainy day in March 1993, from a hillside above the Kakavia border-crossing point. The view looks into Albania and shows a long line of trucks, apparently in the middle of an otherwise empty, shrubby, and hilly area, waiting to get through the border post and cross into Albania. There was always a queue, but during this period it was much longer than usual because the Greek border guards were on a slowdown in protest over one of the guards' having been shot by what was termed in the Greek-language Epirot newspapers an "Albanian Mafioso." The border guards felt they were not being protected sufficiently by the Greek government, and therefore staged the slowdown. It became something of a cynical joke in the area that "Albanian Mafiosi" regularly used Kalashnikovs or small arms as their passports and visas to get into Greece. Regular reporting of such incidents in the media contributed considerably to the "Wild West" image that Pettifer evoked of the place during the 1990s.

Figure 7. Kakavia Greek-Albanian border post area, March 1993

There were many such incidents involving the border during my time in Epirus, but I will mention just two of the ones most noted in the Epirot as well as Athens-based media. The first also occurred in 1993, when the Albanian government expelled a Greek Orthodox priest who, the government claimed, was fomenting ethnic hatred between Greeks and Albanians. Of course, during 1993, there was a great deal of nervousness about ethnic tensions in Albania, as this was at the height of the conflicts that were raging in several parts of former Yugoslavia, to the east of Albania. The Albanian government was clearly anxious to prevent the explosion, on their patch of the Balkans, of what was widely reported as a Balkan "tinderbox." And as I mentioned in the previous chapter, the Greek Orthodox Church in this region made it its business, especially during the period the border was closed, to remind Albania continually of its (Greek) Orthodox population. A small example of this can be seen in figure 8: it shows the chapel at the Kakavia border post sporting a prominent evil eye looking suspiciously toward Albania (one of the metropolitan Sevastianos's constructions).[13] In any event, the Greek government responded to the expulsion of the Orthodox priest from Albania by expelling thousands of Albanian immigrants from Greece, which also caused considerable queues at the border post. This is one of many incidents involving the Greek Orthodox Church alluded to by Michalis, the man in Ktismata who felt fairly cynical about the usefulness of priests (chapter 2), when he suggested that the Church caused "chaos" in this area.

Figure 8. Chapel at Kakavia Greek-Albanian border post (Greek side)

The second incident occurred in April 1994, when two Albanian border soldiers (conscripts) were killed and three others injured, apparently by five Greek men who were members of Omonia, a political party representing Northern Epirot (i.e., Greek) rights in Albania. The Albanian authorities arrested and imprisoned the five men, which resulted in enormous tensions between the Greek and Albanian governments, particularly as the then president of Albania, Sali Berisha, accused the Greek government of involvement in the Albanian soldiers' deaths. Again, the Greek government began to expel thousands of Albanian immigrants, most of whom were sent back through the Kakavia border post. The whole saga captured headlines in the Greek press for weeks, again constituting this region of the country as deeply problematic and politically unstable.

All of these events during my earlier fieldwork period meant that the disruption, as it were, of the geomorphological story on the western side of the Kasidiaris, and its interweaving with other scales, was much more starkly obvious than it was on the eastern side. Nevertheless, that interweaving did occur on both sides, and this is where the geomorphological story does directly overlap with the stories told by people in the area. The story of the formation of the plain on the eastern side was told in terms of how the plain became productive for cultivation, and within this story, that explained why a higher population and all the best asphalt roads were now located on that side. This focus on the productivity of the land was also the reason for the importance in this story of the continuing landslips, cracks, and gullying: these processes could negatively affect that productivity. The story of the formation of "poor soils" on the western side was told in terms of how that area, over millennia, became relatively unproductive, which explained the lower populations and relatively large amount of abandonment of productive use of the land on that side. On the basis of these criteria, the instability of the land surface on the western side of the mountain was less significant in contemporary terms, since the place was not really productive enough to enable people to make a decent living these days. Within this kind of "economy of geology" account, there was of course no explicit discussion of how the western area was also constituted as unproductive by the much more recent closure of the border and thus the "disappearance" of the fertile plain: the border simply represented the limits of the geomorphological story. But as I have said, that gap is visible in the maps.

In any event, the upshot once again was that the Lower Pogoni area, which constitutes most of the western Kasidiaris, was made relatively unimportant in this story: not all its story could be told because of the Greek-Albanian border, and what could be told rendered the area a place of little productive import. The story thus ended with the same conclusion as was drawn by many people associated with the Lower Pogoni region: even though the Kasidiaris was a key part of the geomorphological account of this place, and was constituted as being contiguous to it, the interweaving of political and economic scales into the story made Western Kasidiaris, once again, of relatively little significance.

CONTINUITIES AND DISCONTINUITIES

This brief survey of some of the accounts involving the embodied aspects of Epirus and the Kasidiaris region gives a sense of how phenomena apparently occurring at completely different spatial, temporal, and discursive scales—such as tectonic activity, geological processes, climate, productivity of the land, and political disputes between nation-states—continually and inevitably interweave. In physically experienced as well as conceptual terms, these different scales become involved with one another, despite the varieties of ways in which the story of the place has been told and what aspects are rendered visible or invisible, peripheral or central. The geomorphological studies, seen in their own epistemological terms, emphasized that the physical surfaces shift and move regularly: even though the underlying processes involved occur so slowly that they are thousands of times beyond the human life span (let alone social memory), there are many continuous small shifts and movements that are experienced within historical memory, within lifetimes, or even within weeks and within a few minutes or hours, such as sudden landslips or occasional earthquakes. They also show that the moving and shifting character of this place means that most of the soils in Epirus, with the important exception of the few areas of alluvial deposits on some plains, are relatively poor and thin (Sturdy, Webley, and Bailey 1994; Sturdy and Webley 1988; Bailey, King, and Sturdy 1993). There are few places where things stay put long enough for a good quality, deep soil to develop. The Western Kasidiaris area was seen as being at the bottom of that particular constructed hierarchy: not only highly tectonically active, but also poor in "economy of geology" terms, in that relatively unproductive soils develop there. In these terms, when mixed cultivation and pastoral peoples around the Western Kasidiaris complained about the quality of their soils, they did have something to complain about, given that they were now cut off from the Drinos Plain in Albania. And also in that sense, the geomorphological research continually highlighted—by leaving an obvious gap in—what it could not explicitly discuss: the imposition of political and economic "realities" that constituted the geomorphological story as being a part of those realities.

All of these stories also generated a continual sense, in different ways, of Epirus as a place of instability, movement, and shifting. None of them implied that the physical place formed a static stage for people, a backdrop for their activities, in the sense described by Eric Hirsch (1995); indeed, in the geomorphological account as well as some of the sociopolitical accounts, a considerable amount of agency was ascribed to the place. People around the Kasidiaris were familiar with the sociopolitical accounts, but unfamiliar with the geomorphological accounts. One could argue that in embodied terms, they experienced the geomorphological story whether they were aware of that particular story or not, and therefore they would "know" about it, even if the experience was expressed differently; but they also simultaneously experienced the other kinds of accounts, the ones excluded from the geomorphological accounts, in embodied terms as well: the imposition of administrative and state boundaries, the account of the place as being in the "middle of nowhere" and as a place of political "tectonics," and so on. The lack of productivity of some soils compared to others was not separate from all these other accounts and impositions.

Here, the focus of the geomorphological story, in not being able to include these other accounts explicitly, is what differentiates it from the stories told by the people around the Kasidiaris. As I have outlined, the processes causing instability within tectonics—"faults," "slips," "contractions," "folds," and so on—are analyzed in terms occurring so far beyond the spatial and temporal scales of political instabilities that neither appears to have anything to do with the other; they are rendered both incompatible and incomparable scales, in Strathern's terms (Strathern 1991: 35–36). That points both to the particularities of the discourse that geomorphology uses to describe this place and to the particularities of the discourses that were used by other accounts about it; it points to what such discourses pay attention to and what they are indifferent about, as well as what they cannot pay attention to. At the same time, as I have shown, these scales do in fact come into relation with one another: they interweave, both on a discursive level (the Albanian blank fragment on the maps, the focus on the "economy of geology") and on an embodied level (the inability of the research team to travel to Albania in the 1980s).

This kind of interweaving was self-evident to peoples around the Western Kasidiaris; it was the manner in which they narrated the experience and construction of this place. In that sense, the "environmental forces" that contributed both to their continual coming and going and to their relatively undistinguished status involved the continual interrelation of many things, whether or not they were intellectually compatible. The language used by geomorphology, which focuses on the physical characteristics of the place without bringing other things into account, would not do to describe such forces. Instead, the language of "impoverished," "hostile," and "unproductive" was used by some people and "remote wilderness" by others, all of which pointed less to the apparently anomalous activities of the physical surface of the earth than to interwoven processes of social, economic, and political marginalization and/or embattlement (the language of war was rarely absent).

In these terms, "environmental forces" added to conditions that meant the people in and around Epirus frequently described the place(s) as existing "on the edge" and on a periphery, both literally and metaphorically. For most people associated with Epirus, that was an image with which they had to engage in one way or another, whether they wanted to or not. For many associated with the Lower Pogoni region, such an image was often used to describe the reasons for continual coming and going: either a general state of affairs that kept repeating itself in different ways across time, or some specific event or another that tipped the balance, meant that movement had to happen to enable them to survive. That contrasted with the stories told by those living on the eastern side of the Kasidiaris, who moved to improve things, or who even returned once things had improved. Either way, this notion of "environmental forces" was not the same as imagining nature to be an independent agent affecting the way people lived. It was not so much that people failed to make a distinction between nature and culture; rather, they understood that most "environmental forces" were always entangled with other things, especially with what were seen as political and economic forces. In that sense, there was more of a notion of the environment as an "actor" in actor network theory terms (Law and Hassard 1999). The environment was different but not separated from such forces: the scrubby or beautifully mountainous vistas; the naked badlands; the representation of the region as remote, wild, and rugged; the contested border; the various political histories; the ambivalence embedded in *Gréki-ness*; and the tensions around Northern Epirots, Tsamides, and the rest—all were actively part of the particular ambiguities, instabilities, visibilities, and invisibilities of place(s) and the peoples associated with Epirus. The diverse scales involved and the relations between them meant that the notion of separating out nature so that it stood independent of anything else did not make a great deal of sense; or more accurately, when something to do with the environment *was* regarded as being independent of anything else, then it was not taken into account; it had no meaning.

This is where the form in which people around the Kasidiaris told their stories, the focus on the interweaving of scales, particularly through a political discursive approach, becomes important. In those terms, the very ubiquity of land slippage, soil erosion, and gullying, the fact that it has always happened and continues to happen everywhere, meant that it was generally regarded as being *just* "natural," as opposed to nature entangled in other things. And that meant it did not mark anything, did not distinguish anything, and therefore it was not re-markable in the way it was within the geomorphological story. It is in this context that the widespread apparent indifference toward land degradation began to make some sense to me; the accounts people gave me of the physical characteristics of their area repeatedly ignored land degradation of the type analyzed by the geomorphological account and brought other things into the story; they repeatedly rendered the place, even in its embodied, physical form, as the outcome of multiple scalar relations. So it is finally time to give a brief account of these kinds of stories of indifference, as well as the way other things were brought into the conversation.

Interweaving the Gaps

Talking about Soil Erosion

Some of the first people I tried to talk with in Epirus about land degradation lived outside the Kasidiaris region, but as I learned later, their accounts took much the same form as those around the Kasidiaris. During the earliest part of the research in 1992, and as part of a multidisciplinary team, I paid several visits to the inland area of Preveza (in the south) around the Louros River. Among those I met there were the Rentzios and Maris families, who had neighboring pastoral farms located near Kokkinopilos (map 6), a significant Paleolithic site, but also one of the largest areas of *terra rossa* badlands. The Rentzios family kept some 950 sheep and goats and seasonally took the sheep up a nearby mountain to an area called Annogio during the summer months, from May to September. There was a village up there and a school, and the Rentzios family said that they considered Annogio to be where they came from, as they had grown up there. The Maris family used to have sheep and goats and also used to move seasonally with them, but now kept around a hundred beef cattle, so as to avoid having to move up and down the mountain every year. Both families also carried out a small amount of cultivation in the lower area, growing mostly fodder for the animals. They rented most of their grazing and cultivating lands.

As I was aware of Geoff King's and Derek Sturdy's geomorphological studies, the numerous visible indications of land surface movement scattered around the Maris and Rentzios farms instantly attracted my attention: bare, red dunes of *terra rossa* badlands could be seen from the verandas of their houses, not ten feet away; there was also gullying and cracking of the land near their houses, and badlands were scattered around their entire landholdings. So it seemed a good opportunity to ask what the Maris and Rentzios families thought about all of that.

Anastasios Maris, who said he was born in 1907 and had lived in the area all his life as a shepherd, gave me a puzzled look when I pointed to a section of badlands from his veranda and asked him to tell me something about it. "Tell you something about what?" he asked. I replied, "About the soil erosion over there, where there are no plants growing. Has it always been like that?" He looked at the area where I was pointing, and eventually said: "That's not erosion [διάβρωση/*diavrosi*], it's always been like that. That red soil has always been like that." Eleftheria, his wife, who had been in the area since 1941, agreed; but she could see that this response troubled me, and asked me to be more specific. I asked whether it had changed at all over the years, whether it had become worse. She replied: "Worse? No. I remember that the red soil there has always cut down and gullied, all my life. It's always been the same." I asked whether anyone had tried to stop it happening. She gave me a look of incomprehension. "No, nobody ever tried to stop it." So what, I asked, did people do when the erosion affected areas where they were cultivating? Eleftheria looked puzzled again and replied: "Well, we never grew much down here. We cultivated everything up in the mountains, since we were up there in the summer months. Here, it was mostly grazing land." She paused and then added, "Ah! There *is* soil erosion in the mountains, so maybe you should go up there; you will see erosion there. Where we had fields on the hillsides. We built terraces there. If you don't build terraces for fields that are on slopes, the soil slips down the mountain when it rains. It erodes."

Eleftheria was clearly pleased that she had finally understood what on earth I was talking about. I, on the other hand, stared at the badlands and gullies across the way, which looked an awful lot like erosion to me at the time; yet I was being sent up a mountain to find erosion, for there was none here. For Eleftheria, slippage on slopes caused by rain pushing the topsoil off hillsides that had been tilled did constitute erosion; in contrast, the *terra rossa* badlands, the cracking, and the formation of gullies on flatter areas, which "just happened," did not constitute any kind of erosion at all. What it constituted was the natural characteristic of the land; it is what this land is, inherently. After dozens of such conversations with others, I began to gather that Eleftheria, along with most others, understood "erosion" as a process that was anomalous, a process that does not always happen but does occur under certain conditions. On those grounds, the badlands and gullies around the house did not signal erosion because they resulted from a process that always happened under all conditions.

Anastasios and Eleftheria's son, Kostas, responded in much the same way. The badlands and gullies had been like that as far back as he could remember. He added, when I persisted in asking whether they had changed at all over the years, that the badlands around his house "lose around a meter a year, from the rain." If change was involved, it was, once again, an additional process, the rain, that caused change, not the land in itself, which never changed. Moreover, for Kostas, there was nothing to be done about the badlands: how could you do something about a fundamental characteristic of the land?

The accounts given by members of the Rentzios family seemed initially somewhat different, in that they agreed with my suggestion that some of what was occurring around their farm constituted erosion. Yet, as for the Maris family, this referred to areas on a slope, or just below a slope, and what was called erosion was attributed to rain. The process began, Mrs. Rentzios senior recalled, around 1933–34. That was the period when smaller "cuts" appeared in the hill to the east of the house. She added that when she first arrived here in the 1920s, there was no gullying there; it had been a clear slope with scrub on it. When it did begin, very slowly, it fell more and more each year with the annual rains. Gullies appeared on the slope and then continued on to the flatter areas, as a result of water streams cutting through the land. The problem, her son Yiannis added, was that these red soils have no stones or gravels in them, and once such soils on a slope begin to slide gravitationally with the rains, there is nothing to hold them up or back. "When it rains, that red soil is like blood. What's more, you can't get it out of your clothes; it's so fine, it doesn't come out, it stains your clothes."

I asked whether the Rentzios family had done anything about it. Yiannis responded that—as they had done in the mountains with their fields on hillsides—they had at first attempted to build stone or brushwood terraces to hold the soil up on the hill, and had also built some dams in the gullies to prevent the gullies from opening wider, as they had some cultivated fields there. However, neither activity had really worked, so they gave up. "It's the way this land is," Yiannis said, "there's nothing that can be done about it."

Of the dozens of people I spoke with about this topic over the months, the Rentzios family came closest to agreeing that there was erosion, and that they had initially attempted to do something about it; but even they distinguished between something caused by the additional action of water and what happened more generally with the land, which did not consti-tute erosion. The vast majority of conversations I had did not go even this far: people simply blankly denied that there was erosion, denied doing anything to repair fields affected by gullies, sinkholes, or erosion, and had no interest in discussing the topic further, as it did not constitute a topic in the first place. There was nothing to discuss.

Responses around the Kasidiaris, on both the western and eastern sides, were much the same as those of the Maris and Rentzios families, irrespec-tive of whether I was talking with pastoralists, pensioners, people who lived in cities most of the time, people who were involved in cash-crop cultivation, or those who still engaged in mixed cultivation and pastoral-ism mostly for their own consumption. The only real difference between descriptions was that for those living near flysch, most added that the flysch generated awful soils for cultivation and not much better soils for grazing, and that when the fine gray, dustlike flysch badlands got wet, the dust went hard like cement (indeed, it looked like cement). Those living near *terra rossa* said they had good soil, but that it was very "thirsty," needing a great deal of water. Almost invariably, whenever people tried (out of politeness, I suspect) to engage with my questioning about the issue of erosion—rather than, as was more common, avoiding the issue and talking about something else—they associated it with water: either the action of rain on the surface or the action of underwater springs. In the case of Katarraktis, whose territory includes a section of the Kalamas River that has cut down around thirty meters in some of the villagers' lifetimes, and resulted in the loss of many people's fields down the gorge, it was this to which the villagers pointed persistently as an example of erosion. The fact that the territory was also covered with large sections of bare *terra rossa* badlands was something nobody mentioned, and when I brought it to their attention, they invariably said it did not constitute erosion. One morning, after a walk around the area with the only teenage permanent resident of the village, the priest's daughter, who was fourteen at the time, we came across one of her uncles in the village *kafeneio*. She asked him about the *terra rossa* badlands on my behalf; he gave her a blank look and asked her what she was talking about. We went out onto the veranda of the shop, which was located on a small hill, and she pointed out an example to him. "That's not erosion," he said, "it's always been like that." These kinds of conversations were repeated hundreds of times, in every area around the Kasidiaris and, for that matter, anywhere else in Epirus that I asked about it.

Having spent both the summer of 1992 and the first three months of my period in Epirus in 1993 trying and (as I then thought) mostly failing to get people to talk about this issue, I went to see a specialist on the Epirot environment in Ioannina in late June of 1993. Mr. Papathanasiou was the overall manager of the Department of Land Improvements for Epirus, as well as the islands of Lefkada (Lefkas) and Kerkira (Corfu). The department coordinated all projects that involved infrastructural work on areas that could be made more agriculturally productive (i.e., the larger plains). At the time, I thought that I could at least get a story about official attitudes toward all this shiftiness of the land surface, even if I could not get a story about it from people around the Kasidiaris. As usual, I was wrong. This was not because K. Papathanasiou was unhelpful; on the contrary, as on almost every other occasion when I asked to see someone from one of the many government offices in Ioannina, I was given an interview at once rather than having to make an appointment, offered something to drink, and treated with enormous generosity, patience, and friendliness. Over time, it became clear that most people visiting government offices were given much the same "open-door" treatment by the directors and managers. Indeed, their doors were usually literally open, and people could just walk in and request an audience. Although people often complained to me about the level of bureaucracy and paperwork required by the Greek state, as well as a perceived failure of the state to take effective action (complaints that were made as much by civil servants as they were by anybody else), nobody complained about the lack of access to officers of the state, even high-level ones.

In any event, after going through many details about land improvement programs in Epirus with K. Papathanasiou, I broached the subject of land degradation and soil erosion. He kindly allowed me to tape the interview, and this is an extract of that exchange:

> SARAH: Can you tell me whether there is any soil erosion and landslips in the areas where the improvements are being done?
>
> K. PAPATHANASIOU: Of course there is land erosion; erosion occurs everywhere.
>
> SARAH: In other words, it occurs naturally?

K. Papathanasiou: Yes, naturally. Erosion occurs in places where the land is bare—it rains, and the land erodes. Where there aren't trees, the land doesn't hold.

Sarah: Is that a bigger problem in Epirus than in other places—the land being bare and that causing erosion?

K. Papathanasiou: Not that I know of.

Sarah: Has anybody studied what causes it?

K. Papathanasiou: Studied it? No. There have been some studies, I think, on looking into protecting improved land from erosion, that sort of thing.

K. Papathanasiou had spent the previous forty minutes providing me with reports, statistics, maps, and studies on every aspect of land improvement programs, yet on the topic of land degradation, he was as bemused by my questions as was anyone else. So I gave up on that specific issue and asked K. Papathanasiou whether in general he thought there were any particular environmental problems in the area. He responded thus: "Epirus is a problematic region—God has not been particularly bountiful around here. What we've got is stones, a lot of stones, and very big ones, too. A lot of mountains, a lot of rocks, not much good soil. The choices here are very limited. For that reason, people have been forced to find other work, to go elsewhere, to spend a lot of time in cities. They return to retire." He went on to explain that as far as he was concerned, in recent years, one of the biggest environmental changes had resulted from a dramatic drop in people's using the land as they had done previously. Fewer people cultivating and grazing except in the large plains meant overgrowth of the hills and mountains; with the aging population living around those areas, people were no longer able to cultivate or take care of large numbers of animals, so that too was contributing to reforestation; and because of a *philoxera* (grapevine disease) epidemic in previous decades, cultivation had not been permitted in the affected areas for some years, so those areas became forest as well. In any case, he added, a widespread *astifilia* (love of cities) and an emphasis on professional and service-sector work within education meant people were not returning from cities to use their parents' fields and grazing areas; so the place was likely to continue to become even more forested. Except, of course, in the plains that K. Papathanasiou's office had worked hard to improve to make them more economically viable.

Abandonment

It is here that I will move away from looking at the kind of land degradation I was trying to get people to discuss, and on to the kind that people wanted to discuss, often without any kind of prompting. The widespread abandonment of pastoralism and cultivation in the hillier areas of the region was mentioned by almost everyone I met. Among a number of other things, *that* is what constituted "land degradation" (though not erosion) for many people. Whereas the land degradation I had been trying to get people to discuss was regarded as "just natural" and not worth discussing, this kind of land degradation was anything but "natural" and was very worthy of discussion. For many, it visibly marked the interweaving of a range of "forces"—political, economic, social—that together always constituted the place, and had done so now in this particular form.

For some, the abandonment of mountain pastoralism and cultivation and the widespread movement of people to live permanently in cities marked the disappearance of an era during which people had used the land to live, had grown up in the villages, and had had "proper communities" there. Within this perspective, people's contemporary relationship with cities was regarded as being very different from what it had been in the past, when men would travel for periods of a time to cities, occasionally returning. Nevertheless, one of the key tropes in which this "new" relationship with cities was discussed was much the same as others used to discuss *both* past and present relations with cities: a sense that cities constituted a form of alienation. This was not a matter of people's feeling that they did not "belong" in cities as much as others: most people I spoke with felt they belonged in cities as much as anyone did. The point was rather that cities were cast, within this particular rhetoric, as being bad for people in general. Vasiliki, a woman in her fifties living in Ktismata, expressed this view particularly strongly:

> Cities haven't given people anything for them to understand what culture means, what purity means, what the meaning of history is, and we should do with them what? Put people to work on the European Community's computers, and tell them this is what it's about, this is what life is? Get on top of the next person, take care of yourself and don't care about anyone else? Is that a system? I have different ideas about life. I live here [in Ktismata] and I like it.

Here, the idea of being outside of a city was equated with the familiar argument that, somehow, being in a village allows one to avoid the more brutalizing aspects of (capitalist) modernity: what one could call the Fordist aspects, the aspects that standardize, overtechnologize, and encourage unrestrained self-interest.[14] Kostas, Vasiliki's husband and the president of the village (who was explicitly left-wing), waxed lyrical for a long time one afternoon about his memories of how things were during his childhood in the village, starkly drawing out the contrast between what he saw as city life and village life. This is a small extract:

Until the 1950s, the husking of the corn resulted in a celebration, a party for the residents. They used to come together in the evenings, and because there weren't any other available forms of entertainment, they would husk the corn and remove little black parasites that used to be in the ears of corn, and quite often they'd smear dirt, from the husking, on one another and they'd laugh and they'd sing of an evening. And it was a tradition that they'd always husk the corn in the evenings, as they worked during the day, and in the evening they had the time to sit at home and husk corn. Neighbors would get together all the time—and in that way the husking of the corn got done, as well as a number of other jobs, got done in the manner of a celebration. In other words, agricultural jobs took on a celebratory, communal character.

Both Vasiliki and Kostas felt that the ending of all of this "communal spirit" and its replacement by the alienation of cities was the result of "big politics": the closure of the border, the Second World War and the civil war after it, the lack of investment or interest in the region, especially for those villages such as Ktismata that had close relations with Northern Epirus on the other side of the border. All of that added up to a level of indifference about Epirus and the Pogoni region in particular that meant people could no longer live as they once did here. Kostas went on: "So the young people were forced to leave again to find jobs, either in Athens or in other cities—and in Ioannina, some of them—and internationally. And the result is that, except for a few who are involved in animal husbandry and two or three families who are farmers, all the others are pensioners." Like Theo in Zavroho, Kostas particularly complained that the Greek state, which he explicitly thought of as an Athens-focused institution (as did many people in Epirus), did not care about Epirus, and particularly did not care about the Pogoni area. That lack of care could be seen in the abandoned fields and grazing lands. Kostas was one of the people trying hard to promote the idea that the Pogoni area had as much cultural heritage as anywhere else, particularly in terms of polyphonic singing, but felt that his efforts fell on deaf ears:

I still try to keep hold of the musical culture, which they had in the old days here—the polyphonic songs, those incredible polyphonic songs. I'm sorry for the Ministry of *non*-Culture of Greece—not the Ministry of Culture—which doesn't care about it. When you go abroad, though, they request Ktismata to take a medal at the Bach Festival in London in 1978. In 1984 in Paris, as well. Little by little, these things are disappearing. I wish they'd do something so that we could keep hold of our culture, and the life that we had before. That polyphonic song, which they still sing in fourteen villages in the Middle East, from the period of Alexander the Great—a type of song that has five thousand years of existence, and it's in danger, it's in danger today of being forgotten, because the state doesn't care.

Even Kostas, who had a particular interest in folklore and cultural heritage, as well as a tendency to reproduce the Hellenistic version of Greekness (particularly when talking to people like me in his capacity as village president), nevertheless still kept using tropes of movement and interweaving scales in his conversations. Apart from his leapfrogging over Athens to London and Paris to have his cultural distinction recognized, at other times he continually emphasized the Lower Pogoni area's connections with Albania, the previous long-distance travels to distant cities undertaken by the men associated with Ktismata and the Lower Pogoni area as a whole, and the many ways political and economic "forces" kept rendering this place neglected and of no account, which continually affected how the place was constituted.

Kostas's perspective was only one kind of account of how the "land degradation" of the area was entangled with other things, and on the whole in the Lower Pogoni area it was not a very commonly expressed view. Kostas's approach was associated by many with a kind of cultural heritage/folklore "snobbery" that was closely related to the Athenian "snobbery" about Greekness discussed in the previous chapter. It was also associated with local politicians' trying to "talk up" the area to attract funding: these days, many assumed that people and places had to be recognized as culturally and environmentally distinct to secure financial support. That was part of the political process; in order for the Pogoni area to "have a future," it had to become "culturally" and "naturally" attractive. For example, during a taped conversation with a group of men in Pontikates, in Upper Pogoni and next to the Greek-Albanian border, I raised the question of what people thought about the area's future. Here's an extract of their response:

SARAH: And what do you see for the future here?

DINOS: What's there to see? It's black.

NIKOS: As it's going now . . .

DINOS: Black. Why, do you see anyone else coming here, returning to the villages, saying that there's a future here?

SARAH: The president of Pogoniani.

DINOS: He said that there's a future here? *To kako tou kerato!/* Το κακό του κέρατο! [loosely translated: "That so-and-so!"].

SARAH: And the mayor of Delvinaki as well.

DINOS: Oh, him, he's *another* one.

NIKOS: Look, there are a lot of problems for the people who live here. The schools have closed, so people with children can't live here. Plus, people need work to live, and there's no work here.

Plus, if you want to build a house here, it costs many times more than building one in a city, because you have to bring all the materials here, and it's very expensive. These people who say there's a future here, that we have a lot of cultural heritage and natural beauty that people will want to return to or come to visit—well, you have to understand, it's a political thing that they say that.

For others, the widespread abandonment of cultivation and/or pastoralism and the subsequent reforestation was regarded as having its positive sides, because it marked the passing of a period when people had to live hand to mouth, had to scrape a living from this "hostile" (εχθρικός/ *echthrikos*) and "unproductive" (άγονος/*agonos*) land. A comment from Dimitris, who was spending his retirement in Dolo, a tiny village very close to the border and just to the north of the Kasidiaris, provides an example of that: "There's a lot of nostalgia about the past and a lot of stupid attitudes about the environment. You know, the idea that we all lived idyllic lives before everyone left for the cities, and that Epirus is all unspoiled nature and cultural heritage. It's crap. Excuse my language, but we had to piss in the bushes in the past; there weren't any toilets in the houses. And since Chernobyl, I wouldn't say the natural environment here is so unspoiled, would you?" Dimitris was not only being deliberately cynical about the kinds of views Kostas asserted; he was also making a reference to the many EU-funded projects being carried out in parts of Epirus at the time with the aim of helping to develop tourism there—projects based on conserving nature and preserving the cultural heritage of the area (see chapter 7). Dimitris thought these projects were at best a naive idealization of Epirot "nature" and "cultural heritage" born of misplaced nostalgia for something that had never existed in the first place, and at worst yet another example of the murky things that go on when politics are combined with funding.

Although Dimitris's opinion contrasted starkly with that of Kostas, he shared Kostas's cynicism about powerful "political forces" that were always visibly or invisibly operating and affecting this area—whether by direct intervention or, more often, by blundering through or across Epirus in the course of pursuing something else, wreaking havoc through neglect and indifference in the process. For Dimitris, Epirus constituted a crossroads between more important places, and that meant political power was continually operating here, but not with Epirus or Epirots in mind. As far as he was concerned, the interests of the region and the people associated with it were rarely served by its being constituted as a crossroads, unless those interests accidentally coincided with the interests of the "political forces" that were passing through. The reason for this was self-evident to Dimitris: Epirus had been constituted as a marginal place—environmentally, geographically, socially, and economically—and therefore "political forces" would never be interested in the place or the people; if such "forces" intervened, it would always be for some reason of their own. To him, the apparent concern over the environment and cultural heritage of Epirus was an outcome of policies and ideals designed for somewhere else and on behalf of others, and then imposed on this place and people like himself.

The habit of people in Greece as a whole of being cynical or ironic about the state (and various Great Powers) has been noted repeatedly, most particularly by Herzfeld, who is much concerned with the interplay between official and unofficial accounts of Greekness. For example, in *Cultural Intimacy*, which outlines how people can be fiercely patriotic and nationalist but simultaneously deeply cynical about the Greek state, Herzfeld suggests that cynicism about the state's activities also in some senses reinforces the state's power: "The option of blaming the state gives definition and authority to its shadowy power" (Herzfeld 1997: 10). Yet for Herzfeld there is also potential for subversion in this, for mockery can serve to challenge state authority. Such cynical comments, he suggests, "often call the bluff of official rhetoric. In so doing they raise the possibility of an alternative, critical perspective, one that peers into the semantic intimacies that notions of pure referentiality conceal" (ibid.: 54). It is within this epistemological "militant middle ground" (ibid.: 55) that there is a potential for people to exercise agency, to practice the human capacity for "symbolic invention" (ibid.), in Herzfeld's view.

Yael Navaro-Yashin provides a somewhat similar account that reaches different conclusions about the popular use of cynicism and irony in relation to the state, in her study of people's relations with the contemporary Turkish state (Navaro-Yashin 2002: 159–71). Like Herzfeld, Navaro-Yashin looks at irony and cynicism as a demonstration that people are entirely conscious of the constructed character of their state's assertions and hence do not generally suffer from nearly as much "false consciousness" as other scholars have suggested (e.g., Taussig, in his analysis of mimesis). At the same time, most people do reproduce the state's ideology, though not despite the cynicism, but because of it. As Navaro-Yashin puts it, "cynicism, or doing as if one doesn't know, is a technique of contemporary Turkish state power" (Navaro-Yashin 2002: 163). Using the work of Slavoj Žižek (2002 [1989]), she analyzes the state as a constructed fantasy in which everyone is engaged, and in which people's carrying on with life as if they did not know that the state's ideology is "hot air," that the state in practice operates in a "corrupt" manner, is a means by which the state reproduces its own power:

Žižek draws our attention to the habitual performance of everyday life practices that is done in full consciousness of their counterproductive (or self-destructive) quality. This is the cynical contemporary agent. This is what more characteristically describes political subjectivity today. We are automatons and we know it. (Navaro-Yashin 2002: 162)

Where Navaro-Yashin departs from Žižek is in his implication that everyone eventually becomes a genuine "believer" in the state's ideology by habitually acting as if they believed in it, while knowing it is a false construction. Instead, she suggests that many people never become "believers," but they end up reproducing the authority of the state anyway. This is because they have little choice, often in economic as much as administrative terms (people still have to make a living and fill out the state's forms). In other words, the state might be a fantasy, and everyone might know it is a fantasy, but it is a fantasy with teeth. In one respect, this describes quite well the perspective of many people in Epirus, including Kostas (who reproduced part of the fantasy) and Dimitris (who tried to poke holes in the fantasy). In this case, it was not that they were "automatons" and knew it; it was more that they were irrelevant and knew it, while at the same time acknowledging that this ideology which rendered them irrelevant had teeth; they had to live with it, whatever they thought about it.

Herzfeld sees the interplay between the formal, state-sponsored, version of Greekness and the informal—cynical, ironic, self-parodying—versions as potentially generating a creative space for people, which they could use to challenge and undermine the state's intentions. In arguing that people can creatively undermine the state while simultaneously being fiercely nationalistic, he suggests that other theorists have been far too deterministic in the way they suggest power (or culture) constructs and constitutes people (for example, he argues that Althusser's concept of interpellation is far too deterministic).[15] This is what Herzfeld means by "social poetics": what things mean is neither stable nor fixed, and therefore people are able to creatively make things mean in a different way; official state ideologies have a tendency toward "definitional" and "legalistic" approaches to what things mean; in practice, how things come to mean what they do cannot be controlled in that way. While I broadly agree with this, I also find useful for my purposes Navaro-Yashin's additional point—that the contradictions and complexities of poetics as they are messily constituted in everyday life are frequently not quite sufficient to change one's life, particularly in relation to the state, where "definitional" and "legalistic" ideologies tend to be given political, bureaucratic, and economic "teeth."[16]

There was yet a further element to conversations about "political forces" that I had with many people around the Kasidiaris and which referred to "ideologies with teeth," an element that went considerably beyond the Greek state. There were continual references in particular to the European Union, to Albania, to the former Soviet Union, and to the United States (as a particularly powerful political, social, economic, and military force in the world today). What this place (Epirus, Pogoni, the Kasidiaris, the borderland area) and its people "meant" was embroiled in many more things than the particularities of the Greek state's official rhetoric as compared to cynical and ironic pokes at that rhetoric by its citizens. And that gets me back to the issue of this place's being constituted as being more Balkan than more southerly parts of mainland Greece.

Dimitris's mention of the Chernobyl nuclear power plant disaster in Ukraine (which occurred on April 26, 1986, eight years before he made this comment) exemplifies how people expressed this sense of the intimate interweaving of the relations between large "political forces" and regions such as Epirus. The Chernobyl disaster was a very large event that involved a very large power (the former Soviet Union), and both its source and its causes had little if anything to do, directly, with Epirus. Yet for Dimitris, the activities of such powers are always invisibly present in Epirus, and Chernobyl constituted a perfect metaphor as well as an embodied example of that. Being at the crossroads between big powers meant you were continually buffeted by their neglect. And Dimitris was by no means alone in evoking Chernobyl: when I had conversations with people about the environment and any changes they might have noticed about it, time and again Chernobyl was mentioned, despite the years that had passed since the event, and despite the fact that I could find no reports suggesting that Epirus was affected any more seriously than, say, Wales. Even Kostas Maris mentioned it: "The weather has changed a lot. It's become hotter and there's been a lot less rain in the last six or seven years. After about 1985, the change was really noticeable. I think it's from the time of the Chernobyl disaster, I think that's what changed the weather." A goatherd from the Zagori, someone I had known since the early 1980s when I was an undergraduate working on a Paleolithic rock shelter excavation in the summers, also said in 1995 that things had changed in this way: "The climate has changed a lot in recent years, because of international pollution problems, particularly Chernobyl. It's having a bad effect on this area." The vice president of Argyrohori also believed that the dramatic drop in water supplies that his village had experienced in recent years, as well as a number of other environmental problems he identified, had been caused by Chernobyl. Theo, the president of the Mavropoulo commune nearby, expressed the same opinion:

SARAH: Do you think the climate has changed here at all?

THEO: Yes, it's changed. We had a lot of rain before ten years ago, and now it's rare for it to rain. And a lot of us worry that maybe Chernobyl has altered the climate for us here. Before ten years, we had a lot of water. Now, we don't. We have very little water now.

The president of Pogoniani also suggested that the wild tea on the surrounding mountains, considered a specialty of the region, had been affected by Chernobyl.

There were dozens of others who mentioned Chernobyl as contributing to, or being the entire cause of, recent environmental changes in Epirus. For many, the radiation cloud that wafted across much of Europe following the accident was a perfect example of how any asserted autonomy, separation, or purity of "nature" was naive; Chernobyl demonstrated how political and economic "forces," despite operating at different scales from the immediacy of the here and now, always interweave and intervene, and are always already there. In the case of this region, the *way* in which all these scales intervened had, once again, to do with the constituted "where" of this place; the continual shadowy presence and ambiguities of the Balkans as a crossroads on the way to somewhere else, which always seemed to account for much of how things seemed and how they were. Having begun this research project with one kind of fractal—the geomorphological account of the way the mountains were constituted as unstable and continually shifted in interrelation with other things—I ended up with another kind of fractal: the way the mountains were constituted as unstable and continually shifted in political terms, which time and again seemed to be encompassed within this deeply politically inflected and ambiguous concept, the Balkans. So before going on any further with this story, I need to explore that fractality.

CHAPTER 4

The Balkan Fractal

> The Balkans seem destined to remain in a kind of deconstructionist *mise-en-abîme*. Jacques Derrida's concept of *différence* [sic] . . . seems to be translated into symbolic geography. There is no part of the Balkans which represents a stable identity, everything is defined through difference.
>
> (Goldsworthy 1999: 114)

> Macedonia . . . was seen as the Balkan of the Balkans . . . a place of chaos and confusion, a veritable fruit salad.
>
> (Irvine and Gal 2000: 63)

> Bucharest [was] being taken as a paradigm of Roumania, that country offered likewise a model for the totalising treatment of the Balkans. (Pippidi 1999: 94)

> In the Balkans, history is not viewed as tracing a chronological progression, as it is in the West. Instead, history jumps around and moves in circles. (Kaplan 1994: 58)

> The question still remains, is there any *there* there? The Orientalist/post-colonialist/post-structuralist critique has no real answer to this question. . . . If the imputed differences that define "the Balkans" are simply the markers or epiphenomena of power politics, then the implication can be that there is no reason to single out anything that is specifically Balkan.
>
> (Bracewell and Drace-Francis 1999: 59)

> A fractal person is never a unit standing in relation to an aggregate, or an aggregate standing in relation to a unit, but always an entity with relationship integrally implied.
>
> (Wagner 1991: 163)

THE BALKANS HAVE COME to epitomize fragmentation over the years; for many, it seems as though there is nothing but a "Macedonian Salad" of difference there, a state of permanent disconnection, of essentialist and dangerous gaps between peoples and places that can never be fully closed, just papered over for a time. It is these gaps full of hostility that many focus upon, wondering how to close them, how to resolve the apparently endless moments of conflict that never seem to entirely resolve anything at all.

At the same time, the Balkans as a whole are also regularly described as another kind of gap, a bridge or a crossroads, and it is this that apparently makes them into a "Macedonian Salad": a place that is in between a diversity of other powerful places, so that they themselves contain too many differences that are too close and too mixed up together, never resolving themselves into clearly separated-out entities.[1] Yet the thing about bridges and crossroads is that while they constitute gaps in between places, they are therefore also gaps that connect, and so they are not empty, just as the gap that constituted Albania in the geomorphological maps discussed in the previous chapter was not empty: crossroads and bridges are spaces traveled through where people and places cross paths. Bridges and crossroads epitomize relationships, not disconnection. My argument in this chapter is that the "problem" of the Balkans, as they are currently constituted in hegemonic terms, is not too much fragmentation, as many suggest, but too much connection, too much relationship; the Balkans always seem to generate ambiguous and tense connections that ought, in modernist terms, to be clearly resolved separations.

To make that argument, I will use the trope of fractals in two different ways. First as a descriptive device, to outline how current hegemonic discourses about the Balkans focus on fragmentation, but that this is done through the notion of too much connection. That will take up the first part of the chapter, which explores how the Balkans came to mean fractality in hegemonic terms, something that seems monstrous to a modernist way of thinking, despite having been generated out of that way of thinking. Second, having shown how the Balkans constitute problematic connection rather than problematic fragmentation, I shift to using this imposed sense of fractality as an analytical device. Given that fragments create gaps, and gaps constitute relations between things (rather than being empty space that separates things), one should focus on the relations in and across gaps, not the fragmentations.

It is important to note here that my understanding of "hegemonic" combines how things seem with how things are. As Crehan argues, Gramsci never intended "hegemony" to be simply another word for "ideology": in regarding ideal and material existence as always entangled, Gramsci used the term "as a way of mapping an ever-shifting landscape of power that includes both accounts of 'reality' as these confront particular people in particular places, and the hard realities that lie outside of discourse" (Crehan 2002: 174). I take this to mean that "hard realities" are as thoroughly constituted by this "landscape of power" as are the accounts of such realities. In that sense, I would argue that one of the more powerful contemporary understandings of the "Balkans" is hegemonic in this combined ideal-material sense: the concept not only asserts an ideological account of how things seem; it has also become entangled with, and has at the very least partially constituted, the practical conditions of how things are. The somewhat ironic twist is that in this case, the contemporary hegemonic understanding makes it difficult to conceive of the Balkans as a particular place, or of the people associated with them as particular people, in the modernist sense of being able to separate them out and thereby make them clearly bounded entities. So in exploring the discursive aspects of the hegemonic understanding of the Balkans, my aim is to understand how this particular entanglement between how things seem, and how they are made to be, resulted in such a lack of particularity.[2]

The Balkans Described as Fractal

It is easy to see a resemblance between the way fractals are described by chaos theorists and the way the currently hegemonic concept of the Balkans—and the intimately related concept, Balkanization—have been described. In one sense, fractals are about fragmentation and fault lines; but in another sense, fractals are about relational fragmentation: every fragment is a fraction, a part of something else, and it is the relationship between the parts, their fundamental interrelationality as it were, that renders something fractal.[3]

The currently hegemonic discourse on the Balkans carries both these characteristics: on the one hand, the Balkans are said to be in a continual state of fragmentation, parts proliferating into ever smaller parts, and then recombining and fragmenting again (and for that reason, few commentators agree entirely about exactly where the Balkans are, and the names of the parts are both multiple and contested).[4] At the same time, each part is seen as utterly relational: the way the parts proliferate (generate more fragments) is imagined to be entirely caused by the way they are interrelated (or "networked," in the actor network theory sense of the term [Law and Hassard 1999: 6–7]). This has been asserted to be either due to the way all parts of the Balkans constitute a "Macedonian Salad" or "mosaic," in which the (sub)parts can never be fully separated out (into distinct nationals and nations, for example); or due to the way the Balkans have been the location of a particularly large number of battles between "Great Powers" (Britain, Russia, France, the Hapsburgs, the Ottomans, etc.), and therefore constitute a kind of fault line, or a crossroads or bridge between them. Whichever way you look at this place, and at whatever scale (within the parts of the Balkans or at the Great Powers level), it apparently behaves fractally.

There is an important difference here, however. Unlike fractals in chaos theory, which generate the most beautiful geometric shapes, and which also apparently have high potential for use in inventive approaches to some of the most complex phenomena in the world, the Balkan fractal is described as neither beautiful nor potentially inventive. Rather, it is variously regarded as monstrous, a virus or toxin that could proliferate, and sometimes has proliferated, to the rest of the world (Gunther 1940: 437); or a site of the tragic consequences of the Great Powers' political machinations (Gallagher 2001; Glenny 1999); or an example of meaningless, even "primitive," savagery and violence, a place where "backwardness" and bloodletting are allowed to run amok unless stopped by external forces (Cohen 1995; Brown 2002); or an example of how that level of deconstruction (tearing things apart and recombining them continuously) will always lead to a sense of meaningless fragmentation and combination (Bracewell and Drace-Francis 1999); and so on.

In short, the contemporary Balkans end up appearing, to many contemporary commentators at least, as a monstrous miscegenation between the premodern ("primitive savagery") and the postmodern (deconstruction to the point of meaninglessness). What the Balkans definitely are not, within this discourse, is modern—that intellectual and political-economic space which continually attempts to separate itself from the premodern and the postmodern (Latour 1993); the modern is the gauge by which the Balkans are both defined and judged within this particular hegemonic concept of them. And the impossibility of properly separating out the Balkans, permanently disentangling them from their intra- and interrelations, seems to be the key to what makes them appear fractal to a modernist frame of mind.

In fact, Irvine and Gal use one aspect of the concept of fractals (what they call "fractal recursivity") to describe how Western European commentators were horrified by what they saw as the level of "chaos" existing in the region of Macedonia during the nineteenth and early twentieth centuries (Irvine and Gal 2000).[5] In their analysis of the way multilingual practices in many parts of the world have been separated out and classified into single ("pure") languages, both by "Western" scholars and by political elites, Irvine and Gal note that Macedonia caused a particular challenge. Not only was there a "Babel" of languages spoken in Macedonia; even worse, the multilingualism of many peoples and the way in which these diverse languages were spoken did not match the ("Western European") ideologically inflected belief that languages can be separated out into pure forms that can be associated with single ethnonational/racial identifications and particular territories. Irvine and Gal quote Karl von Östreich complaining about this in 1905: "Instead of racially pure Turks and Albanians we find people who are racially mixed . . . and whose multilingualism misleads us about their real origins, so that they can be counted sometimes as Greeks, sometimes as Bulgarians, sometimes as Wallachians" (quoted in ibid.: 64).

The concept of "fractal recursivity" comes in where Irvine and Gal argue that this perception of "chaos" led commentators of the day to construct an opposition between the Balkan region as a whole and "Western Europe." While in Western Europe languages, people, and territories were asserted to be neatly separated out and neatly aligned with one another, in the Balkans they were "chaotically" blended and intermingled (ibid.: 65). The same kind of "chaotic intermingling" was regarded as being recursively repeated at every level within the Balkans: just as the Balkans as a whole were "chaotic" in this way, so too were all parts of the Balkans, and even individuals within the Balkans. Irvine and Gal quote Ehrenpreis writing in 1928 that the kind of person living in this region was "truly a 'wavering form,' a composite of Easterner and Westerner" (quoted in ibid.).

These authors' work provides an important corrective to the commonly held belief that the Balkans are somehow inherently "chaotic"; they demonstrate how the Balkans came to appear that way to Western European commentators because of these commentators' inability to classify this place according to the principles of nineteenth- and early twentieth-century modernist ways of thinking about things. However, my argument about how fractality relates to the Balkans is different from theirs in one important respect. The assertion that a place is so "chaotic" that it cannot be classified through modernist techniques also renders it a challenge to modernity itself, in that it implies there are some phenomena that cannot be accounted for through a modernist approach. That this "chaos" is generated by things' appearing to be too "intermingled" makes matters even worse, in that it implies the Balkans cannot be kept fully separate from other things, as their boundaries are not clear. So the oppositions discussed by Irvine and Gal are themselves "chaotic" and "unstable," which means the separations asserted between the Balkans and other parts of Europe do not constitute complete separations but also involve relations. The Balkans might be opposed to Western Europe on one level, but on another level they are also a part of Europe, and these levels cannot be kept entirely discrete. This combination of the inability to fix the boundaries of the Balkans and the intermingling of separations and relations (things being both different and the same) makes it difficult to establish whether there *are* any "Balkans" that are distinctly and clearly different in any fixed way. While Irvine and Gal note that oppositions generated out of "fractal recursivity" "do not define fixed or stable social groups" (ibid.: 38), in the case of the Balkans they do not define fixed or stable conceptual *oppositions* either (e.g., between "West" and "East," or "more European" and "less European"); what appears instead is a "wavering form," as Ehrenpreis put it in the assertion quoted by Irving and Gal.

As a result, the Balkans came to appear to have fractal properties *in themselves*: it was not simply that the hegemonic understanding of the Balkans constructed fractally recursive relations of "chaos" between one level and another; it was also that the Balkans were ascribed fractal properties, properties that worked to render them inherently not modern. At the same time, however, this ascription of fractality could equally render the Balkans the most modern of places, the place where the underlying contradictions of modernity become most visible and explicit in all their "we have never been modern" messiness (Latour 1993). I suggest that the attempt to resist this implication is one of the most important dynamics driving this particular hegemonic discourse: the attempt to keep modernity out of the Balkans, to stop them from appearing modern, until they cease to appear fractal. Yet the use of the notion of fractality in this construction of difference, a notion of the inherent interrelationality of things that ought to be kept separate, means that modernity could never be entirely disentangled from the Balkans.

It also means that the hegemonic construction itself is somewhat unstable, as bits and parts of the Balkans have drifted in and out of appearing appropriately modern. When the Balkans *could* be separated out into distinct, and distinctly different, parts (e.g., during the Cold War, when Europe was neatly divided into Capitalist West and Communist East), or when they did not appear to be currently behaving in a fractal way (i.e., not currently engaging in conflicts leading to fragmentation into smaller parts), the Balkans could appear to disappear, or parts of them could cease to seem Balkan, at least for a time. This returns me to the point of not being certain whether they exist or not. Many political representatives of regions designated as "Balkan" habitually either deny this designation or claim it to be a "merely" geographical label, rather than a cultural or political one; this means there are continual attempts both by those labeled Balkan and by those labeling the Balkans to make the Balkans disappear, or at least shift their location. This has sometimes been referred to as "nesting orientalisms," where each country's citizens claim that the next one along is Balkan, but their own country is just beyond the Balkans (Bakić-Hayden 1992; 1995; Goldsworthy 1998: 9; Todorova 1997: 58).[6] The habit of defining the Balkans so that they exclude the definer is so common that it has led, Goldsworthy argues, to the possibility of there being no such place at all: "Such taxonomic subterfuges . . . might leave Bulgaria as the only . . . Balkan country, unless we accept the suggestion that it belongs to South-Central Europe, thereby embracing the idea of the Balkans emptied of the Balkan states" (Goldsworthy 1999: 113).[7]

Things being the same and different, things appearing, disappearing, and reappearing, are involved once again. To get to what all of this might mean for what I have been exploring about Epirus and the Pogoni region, I need to take this fractal notion as a descriptive device a little further.

Fractality: Relational Fragments and Wholes

James Gleick recounts how Mandelbrot, the mathematician who coined the word "fractal," took it from the Latin adjective *fractus*, which derives from the verb *frangere*, "to break." Mandelbrot decided that "fractal" appropriately evoked "fraction" and "fracture" in English, and so captured what he intended by the term (Gleick 1996: 98). Gleick goes on to suggest that "[i]n the end, the word fractal came to stand for a way of describing, calculating, and thinking about shapes that are irregular and fragmented, jagged and broken-up. . . . A fractal curve implies an organizing structure that lies hidden among the hideous complication of such shapes" (ibid.: 114).

The idea of the Balkans and Balkanization as constituting "fragmentation," the breaking of parts into smaller parts—the idea of the region as being made up of irregular, jagged places and peoples—is so commonplace that it is hard to find a reference to the Balkans which does *not* discuss these asserted characteristics.[8] And the idea of the Balkans' being impossibly complicated is a common theme as well; there is, as Goldsworthy notes, "an enduring perception of the area as somehow much more complex than any other in Europe" (Goldsworthy 1998: 31). The important point here is that the Balkans are explicitly *ascribed* such complexity within this particular hegemonic discourse about them; within fractal theory, everything in the world is probably as complex (or as simple) as everything else. So what it is that makes the Balkans appear so complex in comparison to other things or places is an interesting question to ask.

Connected to that is the second characteristic of fractals that they share with the way the Balkans are described: all fractals display a quality of self-similarity, even though they also appear to be different, depending on how you look at them. The similarity is due, according to chaos theorists, to the process by which fractals replicate themselves: parts of fractals are complete replications of the whole, and the whole is simply another version of any one of the parts and was formed by the same process of replication as are all of the parts. For example, a single leaf looks different from a cluster of leaves on a branch, but they were both formed through replication of the same pattern of branching—veins on the leaf, branches on the stem. Equally, and returning for a moment to the theme of tectonics explored in the previous chapter, a small earthquake is an identical replication of a big earthquake, even though the first has little discernible impact and the second can be devastating. Each part of a fractal is simultaneously both a part of, and the same as, the whole. As Gleick puts it, "Above all, fractal meant self-similar. . . . The self-similarity is built into the technique of constructing the curves—the same transformation is repeated at smaller and smaller scales" (Gleick 1996: 103).

It is this relational, self-similar, quality of fractals that has particularly interested anthropologists such as Marilyn Strathern (1991) and Roy Wagner (1991): the way phenomena with fractal properties replicate themselves potentially infinitely, and do so in the same way across a diversity of scales, so that the whole is the same as each of the parts, and each part is in itself a whole. Indeed, the whole could be seen as just one example of any one of the parts, so it is in fact less than the sum of the parts.[9] As Wagner puts it, "Fractality deals with wholes no matter how fine the cutting" (Wagner 1991: 172). And this means that fractals have no centers, no tops or bottoms, no clear edges, no beginning or end: you cannot add all the parts together and come up with a different "whole" that is greater than this sum.

Wagner's focus on the self-similar and relational characteristic of fractals, rather than their fragmentary and "jagged" characteristics, contrasts with Irvine and Gal's use of the concept in some significant respects. Most important for my purposes, Irvine and Gal focus on ideologically inflected *assertions* of the existence of "fractal recursivity," and so they include an exploration of how such assertions can impose inequality. While their concept of "recursivity" also evokes the idea of self-similarity, Irvine and Gal focus on how, when used ideologically, this self-similarity is made up of hierarchical oppositions that are asserted to recur (be self-similar) at different levels. For example, in their study of the nineteenth-century classification of Senegalese language groups, they argue that European scholars of the day imagined that the "natural" opposition between "European" and "African" recurred between diverse African groups within Africa (Irvine and Gal 2000: 55). The assumed inherent opposition (and difference in status) between "European" and "African" was mirrored, at a different level, in the assumed oppositions between different African groups in Senegal. The importance of this point is that when a fractal relationship is ascribed to something, that ascription can include, and even be made up of, (modernist) essentialist oppositions and hierarchical assertions: it illustrates how essentialist oppositions can simultaneously generate an assertion of self-similarity.

However, where such assertions of essentialist opposition proliferate, each contesting the claims of the others so that it cannot be clearly established where the boundaries of the oppositions are located, then the relational, rather than oppositional, self-similarity of fractals returns. Here, it is important to remember that not only "Western European" observers but also many groups designated as "Balkan" used (modernist) ethnona-tionalist logic to make political claims to territory. As Scopetea put it, "in the fabrication of Balkan stereotypes the West does not act singlehand-edly" (Scopetea 2003: 175; see also Bjelić 2002: 4). The same arguments were made again and again (they had a self-similarity about them), but each one contested the boundaries of the others. As I have already im-plied, it is this contestability of boundaries that leads to the ascription to the Balkans *themselves* of fractal properties within the hegemonic con-struction of them. This is important because, as Irvine and Gal note, "con-tested boundaries" are incompatible with an approach that believes it is possible to eventually purify and separate everything out (Irvine and Gal 2000: 51). Self-similarity in this sense, the inability to finally separate things out, challenges modernist ways of thinking about things.

This is also, not coincidentally, the characteristic of fractals that chal-lenges Euclidean geometry. Euclidean notions of the world are three-di-mensional and fit well with modernist notions of the world in Latour's sense (Latour 1993). A Euclidean approach measures length, depth, and thickness, and assumes that all matter in the world ontologically has these characteristics and can be classified by them. But to be classified in this way, things have to have edges, boundaries, and clear shapes (Gleick 1996: 96–97). Things with fractal properties do not: breaking fractals down into parts simply gives you more parts and more wholes; however small you break it up, each part is still a complete replication of the whole. So one can never find the characteristics of the fractal by breaking it up, only by looking at the relations between the parts.

Interestingly, John Law notes that actor network theory challenges Eu-clidean geometry in precisely the same way, by suggesting that phenomena in the world are generated by the interrelations between things, rather than by the essential characteristics of things themselves (Law and Has-sard 1999: 7–8). And actor network theory—particularly as deployed by one of its strongest past advocates, Bruno Latour—has been accused by critics of being antirealist, of advocating "meaninglessness" (Sykes 2003: 161). That is worth noting, as it bears a close resemblance to the way the term "Balkanization" has been used as a negative metaphor to describe other intellectual approaches that also apparently share these combined fragmentary and relational characteristics. Not only multiculturalism, but also interdisciplinarity, postmodernism, and poststructuralism have been accused of being "Balkanizing."[10]

To return to the fractals of chaos theory—Gleick notes that for mathe-maticians who thought in Euclidean terms, fractals were monstrous: they defied, perhaps even mocked, the (modernist) logic of being able to clas-sify and categorize the world into its three dimensions (Gleick 1996: 100).

Even worse, fractals apparently replicate these characteristics potentially infinitely, across any number of scales. As Strathern put it, "Attempt to produce synthetic configurations from the scrutiny of individual cases runs into the chaotic problem that nothing seems to hold the configuration at the center—there is no map, only endless kaleidoscopic permutations" (Strathern 1991: xvii).

Strathern was speaking about anthropologists' attempts to come to grips with the complexities of Melanesian ethnography; but the phrase equally well describes the assertions of many commentators on the Balkans: this part of the world seems to behave (as it were) in a way that is anomalous to a Euclidean mind—that is, one that makes sense of things through dissecting the parts into essential bits. The attempt to analyze the Balkans leads to potentially endless permutations, a proliferation of parts. It does not seem to matter in how much detail you look at this place; the same thing seems to replicate itself. Bucharest was "the same as" the Balkans as a whole, as Pippidi notes in the third epigraph at the beginning of this chapter. Images of Russian dolls pervade many descriptions of the Balkans: at whatever scale you consider the place, the same thing seems to happen.

Moreover, the potential endlessness of it—the parts continually proliferate more parts, more fragments—has been at the heart of the accusation that the Balkans constitute a "virus" or a "toxin" that could threaten, and apparently occasionally has threatened, the stability of the entire (modern) world. These kinds of views bear a strong resemblance to what Cecil Helman calls "germism": a fear of invisible malign forces that attack and breach our bodily boundaries, that make a mockery of the idea that our boundaries are hermetically sealed (Helman 1991: 32). A similar idea is expressed in the Western medical understanding of the human body's immune system, which is described as a kind of "police state" trying to keep out all "alien matter" (Martin 1989: 147). Furthermore, the way in which people and places seemed to be hopelessly mixed up in the Balkans, leading to the impossibility of ever fully separating them out, has led to numerous metaphors evoking the idea of impurity, pollution, mongrelism, miscegenation, and so on (Todorova 1997: 123–27). Metaphors describing the Balkans as a "Macedonian Salad" sum up this kind of image nicely.

There have been several responses to these kinds of assertions of the combined fragmentation, complexity, hybridity, and fluidity of the Balkans. One has been to give up and say that the self-evident fractality of the region is simply horrific in and of itself, and the solution is to try to control it externally, to put a lid on the potentially endless proliferation of the fractal. Another has been to state that it does not really exist—that this fractality is not real but simply describes a fantasy—and is in itself meaningless. A third response has been to carry on endlessly analyzing the details, endlessly looking for an answer, however complicated it might be, by rearranging the bits in this way or that.[11] All these responses, to my mind, reproduce the current hegemonic discourse that is behind these forms of explanation. Let me briefly expand on this point.

An unusual example of arguing that the Balkans are a fantasy can be seen in the work of Slavoj Žižek, whom I mentioned in the previous chapter with reference to ideologies of the state. Žižek uses the Bosnian crisis of the early 1990s to argue that the assertion of the Balkans' extreme complexity, the need for decades of detailed study to understand them, is an example of an "inverted" Western ideology, one which blames an external cause (the Balkans) for something that is actually generated internally by the (Western) ideology: ". . . , the evocation of the allegedly intricate context of religious and ethnic struggles in Balkan countries, is here to enable the West to shed its responsibility towards the Balkans—that is, to avoid the bitter truth that, far from presenting the case of an eccentric ethnic conflict, the Bosnian war is a direct result of the West's failure to grasp the political dynamic of the disintegration of Yugoslavia, of the West's silent support of 'ethnic cleansing' " (Žižek, Wright, and Wright 1999: 58).

Elsewhere, Žižek suggests that we should therefore not even *try* to understand the conflicts in the Balkans; one should not try to read the entrails, to search in the endless details of particular disputes, particular histories, particular convoluted interrelations and interactions to explain the current conflicts:

> [O]ne should avoid the trap of 'trying to understand'; what one should do is *precisely the opposite*; with regard to the post-Yugoslav war, one should . . . put in parentheses the multitude of *meanings*, the wealth of specters of the past which allow us to 'understand' the situation. . . . It is only such a suspension of 'comprehension' that renders possible the analysis of what is at stake—economically, politically, ideologically— in the post-Yugoslav crisis: of the *political* calculuses and strategic decisions which led to the war. (Žižek 1997: 62; emphasis original)

In one sense, I entirely agree with Žižek: looking at the intricate history of the Balkans and the range of disputes that have occurred there over the centuries, treating them as if they are internal to the Balkans themselves, will never lead to an answer to the Balkans, in part because the Balkans themselves, as an idea, are an invention, and an unstable invention at that (Todorova 1997; Goldsworthy 1998; Ballinger 1999: 77; Bjelić 2002: 5– 7). But it is also because the Balkans have always been regarded as a "problem" for others owing to their relations with, not their disconnections from, other places and other things: if the Balkans were not regarded as potentially spreading their conflicts (their "chaos") elsewhere, it is doubtful that they would have attracted nearly so much attention.

Where I disagree with Žižek is in his implication that the hegemonic concept of the Balkans does not include a notion of meaninglessness. As I have already suggested, there is a strong strand of trying to "explain" the Balkans by explicitly asserting their meaninglessness. This is done in a range of ways, sometimes in combination with one another. First, by asserting that the Balkans are fundamentally premodern; here, commentators assert that the peoples are "primitive," lacking in "civilization," with a tendency toward bloodletting "savagery," that they simply fight for fighting's sake, using the excuse of "ancient tribal hatreds." Todorova describes how this kind of approach, an idea of the "superstitious, irrational, and backward rural tradition of the Balkans, whose sole value lay in providing the open-air *Volksmuseum* of Europe" (Todorova 1997: 111), is rife within hegemonic expressions of "Balkanism." In this assertion, the conflicts in the Balkans are meaningless because they lack a modern rationality. As Bjelić puts it, "any reality imposed upon the Balkans by *Balkanism* [is infused with] pernicious instability" (Bjelić 2002: 7, emphasis original).

In contrast, a second way meaninglessness is asserted is through an appeal to what today might be phrased as the Balkans' apparently *postmodern* character—the continual deconstruction of borders, boundaries, and names for things, and continual conflicts over the truth of history, origins, legitimacy, and so on. The consequent continual interrelationality of everything, its never being clearly separated out, in the end makes none of the bits appear to be ontologically real: they are all fluid, unstable, historically contingent, and continuously contested, as reflected in the Goldsworthy epigraph at the beginning of this chapter. That is usually represented as continual fragmentation; I would say it epitomizes interrelationality (between what is and what is not modern, as well as what is and what is not "Western"), and that this is the key "problem."

These two versions of asserting Balkan meaninglessness (through asserting either premodern or postmodern characteristics, or both) closely relate to a third: the diversity of explanations for the Balkans have led many to conclude that there is no final explanation to be had. For example, S. G. Mestrovic, in a review article covering the outpouring of writings about the 1990s conflicts in former Yugoslavia, comments that there is a distinct "Balkanization" in the analyses themselves: "The present state of understanding vis-à-vis this Balkan War is, at best, fragmented, disjointed, incomplete, and full of prejudices and factual errors. In a word, Balkanization has afflicted the writings of journalists and scholars who try to make sense of this war" (Mestrovic 1996: 70).

In frustration, Mestrovic concludes: "What is needed is for someone to shout: 'You're never going to figure it out. It's not a riddle. It's a crime. You're supposed to put a stop to it' " (ibid.: 80).

This level of disagreement about what the Balkans are about, let alone what to do about them, has been a marked characteristic of descriptions and debates about the Balkans ever since the Balkans were named as such—in fact, even the name itself is argued about (Bracewell and Drace-Francis 1999; Lambropoulos 2003). Goldsworthy, among many others, notes that in the late nineteenth century, there was as much disagreement about what was going on in the Balkans as there has been more recently (Goldsworthy 1998: 31). Just as the Balkans are regarded as a multitude of proliferating fragments and continual changes in boundaries and names, so are the explanations for the Balkans.

That, I suggest, is a key aspect of the currently hegemonic element in the concept of the Balkans. While some people blame "ancient ethnic hatreds" (Gunther 1940), others blame "Great Power" politics (Glenny 1999); while some are convinced that there is something about the topography and climate that makes the Balkans inherently fragmented and chaotic, particularly the region's highly mountainous character (McNeill 1964),[12] others are convinced that the problem stems from the clash of Islam against Christianity; while some think the Balkans have been shaped by Ottoman ideals (Todorova 1997), others think the real intellectual driving force of the Balkans was Orthodox Christianity (Kitromilides 1996; Tziovas 2003). However, and this is my point, everyone *knows* that his or her perspective is contested, and that each view has always been contested. No perspective has really ever had the privilege of being considered to be the authoritative, let alone self-evident, truth about the Balkans. What *is* self-evident, and is therefore where the hegemonic discourse is located in my view, is that everything about the Balkans is contested, including explanations for that state of affairs. While Mestrovic argues that means the explanations are "fragmented," one could equally see that the issue is too much connection between the explanations: that the gaps between them are not empty but generate relations, a crossing of perspectives that makes none of them seem *clear.*

In short, the idea that you can never get to the bottom of it, that it will always be either too complicated or too meaningless to ever be understood, *and* the observation that analyses or arguments about the Balkans are as "Balkanized" as are the Balkans themselves, together point to what constitutes the essence of the current hegemonic concept of the Balkans: that in political, intellectual, historical, cultural, and even topographical terms, the Balkans are fractal. Therefore, to suggest "switching the sound off," as Žižek does, to grasp more clearly what is going on, is in a sense to reproduce the hegemonic concept itself, rather than to critique it, as

Žižek intends to do. Žižek says, "One should resist the temptation to 'understand' [the Yugoslav wars], and accomplish a gesture analogous to turning off the sound of a TV: all of a sudden, the movements of the people on the screen, deprived of their vocal support, look like meaningless, ridiculous, gesticulations" (Žižek 1997: 62).

This metaphor has interesting parallels with one used by Mitchell Feigenbaum, one of the earlier mathematicians working on the idea of fractals, in an effort to describe what fractals might help to explain:

> The ceaseless motion and incomprehensible bustle of life. Feigenbaum recalled the words of Gustav Mahler, describing a sensation that he tried to capture in the third movement of his Second Symphony. Like the motions of dancing figures in a brilliantly lit ballroom into which you look from the dark night outside and from such a distance that the music is inaudible. . . . Life may appear senseless to you. (Gleick 1996: 163; emphasis removed)

In other words, Žižek is encouraging us to look at the Balkans as a fractal effect to critique *one* of the ideologies that describes the Balkans. For Feigenbaum, what makes something meaningless when you have too little detail (switch off the sound, look at things from a very long way away) is the same as what makes something seem incomprehensibly complicated when you have too much detail (looking at something under a microscope): it is the effect of fractals operating in the same way across different scales (it is their relationality, their lack of separation). Žižek felt he knew what was the underlying cause of the wars in former Yugoslavia (the involvement of the Great Powers in this region, both ideologically and politically); he also felt that if you just switch your scale of attention, if you just stop scrabbling around in the details of particularistic ethnic hatreds, then that underlying cause will become clear.[13]

In contrast, my approach has been—and will continue to be in the rest of this book—to switch to and fro between scales, to switch the sound off and switch it back on again repeatedly, to try to understand the relations between them, rather than the fragmentations. One way to do that is through exploring the scalar characteristics of fractality—the notion that one of the things that typifies fractals is that when you switch scales, things look and indeed are different, but actually the processes affecting them (hegemonic constructions and practices) are the same. That idea is one I have already attempted to explore in the previous chapter in bringing together sociopolitical commentaries, geomorphological accounts, anthropological accounts, and the accounts of people around the Kasidiaris. In the next chapters, given that people in Epirus expressed this fractal notion of the Balkans as often as did people in the media, in academics, and in national and supranational politics, I explore what is both different and the same about these expressions at different scales (of magnification in this case). Being on the Greek-Albanian border is different from talking about the Greek-Albanian border from Athens or Brussels, while it is also part of the same thing. Representing things statistically seems different from giving narrative accounts of things, but they are also part of the same thing (Munro 2001). They look different, they are experienced differently, they generate different perspectives, but each is also a fraction (a relational part) and a whole in itself; it is simultaneously both generic and different.[14]

In that sense, and to return to my concern thus far in this study, marginality both appears and disappears in the Balkan fractal effect, just as the Balkans themselves both appear and disappear. It depends on the scale, and the moment, at which you are looking at them. The Greek-Albanian border is both distant (far away from the heart of things) and generic (a detailed part, a not-quite-replication, of an assumed jagged, fragmented, and chaotic whole). The frequent dichotomy drawn between local and global (let alone that awful neologism "glocal") does not capture that relation; in the assertion of an absolute, rather than partial, distinction (local is the opposite of global), their entanglement and self-similarity are made to disappear.

I should emphasize again that unlike Gleick's descriptive approach to chaos theory, which is concerned with patterns that are asserted to exist ontologically in nature (fractals were "discovered" in nature as well as in mathematics, in Gleick's terms), I am looking at the expression of a hegemonic discourse which asserts that a particular part of the world is fractal, and I am attempting to understand how that makes people think about and experience the world in which they live ("This is the Balkans, Sarah; what do you expect?"). I do not take the fractality of the Balkans as a self-evident ontological truth; I take it to be a hegemonic construction.

THE APPEARANCE, DISAPPEARANCE, AND REAPPEARANCE OF THE BALKAN FRACTAL

My second approach in switching the sound on and off again repeatedly does take more of a stab at explanation rather than descriptive exploration, and it is here that I take the notion of fractals as implying fundamental relationality, rather than fragmentation, as an analytical trope. In this, I take the same approach as Wagner (and others, particularly Strathern), in being primarily concerned about *how* things mean, as opposed to *what* they mean (Wagner 1991: 166; Sykes 2003: 157). The assertions that there is no ultimate meaning to the Balkans and that their meaning is too complicated ever to be fully understood are both valid in their own terms, but the problem is that these kinds of statements are valid for any part of the world, and for any hegemonic concept. Making such comments leaves open the question of how this part of the world was picked out as being fractal in its very essence, as its monstrous defining characteristic; how it was made to mean fractality, and how that characteristic might have changed over time, while also being the same.

My interest here involves looking at the scalar effects of the Balkan fractal in terms of domain, as well as magnification. As Strathern describes in *Partial Connections*, fractal scaling not only concerns how close or how far away things are in space and time; it also concerns boundaries and interactions between one type of thing and another type of thing, their relationship as opposed to their fragmentation (Strathern 1991: xiii–xxvii). As Gleick puts it, "Fractal descriptions found immediate application in a series of problems connected to the properties of surfaces in contact with one another. . . . Contacts between surfaces have properties quite independent of the materials involved. They are properties that turn out to depend on the fractal quality of the bumps upon bumps upon bumps" (Gleick 1996: 106).

Bumps upon bumps upon bumps. That sums up quite a lot of what is said about the Balkans in terms of their intra- and interrelations, both literally and metaphorically. The region is notoriously mountainous, a fact that has been regularly blamed for the inability of military forces to permanently secure the area, for the small-scale divisions and mutual hostilities of peoples who live between narrow valleys or between mountains and valleys, and for the asserted/ascribed uncontrollable "savagery" and nomadism of people who flit around in the mountain underbrush. It is, moreover, represented as a fault line, as the geographical site where sudden explosions of violence, relatively often described as "earthquakes," occur between differing parts and powers (Goldsworthy 1999: 114; Ballinger 1999: 73; Winchester 1999).

The tectonic theme thus returns. How the Balkans came to appear so politically tectonically fractal clearly had a lot to do with the "where" of these mountains in relation to other places. They are not just anywhere—they are located on the European continent—and as I mentioned earlier, they have been constructed variously as a "buffer," "crossroads," or "bridge" between East and West, geographic terms ascribed a range of metaphorical connotations. "East" was sometimes taken to mean "Oriental" (Ottoman control of some European regions, frequently referred to as "Turkey in Europe"), sometimes taken to mean "Byzantine" (Russia's involvement and involvement of the Orthodox Church), and sometimes taken to mean "Communist" (former USSR). "West" was sometimes taken to mean benevolent or malevolent (Occidental) imperialism, sometimes taken to mean modernity and Enlightenment, sometimes taken to mean economic and technological progress, and occasionally taken to mean democracy (but not very often in this part of the world). At times in the past, the British government supported Ottoman control of the region on the grounds that it would keep the Russians from gaining any further foothold in Europe; at times, the Russians made alliances with the Ottomans, as did the Hapsburgs, in trying to keep out the French or the British; at other times, the Russians and Hapsburgs were at war with the Ottomans; at times, the British supported campaigns for independence from Ottoman rule by various groups within the Balkans in the endeavor to get the Ottomans ("Orientals") out of Europe (Todorova 1997: 109–11; Roessel 2002: 132–36); at times, the Austro-Hungarian Empire switched between these choices as well, and the Russians did too. If anything appeared to be happening in this region—in terms of British, French, Ottoman, Hapsburg, or Russian activity, especially during the period of the weakening of the Ottoman regime in the nineteenth century and the rise of nationalist campaigns in the region—all the other neighboring major powers paid a great deal of attention. During each "earthquake," whether it was relatively small-scale (e.g., shifting one territory from one empire to another, or a campaign for the [national] independence of a territory) or large-scale (e.g., the First World War), the borders were shifted, as were large numbers of people. In each case, the Balkans came to be represented as existing on the fault line between different powers and ideologies—Islam and Christianity, Byzantine and secular, imperial and nationalist—but in themselves constituting neither one of these oppositions, in full; the Balkans were simply the site where all of this came together (bumps upon bumps) and was continually fought out. The Balkans themselves represented a mixture, neither one thing nor the other, or alternatively altogether too much both one thing and another—or, perhaps, and therefore, nothing in particular, in themselves and by themselves.

Scopetea wonderfully evokes a sense of this in her brief account of a novel by Ivo Andrić (*A Bridge over Drina*), which concerns the building and then constantly contested fate of a bridge in Vishegrad, a small Bosnian town. "By the end of the novel," Scopetea recounts, "Vishegrad is caught in the crossfire, which supersedes any notion of East or West, and eventually the bridge is blown up" (Scopetea 2003: 173).

In this focus on Great Power politics, the Balkans could be seen as what was left over after the Great Powers resolved whatever disputes they had among themselves; the Balkans were the messy remainders, lacking in clear distinctions between one thing and another thing.[15] In fractal terms, that is rather appropriate, given that fractals focus on fractions, the leftovers of whole numbers.

There are various interpretations about when and how the idea of "Balkan" in this fractal sense began to explicitly emerge. In David Roessel's view, the genesis occurred in the late 1870s, when a range of political "earthquakes" in the region had occurred one after the other, an upheaval that came to be known in Britain as the Eastern Question (though there had also been earlier Eastern Questions), and culminated in the Balkan Wars (1912–13) and then the First World War (1914–19). These events, Roessel argues,

> significantly changed the map of southeastern Europe in the mind of the West. . . . The new perspective can be summed up in a single adjective, Balkan. . . . [W]e often forget that it has only been used to refer to a particular region of Europe for a little more than a century. (Roessel 2002: 141–42)

In any event, everyone seems to agree that the idea of the Balkans as a peculiarly unstable kind of region was in place by the end of the First World War. By then, there was a scatter of new states where the Ottomans had once administered territory, along with ongoing disputes between neighboring states about where the boundaries should be placed, now couched in explicitly nationalist terms.[16] It was also at this time that the region first began to be described in explicitly fractal terms by many commentators—including, interestingly, Leon Trotsky, who argued that the greatest cause of the problems in the Balkans was the recurrent involvement of Great Power politics combined with the peculiar diversity of Balkan peoples, living cheek by jowl (Trotsky 1980: 57–73).

Trotsky was in favor of a Balkan federation, not a scatter of nation-states. For others, who were more nationally inclined, the Balkans came to appear as something of a monstrous anomaly: the different peoples were too mixed up, too much of a "mosaic" or "Macedonian Salad" to permit clear distinctions as to which places "rightfully" belonged to which people in national terms. The result was continual contestation, continual dispute, continual vociferous assertions, backed up with appeals to this or that reading of origins or histories, to "prove" that this or that place was the "nation" of this or that group of "nationals." And every claim about a particular territory, a particular history, a particular people, was met by a counterclaim, making opposing assertions, combining people, place, and history in different ways (a proliferation of overlapping, intertwined, bits). Moreover, different members of the Great Powers supported this or that group, for a variety of differing reasons, which was interpreted as involving a moral/ideological commitment to either the group being supported or, alternatively, to the Great Powers' self-interested concerns about the geopolitics of Europe. Todorova notes: "All Balkan nations at one time or other have served as pet nations for the great European powers. The Greeks, due to the magnetism of their ancient history and the influence of Enlightenment ideas, have been the chosen ones" (Todorova 1997: 82). Later, Todorova adds, "just as Europeans were discovering *their* Greeks as the source of their civilization, Russians were discovering *their* Bulgarians as the roots of Slavic culture" (ibid.: 84). And David Roessel titles an entire chapter of his book on British and American perceptions of modern Greece "Pet Balkan People" (Roessel 2002: 132–58). Roessel quotes from Rebecca West's *Black Lamb and Grey Falcon* to make the point:

> English persons . . . of humanitarian and reformist disposition constantly went out to the Balkan peninsula to see who was in fact illtreating whom, and, being by the very nature of their perfectionist faith unable to accept the horrible hypothesis that everybody was ill-treating everybody else, all came back with a pet Balkan people established in their hearts as suffering and innocent, eternally massacree and never massacrer. (Quoted in ibid.: 145)

In terms of the Balkans *themselves*, it all began to look hopelessly complicated and a bit meaningless, all these claims and counterclaims. The region's process or pattern of conflicts had been understood by some, before the First World War, to be simply about battles between empires (British, French, Ottoman, Hapsburgs, Russians); or about "backward peasants" who nevertheless had the right to their own autonomy; or about the fact that once-great peoples had fallen into a state of degradation as a result of centuries of Ottoman rule and needed to reclaim their right to their previous glory (e.g., the Greeks). It now came to be seen as a process or pattern of conflict that, in addition to all those explanations, *also* appeared to be inherent ("natural") to this region as a whole, and to all of its bits and parts.

Here entered the sense of "self-similarity," and a perceived division between inter- and intrarelations (previously often seen as part of the same thing), and processes of conflicts that proliferated parts. There was something that appeared distinctly fragmentary as well as overly mixed together about the place and/or the people, and whatever it was, it generated continual explosions of violence and instability. It was the combination of making this explicit, and the sense that there was something "natural" about all this continual chaos, something that related particularly to this region and these people—or, alternatively, to the region's location in between a scatter of Great Powers—that rendered the hegemonic concept of the Balkans fractal.

In short, what eventually developed into a sense of this place as fractal during the nineteenth and early twentieth centuries was a sense of its being the location of repeated clashes of scalar domains: bumps upon bumps upon bumps. It was not only that differing ideological views and different forms of exercising power (and differing opinions about such exercises, both within and outside each power base) clashed and intermingled here; it was also, and importantly, that different structural arrangements, ways of governing, that flowed from those views, clashed and intermingled here. Let me take a brief look at this element.

During the Ottoman era, people and places were distinguished and organized in a way that was unsuited to easy transformation into a "nation-state" mode of organizing people and places (Todorova 1997: 121–27). First, there was the millet system: non-Muslim people within Ottoman territories were divided for legal, administrative, and tax purposes into groups, called millets, according to their religious affiliation, regardless of where they lived, what language(s) they spoke, or what was the color of their skin. Moreover, people could change this religious affiliation, and in many cases they did (Clogg 1992: 14). Unlike some authors who argue that the millet system was an early form of enlightened "multiculturalist" benevolence on the part of the Ottomans,[17] one that allowed non-Muslims to follow their own "traditions," I prefer the view that it was an alternative way of classifying and stratifying people, not a way of encouraging "plurality." Certainly, Frazee, in his study of the Greek Orthodox Church in the run-up to the Greek War of Independence, does not think the Ottoman motivations for organizing people into millets were particularly enlightened. By placing Orthodox peoples "under the religious and civil authority of their own church leaders . . . the Ottoman officials could count on using the services of the natural leadership of the Christian communities throughout their domain for their own purposes. The Christian hierarchy thus became, paradoxically, a very important arm of the Ottoman political administration" (Frazee 1969: 1). In short, this was a different way to organize the populations of empire, one that contrasted with British and French forms of colonialism, for example. But that difference did not necessarily make matters any more pleasant, nor did it provide any more of a sense of an official acceptability of diversity for the subjects of the Ottoman Porte; there is nothing in accounts about the Ottoman regime to suggest it was particularly benevolent, let alone a form of cultural liberalism as that phrase is understood today. People in millets were often disadvantaged in tax and other terms, and the religious organizations that ran the millets were not generally noted for their encouragement of autonomy on the part of their subjects; after all, the power of millets originated in the Ottoman Porte. Certainly, people in Epirus recalling stories about the final period of Ottoman rule in the Epirus region, stories they learned from their grandparents, did not suggest there was anything positively "multiculturalist" about the arrangements; on the contrary, most reported it as a form of often fairly extreme discrimination against them.[18] Although one could argue that subsequent Greek nationalist discourse made it inevitable that people would "remember" the Ottoman period in a particularly negative light, many people had equally negative things to say about a range of conditions during that period, irrespective of whether these were identified as being part of the Ottoman administration.

In any event, the main point is that the millet system did not distinguish people in the same way as the idea of "nation" distinguishes people: "Greek" referred to people who belonged to the Orthodox millet, whatever language they spoke and wherever they were from. The idea of "ethnic" Greekness was a separate matter altogether, and the difference between that and other kinds of Greekness was highly ambiguous (Pippidi 1999; Agelopoulos 2000).[19] As Irvine and Gal note about the Ottoman period, "in the understanding of identity, the criteria of religion, region, occupation, social stratum, and language group had not been aligned, hierarchized, or regimented on the model of the Western, nationalist imagination" (Irvine and Gal 2000: 67).[20]

The second element that made it difficult to transform the previous Ottoman system into a "nation-state" system (a switch of scalar domains, in a fractal sense) was the particular way in which the Ottomans relied upon trade and travel. As in other imperial regimes, there was a great deal of dependence upon long trade routes, and people moved around continuously and in a range of different ways, as I have already been describing at some length through people's stories in chapter 2. Importantly though, in the Ottoman case, there was no focus on a network of "hub" cities—centers of regions and places for a bourgeoisie to develop—like the cities that had grown in other parts of Europe (Todorova 1997: 173–74; Pippidi 1999: 101). Until the "Young Turk" revolution in 1908, the empire manifested a strong emphasis on divide and rule, maintaining a powerful center in Constantinople, where the headquarters of all the millets were also located (Palmer 1992: 200–211; Glenny 1999: 216–19).

The combination of the millet system and this network of traveling with no dominant urban centers that could challenge the Ottoman Porte meant that people might be considered to be "from" one region or another, but they did not "belong" to it in the sense of being rooted in it; the "belonging" was according to religious affiliation and a range of other criteria such as occupational specialism, none of which were based on territorial location, on language spoken, or on skin color. In other words, the Ottoman way of distinguishing people involved a different form of relations and separations from those imposed or asserted within the "nation" form. And just to confuse matters further, the word "millet" is often mistranslated as a Turkish word for "nationality" (Irvine and Gal 2000: 65).

So, during much of the nineteenth and early twentieth centuries, when there was a movement for independence on nationalist grounds (based on the notion of combining a single language, ethnonationalist group, and territory) in one or other part of the Ottoman regions, and when borders were drawn around an area and a population, the people thereby enclosed explicitly *appeared* to be a mixture, for the Ottoman system and the nationalist system interwove here: speaking different languages, of different religions, with differing occupational specialisms, different names, different habits of travel and movement, a range of relations to different places, and a different notion from the nationalist one about how people and places "belong." For many, the new nationalist way of distinguishing people did not quite fit, and I gave two examples of that in discussing Tsamides and Northern Epirots in chapter 2. When that was combined with the obvious interests of various "Great Powers" in achieving territorial divisions of one kind or another for their own purposes, it could appear that it did not really matter *who* the people in these (new, national) places were; what mattered was *where* they were—the assumption being that they could be "made" into nationals, to fit the territory.

That was done in practice in a variety of ways: nationalist logic attempted to generate a fit between people and place by either moving the borders, or moving people, or killing people, or changing people's names and the languages they spoke.[21] These attempts at separation were also notably carried out through the use of mapping techniques. Wilkinson's detailed study of the plethora of competing "ethnographic" and linguistic maps drawn by a range of groups in Macedonia demonstrates this in a particularly clear way (Wilkinson 1951). Peckham also notes this for a much wider region, suggesting that from the 1870s onward, differing nationalist movements drew up these competing maps, in what he refers to as "map mania": "[C]artographic techniques and, in particular, the tendency to depict ethnic groups in color codes as homogenous blocs, obscured ethnic diversity. . . . Often substantial minority populations . . . and dispersed communities were omitted so as to give an impression of stability and uniformity" (Peckham 2001: 142).[22]

Yet it seemed as though no matter how much rearranging and map drawing went on, every outcome was (implicitly or explicitly) contested and could lead to a proliferation of more of the same, generating that sense of Balkan fractality.

The major "bump on bump" that coincided with this earlier explicit ascription of fractality to the Balkans, then, was the Ottoman bump against the nineteenth-century nationalist bump, in which both the campaigners for independence and the Great Powers were thoroughly espousing ideas of nationality (as well as notions of modernity and Enlightenment, which went together at the time) as self-evident and authentic truths about who people are, and the morally correct way in which they should be governed and should develop their collective futures.[23] Modernist political ideologies became explicitly entangled in the Balkans, and it was this entanglement that seemed to be causing all the trouble.

This was also a period when intellectual and political elites were becoming attracted to the ideas of eugenics (the biological separation and purity of people). It was these elites (both within and outside the Balkans) that became regularly involved in trying to "resolve" things in the Balkans in a manner that suited their purposes. For example, during this period, commentators began to despair of sorting out the region into discrete bits—nationals with their nations—and started to be concerned about "mongrels" and "cross-breeds," the polluting character of mixture that was to be found in the Balkans. Todorova makes explicit what the problem was perceived to be: "Thessaloniki was . . . an uncouth Tower of Babel . . . 'Bulgarians, Servians, Albanians, Vlachs, Armenians, Anatolians, Circassians, Greeks, Turks, Jews, infidels and heretics of every land and language. Between and among these are sprinkled the races of civilized Europe.' . . . Sarajevo 'swarmed with strange nationalities': Bosnians, Croatians, Serbians, Dalmatians, Greeks, Turks, Gypsies" (Todorova 1997: 123). This frequently noted characteristic of the Balkans produced "feelings of revulsion and impurity" (ibid.: 124). Todorova adds: "Practically nobody . . . emphasized the fact that it was not ethnic complexity per se but ethnic complexity in the framework of the idealized nation-state that leads to ethnic homogeneity, inducing ethnic conflicts. Not only was racial mixture conducive to disorder, racial impurity was disorder" (ibid.: 128).

In sum, this was a scalar meeting of domains that developed into an explicit conclusion that the Balkans constituted an impossible, and therefore monstrous, shape: a fractal, in which no matter how small a scale was considered, or how large, the pattern was replicated, and the level of complexity, and impurity, was also the same. Each boundary stood for many other competing boundaries; each division led to further divisions; each moment of quiet was inevitably (if unpredictably) followed by conflict. There was no center, no clear edges, no apparent beginning and no end—or rather, at whatever scale you looked at it, it all looked the same. There was no way to *classify* this place, to separate out the discrete bits, in modernist terms. A period that strongly promoted ideas of modernity and Enlightenment thinking in the region, inextricably linked to the idea of national independence, also led to the conclusion that the region was "impossible." And as discussed in the previous chapter, the predominant areas marked out as constituting this "problem" for Greece were the northern borderland regions of Macedonia (in particular), Thrace, and Epirus.

Many have suggested that this view of the Balkans' impossibility developed because the region was judged by modernists to be premodern, on the basis of Orientalist stereotyping (e.g., Gallagher 2001). I suggest instead that it was the essential *ambiguity* which the Balkans represented to the modernist approach that rendered it problematic, and the place was ambiguous because of the relations between things, not its fragmentations. As Todorova put it, "Unlike orientalism, which is a discourse about an imputed opposition, balkanizm is a discourse about an imputed ambiguity" (Todorova 1997: 17).[24] Todorova relates this ambiguity largely to the way the Balkans were regarded as too Western to be cast as being entirely Eastern; too European to be cast as entirely non-European; too Christian to be cast as entirely Muslim; never fully colonized enough to permit a distinction between colonial and postcolonial; and geographically altogether too close by to be somewhere else. She concludes that what the Balkans represented was "disheveled" Europe, a kind of "premodern" (in Todorova's terms) version of the *self*, not a depiction of the other (Todorova 1997: 14).

I largely agree with Todorova on this point; but my argument has been that there is yet more to this ambiguity, because it was not possible to fully maintain the assertion of "premodernity" in its "pure" form, to keep the Balkans separate from modernity. A key element that disturbed the modernist approach was the way the Balkans apparently combined the "premodern" with fractality: continual contestation and proliferation of the parts, none of which could be guaranteed stability, makes a mockery of the modernist notion of purification and separation (Strathern 1999: 122–24).[25] This is why, I suggest, the hegemonic concept so strongly associates the essence of the Balkans with a *process* (continual conflict, instability, and fragmentation), and not with some more static notion of essence. It is also why the Balkans (or parts thereof) can appear, disappear, and reappear within this discourse, which is the final point I want to address regarding the "how" of the Balkan fractal.

The Disappearance and Reappearance of the Fractal

Retrospectively, the First World War came to be blamed on the Balkans (the fractal was in place by then). And although some authors, most notoriously Robert Kaplan, have argued that the Second World War was also the fault of the Balkans, there is so little basis for that argument that few historians take it seriously. Kaplan's argument relies on Hitler's having been Austrian, and Austria's being included in the Balkans, on the grounds that the Hapsburg Empire controlled a large part of the Balkans for a considerable amount of time and the Hapsburg Empire was Austro-Hungarian.[26] In any event, Kaplan was certainly convinced of the fractal characteristics of the Balkans, as indicated by the epigraph from *Balkan Ghosts* at the beginning of this chapter (history in the Balkans, in his view, is not linear but jumps around in circles, being altogether too interrelated). He also argued that the Balkans were the "original Third World," and that the region "produced the century's first terrorists" (ibid.: xxiii). It is a rather extreme example of what constituting the Balkans as fractal is liable to do to the reputation of the place.

I am getting away from my point. The Second World War also led to a continuation of skirmishes about borders in the Balkan region, as had all previous conflicts, both large and small. But following the end of that war, a strange thing happened: the Balkans disappeared, as Europe was neatly divided into capitalist West and communist East, and relations between them were severed. The Balkans were rather messily and ambiguously split across that line; by then there had been so many debates about where the Balkans are, which countries were and were not included, that it was difficult to discern exactly where the Balkans had gone, as it were. There were the places that were now behind the Iron Curtain and therefore unambiguously classified as East in socialist terms (Albania, Romania, Bulgaria, and possibly Hungary if you include Hungary in the Balkans, which most Hungarians do not); there was Yugoslavia—which, although not behind the Iron Curtain in the sense of being a part of the USSR, was nevertheless socialist; there was Greece, which was ambivalently located in relation to West (Occident/Hellenic) and East (Orient/Byzantine); and there was Turkey, which was, to Euro-American minds, more East than West (in Orient versus Occident terms), but under Attaturkist secularism considered itself to be more West than East (Navaro-Yashin 2002). And Austria (for those who include Austria in the Balkans) was at the farthest end of West. The point is that the fractal had been fragmented into constituent parts (the bits had been separated out in linear, statistical terms, an impossibility within fractal thinking) and had therefore ceased to be a Thing, a relational fractal geometric shape, at all.

That set in train a kind of "timelessness" perspective about the Balkans, an idea that they had moved into the realms of history and/or myth—until, that is, they were deemed to have returned. The first indications of this occurred after 1989 with the collapse of the former Soviet Union; but it was really with the wars in former Yugoslavia, and various other moments of political unrest, as well as large population movements (peoples variously labeled asylum seekers, refugees, economic migrants, etc.), in other parts of the region throughout the 1990s, that people began to talk about the region as Balkan again, and began to talk about that in fractal terms again. Both the media and many academics started to blame all these new violent "earthquakes" on a reappearance of the Balkan fractal (on "Balkanization").[27] The process of conflict was asserted to have exactly the same properties—a self-similarity in the way it proliferated—as it had had during the nineteenth and early twentieth centuries. As Keith Brown put it, "The violent break-up of Yugoslavia in the 1990s . . . came to appear as a case of Balkan history repeating itself" (Brown 2003: 23). The fractal had apparently not been destroyed—it had just been held in suspension for a few decades—and now it was released to carry on doing its Balkan Thing, as if fifty-odd years of socialism and other factors had not changed the place or the people by one iota. And the arguments and disagreements about what was causing it began again, apparently repeating the same process of disagreements and fragmentation/relationality of explanations as had occurred in the nineteenth and early twentieth centuries.

A Not-Quite-Replicating Fractal

While the more recent version of asserting fractal properties for the Balkans was a replication, it was a not-*quite*-replication, for it was explicitly represented as a replication. This is where I have reached the limits of borrowing fractality as a descriptive concept from chaos theory. In descriptive chaos theory, fractal patterning remains mathematically constant, even if things bifurcate (suddenly take a different direction); in a hegemonic fractal discourse about places and people, on the other hand, fractal patterns can change if what is said about them changes, even while it is asserted that nothing has changed (or rather, because of that). This gets me back to Strathern's point in *After Nature* (1992a), mentioned in chapter 1: what can change things is what events in the world cause you to think about what you know has always already been true. In that sense, the first Balkan fractal and the second are not-quite-replications of one another.

First, the initial explicit ascription of fractal properties to the Balkans did not, of course, have a precedent. The next time, it did have a precedent; so historical as well as cultural anachronism could be ascribed to the 1990s wars in former Yugoslavia and the uprisings in Albania in 1997 in a way that was not possible in the earlier period. Second, and as important, by the time the Balkans reappeared in the 1990s, the concept "Balkanization" had been used as a metaphor for decades to describe a whole range of "new" phenomena and theories whose combined fragmentary and relational characteristics were disliked, by some. As I mentioned earlier, these included multiculturalism, postmodernism, and interdisciplinarity; none of these discourses existed, at least in their current form, in the late nineteenth and early twentieth centuries. So Balkanization had proliferated by the time the Balkans apparently started Balkanizing again.

Balkanization was therefore no longer something assumed to be specific to this part of the world; because the concept had been constituted around the idea of a fractal—which, above all else, constitutes a process and a particular kind of interrelationality, rather than an idea of static essential identity—it became a particularly useful metaphor for critiquing theories and approaches that emphasized the unstable, fluid, and hybrid character of existence (from a modernist perspective). This means that the concept "Balkanization" was reimported, as it were, back into the Balkan region once conflicts of the "appropriate" kind began to arise there, after a long interval of the term's being used for other things elsewhere. So it was not only that these places and people had continued to exist for around fifty years in between the disappearance and reappearance of the Balkans: the hegemonic rhetoric itself had continued to exist, elsewhere, for the same period.

That goes some way to explaining my strange sense of déja-vu when I read descriptions of the asserted characteristics of the Balkans and compared them to descriptions of some kinds of postmodernist theory, particularly those interested in the potential inventiveness of ambiguity, gaps, networks, and hybrids.[28] For example, "Macedonian Salad" suggests an inherent and irresolvable diversity, a situation of cultural identification that is "polycentric, multiple, unstable, historically situated, the product of ongoing differentiation and polymorphous identifications." Yet this is the phrase I invoked in chapter 1, which Turner cited approvingly in discussing "critical multiculturalism" (Turner 1993: 418). And "crossroads" or "bridge"—two terms used incessantly to describe what constitutes the Balkans in Europe—seem to me to be very similar to what Roy Wagner describes as a "hinge" in his paper on the "fractal person." He used the word to refer to the way babies among the Daribi who remain unnamed for too long come to be perceived: "an embodied hinge between the world of names and that of unnamed things" (Wagner 1991: 164). In that sense, one could say that what currently constitutes the Balkans is a name for that which cannot be named in Europe because it is neither one thing nor another or, rather, altogether too much *both* one thing and another, and therefore perhaps also nothing in particular. Postmodernist theory seems to be made for the Balkans.

Once again, though, there is a not-quite-replication here. Turner's call for the use of the universal inventiveness of people as a revolutionary force in promoting cultural diversity and thus undermining hegemonic cultural constructions makes little sense in the contemporary Balkans, because the hegemonic construction precisely defines Balkan peoples as "polycentric, multiple, unstable," etc.—all those things Turner wishes to promote—and it is this very polycentric, multiple unstableness (as it were) that is deemed to continually generate attempts at purification, essentialized notions of cultural identity that lead to ethnic cleansing and threaten to destabilize the entirety of Europe, if not the world. This is why it has been important to emphasize that it is the relational character of the Balkans that is constructed as their problematic characteristic, not the fragmentation.

Turner himself repeats the negative view of the Balkans as representing fragmentary and essentialist (rather than relational) multiplicity by quoting two authors in favor of "critical multiculturalism" as defending themselves against accusations that their approach would "Balkanize" (*sic*) the (U.S.) nation (Turner 1993: 417–18). Whatever is the "right" way to do culture and hybrids, "Balkanization" is clearly the wrong way to do them, whether one is modernist or postmodernist (with the exception of the circle of radical theorists represented in Bjelić and Savić 2002). In fact, it seems to be the blending of modernist ideas (purification, essentialism) with postmodern ones (fluidity, instability, hybridity) that is at the root of the problem of "Balkanizing." Reimporting "Balkanization" into the Balkans after the term had been used as a modernist critique against postmodernism seems to have led to a very odd hybrid indeed in the Balkans themselves; they are altogether *too* hybrid.[29] Here, it is important to note Ballinger's point that "the notion of hybridity rests on the myth of pure wholes whose intersection generates intermixture" (Ballinger 2003: 248). In that sense, "the Balkans," as a construction notion, demonstrates how hybridity can be simultaneously modernist and postmodernist.[30]

I am arguing that the more recent debates on multiculturalism[31] have generated a notion of culture that is being used against the Balkans, and because these debates on multiculturalism were absent during the earlier period of the assertion that the Balkans are fractal, the more recent Balkan fractal is once again a not-quite-replication of the previous one; it is both the same and different. Those Balkan politicians who are currently being cast as having an essentialist attitude toward ethnicity are once again being defined as anachronistic, as were their predecessors in the early twentieth century. However, this time these Balkan politicians are not being sufficiently multicultural for today's version of modernity, in that they are represented as having an attitude toward nationalism that arose at the end of the nineteenth and in the early twentieth centuries, an attitude that is no longer ethically/morally appropriate in a transnational, global world. In other words, essentialist Balkan politicians are being cast as premodern as a result of their apparently promoting an earlier version of modernity.[32]

Moreover, many of those Balkan politicians who are not being essentialist, who espouse an acceptance of diversity within their territories (and who should therefore be regarded as appropriately modern) are nevertheless often cast as "disheveled" Europeans, generic peoples who have little in the way of distinctiveness to sell on the cultural heritage market: they might have the "right" approach, but they don't have the appropriate economic, technological, or political structures.[33] That sounds, and is, much the same as the earlier idea that the Balkans have not "modernized" enough; but the form of modernity that is supposed to be lacking is no longer what it was imagined to be during the earlier period. Rather than a clash of Ottoman "premodernity" against European modernity, now there seems to be a clash between earlier and later modernities. The resistance against the implication that this makes the Balkans archetypically modern (simultaneously both modern and not modern in Latour's sense) is once again reproduced in this discourse.

What remains the same for both the previous and more recent versions is the sense of fractality. What is different here is that this fractality can now be explicitly imagined to be postmodern as well as premodern. And that generates relations between the Balkans (and their Balkanizing) which are both the same and different from their previous relations. They are the same in that they are still constituted as being fractal, as fundamentally about complex intertwined relations (internal and external) and fragmentations; they are different in that the means for causing the fractal to disappear is currently as much about culture as it is about fixing stable state boundaries and territories.

One contemporary way to be cut out of the networked interrelationality of the Balkan fractal (to make it disappear) is to constitute a group of people as standing for themselves, rather than standing for the Balkans (e.g., the Sarakatsani), in the manner described by Turner as "difference multiculturalism" (Turner 1993: 414).[34] Yet this kind of separation does not work for peoples marked as Northern Epirot; while labeling a group of people as Northern Epirot could be regarded as a form of cutting, in that it asserts a distinctive characteristic of these people, it is not a separation: it is both a relational and contested distinction, and implies a cultural shifting of existing state borders. Northern Epirots are such because they are constituted as Greeks living in Albania; in that sense, the designation "Northern Epirot" is not cut out of the Balkan fractal; it remains archetypically Balkan in the hegemonic sense.

Even more ambiguous is the situation for people such as the "undistinguished" "just Greek" population of Pogoni living on the Greek side of the border, who neither constitute a Balkan "problem" in terms of boundaries, as do their Northern Epirot kin and neighbors, nor constitute a minority or other kind of distinctive group in terms of cultural politics, as do the Sarakatsani. The important point here is that it is not an ambiguity about *who* they are which makes the difference (there is little question that Pogoni peoples are Greek and that this makes them different from people who are constituted as being something else);

rather, it is their interrelationality, the things which also make them the *same*, not different, that is at issue. And as I have been arguing repeatedly already, the key here is the "where" of Pogoni. Given Pogoni's location on, or straddling, the Greek-Albanian border, attempts to disentangle the fractal—to remove the ambiguity that generates a sense of things' being both unclear and the same while also being different—are hedged around with a sense of danger: a host of memories and stories about previous impositions of difference and distinction, as well as the current examples of Northern Epirots and the even more difficult example of Tsamides, demonstrate the still-existing tensions attached to cutting things out of this fractal. The Pogoni "just Greek" population on the Greek side of the border, able to avoid the assertion of "displacement" in nationalist terms, also find themselves unable to assert "distinction" in "difference multiculturalism" terms.

The point here is that the way multiculturalism is currently used, in practice, as a means to creatively garner recognition, resources, and rights, or even to challenge current orthodoxies, is inevitably the currently hegemonic form, since the resources come only from powerful institutions with investments in the hegemonic form: one cannot be inventive in a vacuum.[35] This is the same form(s) that has/have consistently been used, in not-quite-replications, against the Balkans (they have been borrowed). The response has been continual attempts, both within regions defined as Balkan and outside of them, to make the Balkans disappear, to dissipate their fractality and therefore to render them not a Thing anymore, to remove the interconnections, the fluidity, and the hybridity that make the place an impossible, ambiguous, and dangerous shape.

The significance of this, for my purposes in this study, is that the contemporary Balkans, within this hegemonic context, are generating a particular kind of proliferation: of peoples who are unable to reconstitute themselves appropriately, being located in the midst of a scalar, hybrid (interrelational) clash between modernisms and postmodernisms, and who therefore either remain unnamed (and hence "invisible") or have a name that cannot, on moral grounds, be given resources—unless they are reconstituted as peoples who are the victims of Balkan essentialisms (e.g., the Albanian victims of Milošević's Serbian nationalism in Kosovo). But, as is regularly asserted by the media and Western European politicians commenting on the Balkans, these victims often also generate victims of their own at other times—there is a continual reconfiguring of the parts, an endless chain of separations and relations, purifications and hybridizations.

The implication of the more recent political attempts at the reduction of fractal proliferation in the Balkans (e.g., U.S. and UK interventions in Kosovo; proposals to have Balkan countries join the European Union) is this: where hegemonic constructions in fact make it impossible to cut the network in Strathern's terms (Strathern 1996)—indeed, pointing to the terrible consequences when it is cut ("Balkanization," world wars)—the only possibility is to make the whole thing disappear, and this is as restricting on the "freedom" to be "inventive" as is the opposite. In the hegemonic concept of the Balkans, the proliferation of hybrids, cast as problematic interrelations (fragmentation) is not regarded as "inventiveness" at all; it is neither productive nor creative but is instead represented as chaos, the outcome of a fractal, and the only thing you can do about that, within this hegemonic discourse, is to break it up into discrete bits that do not look like fractions of the whole. When Savvopoulos, one of the most famous contemporary Greek singers, sang, "Εδώ είναι Βαλκάνια, δεν είναι παίξε-γέλασε" ("This is the Balkans, it is not fun and games"), he was quite right, and that is the reason I have used the term "hegemonic" for this understanding of the Balkans: it is not only a fantasy (an ideologically mediated invention that generates an image of how things seem) but a fantasy with teeth (an ideologically mediated invention that affects how things are, whether or not people believe the invention).[36]

In sum, the hegemonic understanding of the relational, the self-similarity character of the Balkans, its inability to be differentiated and untangled (most particularly from modernity), has been a key aspect of all the trouble in the ability or desire of some of the people with whom I worked to make appropriate, or at least profitable, use of more recent ideas of multiculturalism and cultural heritage. That is something I will explore in this book's final chapter, in an examination of EU-funded agrotourism development programs in the Epirot region. Before that, I will continue to spend some time exploring the appearance and disappearance of things, the relationality of sameness and difference, across a range of scales.

CHAPTER 5

Counting

OVER THE LAST CHAPTERS, I have made a great deal of how things come to appear and disappear, how they come to seem important or irrelevant, and how this works across different scales, of both magnitude and domain. In this, I have emphasized gaps and how they are never empty, taking that to the level of the entirety of the Balkans in the previous chapter, in looking at how the Balkans, too, have been constituted as a gap, or a plethora of gaps. Before that, I considered how Epirus was considered something of a gap, as the least visible and least noted of the three Greek mainland regions that are rendered more Balkan than other regions in mainland Greece; and within Epirus, I considered how the Pogoni area as well as the Thesprotia region were gaps of a sort, the first in terms of its lack of distinction and its ambiguity, and the second in terms of the distinctive, troublesome ambiguity of some of the people associated with the place; and within the Kasidiaris area of Pogoni, I considered how the ambiguity and ordinariness of some people, the "just Greek" people, rendered them something of a gap as well within the discourse of distinctive identities, so that *Gréki* constituted a name for something that was unnamed, that marked a lack of distinction, in wider discourses about Greekness. The gaps, I have argued, inevitably contain relations, an interweaving of things—people, places, moving around, stories, events, boundaries, geomorphology, hegemonic discourses, and so on.

That is not a new approach, of course, either in anthropology or in other social disciplines, and I have already mentioned fractal theory and actor network theory. Another pertinent example for this chapter and the next one is Mary Poovey's study of the way the British public came to be constituted as an aggregate, a "social body" in modernist terms, during the Victorian period (Poovey 1995). Poovey argues that the attempt to encompass the totality of what could be known about the British public, now cast as a "mass population"' through modernist techniques such as statistical accounting, never entirely succeeded because these techniques incorporated previous ways of thinking—different domains, as she calls them—that preexisted a statistical form of thinking about the world (ibid.: 14–15). Thus Poovey also points to the gaps in the modernist story of homogeneity, the interweaving of temporal and conceptual domains. In a different way, James Scott's study of "high-modernist" development and state-sponsored planning projects suggests that all such projects are liable to fail because they persistently and deliberately ignore things that exceed the self-imposed, homogenizing parameters of such projects—and what is more, both planners and everyone else are aware of this (Scott 1998: 345–48).

The issue of gaps and what they contain became a focus for me because people around the Kasidiaris and elsewhere kept referring to things that seemed to exceed, or constitute gaps in, other accounts I had available to me at the time: gaps such as Albania in the geomorphological accounts; gaps such as the invisibility of one kind of land degradation as against the visibility of other kinds; gaps such as the "whereness" of the Balkans in accounts about Greece, and gaps such as *Gréki* in accounts about Greeks. I kept encountering stories, events, and relations that seemed to go beyond any of these accounts, which referred to things that such accounts rendered invisible or irrelevant and/or could not account for. So I have focused, time and again, on bringing these accounts into relation with one another, as a means to render visible the gaps and the interrelations they invariably contain.

This chapter and the next one continue that approach, in focusing on techniques and processes of accounting for things through counting them, turning them into numbers, and considering how such accounts interweave with other things. It will involve dipping into the reams of the Greek state's statistical data I collected for the purposes of the wider research program of which I was a part (the appendix contains a smattering of these), and looking at how such accounts again always exceeded what they purported to account for. I will argue that statistics were rarely treated entirely statistically in Epirus, in the sense that it was assumed there were always other things that exceeded what statistics can account for in their own terms, or which statistics deliberately rendered invisible; and these other things were also always assumed to be involved in the creation of the statistics themselves. In other words, the numbers that actually appeared always revealed traces of other things that went into arriving at those particular numbers.

Once again, this understanding of what constitutes statistics around the Kasidiaris area was related both to an emphasis on the idea that statistics are tools of political activity and to a sense I gained from talking with people in Epirus that statistics, along with other kinds of accounts, are always the outcome of negotiations as a result of conflicts of interest. Of course, few people in the contemporary world can fail to be aware that political decisions and assertions are often made on the basis of statistical accounts of places, people, and activities: a perusal of just about any policy document, from just about any political entity in the world, shows quite how strongly this is the case in contemporary life.[1] What many people in Epirus emphasized about this is that it does not matter whether the numbers are "accurate" in their own terms: if they are used to guide actions at the level of the state or beyond, then they can alter people's lives as well as the places in which they live, and that makes them into powerful "facts."[2] In that sense, how things are made to seem through statistical accounts can have a direct effect on how things are made to be.

This is a point I made in a different way in chapter 2 in discussing Navaro-Yashin's work on people's relationships with the state, and the way people can be cynical about the state while simultaneously recognizing the state's power to make things happen in practical terms. In that sense, Holt's argument that statistics have to be trusted in their own terms in order for them to be used did not seem to be borne out in Epirus (Holt 2000: 1011); nor did Porter's argument that statistics have to be constituted as being more "objective" than personal opinion or expertise in order for them to overtake the authority of professional knowledge in making the world meaningful (Porter 1995).[3] Rather, statistics tended to be understood by many people in Epirus in much the same ways as they understood maps: they constituted politically inflected constructions of how things seem, and formed part of a political tactic (in de Certeau's [1988] terms) in attempts to control or alter the way things are. And as with maps, people also tended to assume two things about statistics: first, that they would account for this place, the people there, and their activities using criteria established elsewhere and with others in mind; and second, that there will always be different and competing versions of statistical accounts, so no account would ever stand as a self-contained ontological "truth." That was reflected in the pervasive sense that all statistical accounts are the outcome of negotiations, where one version of how things seem wins out over another version; but there will always be other versions available, so whatever reality the accounts currently show is inherently contested and could be overturned tomorrow.

Moreover, unlike maps, which take a long time to construct and tended to have restricted access in this area, as well as being expensive to reproduce, most official statistics are enormously accessible and exist in copious quantities, with few restrictions on their availability: they are collected and collated year in and year out, and regularly directly involved most people (who were obliged to provide data) as well as every level of government. Among the sources of such numbers that I used was the Ioannina Prefecture's branch of the Department of Agriculture, which provided the bulk of data on animal husbandry and cultivation; the Forestry Commission, which provided information on fires and forest cover; the local office of the Statistical Service of Greece, which provided most of the demographic data and various other odd collections of figures; the offices of Land Improvement and Development, which provided data on agricultural land redistribution and irrigation system programs; the offices of the Union of Communes and Municipalities of Epirus, which provided information on research and audits carried out for development projects; and, finally, many data were collected from commune offices themselves, either from records or from the memories of commune presidents and secretaries. The data actually shown in the appendix and described in the following chapter represent just a small selection of many similar types of statistics gathered in these regular visits.[4]

The pervasive collection and availability of official data provided repeated opportunities for negotiation and reinterpretation in Epirus, both about past statistical accounts and about the collecting of data for current statistical accounts. And in those negotiations and reinterpretations, people drew back in many of the elements that statistical accounts in themselves leave out, repeatedly making explicit the partialness of such accounts. The continual process of contesting and being cynical about statistics, of pointing to the nonstatistical elements that are embedded within them, once again constituted these accounts as always already embroiled with other things.

There was an interweaving of three different scales here: one of magnitude, in which the overall impression of Epirus and its subregions generated by such accounts constituted powerful images of the place that could affect both state and European Union policies toward it; a second scale, of domain, in which the (modernist) statistical ideal of neutrally and objectively reflecting "how things are in the world" interwove with the political imperative to create certain assertions about "how things are" in order to make them that way; and a third scale, of magnitude, in which both personal interests and larger-scale political interests interwove in the negotiations over *which* numbers would eventually be written down and come to take on the authority of being "The Number," against a range of competing numbers that could have been put there. This third scale involved people and institutions at every level: an individual shepherd reporting how many sheep or goats he had, a commune president reporting how many residents existed in the commune, the Forestry Commission's definition of forest against the rather different definition provided by the Statistical Service of Greece, and so on.

Rolland Munro suggests that this negotiation process always occurs, and it always points to things that exceed numerical accounts, and thus renders the difference between numerical and narrative accounts one of no difference at all. The example he uses is executive negotiations about company budgets as compared with accounts showing the results of the company: what is to be included and what cannot be included as an explanation for discrepancies between budgets and results is a matter of negotiation (Munro 2001). Because of this, Munro argues, even company budgets and accounts are constituted by the interweaving of social relations that brings them into existence. He further argues that the documents themselves, as things, continually act as reminders of social relations and are therefore integrally embedded in social relations. The usual mistake, he says, "is to essentialise the social into *either* things *or* humans, as if one could wash out the socially constructed nature of the former and bracket off a prosthetic 'extension' . . . of the latter. If it is an ability to invoke presence, or to make things seem absent, that determines, for all practical purposes, social relations, then 'things' will often do as well as 'people' in forming, or re-minding people of significant others" (ibid.: 488, emphasis original).

In the example Munro uses, the whole aim of attempting to account for the gaps between budgets and actual expenditure and income was to render invisible the underlying personal relationships involved in such negotiations about accounts, to render them literally of no account, and to emerge with a set of numbers that appeared to encompass the totality of what could be said (in his terms, to prevent the "monster" of other things' coming into the accounts). In contrast, in the negotiations that I will be discussing, the whole point was to make those other things, the relations and the partialness embedded within the numbers, continually explicit. Doing that not only challenges the claims to objective truth of such accounts; it also means that any truth would always already be partial, because it could always be contested.

Here, I need to pause for a minute to bring fractals back into the story. Roy Wagner makes a useful distinction between the ideals of a statistical way of thinking and a fractal way of thinking (Wagner 1991: 167). A statistical account treats each piece of raw data as a discrete unit, then aggregates hundreds or thousands of such units together according to some (modernist) system of classification, and finally generates an abstraction, a pattern, that is not fully contained in each unit; this pattern can be seen only in the aggregate, and its representation in the form of numbers. Of course, what is generated out of this process, as a technically, socially, and politically constructed form of reality, has been the subject of considerable debate within anthropology and elsewhere (Appadurai 1996c; Kertzer and Arel 2002a; Urla 1993; Cohn 1990; Friedman 1996; Scott 1998; Poovey 1995; Porter 1995). Leaving that aside for the moment, statistical techniques, in their own terms, assert that the result of treating data statistically is to expose or reveal patterns in the data that are greater than the sum of the parts, underlying or encompassing "realities" that are different from any bit of the raw data taken individually.[5] In contrast, as I described in the previous chapter, a fractal way of thinking assumes that each bit or part is a complete whole in itself; if they are aggregated together, the result is another version of the whole, not something different from each individual bit. The only way to understand fractals is by looking at the relations already contained both within and between the parts (as it is these relations that generated the fractal in the first place), not by aggregating them together and hoping that some encompassing relationship among all the parts will reveal itself.

While this is a useful starting point, it does not go quite far enough for my purposes, as it is the way the statistical (one way of accounting for things) and the nonstatistical (a different way of accounting for things) are almost always combined *within* statistical accounts that interests me. Wagner takes the asserted ideals of a statistical way of thinking as the definition of statistics; this ideal imposes a certain kind of numerical knowledge about the world, and he argues that for peoples who think in more fractal terms (e.g., the Iqwaye described by Mimica [1988]), statistical thinking does not account for things, and, most particularly, it does not account for persons. In Epirus on the other hand, where people were entirely familiar with statistics and talked about numbers in those terms all the time, it was assumed that a statistical way of thinking is never what it asserts it is in *ideal* terms (i.e., a technique that is separated out from the world that it accounts for), because in practice every aspect of collecting, classifying, compiling, disseminating, and interpreting statistical numbers is always already embroiled with other things. This means that each statistical account will contain within it the same kinds of relations to other things as any other statistical account (or indeed, any other kind of assertion about how things are). In that sense, statistical accounts, for people in Epirus at least, constituted complete wholes in themselves, containing both statistical and nonstatistical elements in the way the numbers that appear in them were calculated; their characteristics could be understood only through examination of the relations between statistical accounts and other things, relations that were always embedded within the numbers. In short, most people I met around Epirus treated a statistical way of thinking as being as "fractal"—in Wagner's use of the concept this time—as anything else, even if those citing or producing statistics claimed them to be something different (or, rather, because of that).

LIES, STATISTICS, AND INTERESTS

Unsurprisingly, the kind of cynicism expressed about how official statistics were generated and what was embedded within them bore a close relation to the cynicism expressed about many things, and three in particular interest me here: the widespread assumption that everyone lies; the way the place (Epirus and the Kasidiaris area) was constituted as being more "Balkan" than other parts of Greece; and the sense of neglect and indifference shown toward many parts of Epirus. I will start with lies.

One afternoon in 1994, I was in a *kafeneio* in Sitaria, a village on the eastern slopes of the Kasidiaris, and got to talking with a man there about my research and what I was hoping to achieve. Like many other people, Spiros thought it was important that he caution me:

SPIROS: You need to be careful; people will always tell you lies around here.

SARAH: Does that include you?

SPIROS: (raising his eyebrows in mock shock and offense): Me? I'm trying to help you; I'm telling you not to believe what people tell you. They say a lot of rubbish[6] most of the time. You need to check up on what people tell you. You need to get the facts, get proper information, and not listen to rubbish.

SARAH: Why do people tell lies?

SPIROS: What kind of a question is that? Because people are ignorant and want to make you think they're smart.

SARAH: So smart people will tell me the truth?

SPIROS: I already told you. Nobody tells the truth.

SARAH: So why do smart people lie?

SPIROS: Politics; interests; to pass the time; because they think you'll believe them; all kinds of reasons. You don't believe me?

As usual, irony and cynicism were key parts of this conversation. In this case they reflected a widespread assumption that people regularly and deliberately embellish, alter, conceal, or are conservative with "the truth": almost everyone I met in Epirus, both men and women, young and old, were convinced that most people did this most of the time. It was a fact of life, a general truth about the way people interact with each other, and Greeks in particular.[7] That has been noted by most ethnographers of Greece, particularly du Boulay (1974: 189–97; 1976), but also Friedl (1962: 78–81), Hirschon (1989: 179–81), and Campbell (1964: 282–83), to name but a few. Herzfeld devotes some time to investigating solemn oaths, as a means used to deal with this assumption at times when a constructed version of the "truth" is particularly important to establish (Herzfeld 1997: 121–24; 1990).

Many of these analyses consider aspects of lying that involve secrecy, aggression, or defensiveness. Here, however, I am more concerned with the general assumption that lying is pervasive in social relations.[8] In that sense, being "imaginative with the truth" as a practice seems to be one of those "cultural intimacies" that Herzfeld outlines as "the recognition of those aspects of a cultural identity that are considered a source of external embarrassment but that nevertheless provide insiders with their assurance of common sociality, the familiarity with the bases of power that may at one moment assure the disenfranchised a degree of creative irreverence and at the next moment reinforce the effectiveness of intimidation" (Herzfeld 1997: 3). In similar fashion, John Barnes, in noting Ernestine Friedl's description of how Greek parents in Vasilika deliberately lie to their children to teach them not to trust what anyone says, suggests that in the Greek context, lies are perhaps best regarded as "untrue stories that only a stranger would think were true" (Barnes 1994: 2). This echoes the advice that Spiros had given me: being a "stranger," I should learn not to believe anything I heard.

This general sense that lying happens at all times applied to official statistics as much as it applied to people's talk. In fact, it was many people's repeated attempts to help me in my research by warning me against taking statistical records too literally that alerted me to the pervasive sense that official statistics were, in themselves, only part of the story; they could be properly understood only through the addition of a lot of other (nonstatistical) ways of representing how things were, which were embedded within the statistical accounts. The irony here is that in practice, many people took Spiros's attitude toward my endeavors: they repeatedly tried to help me see the combination of things that contributed to any asserted truths. I was not only regularly warned about lies; I was also taught how to read statistical accounts in the appropriate way: people trained me to spot the gaps and explained what I should and should not believe. This was often based on people's gauging what *my* interests were: one kind of account would do for one kind of interest, but another kind of account had to be constructed for another kind of interest. Many concluded that I was a "scientist," which was different from being a civil servant, a politician, or somebody filling out a form to get subsidies or to pay tax. So, given my ignorance of how the numbers were constituted in this place, people felt a need to tell me about it so that I would not make the mistake of reading the numbers, or of believing what people said in general, as if either statistics or assertions were "pure" "scientific facts." This kind of warning was as frequently given by civil servants in government offices who were in charge of compiling the statistics, and by presidents of village communes, as it was by anyone else. The only exceptions were during debates and arguments, where people would cite certain numbers as support for their argument and assert that these numbers were the "true," "pure" ("unadulterated") facts. What was meant, as I learned over the years, was that these facts were the ones that were true for the particular perspective being supported; nobody was expected to believe that they were the only facts available.

A couple of examples are worth giving here. The first comes from Pontikates, where I went to visit the secretary of the commune to gather some information about the village, mostly as a means to introduce myself. I asked him about the current population of the village. This was his response: "According to the 1991 census, it was 115. But the permanent residents are 30. The 115 at that moment was because of the movement of people and I don't know what. You know, people come to the village on census day, that's why it says 115. Permanent residents in the village today, in the year that's just gone by, was 29, 30."

I had similar conversations in many communes about the caution with which I should treat the census, and will discuss that further in chapter 6. Worth noting here is that the secretary did not say the census was entirely a "lie"; it was more that it was one kind of truth, which contrasted with another kind. A second example, this time not about official statistics, came later in the same conversation, as we were discussing the period when people from Pontikates had begun to emigrate. Another man present felt the need to intervene in the secretary's comments:

SECRETARY: Some went [emigrated] from 1950, and to Germany, they went from 1960.

YIANNIS: To Germany, very few went. Hardly anyone went to Germany.

SECRETARY: [Spiros, Manos] went to Germany . . .

YIANNIS: Eh, very few. We don't have Germany, us.

SECRETARY: Don't we have [Georgios]?

YIANNIS: Which [Georgios]?

SECRETARY: The child of [Mitsios], isn't he in Germany?

YIANNIS: In Germany?

SECRETARY: The child of [Mitsios], isn't he in Germany?

YIANNIS: Oh, right [sarcastically], come *on*.

SECRETARY: The lady asked me who left, and who didn't leave. She's doing a scientific study. Should I tell her lies just because you don't like Germany?

And a final example: Theo, the president of the Mavropoulo commune, was talking to me one day about how many of the young people of the village had gone on to college or university. He said that some had, but that most had not. A man who overheard this statement objected, saying that large numbers of the "children of the village" had gone on to become "scientists," and so this was a village that had produced many educated people. That was a common assertion in many villages in Epirus: a marker of a commune's relative status was how many of its population had been highly educated (and therefore were not "peasants"). Theo told him to be quiet and then added: "The young lady here is collecting information to write a scientific book. What should I tell her? Lies?"

The point for most people in talking to me about numbers and how I should "read" them was to locate the συμφέροντα/*simferonda* (literally, "interests"), both mine and those of others. In practice, this meant identifying the motivation underlying the desire for "facts" or representing "facts" in one way rather than another. There could be any number of such motivations, depending on the individual or organization involved, but they were all related to one basic concept: self-interest. Sometimes, the "interests" were thought to be those of people regarded as powerful, and these kinds of interests had the authority to make their assertions about the world stick, both in how things seemed and in how things can be made to be. At other times, the "interests" were those of people regarded as individually powerless, but who collectively had the effect of "molding" the aggregated statistics, through their each reporting "self-interested" numbers as if they were "genuine facts." It was also accepted that such "entangled facts" could become "genuine facts" in practical terms, because political organizations often acted upon them as if they were "genuine facts," even if they were aware that they had been "molded." In any event, "interests" were assumed to be something everyone, and everything, has; "interests" are specific and they are personal; "interests" peel away the assertion of disinterested abstraction, of the apparently bland, decontextualized, factual objectivity of numbers, and of their anonymity; they make statistics personal. Each unit, each piece of raw data, as well as each aggregated number, contained these kinds of relations. That meant there would always be an imperfect fit between what the statistics asserted they represented (objective, separated-out, disinterested truth) and what they deliberately concealed (subjective, embedded, interests), a gap in which the relations that constituted them were located and would shine through, if you knew how to look for them.

That points to another kind of gap that generated a sense of the Epirot "context": in Epirus at least, it was obvious that official statistics have important (and self-imposed) limits—and that certain significant realms exist which go beyond these limits. As in the case of the tectonic and geomorphological data discussed in chapter 3, many things are rendered invisible by failing to be counted, and here the particularities of Epirus in relation to other places that I have been discussing in previous chapters become involved.

THE BALKAN AND OTHER SHADOWS

One of the most obvious elements missing from the numbers that concern me here is the same as what was missing from the geomorphological maps: any information going beyond the Greek-Albanian border into Albania. And the reasons for that are the same as well: although I collected most of the data after the reopening of the border, in the early to mid-1990s, I found it almost impossible to gather from Albania the kinds of data I collected from the Greek side or, more important, any information about the process of data creation and their current use in Albania. At the time, almost everyone, from border guards to people from Albania, convinced me that things were so "chaotic" in Albania that there would be little point in even trying. And since official statistics literally belong to states and give accounts only of state territories, the existence of the border and of Albania again become starkly visible through their absence in the Greek official statistics of the region.

At the same time, and as I have already discussed, Albania (as part of the Balkans) was entirely present in the way Epirus as a place was distinguished from others in Greece in sociohistorical accounts. That was reflected in conflicts over other kinds of numbers that did stretch beyond state boundaries: there were not only multiple maps showing different boundaries of this place, but also multiple statistical accounts of the people. This competition over numbers has continued into recent times, as Friedman notes for Macedonia (Friedman 1996), and as Kertzer and Arel note for the Balkans as a whole (Kertzer and Arel 2002b), though once again Epirus is rendered somewhat invisible in these accounts. An example used by Kertzer and Arel to demonstrate the problems the Balkans posed for statisticians was the efforts by European statistical experts to "sort out" the statistical accounting of people in Macedonia in 1994: the area stumped specialists who were trying to clarify things by separating them out and accounting for them in modernist terms. The experts were apparently "shocked by the level of political passion their very exercise reignited, and baffled by the sheer ethnographic complexity of the area. How is a Macedonian-speaking Muslim to be counted? As the experts discovered, two diametrically opposed views existed on the matter, and statistical realism was of little help to adjudicate the issue" (ibid.: 19).

Kertzer and Arel go on to suggest that this example demonstrates how "statistical realism" is something of a fantasy. Moreover, they suggest, the argument that the statistical accounts of peoples around the Balkans had been "fabricated" by political bias more than in other areas "largely misses the point, since it assumes, in the tradition of statistical realism, a correct and objective method of counting identities [exists], whose process is then spoiled by political elements" (ibid.: 22). Instead, Kertzer and Arel argue that the conflicts over how to count people and classify them in the Macedonian case is "not the exception but the *norm* of census politics, if perhaps a bit extreme" (ibid.: 23).

That conclusion was as obvious to most people I met in Epirus as it was to Kertzer and Arel. Past and current conflicts over how to classify people and places in their region made it entirely self-evident that the "norm" was for statistics to be politically inflected. This was not because there was a different "way of thinking" about numbers, counting, or accounts among Epirots, as in the Iqwaye case described by Wagner; rather, it was because of the sense that all accounts—statistical, cartographic, or any other kind—constituted assertions about the way things are that could be, and often were, contested. What such accounts meant, let alone how they were compiled, depended upon the embedded relationships people had with entities being accounted for.

An example of this from Epirus is the range of competing numbers that were floating around about how many "Northern Epirots" there had been in Albania before the border had reopened. The reopening had led to a widespread exodus of people from the Northern Epirot/Southern Albania region, and there was a concern, sometimes expressed in the more nationalist Greek newspapers, that the area was now being "Albanian-ized." One of the numbers cited in Greece of "Northern Epirots" in Albania before the border reopened was 400,000; it was based on a "guesstimate" of all Orthodox peoples in Albania. This particular number, the highest of all available estimates, was closely associated with Greek nationalist claims to Northern Epirus and existed as part of the muddy pool of "popularly known facts." The Albanian government regularly quoted the very different estimate of around 60,000, based mostly on peoples who spoke Greek as their first language. The U.S. government official estimate was in the region of 270,000.[9] Pettifer quotes several different figures: 35,000–40,000 estimated by the League of Nations in 1923, 20,000 by the Albanian government of the period, and 200,000 by Pettifer himself (Pettifer 1993: 181–82). This kind of variation made it obvious to most people that numbers about this place in particular were politically constituted and were used to assert something about the way things are from a particular perspective.

Moreover, the shadow of that Balkan "whereness," the way this place was always tensely interrelated with other places, could also be seen in regular changes in how the official Greek statistics were compiled and published. For example, the languages in which they were written altered across the years, as did the units of measurement; many of the commune names changed, according to this or that government's decision to change any "non-Greek"-sounding names; and in many records, the person filling in the numbers made notes in the margins or added extra columns to account for things that the formal classifications did not distinguish. For example, notes were often made about the time of year that an audit of animals was carried out: timing deeply affected how many sheep and goats would be recorded for a commune, because of the widespread habit in Epirus of moving animals seasonally from one place to another. In other words, clerks in offices often attempted to adjust formal classifications to better suit the Epirot context, at least for the numbers held in the offices of local authorities, even though such notes in the margins did not appear in the nationally published results. As I had been taught by people around the Kasidiaris and elsewhere how to "read" the numbers, those traces became increasingly obvious to me.

Beyond the direct issue of the Balkans, there were other ways in which repeated shadows and echoes of other places, other times, and other people left traces in the numbers, relating the numbers to the place itself. The late Ottoman period was still present, as much in the form of some of the numbers as in people's social memories, in the place itself, and in the way relations between places were organized *now*, as well as "then."[10] In that sense, while I agree with Collard's suggestion that certain moments in northern Greece's history were marked as significant while others were not (Collard 1989), this selective marking was also visible on the surfaces of the place itself: the Ottoman period, the Second World War, and the civil war had all left their marks (and I am not speaking here of deliberately built monuments), which were intermingling with one another and contributing to experiences of the shifts of focus around this place.

In addition, there were marks left both in the numbers and the place by the Marshall Plan, the military junta, Greece's entry into the European Union, and the breakup of communist Europe leading to the reopening of the Greek-Albanian border, all of which I will go on to discuss in the next two chapters. They also intermingled. These marks carried memories of different kinds of comings and goings as well, both within the region and far beyond it—involving traveling to Constantinople, Egypt, Germany, the United States, Athens, Albania, and Romania, all manner of places—and traveling back, and then away again. In that sense, Collard's suggestion that this type of social memory had set up spatial and temporal "dichotomies" between the villages in Evritania that she studied and other times and places (Collard 1989: 99–100) was not quite apt for Epirus. There were differences, and crucial spatial and temporal separations between places (e.g., city and village, Athens and Epirus), but not dichotomies. In fact, that is why the differences and separations mattered: they were here, leaving their marks and intermingling, as well as being somewhere else or having occurred in another time—or, indeed, at another scale. The "marginality" of Epirus could exist only as a relation; it could not be produced by a dichotomy. The events that led to the Grammos's being permanently pockmarked because of the dropping of napalm on ELAS forces at the end of the civil war (Glenny 1993: 544)—which also led people from Katarraktis (Eastern Kasidiaris) to flee to socialist countries, and were further associated with subsequent strong U.S. involvement in the restructuring of cultivation and pastoralism in

Epirus via the Marshall Plan—operated at a different scale from the everyday lives of Kasidiaris peoples, but they were also right there, intermingling with other things, and left their marks on the numbers and the place to prove it.

Also right there were other scales as well, those of people's relations with one another and with various places, many of which were too "noisy" for official statistics to mark at all. That can be seen to some extent within the numbers in the details—which are endless, and can turn and twist back on themselves infinitely, can contradict and confirm, can be read and interpreted in myriad ways. That made them useful to many people, for the numbers reflected back to them what they already knew; but equally, that very flexibility made them incapable of speaking for themselves as "pure" statistics; ultimately, they simply highlighted the differences in people's viewpoints, experiences, and interests. Everyone contributed to these collective and contested stories about Epirus and the Kasidiaris—to the making of them (which involved practical experiences as well as accounts), to the telling of them, and to the interpretation of their meanings—everyone, from the civil servants in Ioannina, to goatherds in the Zagori, to emigrants and immigrants, and even to European policy makers. They all participated in and understood the stories in their own ways; and in retelling fragments of these makings and understandings in chapter 6, I also participate. The stories, combined with various experiences, provided origins, causes for how things were, justifications for the actions people took and the attitudes people held, and they proved capable of absorbing any event, shift, or transformation within themselves. In that process, change, even apparently radical change, was sometimes reduced to changes in content but no change in *form*. And that was connected to the apparently unchanging character of the relations between and within things, which brings me on to the next topic.

INDIFFERENCE

There was one final recurring element in how some people around Epirus (and particularly many in Lower Pogoni in this study) explicitly regarded statistical accounts as only ever partial and always embedded in other things: the sense of neglect and indifference that I have also explored at some length. As Scott (1998) notes, states and other political institutions (such as the European Union) take special care to classify and account for things that matter to them, and—either deliberately or through indifference—render invisible other things that are not defined as beneficial to the political entity (Herzfeld 1992). In the case of the Greek state, there was a steadfast insistence that the vast majority of the population (except in Thrace) has been homogenously Greek, until very recent years (Danforth 1995; Herzfeld 1997; Karakasidou 1997; Hirschon 2003). That rendered the question of the differences between peoples in Epirus as one of ambiguity within unambiguous Greekness (as it were), and in the case of *Gréki*, it resulted in no named difference at all. In the numbers, such differences did not appear; there were no accounts of "minorities," because, officially, the Greek state did not consider that Epirus contained any minorities.

Furthermore, in terms of land (as opposed to territory) and activities relating to the land, the official statistics tended to focus, above all, on productivity, both for tax purposes and also to identify economic conditions in different areas and develop policies about them. On that level, too, most of Epirus was relatively undistinguished: the mountainous areas were becoming less and less "productive," and during the last decades policies aimed at increasing the productivity of the land focused thoroughly on the plains, a matter I will go on to discuss in more detail in chapter 6. Once again, that rendered the Western Kasidiaris area, which has few plains (in official statistical terms, none at all), uninteresting, not a place where a great deal of investment in productivity of the land should be focused. Moreover, in more recent years, during which the European Union has become more actively involved, efforts to develop productivity in mountainous areas have focused on tourism and thus on "natural and cultural heritage"; in this, the Western Kasidiaris area (along with the borderland areas of Thesprotia) has once again received much less attention than have areas such as the Zagori.

People around the Western Kasidiaris area were well aware of all of this, and it contributed, among many other things, to their sense of repeated neglect: different each time, but the same as well. In terms of counting, many concluded that neither they nor their area counted for much. Therefore, the counting—the census, land use statistics, the animal numbers, the cultivation, and so on—that was carried out for such neglected areas would probably be done in a much less careful manner than the counting in other places. Why bother to "accurately" count pensioners, abandoned fields, or grazing lands that were no longer used for grazing? People understood the reasons why counting happened, and that the classifications rendered them and this place of little account.

Counting the Interweaving of People, Places, and Activities

In many anthropological analyses of the effects of official statistics, the focus is on people, rather than the many other things that are counted. In particular, many studies focus on processes of identity formation, on the way statistics classify people as being different from each other in some statistically established way. This includes Bernard Cohn's now classic historical study of the impact of the census instituted by the British in India, which classified people into what were increasingly regarded as objective castes (Cohn 1990), and a variety of studies that pursued this topic, including the collection edited by Barrier (1981) and Appadurai's revision of Cohn's study (Appadurai 1996c). In a different way, anthropologists working in politically highly tense or violent areas have occasionally explored the "politics of numbers," examining how instability and violence come to be represented through statistics as "ordinarily abnormal" for such areas (Ferme 1998), or assessing statistics as one of many sites of dispute between factions (e.g., van der Veer 1997; Das 1985; Verdery 1999). These latter studies seem to particularly focus on "body counts" after violent encounters: an insistence on the acknowledgment, often years after the fact, of who was killed, by whom, and how many were killed; the sheer number of bodies has often been crucial to this process.[11]

All these studies focus on what is rendered visible and objectified by statistics, how they create the realities they purport to merely illustrate numerically, and how this process may hide an underlying complexity that is inevitably part of life. In my approach, that constitutes only part of the story, albeit an important part. First, I give accounts of places and activities as much importance as accounts of people in the construction of how things seem through statistics, and consider how accounts of people and places interweave. But more important, and following Poovey's approach in this respect, I also focus on how such constructions in themselves always interweave different, nonstatistical, scales and domains in the construction of the statistics themselves. So the emphasis is not, as in Cohn's work, on the "objectification" of peoples' identities that occurs in the process of collecting, classifying, and publishing data; nor is it, as in Appadurai's study, an attempt to draw out how the apparently bland and bureaucratic work of collecting statistics has an effect on cultural imagination—how, in other words, statistics make their categories and classifications "real" in people's minds. My focus is more on the process of the relations generated within statistics and between statistics and other things, and not only the outcomes of such relations.

To be sure, outcomes are an important part of that: one particularly significant one in this case was the way the statistics seem both to reveal and to constitute the marginality of Epirus and the peoples associated with it. After having been through reams and reams of numbers, as well as having been taught how to "read" them by the dozens of people I met in the course of collecting them, I gained a sense that there was something strongly mythical about them: out of the endless details, there emerged repetitious patterns, transformations of the same things, again and again, achieved through the abstractions of number and the continual comparison of one example of a classification or time period as against another example of a classification or time period. Read in their own terms, these repetitions are circular and self-contained: the truths will always repeat themselves and will always relate to what statistics can show, defined by the criteria used to compare the numbers. And one repetitious message that was continually produced and reproduced across all these numbers, building up an apparently unassailable and timeless truth revealed by its continual telling and retelling, was that Epirus as a region, Pogoni County in particular, was and would continue to be marginal. Within the domain of the statistics themselves, which focused upon "the state of things" mostly in terms defined economically (in this case, the productivity of places) and demographically (in this case, the numbers and location of people), there was no other conclusion that could be reached, despite the variations between periods and places within Epirus. Yet even this outcome turns out to be as much one of omission (what the statistics leave out or are indifferent about) as it is of inclusion, so it is only part of the story.

CHAPTER 6

Embodied Recounting

THE WAY IN WHICH OFFICIAL STATISTICS about peoples, places, and activities became continually entangled with other things involved embodied experiences as well as accounting for things, both for the people with whom I spent time and for myself. After a few months of speaking with people about these numbers, I began to sense the traces of them in my surroundings: abandoned fields related to certain kinds of numbers in the statistics, to certain government policies, to certain activities of the people involved, and more. I began to regard the numbers as shorthand for all of that; they reminded me of the entanglements that people had described to me, about how things were made to seem and how they were made to be, and which I began to experience in walking around the area. This was not because the numbers in their own terms encompassed what could be known about abandoned fields; rather, as Munro describes for company accounts (Munro 2001), it was as much because of what they left out and could not say, and that included embodied relationships. Abandoned fields do not constitute a category in Greek statistical accounts of "basic categories of land use," but I learned to find them there anyway, in the same way the civil servants in Ioannina compiling or dealing with the statistics and the people living near those fields could find them there.

This embodied element of the statistics' entanglements became particularly evident to me in the two village territory surveys I carried out, during which Geoff King and I systematically walked through the entire territories of the villages of Ktismata (Western Kasidiaris) and Katarraktis (Eastern Kasidiaris), marking what we saw on blueprints of these territories (maps 7 and 8), and which I will discuss in more detail at the end of this chapter. By then, I had already walked around village territories with forest guards, shepherds, and people from villages, and I had learned something of what I should be looking for from the way people talked about these places.

In one sense, this process of "learning to see" was somewhat like Keith Basso's description of learning how to see the Apache landscape in the way the Apaches did so through their stories about particular places (Basso 1996). However, there was also a significant difference: in Epirus, the stories were not only about Epirot peoples and their past embodied relations with the place; they were also about many other peoples' and institutions' relations with the place, which also contributed a great deal to making the place what it seemed and what it was. The marks of their involvement, and Epirots' entanglements with their involvement, were embodied both in the numbers and in the place: for example, where asphalt roads were built and where they were not built during different periods; the land improvement programs on the plains but their absence elsewhere; the border and the differing ways it was controlled over the years; the pockmarked Grammos mountain, which had been bombed during the civil war; the houses that were empty most of the year in some of the mountainous villages; the overgrowth and reforestation of the mountains; the closed schools; and, more recently, the scatter of blue signs with telltale circles of yellow stars posted all over the place, indicating the existence of an EU-funded development project of one kind or another (fig. 12). The numbers themselves were never alone, nor were they merely abstract. As tools of state, they were powerful; how they classified a place or failed to classify it, how they counted people, how they marked some things as important and others as unimportant left embodied traces in the place, as well as encompassing impressions.

This chapter focuses on just a few of these entanglements. As with the other accounts I have explored in previous chapters, I will occasionally provide accounts of the statistics in their own terms, particularly in the appendix: since the language and narratives of statistics involve comparative tables of numbers, they appear as such there.[1] Once again, their appearance does not mean I take them as constituting self-evident and self-contained accounts, let alone accounts that are somehow more "objective" than other kinds of accounts (Porter 1995); it is the interrelations between different kinds of accounts, interrelations that are also embedded within the different accounts, that interest me.

There is an additional point here, which also involves embodiment (the physical experience of number, as it were). I compiled literally hundreds of tables and charts from a variety of sources, so I became painfully aware of the arduous work that goes into producing statistical abstractions, and how that involved leaving a (nonempty) gap in which all the talk that happened while I was collecting the data was placed. Moreover, to work within the paradigm of statistics is axiomatically to work with bulk and, even worse as far as I was concerned, with bulky numbers: every shift of statistical scale required recompilation of the "raw data," producing new tables and new calculations. As a result, the sense of statistics as both a technique and a technology that constitute very particular kinds of stories about the world became starkly and mind-numbingly clear. In that sense, the actual process involved in providing the statistical stories constituted another embodied experience of dwelling, in Ingold's terms (Ingold

1995), and one that incidentally gave me a direct sense of how the idea of a Cartesian mind-body split is not a particularly convincing concept.

Despite the presentation of some statistical tables in the appendix, the task of this chapter is different from the task of compiling official statistics and trying to understand what they "reveal" about underlying or encompassing patterns of what exists in the world. Rather, I attempt to draw out the interrelations that people around the Kasidiaris and elsewhere in Epirus understood as entangling the statistical stories with the place and with themselves—somewhat as Chernobyl was thought to have become entangled with changes in the Epirot climate, as discussed in chapter 3. The official statistics not only reflected or partially represented what happened; they were a part of what happened. I will explore that in three ways here: through the way the numbers classified things, the way the numbers changed along with changes in political and economic conditions, and the way they made things appear and disappear in the place.

Classifying Places

That Epirus was classified in a particular way through official statistics is something I have discussed in chapter 3, so I will not revisit that here in any detail. Overall, Epirus is represented as much more mountainous, more rural, and more wet and cold than the rest of Greece. People in Epirus viewed that general representation as being both true and false: true, in that Epirus as a whole, when compared with other places, was officially treated by both Athens and Brussels as if it were a remote backwater, which meant that in certain respects that is exactly what it was; and false, in that few of the people associated with the place actually lived in the way imagined by such classifications. Most people lived in cities most of the time, and of those who did not, the majority lived on the plains. Of those who lived in the mountains, the majority were pensioners, so they did not engage a great deal with this mountainous area. Most Epirots traveled by road, either by bus or by car, and since the main trunk routes go through plains, any widespread experience of the mountains was relatively limited for those who no longer used the land for large-scale pastoral activities. And most who visited the remoter mountain villages did so in the summer months, so they did not experience nearly as much of the inclement weather as was implied. Moreover, the interrelations people experienced between Epirus and other places were rendered invisible, since comparative data depend on the highlighting of differences between one place and another, not the relations between them (which are supposed to emerge through comparison of statistical accounts).

In sum, the particular focus of the regional figures (tables 1–5) generated one perspective with which Epirots regularly had to negotiate: an overall image of their place that reflected something most considered to be true about the place in comparison to other places and in the terms highlighted by the numbers, but something untrue in terms of what it implied about the people. In any case, that classification had nothing at all to say about the Greek-Albanian border, which was an obvious absence to anyone living near it. These kinds of generalizing classifications were not often challenged in terms of the numbers; rather, what was contested was how to read the numbers, the conclusions to be drawn from the story they told.

Other kinds of classifications within the statistical accounts were challenged more directly. One of the most heated of these was the classification of a place as "forested." This was a matter of continual controversy while I was in Epirus, because areas defined as forested could not be cleared of vegetation without the permission of the Forestry Commission, and this permission was rarely given.[2] On numerous occasions, I heard people protesting that the definition of a place as "forested" was neither reasonable nor congruent with any commonsense understanding of what constituted a forest. The implication was that the official definition of "Forest" had been guided by particularistic interests or deliberate indifference more than by any objective application of knowledge about trees or their use; but it was equally accepted that challenges to the official definitions were *also* guided by particular interests or deliberate indifference: there was no such thing as an objective definition of forest in this context.

Most of the complaints about this issue were closely related to an assertion that the classification of certain areas as forested had the effect of reinforcing the "land degradation" of the area—that is, its abandonment and the subsequent overgrowth of fields and grazing lands. When such overgrowth was classified as "Forest," it meant that anyone who wished to clear the land to use it again for cultivation or grazing would often be prevented by the Forestry Commission from doing so. For example, the president of Argyrohori complained that a planned improvement of the commune's small area of plain was being delayed because the Forestry Commission had defined as "Forest" the overgrowth of what he saw as abandoned fields, so this overgrowth could not be cleared. He pointed down to the plain from the veranda of the *kafeneio*, which was clearly overgrown with prickly oak scrub bushes, and said with disgust, "Does that look like a forest to you? How are we supposed to make a living here if people keep stopping us from being able to?" He went on to complain that when the Greek-Albanian border had been closed after the war, the extent of the commune's part of the plain had been reduced from 500 stremmata (approximately 125 acres) to 400 (approximately 100 acres).

His point was that the way things worked out in terms of the state's involvement in classifying this place never seemed to have his commune's interests in mind.

On another occasion, the postman at Doliana asked me if he could study some aerial photographs I had of the area from World War II, so he could prove that a certain area of land had been cultivated in the past, to support his argument with the Forestry Commission about the commission's decision not to let him cut down any trees there. His view was that if the fields had been cultivated at some time, they could not possibly constitute forest now, and the Forestry Commission would have to agree with him that the "ligneous plants" on his land were not trees that constituted a forest; rather, they were trees on disused fields. For him, a forest was either a place that had been forested for centuries, or one that had been deliberately turned into a forest by someone's systematically planting trees. Neither of those criteria applied in his case.

On a third occasion, a large fire broke out in the summer of 1997 in the hills to the east of the Doliana Plain around the village of Negrades (map 4); it lasted for three days. At its height, the smoke was so thick that it blocked out the sun in many places. I had several conversations about it with people in Doliana, where I was living at the time. The first was with two people in their twenties, Mitsios and Vasso, on the evening the fire started; we saw the flames lighting up the night sky as we were driving back from a new bar that had opened up next to a water mill by the Kalamas River on the plain. Mitsios commented that the fire had almost certainly been started by shepherds to clear hillside areas so as to develop the grazing land there. The following morning, while people were discussing a huge fire in the Thessaloniki area that was front-page news that day (July 7, 1997), the fire around Negrades also came up in the conversation, and everyone agreed that they believed it was set deliberately. Vasso's father, Spiros (who ran the *kafeneio* in Doliana above which I was living), said that this was a "good fire"; the only pity was that the national road had acted as a firebreak and cut access to the other side, so the job had not been completed. The following day, a Doliana resident whom I was driving to Ioannina also brought up the topic of the fire and commented that it must have been set deliberately. He did not see anything wrong in that but felt it was a little irresponsible to go setting fires in the middle of a heat wave, as it could be dangerous.

All these comments were related to the widespread view that the setting of fires in overgrown areas was a sensible practice for pastoralists, as it generated good grazing land, and that the Forestry Commission's attitude, that what was burned constituted "Forest" and its burning was therefore an illegal practice, was either nonsensical bureaucracy or an unjust assertion of somebody else's interests at their expense. This was a continual topic of conversation in my time in Epirus, as was the fact that people were regularly fined for chopping down trees in mature forests without licenses to do so.

As I discovered during attempts to gather data about land use, there was plenty of scope for contesting official assertions of what constituted a forest. This is worth elaborating a little. Table 1 shows two types of forest: "commercial" and "noncommercial." In terms of the numbers themselves, the sum of the percentages of all types of land in the rows of this table (agricultural, grazing land, and both types of forest) should come to 100 percent or less, because land areas are supposed to fall into only one "basic category of land use." In fact, in each case, the totals add up to more than 100 percent. The reason is that the Statistical Service of Greece provided the figures for "commercial use" forest, whereas the Forestry Commission provided the figures for "noncommercial use" forest, and the two institutions used different definitions of "Forest." The Forestry Commission had included as "Forest" some areas that were listed by the Greek Statistical Service either as "Agricultural Land" or as "Grazing Land." As I spoke with people at the Forestry Commission and the Department of Agriculture, and with village commune staff (who were often involved in deciding whether a place counted as forested or not), any idea that a "Forest" was a self-evident type of place or object rapidly disappeared.

Pursuing this issue led me back to the issue of abandoned land; it turned out that officials used not only "Forest" but other classifications of "land use" in accounting for what most people in the area understood to be abandoned land. For example, both civil servants at the Department of Agriculture and village commune secretaries explained that the "Agricultural Land" category includes both fallow and cultivated land; strictly speaking, land that has been fallow for more than five years should be removed from the category and placed instead in the "Grazing Land" category; in practice, this often failed to be done. One of the reasons for that, other than administrative inertia, was that this constituted the first step toward the land's possibly being reclassified as "Forest" by the Forestry Commission. The "Grazing Land" category includes all land that contains wild flora and is not cultivated, fallow, or forested; but if it is left for too long, the "ligneous plants" can come to look a lot like trees to the Forestry Commission. Village secretaries, who were responsible for making the returns, explained that this "Grazing Land" label bears no relation to whether or not the land is actually used for grazing, nor whether it could be so used. As I wandered around village territories with commune secretaries or forest guards, it was obvious that a high proportion of land classified as grazing land in the official records was either no longer used for grazing and/or was so overgrown with thorny underbrush that it would be extremely difficult to use it for that purpose even if people wanted to, unless the area was cleared or burned off first.

In effect, this meant that large portions of what most people familiar with the area considered to be abandoned land was recorded as "Grazing Land" or as "Forested Land," depending on the proportion of "ligneous plants" it contained, there being no category for "abandoned land." The Forestry Commission, which has jurisdiction only over land defined as "Forest," had been carrying out its own surveys and as a result was defining quite a few areas as "noncommercial use" forest, whereas the same areas appeared as either "Grazing Land" or even "Agricultural Land" in the Statistical Service records.

The result of this ambiguity and the formal nonexistence of abandoned land contributed considerably to the numerous disputes I mentioned above. In recent years, the fires were regularly blamed on illegal immigrants from Albania who, in making their way through forests and depopulated areas, were accused of being less than careful with their campfires and cigarettes. Vasso, on reading one such report in a local newspaper, threw the newspaper down in disgust and said, "It says here that the Albanians are setting all the fires. Oh yes! Of course! Before the Albanians came, there were no fires here at all, right?" Vasso did not have much time for people from Albania, but she felt this kind of assertion was too extreme a version of blaming the Other. Every summer, both national and local newspapers were full of stories of fires that were reported to have been deliberately set all over Greece (by Greeks); the intention, apparently, was most often to have the official classification of the land as forest changed so that it could be used either for grazing or for housing development. Attica, the mainland region that includes Athens, suffered particularly from deliberate fires set for the latter purpose; and as that area has a great deal of pine forest, which burns extremely rapidly, such fires could easily get completely out of control.

Forestry Commission officials in Ioannina were well aware of the "convenient" fires in their region, which were most often set to generate useful grazing land rather than to force the area to be reclassified as residential, but were somewhat philosophical about the fires. One such official working in the Forestry Commission in Ioannina shrugged and said, "Well, what can you do? I go to the villages, and I talk to the people, but there's not a lot you can do." One of the things that officials *did* do was to put up notices after a fire, announcing restrictions on use of the land for a few years. One such notice I saw in 1994 was posted in a *kafeneio* of the village of Limni (Upper Pogoni), in part of an area that is still used fairly intensively for pastoralism. The notice said that as there had been a fire in a forest on Limni's land on August 11, 1992, and since "it is the law to protect the forests," the grazing of the following animals for the following amount of time was forbidden on the area that had been burned: goats for ten years, large animals for seven years, and sheep for five years.

The problem, the forestry official went on, was that the shepherds setting fires did not care about the cumulative effects of their actions; if everyone were allowed to go setting fires, there would be no forest left at all anymore. It was his job, as a forestry official, to try to balance the self-interested attitudes of shepherds with the interests of the state in protecting the forest. Similarly, an environmentalist campaigner I met in Ioannina in 1994 blamed the fires on people who had no interest in the environment and a great deal of interest in their own profit. He believed that all the statistical accounts about the land in the region were molded by interests, and that none of these interests coincided with what he considered to be "genuine care" about the environment by anybody in Epirus (i.e., his own interests).

This is just one example of how such data become implicated in people's lives and in altering the shape of the place: many were involved in collecting and submitting the information in the form of numbers (every village commune had a secretary for the purpose); some paticipated in attempts to have areas reclassified as one thing rather than another; most had opinions about the interests dictating the data's appearance in one way rather than another (e.g., the suspicion that it is in the interests of the Forestry Commission to define somewhere as "Forest"; that it is in the interests of pastoralists to have land reclassified as grazing land; or that civil servants are "lazy" and don't bother to reclassify land whose use has changed). These figures were embroiled in a continual process of interaction, interpretation, presentation and representation, agreements and disagreements, negotiations and negations. The way in which these matters were discussed made it clear that most people felt the shape and look of the place itself could shift according to these classifications, or to suit such classifications: the entanglement of how things seemed and how things were was obvious to people in that respect.

CLASSIFYING PEOPLE

If the general regional data show traces of "interests" and relations, such traces also repeatedly glimmer in the data on populations. Tables 6 through 10 provide a numerical account of the range of ways people have been officially located as living within Epirus. It is a story that involves defined fixed territories and the numerical accounts made of their ("legitimate") inhabitants over time. The tables provide accounts of people only through their presence or absence as numbers, and for many in this area, such numbers implied the success or failure of a place, literally through its popularity. That was of considerable concern around the Kasidiaris: comments about the depopulation of a village as an indicator of its "failure" were the most common observations I encountered in conversations about people's relations with the place during fieldwork. For the most recent figures, drops in population, and the ways the numbers were negotiated to show or conceal this, were key issues. For the older figures, the events of the past, particularly the way "political forces" intervened in this place, were more focal. In both cases, the way the numbers rendered invisible people's different ways of moving, of coming and going, was a central element in the sense that the classifications had been made with others in mind.

As I noted in chapter 5, from the beginning of fieldwork I was told repeatedly that demographic statistics had embedded within them a range of different understandings of the presence or absence of people in a place. One conversation I had about this when I first contacted Spiros, the president of Katarraktis, for some details about the village, is an example of what the issue involved:

SPIROS: You know of course that the census doesn't match the residents who actually live here all year.

SARAH: I've heard that. In what way doesn't it match?

SPIROS: In Katarraktis, for example, the census says the village has 143 residents. In fact, the number of permanent residents is 60.

Spiros grinned broadly, and added, "That's how things work here," meaning that they did not work as the official rules intended. Since Spiros saw me as a researcher, it was important for him to make clear that the numbers were not exactly what they appeared to be, just in case I made the mistake of thinking that they were. However, this meant only that the census was "wrong" in terms of the rules of the census itself. In other ways, it reflected an entirely reasonable number for Spiros, as it did for many other people: it constituted the number of people who were willing to come back to the village for census day to be counted, combined with the people who lived in the village all year long. And that was a reasonable account of how many people took a serious interest in the village.

The practice of busing in people for census day was a very common one in many parts of Epirus. Village presidents would often pay for coaches to come from Ioannina and Athens, and would use village cultural associations located in various cities to persuade members to make the trip. This had a practical purpose, in that the amount of public money provided by the state to maintain villages and towns was dependent upon the official population size; but many also saw the busing in of ex-residents both as an entirely reasonable practice and as a moral issue. Kostas, the president of Ktismata whom I mentioned in chapter 3, commented that the "real" population of the village was more than 1,000, even though the 1991 census recorded 235, and the number of year-round residents (after Kostas had calculated it for me in 1993) turned out to be 175: "Those 235 residents are the ones who have been written in the census. The villagers living in Athens, Germany, and so on, they haven't been included in the census. The real figure is over 1,000." There were several interpretations of Kostas's comments within the village, including the assertion that it was in his interests to have a high population over which he presided: a high population was an indication of his success as a president (apart from ensuring higher annual funding for Ktismata from the government). But most also agreed that where people happened to be living at the moment did not really determine whether they were Ktismata villagers. The past and present experience of all kinds of coming and going for the people of this place, as discussed in chapter 2, meant that the relationship between residence at any given time and being "from" somewhere was not straightforward. Kostas was drawing upon that to assert that this should be taken into account in the interpretation of the numbers, irrespective of the fact that one purpose of the national census was to locate citizens within fixed territories, to know where they were. That might be in the state's interests; it was not, to Kostas, in the interests of the Ktismata commune; so he rejected the official way of counting people.

The only official recognition of people's habit of having at least two "locations" (as opposed to a recognition of their movements to and fro) is that since 1940, both the "actual" (census) and "legal" (registered) populations have been listed in official statistical tables. People living in cities often chose to be registered in the village as a sign of their support for the village, so as to have a right to vote there (until recently, voting was compulsory in Greece) and—equally important for many—so that they would have a right to be buried there. This was mentioned explicitly by many commune secretaries or presidents when I asked how many deaths the commune had experienced in the previous ten years (which was one of my standard questions when I first met commune representatives and asked for some information about the commune). One example comes from Koukli, a village in the foothills of Eastern Kasidiaris:

SARAH: And how many deaths have there been in the commune over the last ten years?
PRESIDENT: (picking a number out of the air)
A hundred and fifty.
SECRETARY: A lot of deaths. We have an average of 12–13 deaths a year, lately. Let me look from 1983 [goes

SARAH: through records]. The average over the last ten years is 11–12 deaths per year. But you should know not all of those deaths are permanent residents. They're brought from Athens.

SARAH: From Athens? Oh, you mean people from Koukli who have died in Athens?

SECRETARY: Yes, and some who died elsewhere as well.

SARAH: About what proportion are brought from elsewhere?

SECRETARY: Half and half—about half and half.

PRESIDENT: Around about.

SARAH: They want to . . .

SECRETARY: Yes, they want to be buried here. They bring them from Athens to be buried here.

Movement from one place to another therefore also frequently occurred at death; being registered in a place was one means of asserting a certain kind of being from somewhere, whether or not you were there most of the time in physical terms.

In sum, both census and registered figures had been negotiated in a range of ways, and the people involved tried to find some "reasonable" number that met the formal requirements, but that also met their own interests and moral sensibilities. The final number on any given occasion would constitute the outcome of that negotiation, and therefore left a trace of the entanglement of divergent ways of counting and reasons to count.

In discussing Katarraktis, Spiros also added that in the summer, there was an average of two hundred visitors from Ioannina, Athens, and other European cities to Katarraktis, and that he was not counting the transhumant pastoralists who spent the winter months just across the Kalamas gorge by the village. That was because the area where they stayed, called Melissi, which consisted of a collection of temporary huts surrounded by good grazing land, was part of a neighboring commune's territory (Zitsa). He would not have counted them anyway, he said, even if they had been on Katarraktis territory, because in his view, transhumants should be counted in their summer grazing areas, which was their "home." The logic of this was that summer grazing areas were usually high up in the mountains where nobody else lived at any time of the year, so it was "their" place. This was a common rationale about transhumant pastoralists in Epirus (indeed, it is one that Campbell [1964)]and Wace and Thompson [1972] repeat). However, summer grazing areas were not always taken to be where transhumant pastoralists should be counted. For example, Eleftherios Potsis—the commune secretary at Mavronoros, which is on the slopes of Eastern Kasidiaris—commented that he had not included in his calculations of the village's resident population transhumant peoples who visited his village territories annually during the summer, because these peoples had officially registered in their winter homes in the southern coastlands of Thesprotia (they did so to achieve grazing rights there); anyway, he did not regard them as being "villagers," and he did not think they regarded themselves that way either.

In short, there was little consistency across the region about where transhumant peoples should be counted. The one thing that remained the same was the sense that transhumant pastoralists were different from people who were not transhumant pastoralists, and therefore they did not count in the same way as others; if there was a place associated with them where nobody else lived, then it was "their" place; otherwise, it was not "their" place. In the Mavronoros case, the transhumant pastoralists shared their grazing areas with others both winter and summer, so the Mavronoros commune secretary simply fell back on the formal classification: they were registered in their winter grounds, so they "belonged" there in statistical terms. Since the Greek census makes no mention of such distinctions between Greeks, the only way people could read them into the official numbers was to point to where they had been included and where they had been excluded (the number was either smaller or larger than it would otherwise be).

As important, since the census was designed to record where people are at a given time, it was entirely incapable of rendering visible different kinds of moving—seasonal, long-term migrations, summer visits, or whatever else—which, as I have already discussed at some length, were continually used as important forms of distinction between people and places in Epirus. The invisibility of different kinds of ongoing movement in the numbers generates an impression that being in a place is the starting point, and any "movement" in the figures (that is, a change in the numbers) axiomatically appears as "change." In contrast, many people around Epirus interpreted shifts in numbers from one period to the next as mostly to do with "molding" practices combined with other things; and even when people did feel the figures reflected a change in the location of people, this was usually seen as a change in the way people moved. In short, the numbers were not "woven tight like a fabric with neither rips nor darned patches," as de Certeau put it (de Certeau 1988: frontispiece), nor did they appear that way to people around the Kasidiaris.

Moreover, in all this counting and not counting in villages, and all this traveling to be counted, there is the matter of cities, where most people lived for most of the year. The mayor of Ioannina, and even the mayor of Athens, had gone on public record complaining that their cities were underfunded because significant portions of their populations habitually

decamped on census day and were counted in the villages. Nobody decamped from villages to be counted in cities. While the financial impact
on cities was what concerned these mayors most, this habit of moving for
the census also traced the kinds of relationships people understood between cities and villages: cities and villages were different, but not separated. People's relationships with cities were inflected by their relationships with villages and other places; how people "belonged" in cities (and
most did feel they belonged in them, in one way or another, whether or
not that included a sense of alienation) was interwoven with their sense
of also being from somewhere else. There were people in Ioannina who
considered themselves to be solely "Ioannina people," who did not feel
they were from somewhere else as well, but they were considerably out-
numbered by those who did feel that way.[3] In that respect, most of the
residents of Seismoplikta (the Ioannina suburb where I rented a flat) who
maintained regular contacts with the village of Krapsi, and considered
themselves to be "from" Krapsi as well as belonging in Ioannina (which
affected the way they belonged in Ioannina), were more representative of
the Ioannina population than those who considered themselves to be
solely "Ioannina people."[4]

Given all these issues, the various census and population figures illustrated in tables 6 through 10 show a variety of different kinds of location
practices, as it were, none of which can really capture differing kinds of
moving or the way being in a place, being from a place, or belonging
somewhere was understood by many of the people I met. People's acceptance or rejection of the numbers themselves was always blended in with
memories of events, with ideas about interests and/or indifference, and
thus with the assumption that all these numbers were the outcome of
endless political negotiations or disputes—whether in terms of the molding of the numbers themselves, or in terms of events that led to physical
shifts in the movements of people.

Incidentally, what the numbers failed to demonstrate for any of the
people I spoke with was a sense of a "mass population" in Poovey's terms
(Poovey 1995), or an "imagined community" in Anderson's terms (Anderson 1983). The idea of "a society" as an aggregated abstraction of
something that is internally diverse, but that adds up to a whole greater
than the sum of its parts, did not sit well with the notion that everyone,
as well as every institution, engages in pursuing particularistic interests in
producing numbers. Numbers would always already reflect someone's or
some institution's interests and therefore would exclude others. Nor does
the idea of an imagined "greater whole" sit well with the entanglement
of the Balkans, especially the continually contested boundaries marking
where one nation begins and another ends. In short, things were too ambiguous and too particularistic to allow some abstract greater whole to

emerge from the numbers; rather, there were many different wholes, which were generated in the same way every time. What was taken to be homogenously "Greek" was the way in which the numbers were constructed, not what the numbers themselves "revealed" about a mass Greek population.

The Political Economy of Numbers: Moving Events, 1920s–1990s

That brings me to the issue of shifts in differing ways of counting—to the political economy of counting, as it were. The period for which I managed to find at least some census figures for the Kasidiaris area, from the 1920s to the 1990s, was marked by a series of political and economic shifts, which also changed the way the numbers were collected. In terms used by people around the Kasidiaris, the "interests" changed, so the numbers changed as well—changes that were often accompanied by physical shifts in borders and boundaries, in how people moved around, and in the shape and look of places themselves.

From numerous conversations with people, six events emerged as having combined numerical and physical shifts of this sort in the 1920s–1990s period, and they can be briefly summarized as follows. The 1920s and early 1930s constituted the early years of the introduction of the Greek-Albanian border, involved a major exchange of populations between Greece and Turkey (as mentioned in chapter 2), and also saw a transition between Ottoman ways of doing statecraft and those of the Greek state. The late 1930s to the late 1940s were the period of the Second World War, the Greek civil war, and the Albanian communist revolution, during which the Greek-Albanian border was closed and the Cold War began.

In the late 1940s, 1950s, and early 1960s came a series of attempts to standardize, mechanize, and thus "modernize" both bureaucratic activity and productive activity; during these years the Greek government was highly influenced by Western Europe and the United States. A variety of international aid programs and policy interventions were implemented in this period, particularly the Marshall Plan, which was set up to "assist" some postwar countries, including Greece.[5] Commentaries from most people around the Kasidiaris about international interventions mostly involved statements about the self-interested behavior of the "Great Powers" (in this case, particularly the United Kingdom and the United States), and focused on these powers' involvement in the Greek civil war. This is perhaps unsurprising, as the Truman Doctrine, declared in March 1947, pledged support for "free peoples" in their fight against "internal subversion" and on those grounds provided military aid to anticommunist forces in Greece. Shortly afterward, the Marshall Plan, a program of aid and infrastructural "modernization" for European countries, was initiated by the United States to help these European countries recover from the wars (Killick 1997; Hogan 1987; Jones 1989). In Greece, both programs were introduced during the Greek civil war and thus perhaps were inevitably and explicitly regarded as politically motivated.

In any event, there was no sense that any interventions by these "political forces" were motivated by "genuine" concern about the conditions in which Epirots found themselves. What they did do was to forcibly demonstrate that a new, internationally mediated, political division of Europe into communist and noncommunist had arrived; in the Eastern Kasidiaris area, that went along with development plans for the plain intended to make the area more productive in market economy terms; in Western Kasidiaris, it went along with the imposed invisibility of Albania, and the increasingly difficult living conditions for those remaining on the Greek side.

In both economic and conceptual terms, this period tipped the balance very much in favor of Eastern Kasidiaris, and people often mentioned this. Under the Marshall Plan, the Doliana Plain—along with most large plains in northern Greece, and much of southern Greece—was sprayed with insecticide, which for the first time eliminated most of the mosquitoes, and therefore the malaria, that had plagued them. Furthermore, work began on the Doliana Plain to provide drainage canals and to slightly widen and deepen the Kalamas, so that it would not regularly flood the plain. As a result of this drying out of the Doliana Plain, many of the communes in the more soggy southern section were no longer restricted to cultivating rice as they had been in the past. Gone was not only the standing water in which the mosquitoes had bred, but also the leeches, which the women who used to work those fields still remembered with considerable disgust. More of the plain could now be used for pastoral grazing, both because there were fewer disease-bearing insects and because of the less soggy conditions. None of that was implemented in the Western Kasidiaris; instead, the place remained a no-man's-land, and a buffer zone against communism.

I came to see this period as one of "mechanical modernization." One could also call it "industrializing modernization" and evoke the Fordist ideals of standardization, mass production, and centralized planning that influenced the United States so much during that period;[6] I do not because "industrialization" does not quite capture what was going on in Epirus, though the same kinds of ideas were involved. In any event, the form these "modernizations" took could be seen as being part and parcel of the politics of the Cold War, and in Epirus, that is exactly how they were seen.

The late 1960s to early 1970s constituted the period of the junta (1967–1974, to be precise), during which "mechanical modernization" continued apace and bureaucracy massively increased. People also recalled that the era of the junta further exacerbated the personal animosities that had developed in Epirus during the civil war, in that the Papadopoulos regime was strongly anticommunist, which continually reminded people of the divisions between those who had supported the communist side during the war and those who had not. It also had material effects: those communes or commune presidents who were known to be left-leaning tended not to receive the funds and benefits that others did. This was important, because the Papadopoulos regime erased many people's agricultural debts and installed large amounts of infrastructure (often with the help of international, and particularly U.S., funds), such as asphalt roads, piped water, irrigation systems, and electricity, in the more remote regions of Epirus.[7] Indeed, people in Epirus often credited the junta with the installation of infrastructure that had in fact been installed through the Marshall Plan and other earlier international interventions. However, some places received considerably less of this assistance than others.

Many of those who had been left-leaning during that period remembered it with cynical bitterness. Vasiliki, the Ktismata president's wife, who was a socialist, did not see the junta's interest in Epirus as any kind of improvement: "In those days, if you put one word out of place, you were for it. One man was overheard on a bus saying that he had grown a potato as big as Papadopoulos's head. He ended up in prison." Vasiliki went on to assert that the people in Epirus who said the junta had been a good thing (indeed, many did say that) had "been paid to do Papadopoulos's dirty work for him."

The point here concerning the numbers is that the 1970s marked what people interpreted as a temporary and artificially inflated rise (a "blip") in the recorded populations of more remote and rural areas. The changes made by the junta managed to persuade some people to set up some kind of activity in rural areas, though again many noted that these were not the same people as had lived in the area before, and many also warned me to be wary of the figures for the 1970s in table 6. On the first point, the Sarakatsani family I met on the plain near the Bouna forest was an example: they had been transhumant pastoralists traveling between the Zagori and the southern coasts; they had no previous relations with the Pogoni area. But during the Papadopoulos regime, they set up a farm in Pogoni, with considerable financial and infrastructural help from that administration. They eventually ceased to be transhumant at all. On the second point, Papadopoulos had made it clear that he wanted to see the countryside populated again, and according to quite a few people I talked with, his civil servants delivered the numbers, if not always the embodied people.

It was also during this period that many of the first asphalt roads in the area were built. Apart from the main trunk routes and the roads built for military purposes to protect the border, many of these roads seemed to lack any trace of a central strategy: today, old asphalt roads often snake their way up a steep mountain for miles, only to arrive at a single village at the end, with little else in between; yet in other areas—such as across the length of the western flank of the Kasidiaris, where ten villages are close to one another—asphalt had still not been laid by the time I arrived in the early 1990s. Asphalt was an important issue in this area when I was there: if a commune did not have an asphalt road, it had become virtually invisible (Green and King 2001). Complaints about where asphalt was being laid (and the level of political "networking" this involved) were about as numerous as complaints about the Forestry Commission's views on trees.

Just about everybody asserted that Greeks, including Epirots, had become "city lovers" by the end of this period and were extremely unlikely to return to areas such as Pogoni—which had by now become well established as being a remote region of the Greek state and were increasingly appearing peripheral, in part because the Balkans had disappeared and Epirus was now on the edge of a Stalinist state that had become invisible.

Overall, the impression generated in people's accounts of the period is that whereas at the beginning, Eastern and Western Kasidiaris were fairly evenly populous, the political events that both experienced had different outcomes for the people in the two regions, and once again this had to do with the "where," not the "who." The previous "symmetry" between the two sides of the mountain discussed in chapter 3 first began to be reshaped with the introduction of the Greek-Albanian border, then was totally altered after the Greek civil war, both literally and numerically/administratively. In discussing this, Western Kasidiaris people continually referred to the effects of the Greek-Albanian border compounded with neglect of those remaining on the Greek side, whereas the Eastern Kasidiaris people were more likely to talk about various improvements to the plains and suggest that these, combined with people's moving to the cities to "improve" their lives, were the issues that mattered most. The infrastructural changes—drainage and irrigation systems for the plain, asphalt roads, electricity, and so on—which were much more strongly focused upon Eastern Kasidiaris than the Western Kasidiaris areas, emphasized the ever closer connections between the eastern side and Ioannina, the now rapidly growing capital city. In short, Western Kasidiaris had once again "disappeared" from view, both literally and numerically.

The 1980s and 1990s seemed to witness reversals of these previous events in certain respects, and I will be discussing these further in chapter 7. The 1980s were particularly colored by the coming of the European

Union, after Greece became a member state in 1981. That would set in train the introduction of different kinds of "modernizations," what could be called "organic" rather than "mechanical" modernizations, implemented through funded programs aimed mostly at attracting tourism through developing the cultural heritage of the region while conserving the environment. Rather than mechanizing rural areas, this kind of modernization seemed to be intended to "de-mechanize" and "traditionalize" them. The focus was not on the plains this time, but on the more mountainous areas. That period also ushered in large numbers of subsidies, which enabled people to continue small-scale pastoralism and cultivation, but which also led to a great deal of new paperwork. The auditing of livestock numbers in particular, which was required for the purposes of claiming subsidies, became an ongoing matter of negotiation and conflict between many Epirot pastoralists and increasingly strict European Union regulations. Officials administering the subsidy program at the European Union became so convinced that there had been considerable overreporting of livestock numbers during the 1980s that in 1993 the maximum number of animals that farmers were allowed to claim was pegged at the number they had reported in 1991. Unsurprisingly, this had caused considerable upset in a number of communes around the Kasidiaris.

Finally, in the early 1990s, the Greek-Albanian border was reopened, with all the accompanying reversals I have discussed at length in chapters 2 and 4. All these events involved different kinds of counting and accounting for things, different classifications and enumerations, and different things became visible and invisible. Changing how things seemed was therefore intimately involved with changing how things were; they could not be separated in most people's minds.

Making Numbers

Given all these considerations, I became increasingly interested in how the numbers were differently compiled during different periods, and I began to pay close attention to the notes in the margins, both actual and implicit, as well as how classifications shifted with time. For example, table 7 provides the summary census accounts of the Eastern and Western Kasidiaris communes listed in the table note (some communes included more than one village). Over the period, the names of villages often changed, and I have included former names in parentheses. Thus Gliziani became Katarraktis (Waterfalls), Brigianista became Vasilopoulo (Kingstown), Metzities became Kefalovriso (Headwater), Valtista became Haravgi (Dawn), and Arnista became Ktismata (Buildings). These new Greek names, and their implied Greek populations, simply appeared in the census, and the old names disappeared, without warning or explanation. The majority of commune name changes in Epirus happened during the late 1960s and early 1970s (i.e., during the junta), though others did occur earlier.

Further, included among the Eastern Kasidiaris communes listed in table 7 is one that had not existed at all until the 1970s: Kalpaki. It was located at the crossroads of the region's two main arteries at the northeastern end of the plain and was created out of chunks of neighboring commune territories. Most people, even Kalpaki residents, repeatedly told me that Kalpaki was not a "real" village, on the grounds that it had appeared relatively recently, it was populated by people who did not have particularly close relations with one another, and it was associated with the main asphalt routes—which, in this area, constituted pathways to somewhere else. Kalpaki had developed on the site of a collection of straw huts for people working on their fields in the plain; it was now the intersection of the two main roads, one leading to Ioannina and the other to the Greek-Albanian border post. It had been populated by a mixture of ex-transhumant pastoralists (mostly Sarakatsani) and people who had lived in more mountainous villages before (especially Elafotopos, in Zagori). Incidentally, Kalpaki was also, during my time there, where any undocumented immigrants from Albania, caught by the police or army during the previous night in the area, were gathered to be bused back across the border into Albania. Most mornings, there were at least twenty of these individuals waiting on the steps outside the police station, located right at the crossroads. They were reported simply as numbers in the local newspapers every day.

There are other traces of different ways of making numbers in this table as well. The pre-1950s census taking appears rather erratic in contemporary terms, as indicated by the varied dates they were conducted (1920, 1928, and 1940);[8] thereafter, they were conducted every ten years in the first year of the new decade. This earlier lack of standardization left trace evidence that "political forces" were not, during that period, what they later became (with the help of international advisory bodies). Moreover, people recalled that period (1920–50) as being particularly politically "eventful," encompassing as it did the exchange of populations between Turkey and Greece in the early 1920s and two major wars in the 1940s—it was a period, in other words, when the location and composition of the state's borders, inside and outside, were being questioned and literally rearranged.

During this period, then, the very organization and conducting of the census were part of the process of the political interventions occurring at the time. The numbers themselves also show traces of the state-sponsored shifting of populations undertaken in the 1920s and 1940s in particular.

During that period, one man from Kastani joked, village presidents were not busing people to and fro—governments were.

There are other little quirks that appeared in various statistical records I looked at. In 1938, during the Metaxas regime (1936–41), transhumant pastoralists were legally permitted to register as residents in village communes for the first time, and this boosted the recorded population numbers in both Western and Eastern Kasidiaris, though more so in Eastern Kasidiaris, because of the better grazing lands available there. Interestingly, people also recalled that this period saw a considerable shift in another significant population—the goat population. Metaxas believed that goats caused deforestation and desertification, so he both prohibited their being grazed in mountainous areas (Salmon 1995: 85) and ordered thousands of them to be slaughtered.[9] This also contributed to the decision of transhumant pastoralists to move their animals further down during the summer periods.

Speaking of animals, the records of animal numbers revealed a range of entanglements Epirus had with other places. Up until the mid-1950s, livestock figures were kept in huge, handwritten ledgers that an older employee of the Department of Agriculture remembered had been stuffed in a cupboard somewhere (people are disinclined to throw away numbers). These ledgers, and some of the subsequent printed versions, evidenced a range of ways of making and recording numbers: the earliest had been written in formal Greek (*katharevousa*) on one side of the page and translated into French on the other, and the unit of weight measurement was still the oka, the Ottoman standard. French had been the international lingua franca at the end of, and shortly after, the Ottoman era, and its presence in these ledgers demonstrated the sense that other places mattered, even for numbers of sheep and goats. Certainly, these ledgers were not meant for ordinary Epirots to read, since at the time, most neither spoke French nor understood much *katharevousa* either; had the numbers been intended for them, it might have been better to write them in a combination of demotic Greek, Albanian, and Vlach. But of course communicating aggregated numbers to the people who provided them was not the point at all.

In later periods, the weight measure changed to kilograms, and the ledgers were written in demotic Greek only; still later, during the junta, the ledgers were written in *katharevousa* only, which switched back to demotic Greek after the junta's fall; and in the most recent period, they were written in demotic Greek on one side of the page and translated into English on the other side. All of this provided a clear trace of this region's previous and current entanglements, and also the sense that entanglement was always already there, most particularly in bureaucratic procedures.

Occasionally, the clerk who had filled in the ledgers had added columns to the official ones to make distinctions that he (it always was a "he" in those days) had thought important, such as a separation between "nomadic" and "nonnomadic" sheep and goats; at other times, this distinction had been officially provided in the columns. The clerks had also occasionally scribbled an explanation of a number in the margins, or had crossed a number out and replaced it with another, noting the reason: either to match the numbers officially published in Athens, or as a result of a late adjustment by a commune secretary. Simply going through these ledgers left me in no doubt about the amount of negotiation that had gone into the creation of the numbers. It is a pity that in this age of computerization, few traces are left of such processes.

It was not only clerks and other state officials who were making numbers, though, and this emerges more distinctly if we look at the way "molding" practices varied across areas. This is where the variable "interests" that were involved in generating numbers in different ways become a little clearer.

Variations in Truths and Lies, Comings and Goings, and the Practice of Interests

The variable concept of numerical "population" is demonstrated in a small way in table 8, which represents two methods by which the populations of Western Kasidiaris communes were recorded in the year 1920: registered residents as against the census. I have already discussed the entanglement in the way both registration and census numbers were arrived at, so I will not rehearse that again here. The point of this table is the sheer variation in these differences across communes. For example, in Delvinaki, registered residents were numbered at 1,171, whereas the census for the same year recorded a figure of 2,630 people—considerably more than double the registered figure. In the opposite direction, Kefalovriso had 2,426 registered residents, whereas the census recorded 253, or around a tenth of the registered number. Yet in other communes, there was almost no difference between the registered and census figures, as was the case for Argyrohori, which recorded 221 registered residents and 224 census population. Clearly, different communes were entangling themselves with the numbers in considerably different ways.

When I pointed out these variations to people in the Western Kasidiaris area and asked for some clarification, the responses varied. On the one hand, there were the (by now familiar) exhortations to remain confused: "What do you expect? This is the Balkans"; "Well, neither of the figures is right; they never are"; "How do I know? I don't know anything about bureaucracy"; "Things were different in the 1920s. Who knows how they counted people in those days?" The main implication of these kinds of comments was that such numbers are always constituted according to contemporary interests and concerns, so there was no way of knowing what they meant, because the speaker was not privy to the entanglements that generated them. In short, they were meaningless. This was a rejection of the idea of linear trends, of generating relations across time through comparison of bigger or smaller numbers. Instead, it was assumed that the most relevant relations were the ones in which the numbers were entangled at the time they were produced.

On the other hand, some people offered detailed explanations for the differences. Once again, these circulated around the issue of different kinds of moving, and the fact that both the registration and the census counted people as if they were in one place most of the time—which, in most of Epirus, they were not. One conversation with Takis, the Sarakatsanos resident of Delvinaki I mentioned in chapter 2, and whose family had been associated with the town in one way or another for many decades, gives a flavor of these kinds of conversations. At the time, I had not quite grasped the multiple sense of belonging that many people felt:

TAKIS: The numbers mean different things: the registered residents were not all the same people as the people in the census.

SARAH: Does that mean the village had two populations?

TAKIS: No.

SARAH: Oh. Then I don't understand.

TAKIS: The census covered all the people who were there, in the village, on census day. Like it does today. The registered people could be anywhere—Constantinople, for example. In those days, lots of men were in Constantinople, as you know. Plus, not everyone was allowed to be registered, though they could be counted for the census. Like the Sarakatsani: they couldn't be registered here until way after 1920.

SARAH: So the village *did* have two populations.

TAKIS: No. Yes. Well, sort of. Actually, it had three—no, four—populations, if you want to see it like that. The registered ones who lived here most of the time; the registered ones who lived somewhere else most of the time; the nonregistered ones who lived here most of the time; and the nonregistered ones who passed through from time to time, like the nomadic people.

Takis went on to suggest that the reason the 1920 census figure was so much higher than that enumerating the registered residents in Delvinaki was that the town at the time was associated with a number of transhumant pastoralist families (both Vlachoi and Sarakatsani), who were not registered.

Similar combinations of indifference and explanations based on differing kinds of moving were given in most of the other villages. In Kefalovriso, where the difference between registered residents and census population was so large, almost everyone offered the same explanation: Kefalovriso was, at the time, an almost exclusively Vlach village, and people registered there to maintain their grazing rights.[10] The census must have been taken in the winter, at a time of year when they were somewhere down south with their animals.

As to the communes in Lower Pogoni where the two sets of figures were not so very different from one another, such as Argyrohori and Ktismata: people explained that by saying they were among the mixed cultivation and pastoralism villages, so in terms of this region, it would indeed appear as if they did not move a great deal. Their form of moving was to leapfrog from their village area to somewhere completely out of the region; the fairly static appearance of the numbers was an outcome of their being "sandwiched" into Lower Pogoni; the men who lived elsewhere most of the time would have been registered in the commune and most would also have returned for the census. Another idea proffered in Ktismata was that perhaps both figures had been generated by estimate rather than by any counting of heads, on the grounds that whoever did the counting was trying to compensate for the coming and going of various people—in other words, trying to calculate who "belonged" to the commune rather than who was physically there. Some of the rounded numbers—for example, Peristeri's 600 registered residents as against its 400 census population—do imply that a certain amount of estimation was going on.

In any event, the overall point about the registered versus the census figures in table 8 is that for Kasidiaris people, they showed traces of the differences between places according to the differences in the way people moved. Different kinds of official counting of populations included some people and not others, and the fact that people moved in different ways and therefore affected the numbers in different ways becomes clear through their comparison. Nobody was surprised at these discrepancies; people simply assumed that the official statistics are never self-contained or complete in their own terms.

Table 9 makes a small attempt to explore this numerically for a more recent period: it provides numbers for the 1991 official census populations for some of the Kasidiaris communes, contrasted with the number estimated by people in the village (usually the commune secretary or president) to be actually living there for most of the year, plus an estimate of the number of ex-residents who come to visit in the summer. In effect this table represents three ways of counting people: the census population, the estimated actual "permanent" residents, and the visiting ex-residents.

In every case, the numbers of ex-residents visiting in the summer far exceeded the estimated permanent residents; they usually considerably exceeded the census as well. One of the most notable things about this table is the relative success or failure of village presidents to persuade ex-residents to come back for census day. Katarraktis more than doubled its population, from an estimated 60 permanent residents to 143 in the census; Kerasovo's census figures are almost five times as large as the estimated permanent residents (124 as opposed to 25). Yet Koukli and Mavropoulo show almost no difference between the two figures. The diversity in this "molding" of the census was discussed in three ways: how far away ex-residents lived; the popularity of the commune president and how closely he was connected with Ioannina (and therefore Ioannina residents); and a perceived need to bus in ex-residents. Both Katarraktis and Kerasovo could call upon a relatively large number of ex-residents living in Ioannina (and both their presidents divided their time between Ioannina and the communes they represented); in contrast, most of Ktismata's ex-residents were in Athens, and many others were in Germany and the United States; those of Mavropoulo were mostly in the United States or Australia. As to the perceived need: Koukli had relatively successfully developed its agricultural production in recent years and, as a result, possessed what the villagers considered to be a fairly "viable" population; they did not deem it necessary to bus in ex-residents (and the commune's president lived most of the time in Koukli). The implication is that those communes that bused in ex-residents did not perceive themselves as "viable"—and indeed, people in such villages often explicitly said as much. In any event, all of these population figures, in different ways and at different times, became objects of either active negotiation or passive indifference: there was no single kind of relationship among the numbers, the people, and the places, nor any single outcome.

If there is one entangled political and numerical "truth" that everyone seemed to agree upon, it was that the mountainous areas in the north and the borderland mountainous areas were depopulating, and this, more than anything else, was affecting people's relationship with the place itself, though differently in different places. Of course, people hardly needed official statistics to know that; but the presence of the numbers, and the need to fill in official returns from time to time, provided a range of possibilities and coercions in the "rearranging" of how things seemed and how they were. The numbers allowed people scope for discussions and arguments with one another and with official agencies about (literally) the state of things; those negotiations blended "political facts" and "numerical facts" with levels of commitment and interest in relations people had with each other, with the past, and with the place itself. In this case, some places emerged out of the negotiations as peripheral by almost every definition of the word, but different areas were peripheral in different ways and to greater or lesser degrees—and that mattered. The mountains of the Zagori were set to become a tourist area; the borderland regions of Pogoni were set to become first irrelevant and later problematic.

In the remainder of this chapter, I want to move to a more embodied account of that, to experiences and accounts of shifts in the shape of the place, and to the physical presence or absence of animals.

RECOUNTING PLACES AND ANIMALS

Prickly oak scrub: it is dense; it has extremely tough and deep roots; its dark green, shiny leaves have thorns that can penetrate the thickest clothing—and in the 1990s in Epirus, it was all over most mountainous areas (some of it can be seen in the background of figs. 3 and 5). It was also what most people in such areas pointed to when asked how their environment had changed over the years. The Kasidiaris was now covered with it; older people recalled that the mountain had been bare until the mid-1960s, after which the oak scrub started taking over.[11] This plant, called *pournari* (generally translated as "holly") by people in the area, had changed the look of, and impeded mobility through, the mountains, marking, almost more than anything else, a shift in people's relationship with such places. In the past, paths and tracks used to cover the hills, providing a dense network reflecting continual coming and going, which interconnected with villages, the transhumant routes, the trade routes, and the bridges across rivers and streams at various points. Now those webs of connection were overgrown and virtually invisible (except in many people's memories), replaced by a network of asphalt that mostly ran through the plains and connected to dirt track roads leading to the villages now constituted as the most "remote" (Green and King 2001).

The exceptions, as I briefly mentioned above, were a few of the villages in the high mountains of the Zagori that were considered "remote" but had become tourist destinations, such as Monodendri, Aristi, and Papingo, all of which were located very close to the Vikos gorge and the Timfi/Gamilla mountain, regarded as affording particularly stunning vistas. The asphalt was provided for these routes because tourist coaches needed to get up there. The village of Vikos, which was located on the edge of the Vikos gorge at the opposite end from Monodendri, had somehow lost out on this asphalt for many years (until the mid-1990s, in fact), and the people there were rather resentful: the people of Monodendri had become rich on the combination of the gorge and the asphalt, and the people in Vikos felt themselves to be struggling in comparison. They also felt themselves to be struggling in comparison with Aristi, just a mile or so below Vikos and part of the same commune, as Aristi was located on the main asphalt route up to Papingo. That had resulted in some tense relations between the people in the two parts of the commune.[12]

In contrast to this situation in parts of the Zagori, no tourists were traveling up the Kasidiaris to experience the vista, and there was almost no asphalt on either flank of the Kasidiaris in the 1990s. Its older paths and tracks (generated by the people who used them), which used to weave up, around, and over the mountain on both sides, had long faded from view, replaced by dense prickly oak scrub in most places. As explained in chapter 2, there were differing opinions about whether that fading of past movements was a good thing, but almost everyone agreed it was a bizarre twist of state bureaucracy that if prickly oak scrub was classified as forest, nobody was allowed to touch the stuff. A forest might be seen as naturally beautiful or as a resource for raw materials; oak scrub was neither of those things.

The areas where asphalt was lacking but prickly oak scrub was rife symbolized, for many people, increasing lack of interest in and productive use of the more mountainous areas from the end of the civil war and up to the 1990s. The statistical accounts strongly reflect this notion, for these accounts are concerned with production. In numerical terms, Pogoni County again appears particularly affected. For example, between 1961 and 1991, Pogoni County shows a 55 percent drop in recorded agricultural land and a 26 percent rise in "Grazing Land," a great deal of which will have been oak scrub (table 13). Table 14, which divides recorded agricultural land into plains, semimountainous, and mountainous areas supports the impression that in every case, the major drop has been in the mountainous areas. Again, a significant numerical difference between the Pogoni area and other areas appears: Pogoni is recorded as having experienced the greatest drop in agricultural land by an extremely large margin. For example, in semimountainous areas, Epirus as a whole shows a drop of just 3 percent in agricultural land; in Pogoni County, it was 51 percent. The overall message of these numbers is clear enough: agricultural activity had not only moved to the plains; it had moved south. The oak scrub in the mountains is all over these statistics.

Talking with many different people from around the Kasidiaris about this period, I heard a sense of inevitability expressed about it. For those on the western side, the cultivation that had been going on was small-scale, on bad soils, and anyway had become almost impossible for many because of the restrictions around the border; so people stopped doing it. For those on the eastern side, it made much more sense to use the newly improved plain than to work on a scatter of fields on hillsides. Pastoralists also expressed a sense of inevitability: if you can feed your animals on cultivated fodders—which, according to all the shepherds I talked with, increases their size and health, and obviates going out onto windy, often wet hillsides—then who in their right mind would grit their teeth and face the elements?

The answer, as it happens, was hired shepherds from Albania (whether regarded as Northern Epirot or as Albanian). However, they had arrived only lately and were part of yet another (re)transformation of this place; with the reopening of the border, and the renewed visibility of Albania and matters Balkan, the cheap hired help from "Inside" (i.e., Albania) was beginning to clear the oak scrub away again. Things change—but stay the same.

That little twist is something I will discuss further in chapter 7, because the "hired help" from Albania also provided the majority of stonemasons needed to "restore" the cultural heritage of many areas. I mention it here as a reminder that the sense of inevitability embedded in the story told by many Kasidiaris people about the decline of the mountainous areas should not be taken to mean that people assumed this was a linear transformation; this is a region where coming and going, both expected and unexpected, had happened often enough that people rarely made such assumptions. What it reflected instead was a sense that whatever events might occur, there would be a self-similarity about them; there would be a reiteration of the relations between this place and other places and forces. The Western Kasidiaris had been marked as less autonomous and less significant than others in the past, and it would be again; the Zagori had been marked as more autonomous and more significant, and it would be again. Even if that involved changing the shape of the place, and changing the relations of people, places, and activities within it, the relations between this place and other places would always already be entangled in that, and would reiterate the hierarchies involved.

One of the ways that was expressed was in shifting relations between animals and different kinds of movement; another was in talk about the visible traces in the place left from previous transformations, which continued to be entangled in contemporary relations, and I will move on to these now, starting with animals.

Shifting Animals and Places

I first went to the Department of Agriculture offices in Ioannina in search of animal (i.e., livestock) numbers, for reasons that will be obvious by now: sheep and goats in particular had been at the center of things in the past, and in many ways, they still were. The oak scrub, as far as almost everyone was concerned, had appeared because sheep and goats were no longer chewing the hills clean as they once did. More than that, though, sheep and goats, and occasionally other animals, pervaded the stories people told me about this place: in accounts of different kinds of movement, of family feuds, and of land abandonment, and in most stories about relative status, goats and sheep kept being included in the stories. In the past, they were much more important than any cultivation; the latter, as described in chapter 2, was seen as a somewhat peasant activity and tended to mean many people had to leapfrog out of places in which they were sandwiched. In comings and goings around the immediate region and beyond, sheep and goats were a large part of both the reason and the means; the habit of moving animals around had generated a web of routes across the region, which constituted key routes and relations, shaping people's sense of different places: the northern high mountainous areas with their good summer grazing lands; the southern coasts with their good winter grazing lands; the central areas with their mixtures of good and bad grazing lands and their markets. Those areas with few through routes were also relatively invisible and relatively badly off—and again, that included Lower Pogoni/Western Kasidiaris. Moreover, the places goats and sheep grazed within communes had been central focus points, whereas the cultivated fields had not.

The availability and form of the official statistics on animal husbandry in Epirus also reflect the importance placed on animals by the state in this area. In the Ioannina offices of the Department of Agriculture, I was able to locate detailed crop figures going back only to 1961 (at which point, cultivation began to become more important, in large part owing to the interventions of the Marshall Plan), and these were in officially printed pamphlets. In contrast, the figures for livestock, enumerating every goat, sheep, horse, mule, donkey, pig, cow, rabbit, and chicken, as well as beehives, for every commune, were available back to 1940, and sometimes as far back as the 1930s.

Although the sheep and goats remained central to commercial production in the northern half of Epirus in the postwar years, things began to shift following the end of the civil war. In addition to the rapid increase in use of cultivated animal fodders, new commercially farmed animals began to enter the equation as well, particularly pigs, chickens, and cattle. These had been around before to some degree: one or two pigs in a village in case of food shortages and to eat up the rubbish, a scatter of chickens running around, kept mostly for their eggs, and various kinds of cattle and oxen, used mostly for agricultural work. In recent years, however, such animals have been intensively farmed on the plains, mostly for their meat. Sheep and goats also continued to be farmed, but "improved" breeds had been introduced, breeds that were larger, did not need to be out in the open nearly so much, and did well on cultivated and stored fodders. These breeds could be kept mostly in and around the plain all year long. Tables 17–20 provide numerical accounts of these shifts.

The combination of the shifts meant that it was now possible to have large numbers of animals without seasonally traveling long distances with them: people could now farm animals in the same way as they did crops, by staying put. Moreover, those who did still move their animals seasonally could now do so by truck along the asphalt; there was no need to travel across the region on foot anymore. So the transhumant pastoralism networks of walked (and grazed) routes began to fade; and as most people in the mountain villages were now keeping a few animals for their own use or a small amount of income, the network of paths and tracks up and down mountains began to fade as well.

Considering all I have said about the importance of the trope of movement in people's understanding of differences between peoples and the meaning of places, all of this constituted a significant transformation of the Epirus region, as a place. Continual movement across the region using most kinds of land was becoming the exception rather than the rule, and in the process the shape of the place was being transformed. It was now interconnected through state-built asphalt roads that were routed between cities and state-improved plains, and the area as a whole was divided by state-controlled borders.

Over time, the plains would come to be seen by many as the key areas that were continually shaped, built, and altered by people, as well as the only areas outside cities that now had a significant young year-round population. In contrast, the mountains increasingly came to be constituted, by some, as part of the past and/or part of a wilderness. "Development" and "modernization" were happening on the plains and in the cities to which they were linked; the mountains were increasingly cast as "undeveloped" and abandoned.

The list of land redistribution programs in table 16, which focuses on productive activity, traces some of this story of one kind of "modernization". The table outlines the programs that had been carried out in the Kasidiaris area: all of these had involved the Doliana Plain, and none the Western Kasidiaris area. In fact, Ktismata, along with a number of other communes, particularly Mavropoulo—which had access to the remaining part of the plain on the Greek side of the border in Lower Pogoni—had applied for such a program to be instituted there, but by the end of my fieldwork in 1997, it had not been completed. I will discuss that a little more later. In the Doliana Plain, there were eight projects carried out by the Ministry of Land Improvements between 1968 and 1993; most were imposed compulsorily, and had been planned and carried out by the Greek state. The manager of land improvements in Epirus, K. Papathanasiou, explained that the projects centrally involved installing a mechanized irrigation system, but in the course of this, people who had scattered land holdings (owing to partible inheritance) were forced to accept a redistribution of their plots so that they all became contiguous. After this, agricultural roads would be built in parallel lines across the area, and perhaps some bumpy parts of the fields would be smoothed out. At the same time, agronomists and others provided advice on improved cultivation techniques and the use of various chemical fertilizers and pesticides, and they strongly encouraged a change in animal breeds—all, of course, to improve commercial productivity.

I asked K. Papathanasiou whether there had been resistance against the rearrangement of people's landholdings. He responded that at first there was some resistance, but that once a program had been completed in one commune, "the others realized how profitable it was, so they accepted it easily." People I spoke with from the communes involved did not express it exactly that way, as they recalled prolonged disputes about the quality of the new land they were being given, as contrasted with what they had before. In the course of this series of negotiations, suspicions continually circulated about certain people's having more influence with the Department of Land Improvements than did others about which plots of land they were allotted. However, there were differing experiences of this at different times: Kostas, a goatherd and farmer from Areti in his seventies, recalled that "there were no arguments when those changes were made during the junta. In those days, you just didn't argue with the government."

In any event, the earliest communes to have improvement programs imposed upon them were Doliana, Repetisti, and Parakalamos, the "new town" developing in the middle of the plain. All their land improvement programs were begun during the junta, though none of them were completed until two years after the junta's collapse. Areti, Koukli, and Mazaraki, all located in the southern end of the Doliana Plain (the area that had been soggy before the widening of the Kalamas), had their programs begun in 1979 and completed in 1981; a further program for Doliana and Parakalamos lands, along with Sitaria, was begun in 1982 and completed in 1985; the most recent program to be completed was at Vrontismeni, again in the south, started in 1991 and completed in 1993. In short, all of these most recent programs took about two years to complete; in contrast, Ktismata's efforts at having such a program implemented began in 1986 and had not been realized by 1997, more than ten years later. As I said in chapter 1, it matters where you are in the world.

All this reorganization was part of an explicit development policy that had begun during the Marshall Plan. The increasing importance of cultivation and consolidation of landholdings had highlighted the plains—

not, as in the past, as part of a wider range of interrelations among mountains, cities and plains, grazing areas, forests and fields, but on their own account, as autonomously productive places. That, combined with the increasing importance of new borders and boundaries, had meant that kinds of moving shifted, and what moving meant shifted as well.

That brings me to the final section of this chapter, which explores these kinds of transformations from the perspective of two communes, both in terms of what they meant for the places themselves as embodied, physical entities, and in terms of the accounts people gave of these communes' experiences of the events that were understood as shaping and reshaping them.

KTISMATA AND KATARRAKTIS: RECOUNTING THE (RE)MAKING OF TWO COMMUNES

The first thing that became obvious as Geoff King and I carried out the surveys of the commune territories of Ktismata and Katarraktis was that few if any of the boundaries marked on the blueprints we had obtained were at all obvious on the ground—including the outer boundaries of the communes themselves. The blueprints, which form the basis of maps 7 and 8, were drawn as if each commune is an isolated island, as if its shape is somehow a natural physical boundary. The only indication that the land continued beyond it was the inclusion of the names of the neighboring communes. When we were actually walking around the area, we rarely saw obvious physical divisions—not even deliberately constructed ones, such as fences or stone markers. In fact, there were hardly any fences or boundary markers of any kind, even around fields.

I often asked people I met during the survey to pinpoint the boundaries between one commune and the next, but everyone found this task difficult. Much easier for them was to point to areas belonging to certain families, or to point to communal grazing areas. In short, the administrative commune boundaries were not visible on the ground either to myself or to people from the communes concerned, and they did not mark anything significant. People associated with adjoining villages had tended to intermarry in the past, and as partible inheritance and dowries involving property had been common, there was regular transfer of ownership and/ or use of property across commune territories. In practice, this meant people in the past would continually travel between what are now commune territories, to work on fields or use grazing lands and to make social visits, so the boundaries between territories were interwoven, as it were. For villages along the Greek-Albanian border, this had also involved interweaving territories across the international boundary before the border had been closed. For most people, the land had constituted a scattered patchwork of various kinds of interrelations (and enmities), which did not match the formal boundaries of the contemporary commune territories. That led me to become intrigued about how an interweaving of territories had become an administratively separated out patchwork of territories: how, in other words, interrelations had again become separations. The following account provides a brief story of how that happened in the cases of Ktismata and Katarraktis.

The first Ktismata blueprint had been drawn up in 1933, the Katarraktis one in 1965. These different dates in themselves leave traces of differing past relations: the reason the blueprints were drawn up was to formally establish ownership of property, for which precise boundaries of fields and house plots were required. During Ottoman rule, Ktismata lands had been managed on behalf of the region's pasha by what was essentially a civil servant, a man called an *agas* in this region.[13] After the end of Ottoman rule, such lands automatically became the responsibility of the Greek state, which organized their redistribution among three interested parties: the households in Ktismata, the commune, and the state itself. After the initial distribution in Ktismata had been arranged in 1932, the blueprint was drawn up. Immediately, complaints were made about the perceived inequity of the shares for the lands granted to households: some people from Ktismata had protested that certain households had been "more favored" than others by the *agas* during Ottoman times, and so they had been granted considerably larger plots of land in the Greek state's redistribution, since that redistribution had been based on the lands used by each household during Ottoman times.

These complaints resulted in another redistribution in 1957, in which every household was granted the same amount of land. This made an enormous difference for some households: for example, Tasos, the goatherd whose story I discussed in chapter 2, recalled that his family's holdings were reduced from 140 stremmata (approximately 35 acres) prior to 1957, to 61 stremmata (approximately 15 acres) afterward. Needless to say, this process caused a considerable amount of bad feeling between households in Ktismata, and occasionally arguments still arose in the 1990s about who owned what.

In contrast to Ktismata's experience, Katarraktis lands had been owned, rather than managed, by an Ottoman landlord, locally known as a *tsiflakas* (a word taken from the Turkish *çiftlik*, meaning farm). Unlike the *agas*, the *tsiflakas* could sell his estate, and in Katarraktis's case he did so shortly before the end of Ottoman rule, along with the lands of a nearby village called Sakellariko.[14] The buyer, the new *tsiflakas*, was a Greek Orthodox man from the south of Epirus, and this man was permitted to keep his estate when Epirus became part of Greece in 1913.

As a result, Katarraktis lands were not redistributed to the villagers; instead, the Greek government gave the villagers the right to buy out the *tsiflakas*. They had to work hard to amass the funds to do this, which they finally managed in 1964—with the help, of course, of monies from many Katarraktis people who by now lived in Athens and abroad. However, there was yet another twist: around half of the money collected for this purpose somehow disappeared, along with the Katarraktis man given charge of the funds (a particularly acute expression of self-interest). This meant that only around half as much land was bought up as had been originally planned; hence the relatively small size of the resulting commune's boundaries, and its rather odd shape.

These two different experiences were fairly typical of Western and Eastern Kasidiaris as a whole. During the Ottoman period, the poorer quality lands—found on the western side up to the current Albanian border, which had few plains lands and did not constitute parts of transhumant routes—tended to be managed by Ottoman administrators; the higher quality lands and plains, found on the eastern side, tended to be owned by *tsiflakades*. As a result, what happened after the area became part of the Greek state varied considerably in different places.

There were other kinds of land management arrangements during the Ottoman period in addition to these two main ones. The first concerned the highly mountainous areas, which were sparsely populated; these tended not to be either managed by *agas* or owned by *tsiflakades* during Ottoman times. They included most of the Zagori, and some parts of Upper Pogoni as well. Second, there were a few villages that had bought themselves out during Ottoman times, thus purchasing a certain level of autonomy. This included the village of Doliana. The third variation involved the lands owned by monasteries belonging to the Orthodox Church. Peoples using these lands were effectively in the same position as those who were managed by an Ottoman *agas*, using the land and giving a portion of the product to the monastery, rather than to the *agas*. The difference was that people using monastery lands had no right to buy out their lands following the end of Ottoman rule and were not included in redistribution programs; they depended upon the largesse of the Church to redistribute some of these lands to the people who used them.

In any case, the blueprints of the Ktismata and Katarraktis communes were the outcome of a series of relations and negotiations among people who had used the lands and entanglements with wider political, economic, and legal conditions. Traces of these past negotiations could still be seen both in the blueprints—the dates they were drawn up, and the different sizes and shapes of the two communes—and, more important, in the attitudes of the people associated with these places toward what had happened since.

The blueprints themselves give an indication of what the different parts of the territories had been used for at the time they were drawn up: the small subdivided plots represent fields used for cultivation; the large, fairly blank areas, seen in maps 7 and 8, were commune lands. In Ktismata's case, these communal areas had been a combination of grazing and forest lands (though some of the forest was owned by the state), and in Katarraktis's case, they were all grazing lands. The superimposition on the blueprint of what Geoff King and I learned by walking around these areas in March of 1994—the incorporation of classifications of places based on distinctions made by people we talked with in the villages—provides one kind of account of what had happened in the two communes in the postwar years. Here, the importance of the "whereness" of these places, and the way this deeply affected subsequent understandings of their different experiences and relations with other things, emerges from these combined stories of the place.

Ktismata: Entangled Neglect

In themselves, the map representing Ktismata seems to tell the same story as that representing Katarraktis. Map 7 shows the remaining cultivated and grazing areas in Ktismata in 1994, as well as the overgrown, abandoned, and forested areas. Cultivation was by then limited to the northwest corner of the territory, an area of floodplain, and to scatterings of cultivated fields around the village itself. The remaining grazing land had taken up some of what had been cultivated fields, but by no means all of the fields. People from Ktismata suggested that the bulk of the cultivated northwest corner was in fact rented by a man from Delvinaki, and of the rest, only a half dozen or so Ktismata households were involved. This was the only commercial cultivation in the commune: it was animal fodders, which were for the most part not sold but used to feed sheep and goats, whose meat and dairy products were sold. The remaining cultivation around the village was carried out mostly by pensioners and weekend visitors from Ioannina, for their own consumption. A variety of vegetables, fruit and nut trees, and a few animal fodders were grown on them in small quantities.

The overgrown, abandoned, and wooded areas of the Ktismata territory make up the darker shaded areas in map 7. The shift in land use these areas collectively represent is that the inner parts of the territory, other than the village, had more or less been abandoned; the "mature forest" (that is, not oak scrub, but recognizable trees) covered the eastern and southern portions of the territory. The forest, which everyone called a forest, had been there for as long as people could remember, but had expanded considerably, now covering many areas that had been cultivated and/or grazed, and had become much denser than in the past. Amelia, whose story I discussed in chapter 2, recalled how the forest had been more or less restricted to the northeastern part of the territory when she was a child, and had been much thinner, because people regularly culled the trees both for firewood and to manufacture charcoal for sale. Hardly anybody did this anymore.

The map also indicates some of the ongoing roadwork being carried out by the Greek government to expand and improve the route to the Greek-Albanian border post, Kakavia, reflecting in asphalt terms the importance of the border's reopening. Areas that Geoff and I saw as "eroded" (landslips, cracks, gullies, bare patches, or bare dunes) are marked in black. By now it will be obvious why I was determined to make them appear: they were mentioned neither in the statistics nor by people in Ktismata, and yet that was what I was supposed to be studying at the time. In Ktismata's case, all this erosion was gray-brown flysch badlands and landslips.

Many things are not shown on this map, such as a large number of new houses (constructed within the previous fifteen years), most of which had been built by people returning to retire or as holiday or weekend homes.[15] It will be recalled that after the civil war, the housing area moved down from a hill to a lower area; in that sense, almost all the houses were regarded as "new." The map also does not show that portions of agricultural land were rented out to Ioannina residents by owners living farther afield for most of the year; that much of the rest was owned by people who lived in Athens or abroad and who did not use it for any purpose most of the time; or that there had been ongoing and continual disputes between the Ktismata president and both regional and national administrations about the cutting off of old irrigation systems for the fields, and pressure to institute a land improvement and redistribution program, which was begun in 1986 but had hardly progressed at all since then.

Overall, the Ktismata survey in itself provided me with an embodied sense of a shift in the way people moved to and fro around this place over the years: few had cause anymore to go farther than a couple of hundred yards beyond their houses into the territory, and almost none had cause to interweave Ktismata's territory with neighboring territories. What had once been a place people traveled around to do all kinds of things (collect firewood, graze the animals, tend to fields), and one they traveled into and out of to use neighboring grazing lands, visit kin, tend to fields in adjoining communes, was now something else. Most people, other than the few remaining farmers and pastoralists, stayed within the village confines and traveled from place to place via the asphalt roads. The rest of the territory was becoming separated from people's daily lives. Many in

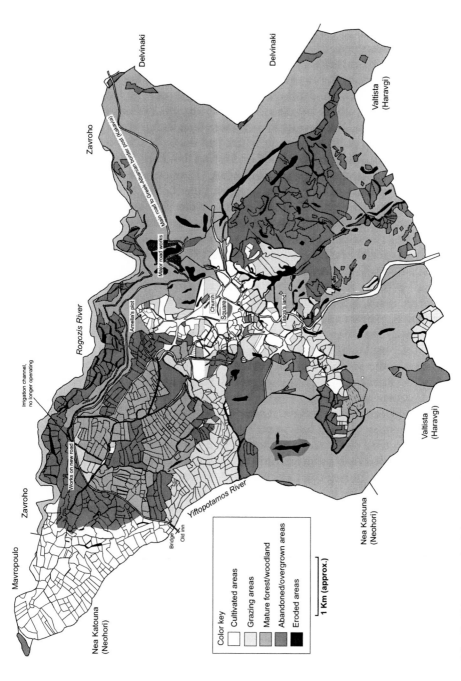

Map 7. Ktismata territorial survey, 1994

Delvinaki

Delvinaki

Zavroho

Valtista
(Haravgi)

Main road to Greek-Albanian border post (Kakavia)

Zavroho

Rogozis River

Major road works

Amelia's plot

Church

Square

Iasqu's land?

Irrigation channel,
no longer operating

Valtista
(Haravgi)

Works on new road

Mavropoulo

Zavroho

Yiftopotamos River

Bridge

Old inn

Nea Katouna
(Neohori)

Nea Katouna
(Neohori)

Color key

☐ Cultivated areas
☐ Grazing areas
▨ Mature forest/woodland
▨ Abandoned/overgrown areas
■ Eroded areas

├─────┤
1 Km (approx.)

the village, and the older residents in particular, regretted this, felt they had lost something.

As might be expected by now, this was not a simple expression of nostalgia, the longing for something that had not existed but had been constructed through a (modernist) conception of the past (Appadurai 1996b: 29–31). Rather, it was associated with a strong sense of injustice, a sense that Ktismata had experienced much more than its fair share of intervention from "big politics," none of which had done the place or the people any favors, in most people's opinion. Having first been "messed around" in the land distribution process following Ottoman rule—which caused no small amount of bad feeling between households in the village that never quite recovered—Ktismata peoples were later cut off from their connections with the Albanian side of the border after its closure in the 1940s; at the same time, their area was made a no-man's-land that required a special pass for entry until the late 1970s. In the 1960s, and while Eastern Kasidiaris peoples were being subjected to "Fordist modernization," with the major infrastructural changes to the plain and with new asphalt roads, Ktismata had to wait. When, as a result of intense campaigning, people in Ktismata managed to get a land redistribution project underway for what remained of their plain in 1986, it was begun half-heartedly and then simply stopped, having destroyed the older irrigation system in the process, but not yet replaced it with a new one. When the Greek-Albanian border reopened, at first things looked hopeful, with the land improvement program being funded once more, this time partly by the European Union; but the money was stopped in 1993, shortly after the irrigation channel had again been cut off. Then the roadwork for the main road to the reopened border post began, and the villagers were informed that their infrastructural changes would have to wait until that was finished. During this time, the levels of illegal Albanian immigration across the border increased considerably, and various violent incidents began to occur. These were splashed across the national newspapers, which represented the border post area as the "Wild West"—an impression that many others in Greece were quite ready to accept without question. People from Albania were strongly marked as "disheveled" Balkan peoples; and this border had become a dangerously leaky entry point, for both the Balkans and the Albanians.[16]

As far as most Ktismata peoples were concerned, various political powers (including the Greek, Athens-centered state) had pursued their own interests throughout and generated conditions that Ktismata peoples were just left to deal with on their own. There was a considerable level of resentment among older people in the village about all of that, which continued to inform their relations both with one another and with the place. To many, the ongoing activities of political powers had repeatedly forced them into marginality through neglect and then blamed the villagers for it; and now, rather than being on the edge of a Stalinist state, they were on the edge of the Balkans, which was frequently cast as a return to something monstrously chaotic, both by the newspapers and by many people living in the area. Ktismata was caught up in a gap once again.

Katarraktis: Inflected Developments

The story provided by people of Katarraktis was quite different, even though what appeared to have happened to the commune lands in physical terms in the postwar years seemed somewhat similar. Map 8 shows the remaining cultivation and grazing on the Katarraktis territory, and again, the darker shaded sections indicate overgrown and abandoned areas. By 1994, large portions of the territory constituted fairly impenetrable oak scrub, which covered much of what used to be the communal grazing lands. The remaining cultivation was mostly concentrated around the river valley, which provided irrigation for the fields—and again, most of what was cultivated was animal fodders. The grazing was scattered in and around this remaining cultivation and around the village, and there was a good deal of "household" cultivation in and around the village. Again, most of this "garden" cultivation was carried out by weekend visitors from Ioannina and a little by retired people living in the village. What is again not shown in map 8 is the considerable amount of new house building and house improvements that had been going on within the section marked as the "village"; that was where the greatest amount of energy and investment had been concentrated in recent years, a concentration that emphasized even further the separation between the village and the territory that had been widening since the end of the wars.

These maps may suggest a similarity between Ktismata and Katarraktis in terms of the shifts they underwent in the postwar years, but the experience of getting there in Katarraktis had not felt nearly as enforced, or as frustrating, as it had done for Ktismata residents. The generally cheerful tone in which people from Katarraktis described their experiences of "big politics," and what had happened to their territories since the end of the wars, contrasted considerably with the bitterness expressed in Ktismata. The major resentment in Katarraktis, insofar as resentment existed, was directed against the man who had run off with their money to buy up the land from the *tsiflikas*; but that was somehow water under the bridge now, something people managed to laugh about. There was also some level of resentment about the past treatment of Katarraktis people as a result of their support for the communists during the civil war, and the intervention of the "Great Powers" into that conflict. But again, this topic

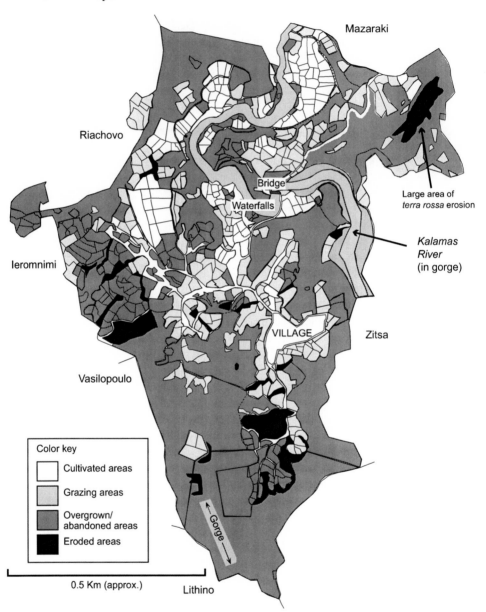

Mazaraki

Riachovo

Bridge

Waterfalls

Large area of
terra rossa erosion

Ieromnimi

*Kalamas
River*
(in gorge)

VILLAGE

Zitsa

Vasilopoulo

Color key

Cultivated areas

Grazing areas

Overgrown/
abandoned areas

Eroded areas

Gorge

0.5 Km (approx.)

Lithino

Map 8. Katarraktis territorial survey, 1994

was usually dealt with in terms of jokes, even if they did occasionally have a slightly sharp edge to them.

Importantly, many Katarraktis residents expressed a sense that they had participated in the shifts that had occurred, rather than had those shifts entirely imposed upon them. Moreover, few regretted the passing of the earlier years. From their perspective, life had been hard when they had scraped a living from a few fields and a few animals before the wars, and since that time, most had gone off, to Ioannina, to Athens, and abroad, and found "something better." At the same time, many did still "dabble" in keeping animals and cultivating, whenever they visited the village. Most described that as something they enjoyed doing; it gave them a break from city life and meant they maintained some connection with their village. Spiros, the commune's president, who was in his forties when I spoke with him, worked in Ioannina for the Greek telecommunications company OTE; while he was committed to the village and was even head of a local group of agricultural cooperatives, he was not terribly keen on 'nostalgia' for the past. "People here had too little land, their families were too big. It was not a good way to live then, it was not easy. And it was even less easy for us, because we were socialist here. Things are much better now; people have easier lives today."

This much brighter perspective than that expressed in Ktismata seemed to be associated with many things: the location of Katarraktis on the eastern side of the Kasidiaris—near good roads, near the plain, and, most important, near the city of Ioannina; the fact that they had bought the land themselves (even if it was only half of what they intended to buy) rather than had to argue with the government about its distribution, as Ktismata residents had done; the lack of any recent "interference" in their affairs by "big politics" that was regarded as particularly harmful or negative; and, as important, not having been cut off from their kin and neighbors, as Ktismata had been prior to being "reconnected" to its neighboring Albanian areas amid Balkan "chaos." All of these differences seemed to impart to the village's way of becoming peripheral in recent years a softer edge, one with which it seemed easier to live and that most in Katarraktis were relatively happy to accept. In a sense, Katarraktis peoples had come to feel that they constituted a part of the shifts in emphasis, rather than being constantly in a state of embattlement with them.

An example of what this meant in terms of how things seemed came from a conversation I had with a group in the *kafeneio* one summer afternoon. They all burst out laughing when I mentioned that I had seen quite a few donkeys around the village. One of the women in the group said: "Yes, we have plenty of donkeys in this village. Well, we can't keep them in Ioannina, can we?"—an assertion that was followed by more hoots of laughter from the rest of the group. In many other villages comments from a visitor about donkeys ran the risk of being interpreted as an insult—it could imply that the visitor assumed that the village, and therefore the villagers, were "premodern," a matter of considerable sensitivity in Greece, as Bakalaki and Herzfeld, among others, have noted (Bakalaki 1994; 2003; Herzfeld 1986; 1987). In Katarraktis, my comment was considered to be hilariously funny. Most people associated with the village, other than pensioners, lived and worked in Ioannina; they visited the village on weekends and holidays because they liked the village, and they liked the donkeys as well; that was part of what the village was about for them. In fact, they liked the donkeys in the same way as many visitors to villages from cities like donkeys: relatively secure in their own sense of modernity, the people of Katarraktis experienced the donkeys in terms of tradition, not premodernity. In that sense, the donkeys were part of a modernity in which Katarraktis people felt they themselves participated: the donkeys were the traditional part of that modernity. Donkeys did not represent premodernity and did not mean, by implication, that the villagers were "premodern." They were something funny and enjoyable, not something embarrassing.

In contrast, in Ktismata, while people felt just as involved in modernity, their particular experience of modernity had generated a sense of being caught up in it, of being embattled by it, rather than the sense of personal participation that Katarraktis peoples expressed. After all, "modernization" had not only been about economic developments; it had also centrally involved political ideology and the tensions over the Greek-Albanian border—which, among other things, marked the fault line between two very different political opinions about how to "modernize." Hoxha was a strong supporter of scientific socialism and was busily carrying out "modernizations" of his own (Pollo and Puto 1981: 266; Biberaj 1990: 68–69; Jacques 1995: 464). Ktismata had been caught in the imposed gap between these two political enmities: cut off from the Albanian side and being only halfheartedly given an opportunity to participate in the "modernizations" going on elsewhere on the Greek side. The sense of uninterested neglect and invisibility that seemed associated with being in a non-empty gap was once again reiterated.

Shifting Whereness

This chapter has skipped to and fro between enumerations, narrative accounts, and the embodied experience of the shifting "whereness" of places and people around the Kasidiaris area. Things did change: people moved differently at different times; the place was accounted for in different ways at different times; the separations and recombinations of places shifted over time; how things seemed, and how things were made to be, shifted over time; what became visible and what became invisible shifted over time. Yet somehow, in all this shifting, there was a reiteration of the relative relations between places, people, and movement. The two communes I have focused upon here, Katarraktis and Ktismata, were both "peripheral" in some senses: Katarraktis was a small Eastern Kasidiaris commune with a relatively overgrown territory that had not been involved in all the agricultural reforms that had taken place on the Doliana Plain from the period of the civil war until the 1980s; Ktismata was a larger Western Kasidiaris commune with a relatively overgrown territory that was exceedingly close to the Greek-Albanian border, which had particularly affected the territory's "shaping" and "reshaping," as well as affecting how that reshaping felt to the people associated with the place. Yet despite the fact that both these communes were on the edge (as it were) of their respective regions, the two different kinds of "whereness" that were involved in the shifts were reiterated, in different ways, across all the communes of both Western and Eastern Kasidiaris; there was a self-similarity about them. And what made them seem to be reiterations was the way in which each shift seemed to repeat the past relative status of these places. For example, Eastern Kasidiaris had been marked as more worth owning than Western Kasidiaris during the Ottoman era; in the postwar years, Eastern Kasidiaris was regarded as more worth "developing" than Western Kasidiaris. While the Western Kasidiaris area had become (again) an ambiguously ordinary place that was of little interest, the Eastern Kasidiaris area had become (again) an ordinary kind of place where people could make something of a living, but not in a particularly large-scale way. In both cases, people had a sense of the repeated involvement of "forces" (political, economic, bureaucratic) that seemed to be pursuing interests that had little to do with the particularities of the Kasidiaris; but somehow, their involvement reiterated the "nesting hierarchies" across the region, repeated them in different forms at different times.

And here enters the final reiteration that I will be considering in this book: the combined entanglement of the European Union and the reopening of the border, two "developments" that once again involved "forces" beyond the particularities of the Kasidiaris area, and that once again reiterated the ambiguous ordinariness of the Western Kasidiaris regions' "whereness."

CHAPTER 7

Developments

BY THE TIME I ARRIVED IN EPIRUS in the 1990s, all the shifting relations of place and people (and their nonempty gaps) that I have explored thus far were there, jostling with one another and interweaving, both visible and invisible, crisscrossing differing accounts of the past and present, as well as the paths between one place and another. Parts of the Zagori had been made into a national park; the Doliana Plain was marked as a place of agricultural activity and contained a couple of growing towns, populated by "ordinary" people, some of whom were engaged in intensive agricultural activity on the "improved" plain, and others of whom disdained such activity as "mere farming"; the asphalt was slowly being extended out from the now rapidly growing city of Ioannina, beyond the national roads and into some of the smaller villages, particularly those with special tourist interest, now mostly funded with European Union monies; work on widening and improving the road to the Greek-Albanian border was seriously underway.

Through all this, the villages and towns of the Western Kasidiaris area had been through repeated processes of becoming virtually invisible and becoming vaguely visible since the reopening of the border, in a kind of ambiguous and neglected way. To paraphrase Bracewell and Drace-Francis, that made it difficult to know whether there was any *there* there (Bracewell and Drace-Francis 1999: 59), for any distinction of the place was unnamed, and otherwise it constituted a lack of distinction; and that too seemed to be a reiteration of things that had gone before.[1] My inability to find an appropriate name for the place in my earliest fieldwork notes was indicative of this kind of combined ordinariness and ambiguity. The different processes of marginalization, of separation and recombining, of making things matter and making them not matter, of moving and fixing in place, were all still there and intermingling when I arrived, marked in the place and in people's accounts of the place and of themselves. And over the years, the people associated with the area taught me how to see all of that.

As a conclusion, I am going make a final and all-too-brief additional note about this ambiguous marginality, in considering the entanglement between two of the most recent "developments" around the Kasidiaris area: the reopening of the Greek-Albanian border and the introduction of European Union–funded development projects, which were scattered across the region. I have already discussed them both in various ways; my interest here is to consider how they interwove with one another. Once again, it is not my intention to closely study their characteristics, let alone to study "development" as a concept; it is more to consider the relations between them and how their entanglement tended to once again reiterate the ambiguity and peculiar ordinariness of this place and some of the people associated with it.

This particular entanglement involved, among other things, a highlighting of some of the tensions and ambiguities in the relationship between modernity and "modernization." In chapter 4, I explored how the hegemonic concept of the Balkans strongly resisted the possibility of imagining the Balkans as "modern." I also noted that in some senses, one could argue this rendered the Balkans acutely modern, in that the Balkans were constituted as such by modernist ways of making things meaningful; but that hegemonic concept of the Balkans led to continued attempts to keep things separate within them that were, in modernist terms, too interrelated in this place. For most people in Epirus, there was a widespread understanding that this region had been subjected to numerous and diverse modernist technologies, ideologies, and policies during this process; and each one of them possessed its own assertion of what constituted "proper" forms of modernization, attempts to impose modernity in a particular way. The European Union's policies that informed the more recent development projects—regionalism as opposed to nationalism (Harvie 1994), environmental sustainability as opposed to industrialization (Baker 1997; Jenkins 2000), the promotion of cultural heritage and an espousal of multicultural values both as a nonnationalist form of (European) cultural identification and as a marketing strategy (Jenkins 2000; Shore 1993 and 2000; Bellier 2000; McDonald 1996)—all these policies constituted one more version of modernization, which would jostle with the others. It would particularly jostle with the reopening of the border and the presence in Epirus of peoples marked as Northern Epirot and Albanian. An exploration of that jostling, particularly in the Western Kasidiaris area, is what concerns me here, for it highlights the numerous gaps left by attempts to apply various forms of "modernization" to places and peoples that could not be conclusively separated out in modernist terms. In particular, it highlights the way modernization practices are always inflected by (diverse) ideological assertions about the way things are, in their pursuit of putting into effect the way things ought to be. The diversity and sometimes the open conflict between these attempts at modernization generated a sense that even "Western" modernity is not a homogenous, ontologically identifiable philosophy and set of practices, but is both singular and multiple simultaneously. In fact, the tension between the idea that it is singular and the experience of modernity as multiple defined quite a lot of what was going on here in the late 1990s: the assumption that modernity is one kind of thing, while the practices involved in modernization in this region were continually informed by competing ideological understandings of how things ought to be, generated gaps, "rips and darned patches" in de Certeau's terms (de Certeau 1988: frontispiece), in the assumption that ("Western") modernity is a homogenous entity.

I will begin with a brief account about Northern Epirots and Albanians, for people marked with these names explicitly dwelled in gaps during the 1990s: gaps left by previous and imagined future modernizations; gaps that were embodied in places as much as in imaginings of how things might become; gaps whose existence kept on becoming visible through these people's presence in them, and kept on constituting things as too interrelated and therefore simultaneously ambiguous in modernist terms. Various official and unofficial attempts to close these gaps, attempts to make things appear clearly separated out, constituted a large part of how people who were distinguished as Northern Epirots and Albanians experienced being in Epirus: various attempts to literally and symbolically police the gaps. But there were other, more muted things going on as well, things that relied upon an unspoken insistence on ambiguity to effectively dwell in those gaps. The cost of that for some, however, was to remain unnameable within whichever modernist rhetoric was used; it constituted a reiteration that the differences made no difference because such differences were always contested, and that in the end, this place and its peoples were "just" ordinary.

Dwelling in the Gaps

One day in October 1994, I was waiting for a bus to take me from Ktismata to Ioannina, being without my car at the time. Two older women and a policeman who were waiting there asked me where I was from, and one of the women asked me whether I had a visa. As usual, I avoided the question and explained what I was doing there, and that was the end of the matter; no one demanded papers from me.

That was starkly different from the experience of three men who arrived at the bus stop shortly afterward, looking rather tired and dusty. They caught the attention of three soldiers, all of them armed, who walked up to them and demanded to see their papers. The men immediately presented these, one of them stating that they were Northern Epirots.

It would be easy to see this moment as a classic act of interpellation in Althusser's terms: the policeman (the soldier) called, and the men responded by naming themselves, thereby being named in the act of being called. In that sense, the soldiers were generating a separation and purification: these men had been constituted as being different from the others standing at the bus stop (including myself) in a particular way, one that gave the soldiers the right to interrogate them and attempt to control their movements. However, that is only part of what was going on, and here I would agree with Herzfeld that Althusser's understanding of interpellation is insufficient (Herzfeld 1997: 29). By stating that they were Northern Epirot, the men acknowledged the soldiers' right to call them, but at the same time, the statement was an attempt at negotiation: being marked as Northern Epirot might not be as good as an assumption that there was nothing to mark, but it was better, in this context, than being marked as Albanian. Self-identification as Northern Epirot claimed some commonality, even some kinship, with these men's interrogators in nationalist terms: the difference—the men's being from another state—should make no difference. The men were able to do this because the distinctions between people in this region were ambiguous; they were open to question, negotiation, contested meanings.

To return to the incident—one of the soldiers, who was carrying a walkie-talkie, inspected the men's papers for a minute, then declared that they were not in good order. One of the passports, he asserted, had a "fake" photograph in it. He looked at the man whose photograph was in the passport and asked, "Why did you change the photograph in this passport, eh?" The man replied that he had not changed it; it was his photograph and his passport.

The soldier changed tack for a while, and the other two joined in, asking repeatedly how the men had got to Ktismata and what they were doing there. The men patiently responded to each question, saying that they were going to Ioannina to work at jobs they had there, and explaining that they had walked to Ktismata, not via the official border post at Kakavia, but using old paths.

"Why didn't you come through Kakavia?" One of the soldiers demanded.

"We just didn't," one of the men replied, and then added, "We came the way we knew, and anyway, it's shorter that way."

"Don't you know it's illegal to cross into Greece except through Kakavia?" The soldier demanded. The men did not reply.

The soldiers then returned to the matter of the documents. Having dismissed one of the passports as a forgery, they turned to a different document belonging to one of the other men. It was a pass that permitted travel into Greece for Albanian citizens if they had secured work in

Greece. However, these passes were no longer valid, since the Greek government had recently revoked them in protest at the trial and conviction in Albania of five members of Omonia (a Greek nationalist organization in Albania); they had been accused of killing three Albanian soldiers and injuring three others in April of 1994. Incidentally, the Greek government's habit of providing visas to people from Albania and then revoking them was a regular occurrence while I was in Epirus; many people from Albania whom I met protested that even if they tried to do things legally, the rules kept on changing, so they invariably ended up on the wrong side of the law. On this occasion, the man who had presented the pass insisted that it must be valid, because he was working for the Municipality of Ioannina, which had given him the papers so that he could get to his job. This did not impress the soldiers at all. The one with the walkie-talkie used it to announce to someone at the other end that he had "three balls," and requested transport to be brought to the bus stop to return them to Albania.

When the public bus to Ioannina arrived, the three men were still standing there, guarded by the soldiers. The soldier with the walkie-talkie got on the bus and asked the conductor if he had anything to report. The conductor replied that he thought there was one "suspicious" passenger, and he pointed her out. This was a woman who looked to be in her early seventies. The soldier looked at her pass and again announced that it was no longer valid. She burst into tears, protesting that she was an old lady and needed to get to Ioannina to buy medicines for a sick daughter, that she did not know anything about bureaucracy, and that she had been assured the papers were valid. The soldier began arguing with her, but then a distant voice on the walkie-talkie announced, "Let her through." Much to the soldier's obvious annoyance, he got off the bus without her and carried on standing guard over his "three balls." As the bus pulled away, the "balls" watched with a look of resignation, one of them staring skyward and sighing. The woman on the bus had slipped through the gap; the three men had not, on this occasion.

This one incident was typical of the continual policing of the border area throughout the time I was in Epirus, and it contained many of the elements of how, in official terms, people from Albania, whether marked as Northern Epirots or as Albanians, were constituted as "matter out of place," to use Mary Douglas's famous phrase (Douglas 1966), or as territorially "displaced," in Liisa Malkki's formulation (Malkki 1992). And it is worth noting that in terms of the state, there was no difference made at the time between "Albanian" and "Northern Epirot" in this respect, even though in terms of the ideology of the Greek nation, there was every kind of difference. In fact, when the borders had first opened in 1991, the then secretary of state for foreign affairs in the Greek govern-

Figure 9. Graffiti in Ioannina. "Hands off the Albanian Workers," signed by "OSE" (Socialist Organization of Greece). "Albanian" was later crossed out and replaced with "Northern Epirot." The original was painted in red, the subsequent edit in blue, colors regularly used to indicate left-wing and right-wing political preferences.

ment had openly welcomed all "Northern Epirots" into Greece; but this policy had been reversed in later years, after the newspapers began to talk about "floods" of immigrants, suggesting that many who claimed to be Northern Epirot were not. The lack of clarity in distinctions between different kinds of Albanian citizens had allowed considerable room for widespread doubt on the matter. In any event, given these continually changing policies (the one emphasizing cultural nationality, the other emphasizing state citizenship), it is perhaps not altogether surprising that many people in Greece also often confused the two, while others continued to insist that the distinction was clear and absolute (fig. 9 provides some interesting graffiti on this issue).

The incident at the bus stop in Ktismata raised this issue in terms of the policing of separations through passports and visas, a means, as others have noted, by which the state continues to assert the power to name people and to control movement in this transnational world (Navaro-Yashin 2003; Goldsworthy 1999: 110; Torpey 2000; Mongia 1999). And the incident also highlights the habit that people from the Albanian side of the border had of using the old and now mostly overgrown paths that in the past interconnected the Albanian and Greek sides of the border—another cause of considerable levels of disquiet. Apart from the fact that walking across the border that way made a mockery of the idea that the border served as a solid separation between Greece and Albania, those old paths and overgrown places had been reconstituted as "wilderness" over the years, places representing a past that was no longer inhabited. Having people officially defined as "illegal aliens" wandering around in such places was not only unacceptable to the state; it also caused many people in the area to feel extremely unsafe (Green 1998c).

In part, that sense of threat was exacerbated by the media-fueled perception in Greece that Albanians (and often, by extension, those named as Northern Epirot) constituted "wild," "desperate," "criminal," and "disheveled" people—or, to put it more briefly, "Balkan" people. Therein lies another ambiguity for people in Epirus living on the Greek side of the border. Bakalaki's observation that negative stereotyping of the newly arrived Albanians in much of Greece has been used as a means to distance Greece and Greeks from being marked as "Balkan" is particularly pertinent here. She notes: "[T]he conflation of Balkan peoples with Albanians reflects Greeks' negation or at best reluctant admission of their own membership in this part of the world. Given the tenacity of the generalized notion of Europe as the touchstone of cultural hierarchy in the Balkans, it is not surprising that one's identification as a Westerner and as a Balkan would be seen as incompatible" (Bakalaki 2003: 219).

Given that Epirus has been marked as more Balkan than other parts of Greece, and that this is largely due to the region's past interrelations with Albania (symbolized by the Greek name, Northern Epirus, for that southern Albanian region and by the naming of the peoples who "belong" there as Northern Epirots), the reopening of the border and the reinvoking of the Balkans as leaking across that border placed the area in a particularly ambiguous position. While the official location of the state border that Albanians crossed was clear (even if often ignored in practice), the precise location of the border, in both nationalist and cultural terms, had never been clear, even at the official level (for the Orthodox Church as well as the state): Northern Epirus was constituted as "Greek" in some senses within Greece, but it was also part of the Albanian state, which was leaking its Balkanness into Greece. That not only resulted in an ambiguity about what kind of persons Northern Epirots constituted (part of the Balkan leakiness or part of Greek purity, to be rescued from that leakiness?), as seen in the changing policies on visas mentioned above; it also resulted in an ambiguity about what the region of Greece next to this leaky border constituted. The use of the old paths that people on both sides of the border had used in the past highlighted that ambiguity: it made visible the gaps, the unfinished business or leftovers, of previous attempts to separate things out in the place, and it therefore highlighted the way the separation had not been, and probably could not be, completed.

There was even more than this, however. Bakalaki also notes that in much of the rest of Greece, people regularly evoked a nostalgic construction of the past as having been entirely safe, a time when people could leave their doors unlocked without any worry that they might be burgled or come to harm (Bakalaki 2003: 212). This was contrasted with the present, in which this Balkan "leakiness" had made Greece unsafe (ibid.: 218). In Epirus, people also said that kind of thing, but the idea of the past as having been "safe" was regularly restricted to a specific time period: from the Metaxas dictatorship (1936–41) until the reopening of the border in the early 1990s, with the exception of the period of the Second World War and the Greek civil war. People regularly suggested that before Metaxas, who instituted strong controls over theft and other kinds of crime, Epirus had not been a "safe" place at all (Green 1998b). This was a view particularly strongly expressed by transhumant pastoralists. For example, one Sarakatsanos from Delvinaki commented: "In the old days, it was very dangerous—there were Turkish soldiers about, who invented their own laws, and there were loads of thieves and other criminals. And until Metaxas came along and broke some heads, as far back in history as you want to go, there were always thieves and corrupt administrators and soldiers. So we got together and cooperated between families for protection, for safety." The same kind of view was expressed by others as well; as I discussed in chapter 2, those in Pogoni particularly marked out Thesprotia as a place of danger. The appearance of people constituted as "illegal aliens" in the overgrown forests and nooks and crannies of Epirus, an appearance that rendered the place "unsafe", was therefore not something new; it was the reiteration of something that had happened before, albeit somewhat differently this time. In fact, one could say that periods of "safety" seemed the least enduring state of affairs here. Again, what I have called the hegemonic understanding of the Balkans as fractal enters into the equation.

Furthermore, a certain proportion of the people "sneaking around in the bushes" were the kin and old friends of those on the Greek side of the border. To people in many villages along the border, if not to the police and army, there was a difference between "sneaking" and simply walking across the border for a visit to buy goods or to see people, an act that rendered the border (and the separations and purifications it asserted) irrelevant. For example, while I was visiting Argyrohori one day, I met three men, who said they were Northern Epirots, sitting outside the *kafeneio*. They were visiting for the day, they explained, having just walked from Albania by passing over the hill behind the village.

Figure 10. Argyrohori president (leaning against railing) with three Northern Epirots at village *kafeneio*

They said they came to shop and to catch up with people and would be returning in the evening. The president of Argyrohori was sharing a drink with them (fig. 10).

Incidentally, one of these men, who was a teacher, discussed changes in land ownership that were then being implemented in Albania, in the postsocialist transition. It was not working, he said, because everyone was to be granted a certain portion of land that was much less than many had owned before the communist revolution; in any case, he went on, it was not the same land as people had owned before, so people thought they were being given lower-quality land. I grinned, explaining that this sounded very much like the land redistribution programs that had been implemented at the end of Ottoman rule and then in the 1960s and 1970s on the Greek side of the border, and that the arguments about these changes sounded much the same as well. He laughed loudly, and commented, "See? It's all the same bullshit, wherever you are."

Under such circumstances, maintaining a clear separation between the Greek and the Albanian sides could be done only through a continual refusal to clarify the ambiguities, through ignoring the leftovers of previous attempts to establish separations that could not be resolved because the location of the separations (as it were) remained contested. The effort to "ignore the border" in this sense did not always entirely succeed, because at the same time, others felt it was as important to make things distinct, which tended to highlight the existence of the gaps, of the ambiguities in the accounts of essential and clear distinction. In short, the many and various contested attempts to clarify, separate, or make claims to purity occurred in the company of the many ambiguous relations and similarities that the two sides shared.

This tension between ambiguity and assertions of purity and separation were occasionally (though not often) directly confronted. For example, I had a conversation one day with a taxi driver, who was waiting to drive a family back across the border into Albania after they had been shopping in Ioannina. He commented that in his opinion, "Northern Epirots" had not helped themselves: they were "lazy" and had not reconstructed their infrastructures since the end of communist rule. He believed this was to do with their having intermarried with Albanians during the communist period. In four hundred years of Turkish rule, he went on, Greeks never intermarried with Albanians. In one fell swoop, the taxi driver had asserted that the Greek side of the border was distinct from and superior to the Albanian side on three counts: the Greek side was more technologically advanced; the people on the Greek side worked harder; and the people on the Greek side had kept themselves "pure," had not become Balkan "mongrels."

Another man in the *kafeneio*, who was from Ktismata, immediately challenged him, saying that his own mother spoke only Albanian when she married his father; was the taxi driver saying that he (the man from Ktismata) was not properly Greek because his mother spoke only Albanian? The taxi driver retorted that he was not talking about *that* kind of intermarriage; he was talking about Christians' marrying Muslims. Well, then, the other man retorted, he should have said so. The conversation then went on to what were considered to be "safer" topics: that some Albanians had been "defiling" Greek monasteries in Epirus in recent months, and that some had intermarried with Chinese people during communist rule.[2] Both of these topics carefully avoided the ambiguities that had previously arisen and returned matters to clear separations that both could agree upon, ones that did not directly entangle the people on the Greek side of the border.

On the other side of the border as well, there had been various efforts to clarify and separate the overlaps. People I met who described themselves as Northern Epirots occasionally commented that during the communist period the Hoxha regime had made attempts to "erase" their Greekness by altering their names, by banning religion beginning in 1967, by moving them away from Northern Epirus, and by forcing them to speak Albanian most of the time.[3] That had the effect, some said, of considerably reducing the apparent number of Northern Epirots in Northern Epirus. This could be seen as another attempted act of interpellation, this time on the part of the Albanian state. However, many of the people I met also added that none of this had "really" altered their Northern Epirot status as far as they were concerned, evoking the notion that nationality is always already there, even before any nation exists (Gourgouris 1996), and therefore whatever happened, there would always be a difference between Greeks and Albanians. As a result, many who regarded themselves as Northern Epirots resented the fact that they were seen by many people in Greece as no different from Albanians. This is one more example of the apparently endless contestability of efforts at purification and separation in this region.

Aside from these continual confrontations with the leakiness and fuzziness of the border in terms of what it meant about the place and the people involved, and the various attempts to "purify" these ambiguities, there were also fairly regular attempts to establish a separation between the two sides in economic and infrastructural terms, as hinted at by the taxi driver. In one sense, that was easier than the question of national and cultural separations, as it could be effectively argued that Albania was more "disheveled" than Greece in this respect. There did indeed appear to be far less infrastructure and poorer standards of living in Albania than in Greece, which was obviously, for most people on the Greek side, the reason that so many people from Albania were crossing the border into Greece. Moreover, since Albania had been communist and Greece had not, Greece was axiomatically more "Western" than Albania. An elision between "modernization," "Westernization," and capitalism, as if each axiomatically implied the others, led to the widespread assertion that Greece was more "modernized" than Albania.[4]

While most people, from both sides of the border, tended to agree with this perspective, there were also complications. As people began to become more familiar with one another, those on the Greek side became aware that a version of unmistakable "modernization" had also occurred in Albania. Hoxha, being a strong advocate of scientific and industrial socialism, intended to transform Albania "from a backward agricultural country into an agricultural and industrial economy" (Pollo and Puto 1981: 26). Biberaj notes that Hoxha's industrialization policies had "led to the creation of a relatively modern multibranched industry, which by 1985 was generating more than 40 percent of the total national income" (Biberaj 1990: 68). Agricultural reforms, apart from a staged program of collectivization and the state's takeover of all agricultural land, were equally major: "Large-scale programs of land reclamation, soil improvement, and irrigation; the introduction of new farm techniques and mechanization; and increased use of fertilizers" had "contributed to a significant expansion and modernization of agricultural production" (ibid.: 69). And education was also overhauled: from 1946 onward, education was to be secular, free, and state-provided, with seven years' primary education compulsory for everyone; vocational and trade schools were set up; a program to abolish illiteracy was established (Jacques 1995: 464).

In short, while there was no doubt that Albania was more impoverished than Greece in economic terms when the border was reopened, it became increasingly clear that what had occurred on the two sides were different forms of the same process; it was not that one side modernized while the other remained as it had been when the borders had closed. As a result, the axiomatic links between modernization, "Westernization," and capitalist political economies began to look a little looser than they previously had. In particular, the interaction between the two sides highlighted the way that different forms of modernization *asserted*, rather than necessitated, a link with certain ideological notions of how things are and how they should be. So, while much of the national Greek media was depicting Albania as a backward place full of backward, desperate, and disheveled people, a place that seemed to have been preserved in some kind of aspic since the border had been closed, in Epirus that depiction was reiterated alongside another one: that the difference between the two sides came down to two ideologies of modernization—one communist, the other capitalist.

What is more, many people on both sides of the border shared a sense that the form of modernization to which their areas had been given access was a lesser version than had been available elsewhere in their respective countries. On the Greek side, as I have already discussed at length, there was the sense that the borderland area in particular had been neglected and abandoned, that there was no industry there, and that the region as a whole had been repeatedly constituted as less "European" and less "sophisticated" than other parts of Greece. On the Albanian side of the border, there was a sense that the region was treated with deep suspicion by the Tirana-based Albanian government, both because of its "Greekness" and because it was a borderland area; and that its agricultural activities, while reorganized and to some extent mechanized, had been kept at a fairly low level of technological sophistication, despite the Albanian government's continual statements to the contrary. Dimitris, a man who identified himself as Northern Epirot—and who was now the caretaker of a technical school, set up in Pogoniani for Northern Epirot teenagers (funded by a $5 million donation from a shipping magnate called Latsis, whose family came from Northern Epirus)—expressed this view particularly strongly. He suggested that living in Northern Epirus during the communist era meant constantly being spied upon, constantly having to use tools that did not work properly, constantly being kept in a state of impoverishment in comparison to other parts of Albania, and constantly being fed a stream of statements from the government asserting that "Albania is the most advanced country in the world." Dimitris had occasionally been able to watch Italian and Greek television stations, he said, for short periods until the Hoxha regime jammed the signals, and these were enough to indicate that things were not as "advanced" in Southern Albania as the government asserted.

The sense of having inadequate access to certain forms of modernization is of course also widespread in Greece as a whole. As many anthropologists have noted, Greeks are perpetually uncertain about whether Greece is considered to be as "modern" as other parts of Europe in "Western" terms; in more recent years, this has been accompanied by a sense that the version of modernity to which most Greeks have access is a sort of copy, a mimesis of something authentic that properly exists elsewhere.[5] As Bakalaki puts it, "That for many Greeks the capacity to maintain a modern lifestyle still rests on access to 'stolen goods' is evidenced by the high demand for cheap-priced commodities (locally manufactured, but often also illegally imported from third world countries) bearing the fake names and logos of prestigious American and European brands" (Bakalaki 2003: 221).

In Epirus, there was certainly a strong element of that expressed by many people; but the way it was expressed included a sense of nested hierarchies, as it were. While Greece as a whole was not granted "authentic" modernity of the "Western" sort, Epirus was granted even less, and Albania even less than that. This generated a widespread aggrieved belief that Epirots, as people, were as modern (in the "Western" sense) as anyone else, but that in Epirus, they did not have access to "proper" modernity. The fact that almost invariably, people in Epirus spoke of "modernization"[6] rather than "modernity"[7] reflected this notion of *being* modern while the place had not been modernized appropriately.

The sense of nested hierarchies is important here: while there was an increasing realization among many people in Epirus that modernization comes in not just one but many forms, the habit of measuring that diversity against a single scale of value ("better" or "worse," "authentic" or "fake," forms of modernity) led to the idea that one particular form of modernity (the "Western" form) was the "best" sort, the standard or benchmark, against which all others were to be measured. This harks back to the point that Richard Wilk makes in commenting on the efforts of people in Belize to participate in international beauty pageants—the "celebration of difference and diversity" involved a standardized measure against which that diversity is valued (Wilk 1995); and to Herzfeld's concept of a "global hierarchy of value" in his study of the artisans of Crete (Herzfeld 2004).

The use of this kind of single scale of evaluation meant that in addition to the notion that Greece and Greeks are always offered a kind of inauthentic copy, or lesser version, of "Western" modernity, in the Epirot region, which was constituted as more "Balkan" than other parts of Greece, that valorized form of modernity would be particularly inaccessible. That people from Northern Epirus felt much the same about their place on the other side of the border was not particularly surprising to those on the Greek side (on the assumption that Albania, having been a communist state for almost fifty years, was bound to be "backward"); what was more of a revelation was that a range of "modernizations," attached to different ideologies of modernity and political economy, had been instituted in Albania as much as they had been, in a different form, in Greece. What is more, the fact that people on both sides shared the same sense of not being given as much access to the levels of modernization that existed elsewhere in their respective countries once again generated a sense of similarity, not difference.

One of the ways that this particular similarity was expressed during my fieldwork was the widespread habit, on the part of people from Albania, of complaining that Epirus was not "modern" enough for them; many said they intended to leave so as to have access to more "Western" forms of modernity. These people were evidently using the same scale of nested hierarchies as were the people in Epirus, but they were also saying that in fact, the Albanian and Greek sides of the border differed very little in this respect. Some of those on the Greek side took umbrage at this. People from Albania, they felt (especially those identified as Northern Epirots), did not express gratitude when they were given secondhand clothes by villagers on the Greek side, and they complained about levels of pay and working conditions after they arrived: this was seen by their critics as a sign of their lack of manners and "uncivilized" behavior. That response drew on the wider stereotyping of Albanians and Albania within Greece as a whole, and it reasserted a strong distinction between themselves and Albanians.

In contrast, others entirely understood the negative responses of people from Albania toward their early experiences in Epirus and even admired these people, thus implying, once again, that the border did not imply a fixed or essential difference between the two sides. The vice president of Ktismata had this to say about the "lack of gratitude": "Well, you can't blame them, can you? They're treated as if they're primitive half-wits most of the time. But people forget. When I was a boy before the war, we used to think the Albanians were far richer and better off than we were. They had much better clothes, and they ate wheat bread, whereas we had only corn bread. Maybe it's the other way around now, but it wasn't always like that." Some people I met who identified themselves as Northern Epirot felt a deep resentment about the way they were treated by many on the Greek side of the border, and younger people from Albania (whether identified as Northern Epirot or Albanian) particularly expressed the notion that Epirus was not "modern" enough for them. I understood this to refer directly to a sense that in Epirus, there was little access to what these young people from Albania identified as the consumer benefits of "Western" modernity. For example, two teen-age boys I met who were attending the technical school in Pogoniani said they hated it there because there was nothing to do—no cinema, no dis-cos, nowhere to go of an evening. They showed me their part of the school, which did look a little run-down. One of the boys suggested that Latsis (the benefactor who had paid for the school) had fixed up all the front part of the building which is publicly visible, but that the students still lived "in a dump." They wanted to go to a big city, where there was some life. Meanwhile, the president of Pogoniani expressed deep pride in the school and often commented on how "healthy" and "well-fed" the students looked, comments that unsurprisingly irritated many of the students even further. Incidentally, the purpose of the school was to train Northern Epirot students in vocational skills such as hairdressing (for the girls only) and electronics (for the boys only); it was a boarding school, and the students were expected to return to Albania after com-pleting their (entirely gender-divided) training to use their skills there to help Albania "develop."

A rather different example that also involved Latsis's generosity was that of a couple from Northern Epirus, Kostas and Maria, who lived in Doliana. Following the reopening of the border, Latsis had bought up a number of empty houses in villages around Epirus, including some in Doliana. He stipulated that the houses were for Northern Epirots only, and that they should live in them rent-free.[8] Kostas and Maria had moved into one of those houses. Kostas was a qualified stonemason and immedi-ately secured a great deal of work in "restoring" the cultural heritage of many villages in the area, particularly those that had received funding from the European Union for the purpose; Maria was a seamstress and had specialized in making wedding gowns, and she had also built up quite a lot of work.

After two years, the houses donated by Latsis became the property of the communes, and after this, the Doliana council began to charge rent. Kostas and Maria decided at that point to move to Ioannina. By that time, they had made enough money to buy a flat there, and Kostas began teaching stonemasonry at a technical school in Ioannina, in addition to continuing his own work. In any event, Maria could get a lot more work in Ioannina and could also charge higher prices.

The point of these two examples is that people from Albania shared the same kinds of aspirations and understanding of the nested hierarchies of diverse "modernities" as most of the people on the Greek side of the border, and like many on the Greek side of the border, they concluded that they could not pursue those aspirations in the villages and towns of Epirus. In that sense, the arrival of these people and their subsequent departure simply reinforced both the symbolic and the embodied constructions of Epirus that I have explored already at some length.

On the other hand, those people from Albania who *did* stay in Epirus contributed a great deal to certain shifts in relations within the place, quite apart from their "sneaking around" in the bushes. Stonemasonry and dressmaking were only two of the skills that they brought with them; they also regularly took on work as pastoralists, tending sheep, goats, and cattle, often taking them up into the hills for grazing as Epirots had done in the past. As I mentioned in the chapter 6, after a few years this was having the effect of clearing a certain amount of the overgrowth from the mountains. Further, groups of musicians were beginning to come over as well, and they began to play regularly at the villages' summer festivals and at weddings, often replacing the Gypsy musicians who used to play at such events.[9] The reasons people in Epirus generally gave for hiring them combined cost and the assertion that they played "truly traditional" Pogoni music. In other words, the view that people in Albania had hardly changed since the border closed gave them the advantage of appearing to be "authentically traditional" (the alternative view, that they had completely changed as a result of communist rule, was quietly ignored in this context). So while there were widespread stories that the arrival in Epirus of Albanians and Northern Epirots heralded a period that was dangerous and chaotic, their arrival also apparently partly "restored," both literally and metaphorically, much of the tradition (in modernist terms) that many folklorists were arguing was in danger of being lost from the region. That meant these people constituted a particularly useful workforce in the many EU-funded development projects scattered around Epirus, all of which had a strong component involving the "sprucing up" of cultural heritage for the purpose of making it into a marketable resource. The irony and the ambiguity here—that people who in other contexts were marked as uncivilized, mongrel, Balkan "others" were in this context cast as representatives of cultural authenticity and traditions that were in danger of being lost—was fairly obvious to many people. Constituting these peoples as both of these things rested on an apparently impossible combination: that they were simultaneously both the other and the self.[10]

Over the years, some people from Albania have stayed for relatively long periods in some of the towns and villages around Epirus; others regularly come and go between Greece and Albania; others stayed for just a brief time and moved on. In short, they have enacted the same variation in movements as those on the Greek side had done. At first, it was mostly those who identified as Northern Epirots (whether or not they were so

Figure 11. Doliana church having plaster removed to restore it to a more "traditional" state. The plaster was applied in earlier years to "modernize" the church.

identified by others) who were settling down in houses in the villages around the Kasidiaris area, though increasingly it had been those who identified themselves as Albanians as well. In some villages, this had considerably increased the younger population and even contributed to schools' being kept open.

That included Delvinaki, the biggest town in the Pogoni region, which was also one of the few places in Pogoni County that managed to secure funding from the European Union to carry out various "developments" in and around the town, aimed at attracting tourism and making good use of its natural and cultural "resources." It is here that I will return to the "just Greek" peoples of Epirus, to those who were not explicitly marked in the way that peoples called Northern Epirots and Albanians had been, in order to consider how the particular version of "modernization" that was being proposed through the criteria of the development projects became entangled with the contested ambiguities of the border area. Although there were many other such projects whose progress I followed in detail while in Epirus, it is this one that I will focus upon in completing this story, for it draws out how the named and the unnamed come together in this most recent reconstitution of the "whereness" of the western side of the Kasidiaris. It does this ambiguously, of course, for it is difficult to directly refer to that which remains unnamed.

Developments in the Gaps

Delvinaki is nestled in a ring of forested hills, about seven kilometers from the Albanian border. It is some way off the main artery road leading to the border and therefore not a place that visitors might happen across; they have to intend to go there, and because of the ring of hills, the town is not actually visible from any angle until you are within about a hundred yards of the first houses. It is the biggest town in Pogoni County, with some six hundred people living there most of the time. It was the only municipality in the area until the recent reorganization of local government in Greece, in which almost all communes have been abolished and replaced by the merging of several old communes into entities called municipalities. Today, Delvinaki is the "head village" of a cluster of Upper Pogoni communes that constitute the Delvinaki municipality. However, my fieldwork ended in 1998, before all these changes took full effect, though there were heated debates about them while I was there.

Delvinaki was given the status of a municipality in 1949, mostly because it was the largest village close to the border, and the Greek state needed an administrative structure nearby to deal with the ongoing border issues after its closure. Until the recent change in the local government organization, it also carried out the administrative duties involving Pogoni County as a whole.

As I discussed in chapter 2, in the past Delvinaki was a major stopover point for transhumant pastoralists; it constituted the summer grazing grounds of many Vlach families who spent the winter months in the low coastal areas in Thesprotia, and of some Sarakatsani, who passed through on their way to Albania or Thesprotia. There was also a long history of some Gypsy families' living there. The others in the town considered themselves to be "ordinary Greeks"; in the past, most of the "ordinary Greek" adult men would travel to Constantinople and other cities for most of their adult lives. Unlike the Lower Pogoni villages, Delvinaki had no plains on which to carry out large-scale cultivation. The hills were used mostly by transhumant pastoralists, with the "ordinary Greeks" keeping just a few sheep and goats for their own use. So the "ordinary Greeks" were mostly dependent upon income from the men who worked away, the rental income from the transhumant pastoralists, and some passing trade from the transhumant route. The Delvinaki people therefore considered themselves rather a cut above those living in the Lower Pogoni area, not being "black-kneed" cultivators.

Today, the majority of the population in Delvinaki are considered to be Vlachoi, families that settled down over the years in the village as transhumance pastoralism began to wane. There are also quite a number of Gypsy families, many of whom have become well-known musicians in the area, a few Sarakatsani families, and a minority of "ordinary Greek" families. In addition, there were fifteen families from Albania (or about sixty people, all identified as Northern Epirots) that had settled there by 1997, since the reopening of the border. None of these families had kin in Delvinaki; they chose the town, I was told, because it is the biggest in the area. In recent years, some families that were identified as Albanian have also moved in. In addition to contributing their labor to the various development projects funded by the European Union, they worked as hired shepherds and did various manual work jobs around the town; the women also worked in a small rug-making business.

Finally, there was a handful of families that still visited Delvinaki seasonally as transhumant shepherds. One group of three brothers, who spent the summer season on Delvinaki lands with their cattle, and who spent the winters in Thesprotia, became quite involved in one of the disputes involving the development projects, and I will return to them later.

Despite the fact that the majority of people currently living in Delvinaki for most of the year are identified as Vlachoi, the town was never marked as a Vlach town either by people from the town or by others, in sharp contrast with some other places in Upper Pogoni, particularly Kefalovriso. The reason for this seemed to be threefold. First, the Vlachoi were considered to be relatively recent arrivals as residents, and therefore they did not "belong" quite as much as the "ordinary Greeks," who had lived there as residents earlier. In contrast, Kefalovriso was regarded as "always" having been a Vlach village. Second, while the year-round population of "ordinary Greeks" was much smaller than the year-round Vlach population, this did not stop the people who lived elsewhere for most of the year from being "from" Delvinaki, so by another measure of population, the town was still mostly "ordinary Greek."

Third, and important for my purposes here, there was the habit of deliberately avoiding openly marking differences between the residents in terms of the public image of the town. This had to do with the wider construction of homogenous Greekness in the development of Greek nationality, combined with that sense of ambiguous ordinariness which I have already discussed. This avoidance of marking difference was present in almost every village I visited, with the exception of two or three identified as being specifically "Vlach." For example, when I was asked to write an article about Doliana for the town's cultural association, I suggested talking about the three different groups that lived there (Vlachoi, Gypsies, and "ordinary Greeks"). These differences were not often openly discussed—though they were sometimes, such as an occasion when I mentioned to some friends in the central part of the village that I was going to attend a music festival in the lower part of the village, and they expressed surprise, as it was regarded as a "Gypsy" festival. Nevertheless, the existence of three different neighborhoods and the marking of these neighborhoods as consisting mostly of one of the three groups, would be clear enough to anyone who spent a few days there. The president of the association was horrified by my suggestion, and spent a full two hours explaining to me that this was not appropriate. This equally strong disinclination to mark differences in Delvinaki meant that any differences remained officially and deliberately unnamed and unmarked, and therefore they were not used as "cultural resources" in applications to the European Union for funds to develop the town's cultural heritage. The development project thus avoided highlighting any kind of explicitly distinct cultural identity; instead, application was made for a few "renovations" and "restorations" of some buildings, which were not in fact hugely distinctive in comparison to similar kinds of buildings elsewhere in Epirus. This was an application for a generic kind of cultural heritage, then. It was a "just Greek" kind of cultural heritage.

Given this background, it is time finally to briefly outline the funded project, which centered on the proposal to build a wild boar sanctuary on Delvinaki lands and would include various "improvements" to the town as well.[11] The mayor at the time first conceived the project in 1993. The territory, much of which is heavily forested and contains a high proportion of oak and oak scrub, also used to contain a large population of wild boar, but in recent years the numbers have dropped considerably, mostly owing to a steep rise in hunting, much of it by city visitors who come for a few days. The boar sanctuary was intended to increase the population of boars and thus increase the area's attractiveness for visiting hunters.

The mayor was an unusually powerful and wealthy man, not only in Pogoni, but in Epirus as a whole. He held multiple positions in political and economic organizations in Epirus; at the time, he was not only the mayor of Delvinaki, he was also the president of the Association of Ioannina Municipalities and Communes (TEDK), the president of the Epirus Board of Timber Products (representing most of the timber producers and processors of Epirus, the second-largest production industry in the area), and the owner of a popular hamburger restaurant franchise in Ioannina. I met him once in the hamburger restaurant, and he spent some time asking me whether I thought the quality of the burgers was as good as in Britain. Even powerful people sometimes checked how well they were doing in "Western modernization" terms: Britain was regarded by most people in Epirus as having achieved considerably higher levels of that kind of "modernization" than Epirus had done, and I was regularly asked to assess the quality of goods or services in Epirus that were particularly associated with this kind of "modernization" against my experience of the same goods and services in Britain. Hamburgers served in an American-style fast-food franchise could hardly have qualified more powerfully as this kind of product (Watson 1997), so I was less surprised by the mayor's question than by the fact that he, in particular, asked it.[12]

In addition to these formal positions, which gave the mayor links to almost every political and economic agency within Epirus, and gave him regular access to information both from the central Greek government and from the EU (concerning, for example, calls for proposals to develop agrotourism), he had numerous informal links with a host of other organizations within Ioannina. For example, TEDK had its offices in the same building in Ioannina as Epirous S.A. Epirous S.A. was the organization set up to carry out research on the present economic, environmental, social, and demographic state of the different parts of Epirus with a view to constructing applications for EU funding for development appropriate to each area. The EU LEADER program, which aimed to encourage "underdeveloped" rural areas to build new projects, and which funded the Delvinaki development projects, was administered through Epirous S.A. Moreover, the research carried out on the current state and needs of Pogoni County, upon which the Delvinaki application for their development projects was built, was carried out by Epirous S.A. In the view of several people I spoke with in Delvinaki, it was through the influence of Delvinaki's mayor that Pogoni County was the first area of Epirus to be researched by Epirous S.A. This study was completed in 1989, two years before the reopening of the border, and in its three-volume report (covering "existing conditions," "development possibilities," and, inevitably, "statistical tables"), it makes little mention of the border, except to note that Pogoni *has* an international border. As usual, the maps in the report show Albania as a blank space in the upper left-hand corner. The report concluded, unsurprisingly, that Pogoni County was one of the most underdeveloped and depopulated areas in Epirus, and that it was in dire need of some development. It also added that the area had considerable potential in that regard, possessing as it did substantial natural and cultural "resources."

Epirous S.A. later worked with the mayor of Delvinaki to put together the applications for LEADER funding to develop the projects outlined above. LEADER (an acronym for Liaisons Entre Actions de Développement de l'Economie Rurale) was the outcome of a policy shift in the European Union. It marked a move away from concentration on particular economic sectors and instead inclined "towards interventions that targeted territories of particular socio-economic disadvantage" (Ray 2000: 164). The program was particularly aimed at "Objective 1 ('lagging' regions with a per capita GDP of 75 per cent or less of the EU average) or Objective 5b (fragile rural economies dominated by agriculture and in need of rural development assistance)" (ibid.). LEADER was also intended to encourage environmentally friendly "sustainable development," and it was further supposed to be designed to be "bottom-up": that is, the program sought "innovative" plans to develop rural areas at the "local" level (which was defined as areas of less than 100,000 population). In this, applicants were expected to make use of their natural and cultural "resources."[13]

The study of Pogoni by Epirous S.A. was commissioned one year after this significant shift in European policy on funds to rural areas, and therefore the Delvinaki mayor was in a very good position to apply for funds when the large-scale LEADER program, LEADER II, was announced in 1993. On the basis of the study demonstrating that Pogoni was highly eligible for these monies, the mayor of Delvinaki, on behalf of the town's council, commissioned a "scientific report" from experts he knew in Ioannina, on the possibility of setting up a wild boar sanctuary, to determine whether it would be environmentally and economically "sustainable." This team drew up the plans for its construction and development.

This background makes it clear that the mayor was in an almost unique position to gain access to information about funds for potential projects and about the political structures and policies that were behind them, as well as access to the organizations in Ioannina that administered them. What is more, since so little attention had been paid to Pogoni County by the more central Greek authorities in the past, for reasons I have already explained at length, the mayor was virtually alone in pursuing EU funds on behalf of the county. In later years, two others in Pogoni would receive some funds from the same source, having watched the mayor of Delvinaki succeed in this way. First, the mayor of Pogoniani, who funded the "improvement" of a small gorge behind the town, which mostly entailed using Albanian labor to build a wide stone slab path through it, with the slabs cemented together; and some small improvements to the "cultural heritage" of the town, which again avoided any specific distinctiveness: it was, again, "generic" cultural heritage. And second, an "entrepreneur" in Dolo, who also opened a path on the other side of the same gorge, built a "traditional" hostel and a "traditional" Sarakatsani hut, and added an open-air bar and disco. I discuss that project further in Green (forthcoming). Suffice it to say here that since Pogoni had not been marked as possessing any stunning vistas, did not have a national park, and was not a major focus of attention for folklorists, there was little formal resistance to these "innovative" approaches to natural and cultural heritage. Some people in Ioannina argued that such projects demonstrated a lack of understanding of "authentic tradition": placing cement in the middle of a gorge and placing a disco in the middle of a tiny remote village blurred the separations that have to be maintained within ("Western," flexible accumulation) modernity to constitute tradition properly. But these commentators did not actively attempt to prevent such projects from being implemented; being seen as lacking in distinction did occasionally have its compensations in that regard.

In any event, the LEADER program was deliberately initially designed by the EU to allow people to construct their own projects, within the limitations, set by the program, of "environmental sustainability" and of being "endogenous." Ray suggests that this gave LEADER an "anarchic" quality (Ray 2000: 165); yet the program also made numerous assumptions about the cultural homogeneity of regions (Kovach 2000; Holmes 2000), and it further assumed that both an area's cultural heritage and its natural environment could be "repackaged" so as to become distinct and recognizable products, as it were, along the lines described by Herzfeld as the "objectification" of tradition (Herzfeld 2004: 195). In the Pogoni area, this was rather more possible with the environment than with "culture," given that the surrounding environment was increasingly being defined as "natural wilderness" and was therefore somewhat less ambiguous. Even on the "nature" front, though, as the region was not marked out as particularly visually stunning in comparison with the Zagori, something else had to be done with it. What the mayor came up with was the wild boar sanctuary: a ring-fenced area of forest with drivable tracks in which wild boar would be reared and protected, and then released to provide good game hunting. This was clearly an interventionist form of modernity; one that intended to "reconstruct" nature to attract the kind of people who wanted not simply to look at nature (for which the Zagori would be a better choice) but to carry out some activity within it.

With the help of Epirous S.A., the mayor of Delvinaki successfully applied for a grant to develop the wild boar sanctuary. In addition, a hotel was to be built in the town to house the hunters, along with a tourist information center, and a path was to be built up to one of the local churches, which was perched atop one of the hills ringing Delvinaki. Various other small improvements would also be made to the church in the center of the town—for example, restoring murals and stonework to their former condition before they had been plastered over during "modernizations" in the 1960s and 1970s. None of these "cultural sites" were marked out as especially distinctive, as I mentioned above; they were simply marked as *being* "cultural sites" (which would automatically make them "unique"), and as traditional to the town.

By the end of my fieldwork, most of the work in the town had been finished, but the completion of the boar sanctuary was delayed, and by July 2003 it was still not operational. This was both because funds had run short and because of a number of local disputes over the ring fencing of what Delvinaki peoples considered to be common land. In the original application, it was suggested that 600 stremmata (approximately 150

Figure 12. Delvinaki European Union Development funding sign

acres) would be ring-fenced. In the event, more than 1,600 stremmata (approximately 400 acres) were ring-fenced. Perhaps unsurprisingly, this led a number of people to accuse the mayor of having been somewhat conservative with the truth when he first announced the project.

Almost as soon as it had gone up, some of the fencing had holes punched through it, and people in the town explained that this was so they could go hunting in the forested area as they had always done. As far as they were concerned, the forest was part of their town's common land, and they had a right to do this. In addition, two large panels of the fencing had been removed altogether, reopening an old path that the fencing had cut across. This had been done by the group of three brothers who brought their cattle every year from Thesprotia to Delvinaki. They had the right to graze their cattle on Delvinaki land because one of the brothers was registered as a resident of Delvinaki. For the past few years, there had been complaints made by the sheep and goat pastoralists of the town about these cattle, claiming that they were not kept to their designated areas, that their owners allowed them to wander where they pleased while the cattle herders drank in the town, and that the brothers regularly brought many more cattle to graze than had originally been applied for and agreed to by the council.

As important from the perspective of many Delvinaki pastoralists, the three brothers were associated with Thesprotia, and that made them a matter of considerable suspicion. Although there was clearly genuine concern about the damage the cattle were doing, and about the brothers' asserted lack of control over the cattle, it was equally evident that a number of the pastoralists did not trust these men on the grounds that they were associated with Thesprotia. To complicate matters even further, when I spoke with the brothers myself, they said some members of their family were from Agoi Saranda—that is, from Albania. I never established whether this meant they were regarded (or regarded themselves) as Northern Epirots, as Tsamides, or as Albanians, for no one in Delvinaki ever mentioned these men's distinction in those terms: such things continually failed to be mentioned in this place, though implicit references were continually made.

The details of this ongoing dispute, which meant that the Delvinaki council was asked every year by some of the sheep and goat pastoralists to revoke these men's grazing rights (a request that usually failed), do not concern me here. What is more important is that in 1994, the men from Thesprotia had punched out two of the panels of the wild boar sanctuary's fence, thus rendering it useless. Their reason for doing this was that the huts in which they stayed during the summer could be reached only via the path that had been cut off by the fencing. But they used two additional arguments to defend their actions: that the ring fencing had encompassed overgrown fields which belonged to absentee owners, and that the path was the "traditional" route used by transhumant pastoralists in moving between Thesprotia and Delvinaki. That second defense was effectively an accusation that the mayor was running roughshod over their "cultural heritage": they were claiming a distinction that had been studiously avoided in the application for the grant, and in so doing, they were using "culture" in a way that was undesirable for the "just Greek" people associated with Delvinaki. The three brothers went so far as to initiate a court action against the council, claiming that the fencing was illegal. When I spent some time speaking with them, they expressed the opinion that the mayor was "corrupt," was interested only in lining his own pocket, and had no genuine concern either for "tradition" or for the environment. What was being implemented in the name of cultural heritage and environmentalism, they said, was "fake": a ruse to make money, nothing more. One of the men explicitly drew on the notion of "nested hierarchies of modernization" in expressing this opinion, when he asked me, "That's not the way they do things in England, is it?" I responded that I suspected it probably was, but the man dismissed this comment as either ignorance or politeness on my part.

Many people expressed similar opinions about development projects in Epirus in general. In chapter 6, I mentioned a Ioannina-based environmentalist who had a great deal to say on the matter. He was an outraged man who said he continually had "doors slammed in my face." He believed that the LEADER program, as it was being implemented in Epirus, was almost all about setting up hotels and hostels. "You'll see," he went on, "after a few years, these hostels will become the homes of those people who took the money from the EU. After all, who would want to stay in a hotel in Delvinaki or Dolo?" He also believed that the "cultural heritage" or "tradition" that was being restored in these places was "fake": "the songs have been changed, people have been made to wear costumes they never used to wear, and the music is fake." He continued by saying that Epirous S.A. was set up to facilitate the creation of these "ridiculous schemes" and to work out how to manipulate the paperwork so that they would get funded. If they told "the truth" in that paperwork, then none of them would be funded.

Clearly, this man did not believe that whatever cultural or natural heritage existed in the Pogoni region (and he was not convinced there was anything there that could genuinely attract tourists) would be either restored or protected; instead, there would be a scatter of ersatz development projects, most of which, he believed, would never be completed anyway. Many people in Epirus who made efforts to "develop" things there, particularly when they used funds regarded as "political," were continually confronted by such expressions of cynical suspicion about their motives.

This kind of perspective, or various milder versions of it, was also expressed by people opposed to the mayor in Delvinaki. The key issue for the opposition was an underlying belief that the mayor was pursuing his own interests (as politicians always do); that it was highly unlikely any "genuine" development would occur in the town, as external interventions almost never worked out in their interests; and, as important, that the mayor's version of "modernization" was being informed by the European Union's idea of what constituted proper modernization, and thus all these schemes were part and parcel of yet another external intervention.

I will look at two other conflicts involving the mayor as examples of how this was expressed in practice. They both occurred during a Delvinaki council meeting that I attended in March of 1994. In the first conflict, a councillor regarded as the leader of the opposition proposed that a disused building (the old school) be converted into an old people's home. This would provide for the increasing number of elderly residents whose partners had died and who could no longer care for themselves. He mentioned that he had spoken with the Greek foreign minister during the latter's visit to Ioannina a few days before, and that the minister had responded positively to the idea.

The mayor responded by welcoming the suggestion but commented that these days, most countries were turning away from institutional facilities for old people and instead paying people to keep their elderly at home. This was an attack on his opponent's level of modernity: he was not sufficiently up-to-date. The mayor went on to suggest that it was a poor reflection on change in Greek society if families were no longer taking care of their old people. The Delvinaki "community" should be encouraged, the mayor said, to respect and care for its elders. This was an attack on his opponent's apparent willingness to discard cherished Greek "traditions." He therefore opposed converting the building for this purpose. The mayor himself had proposed that the building be converted into a residence for the border police, for which the police would pay a considerable sum—on the grounds that the old people's home was a long-term project, whereas his own required immediate action. To the mayor's opponents, this was another illustration of how the mayor was more interested in profit than in local people's needs and concerns. They felt his claim to uphold Greek "traditions" was simply hot air aimed at winning the argument.

The differences in the two perspectives in this illustration are clear. The mayor, while stating he was committed to retaining "tradition," preserving the town's cultural character, and protecting the environment, was doing all of this by introducing some of the most radical changes to the town and its territories—and what is more, for some of his projects he was doing so in the name of the European Union's policies. That identified him squarely with the process of instituting "neoliberal economics in the local scene," as Herzfeld puts it (Herzfeld 2004: 168). His opponent also claimed to be a strong advocate of retaining "tradition," but rather than advocating collecting historical artifacts and restoring local churches, he favored actions that would keep the "community" alive—to live, rather than preserve, the "tradition." If that involved changes, such as the introduction of an old people's home, because the world around the "community" was changing, then so be it. The different rhetoric used by the two men was familiar to everyone; both could argue that they were modernizing by being on the side of "tradition," but they invoked different conceptions of modernization. The mayor's version was an attempt to identify himself as an active and productive participant in the (neoliberal) global "aesthetic," in Herzfeld's terms; his opponent's version was to reject that aesthetic while also using its terms: his opponent "embodied" the tradition, rather than defining it.

In the second disagreement, the mayor and his opponents conflicted about who should be sent as a representative for Delvinaki to the Ioannina Cultural Association. The mayor backed the chair of Delvinaki's cultural association, an energetic young woman who had been trained in history and local folklore.[14] The opposition recommended a village elder, someone with years of personal experience and knowledge. The matter was put to a vote, and the mayor's candidate was selected. He argued later that his opponents were "backward people" and did not realize that the young woman's training and education meant she had far more detailed and accurate knowledge of the town's past than could any single old man who happened to live there. His opponents argued that however much the young lady knew, she could not "be" the heritage of the town in the way that the old man was, because she had not lived it. The mayor clearly supported a move toward cultural heritage as knowledge through education, not cultural heritage as "being."

Again, it would be easy to argue that the mayor's promotion of the European Union's way of "packaging" cultural and environmental heritage could be equated with the spread of a "global hierarchy of value" (Herzfeld 2004). Even though the mayor himself was regarded as entirely "belonging" to Delvinaki in an "embodied" sense (he had been born there and grew up as the only son of a single mother, his father having been killed during the civil war), the "environmental protection" and "cultural heritage" he advocated through the EU-funded development projects was understood by his opponents as involving somebody else's ideals that had little to do with the embodied aspects of life around the Kasidiaris. The tourist center and the expanded and straightened path that led up to their local church represented, in some people's view, an "objectified" and therefore "fake" cultural heritage, which again had little to do with them and was not being fostered on their behalf.

On the other hand, the understanding that the mayor was promoting somebody else's ideals points to something additional going on here. The "whereness" of this region had made it clear to many people that there was more than one form of modernization in existence, and that even the most currently dominant form of ("Western") modernization was not entirely coherent. The "high modernism" of which the "global hierarchy of value" was a part did not encompass all the modernizations that existed, even in "Europe"; there were rips and darned patches, and the Greek-Albanian border area clearly constituted one of them. The mayor, using his own networks of power in the region and combining them with the European Union's intervention in this place, was aligning himself with *one* power, one form of (ideologically inflected) modernization, to be added to a long list of powers that had intervened here in the same way in the name of modernity in the past. Currently, this version might be by far the most dominant form, but people's experiences in the region had made it clear that no version of "modernity," "Western" or otherwise, could entirely escape the ambiguities and gaps thrown up by previous, and different, attempts at modernization. Nor, which is just as important, could any such program of "modernization" escape the internal inconsistencies and contradictions in the various modernist techniques used to generate an account of how things seem and how things are, which I discussed in chapter 4. This part of the world repeatedly seemed, albeit ambivalently, to refute a coherent account of difference and separation, constantly evoking those things that are the same and related, while also being different. In this sense, the "bumps upon bumps" could be seen as problems generated by the internal inconsistencies and multiplicity of modernity itself; it generated, as much as condemned, the "chaos."

So the mayor's opponents were not entirely encompassed by the "global hierarchy of value" any more than the mayor was; what was going on between the mayor and his opponent in the council meeting felt more like a negotiation, an interplay of things that were both different and the same. Which brings me back to the issue of that which remained unnamed, and which made the possibility of fully engaging with the ideals of the EU-funded development projects ultimately untenable. The mayor's development project combined the policies of the EU with the ambiguities of this region, which made it impossible to incorporate the notion of cultural distinctiveness into the project. That the development project made no mention of the differences between people in the town, that much of the work on the project was done by people marked as Northern Epirots and Albanians (in the name of a generic "cultural heritage"), and that the mayor appeared willing to cut off a "traditional" transhumant route to reconstitute nature in the form of wild boars—all this rendered all of the differences literally of no account. The development projects thus once again reiterated the ambiguous ordinariness and lack of distinc-

tion of this place, in the same way as had previous versions of modernization, by entangling, rather than imposing, things that were both the same
and different. And that brings me to my concluding remarks.

Conclusion

The conflicts that occurred during the Delvinaki project were strongly
inflected by a sense that whatever kind of modernization was going to be
implemented, there would be something ersatz about it, something that
was not quite the "real thing." This was partly because this place was
constituted as axiomatically not having access to "authentic" ("Western") modernity; but there were several different issues involved in that.
First, being able to constitute the place and the people as possessing "authentic" tradition depended, for the mayor, on people's being "properly"
modern: only such people would be able to recognize the "real tradition."
Second, there were competing assertions about what counted as appropriate or proper modernity: the mayor argued it must involve "progress,"
a "radical change," while his opponents argued it would emerge from the
pores of those who had lived their "authentic" traditions. I should note
once again that people implicitly understood there was a difference between modernity and premodernity in the notion of tradition: premodernity involved a world that did not understand the value of its own traditions and would therefore also happily shed them without realizing
something had been lost. In that sense, valorizing tradition was a part of
several versions of modernity (there were overlaps there as well) as much
as was placing a value on "progress." In the course of the conflicts, different sides effectively accused their opponents of being premodern, through
suggesting either that their attitudes were "backward" or that their attitudes did not properly recognize the value of tradition. In any case, there
was no final sense that this place had or could achieve whichever one was
the "authentic" version of modernity, because of continual interventions
and practices of "interests." Once again, things remained ambiguous,
both the same and different, by being continuously contested.

Finally, there was the particular "whereness" of the Western Kasidiaris
area, that ambiguous ordinariness, a combination of unnamed distinctions and lack of distinction, that seriously impeded the area's incorporation into the "structures of common difference" (Wilk 1995: 118) laid
out in the standardizing policies of the European Union's notions of culture and nature, structures that Herzfeld refers to as being part of a
"global hierarchy of value." Since the point of these development projects, whatever else they were about, was to transform culture and nature
into marketable commodities, these things had to be made distinctive

and therefore worth buying, as it were.[15] Everything I have discussed about the relations and separations of place and people in the Western Kasidiaris area made it particularly unlikely that this would even be attempted, let alone achieved. And so the marginality of this place was reconstructed once again, and it was both the same and different from what had come before.

Tables

TABLE 1
Epirus and Regions: Land Extent and Land Use

	Land Extent (km²)	% Mountainous	% Agricultural Land[a]	% Grazing Land[a]	% Forest, Commercial Use[b]	% Forest, Noncommercial Use[b]
Greece	131,957	42	31	41	25	24
Epirus	9,203 (7% of Greece)	74	14	52	31	27
Arta	1,662.2 (18% of Epirus)	66	22	24	22	28
Thesprotia	1,514.7 (16% of Epirus)	67	14	72	14	33
Ioannina	4,990.4 (55% of Epirus)	85	9	55	42	24
Preveza	1,035.9 (11% of Epirus)	47	28	51	16	30

[a] Statistical Service of Greece, *Basic Categories of Land Use 1981.*
[b] Forestry Commission of Greece, *Results of the First Register of Forests, 1981.*

TABLE 2
Residence of Population: Rural-Urban, Mountainous (1981 census)

		Urban-Rural Residence			Mountain-Plains Residence		
	Total	% Urban	% Semi-urban	% Rural	% Plains	% Semi-mountainous	% Mountainous
Greece	9,740,417	58.1	11.6	30.3	68.9	21.4	9.7
Epirus	324,541	24.2	9.1	66.8	43.1	18.9	38.0
Arta	80,044	25.0	4.4	70.6	54.8	10.6	34.7
Thesprotia	41,278	0.0	28.3	71.7	8.2	48.2	43.6
Ioannina	147,304	30.4	7.4	62.2	41.3	16.4	42.3
Preveza	55,915	24.4	6.0	69.7	57.0	15.9	27.1

Source: Statistical Yearbook of Greece, 1989.

TABLE 3
Annual Precipitation Levels

Year	Total Precipitation (mm)	% Change from 1956–60
Ioannina		
1956–60	1,236.7	0.0
1961–65	1,228.5	−0.7
1966–70	1,159.9	−6.2
1971–75	1,031.1	−16.6
1976–80	1,178.1	−4.7
1981–85	991.6	−19.8
1986–90	878.4	−29.0
Athens		
1990s	370.8	—

Source: Meterological Service of Greece.
Note: Totals Based on Monthly Averages (mm).

TABLE 4
Average Air Temperatures (°C)

	Ioannina	Athens	Crete	Rhodes
January	4.6	10.2	12.1	11.8
February	6.4	10.6	12.2	12
March	9.1	12.3	13.5	13.6
April	12.7	16	16.6	16.6
May	16.6	20.6	20.2	20.5
June	21.6	25.1	24.3	24.7
July	25.0	27.9	26.1	26.9
August	24.4	27.8	26	27
September	20.5	24.2	23.4	24.6
October	15.0	19.5	20	20.7
November	9.4	15.5	16.7	16.5
December	4.8	12	13.7	13.3

Source: Meterological Service of Greece.

TABLE 5
Average Monthly Days of Snow, Ioannina Weather Station, 1956–1991

	Jan.	Feb.	Mar.	Nov.	Dec.	Totals
1956–65	2.80	3.20	1.90	0.00	0.60	8.60
1966–75	1.50	2.00	1.40	0.40	0.90	6.20
1976–85	2.30	1.20	0.10	0.20	0.80	4.70
1986–91	1.17	2.17	1.17	0.00	2.83	7.33

Source: Meterological Service of Greece.

TABLES ON POPULATION

TABLE 6
Census Populations, 1951–1991

	1951	1961	1971	1981	1991
Greece	7.6m	8.4m	8.8m	9.7m	10.3m
Epirus total	330,543 (4.33% of Greece)	352,604 (4.20% of Greece)	310,334 (3.54% of Greece)	324,541 (3.33% of Greece)	339,728 (3.31% of Greece)
Ioannina Prefecture	153,748	155,326	134,688	147,304	158,193
Cities					
Ioannina	32,315	34,997	40,130	44,829	56,699
Arta	12,947	17,654	19,498	18,283	23,338
Preveza	11,008	12,865	11,439	12,662	15,119
Igoumenitsa	2,076	3,730	4,109	5,879	7,022
Kasidiaris area Counties					
Pogoni County totals	9,453	8,510	5,886	6,727	6,442
Dodoni County totals	124,653	126,156	113,153	125,250	136,670
Dodoni County minus Ioannina City	92,338	91,159	73,023	80,421	79,971

Source: Statistical Service of Greece.

TABLE 7
Kasidiaris Area Census Populations, 1920–1991

	Western Kasidiaris	Eastern Kasidiaris
1920	6,639	5,926
1928	5,730	6,571
1940	7,161	8,074
1951	4,404	7,800
1961	4,240	6,410
1971	3,212	4,511
1981	3,739	5,238
1991	3,698	5,676

Source: Statistical Service of Greece, Ioannina Office, handwritten records.
Note: Western Kasidiaris villages: Delvinaki, Agia Marina (Kousovitsa), Argyrohori, Dimokorio, Kastani, Kerasovo, Kefalovriso (Metzities), Ktismata (Arnista), Lavdani, Mavropoulo, Peristeri, Stratinista, and Haravgi (Valtista). Eastern Kasidiaris villages: Areti (Grimpiani), Vasilopoulo (Brigianista), Vrontismeni, Doliana, Ieromnimi, Kalpaki, Katarraktis (Gliziani), Koukli, Limni (Zaravina), Lithino, Mazaraki, Mavronoros, Parakalamos (Pogthoriani), Repetisti, Riachovo, and Sitaria (Mosiori).

TABLE 8
Western Kasidiaris: 1920 Registered versus Census Population

	Registered Residents	Census Population	Percent Difference
Delvinaki	1,171	2,630	+124.6
Agia Marina (Kousovitsa)	1,026	336	−148.7
Argyrohori	221	224	+1.4
Dimokorio	372	320	−14.0
Kastani	815	543	−33.4
Kerasovo	274	188	−31.4
Kefalovriso (Metzities)	2,426	253	−859.9
Ktismata (Arnista)	299	284	−5.0
Lavdani	715	507	−29
Mavropoulo	368	330	−10.3
Peristeri	600	400	−33.3
Stratinista	364	291	−20.1
Haravgi (Valtista)	389	333	−14.4

Sources: Village commune registration records and Statistical Service of Greece, Ioannina Office, handwritten records.

TABLE 9
Sample Comparison of 1991 Census Populations and 1993 Fieldwork Survey Figures

	Fieldwork Research			Ages (permanent residents)		
Commune	1991 Census	1993, permanent residents	Summer Visitors	Under 18	19–40	% over 40
Katarraktis (Gliziani)	143	60	200	5 (8%)	15	60
Koukli	541	542	1,500	43 (8%)	153	64
Delvinaki	921	650	1,000	30 (5%)	60	86
Argyrohori	39	25	45	0 (0%)	0	100
Kerasovo	124	25	200	0 (0%)	0	100
Ktismata (Arnista)	235	175	800	7 (4%)	17	86
Mavropoulo	173	165	350	0 (0%)	18	89
Peristeri	93	30	100	0 (0%)	0	100

TABLE 10
Katarraktis and Ktismata Census Populations, 1920–1991

	Katarraktis (Gliziani)	Ktismata (Arnista)
1920	154	284
1928	180	390
1940	242	483
1951	232	464
1961	165	430
1971	100	257
1981	115	251
1991	143	235

Tables on Land Use

Table 11
Epirus: Changes in Land Use, 1961–1991 (in 1,000s of stremmata)

	1961	1971	1981	1991	% Change 1961–1991
Cultivated and fallow land	1,395.00	1,398.20	1,298.40	1,249.80	−10
Grazing land, public	3,477.00	3,265.50	3,397.20	3,503.60	+1
Grazing land, private	1,411.90	1,277.60	1,293.90	1,248.60	−12
Forests	2,038.60	2,501.10	2,413.60	2,379.70	+17
Areas under water	238.80	279.10	297.20	296.30	+24
Built-up areas, including roads and squares; other misc.	439.20	481.70	502.90	525.40	+20
Total land	9,000.50	9,204.00	9,203.20	9203.20	+2

Source: Department of Agriculture, Ioannina Office.

Table 12
Ioannina Prefecture: Changes in Land Use, 1961–1991 (in 1,000s of stremmata)

	1961	1971	1981	1991	% Change 1961–1991
Cultivated and fallow land	574.30	532.80	456.90	398.80	−31
Grazing land, public	1,994.30	1,871.00	1,934.20	2,025.20	+2
Grazing land, private	673.80	706.00	755.70	724.90	+8
Forests	1,348.10	1,529.70	1,487.90	1,473.80	+9
Areas under water	95.40	104.60	107.00	106.50	+12
Built-up areas, including roads and squares; other misc.	227.50	246.90	248.50	261.20	+15
Total land extent	4,913.40	4,993.00	4,990.40	4,990.40	+2

Source: Department of Agriculture, Ioannina Office.

TABLE 13
Pogoni County Changes in Land Use, 1961–1991 (in 1,000s of stremmata)

	1961	1971	1981	1991	% Change 1961–1991
Cultivated and fallow land	43.10	35.90	25.20	19.30	−55
Grazing land, public	248.00	240.20	230.60	275.40	+11
Grazing land, private	80.30	88.40	101.70	68.40	−15
Forests	106.10	106.50	107.10	107.30	+1
Areas under water	1.80	1.80	7.90	1.80	+4
Built-up areas, including roads and squares; other misc.	26.70	25.40	25.20	25.60	+4
Total land extent	506.20	499.00	497.80	497.80	−2

Source: Department of Agriculture, Ioannina Office.

TABLE 14
Epirus, Ioannina Prefecture, and Pogoni County Cultivated and Fallow Land in Plains, Semimountainous, and Mountainous Areas, 1961–1991 (in 1,000s of stremmata)

	1961	1971	1981	1991	% Change 1961–1991
Epirus, all					
Plain	417.20	435.30	440.50	432.50	+4
Semimountainous	327.10	320.30	329.80	316.50	−3
Mountainous	650.70	642.60	528.10	500.70	−23
Ioannina Prefecture					
Plain	64.90	59.90	69.40	58.00	−11
Semimountainous	130.90	116.90	136.70	124.70	−5
Mountainous	378.50	356.00	250.80	216.10	−43
Pogoni County					
Plain	0.00	0.00	0.00	0.00	No plains
Semimountainous	8.00	4.90	3.50	3.90	−51
Mountainous	35.10	31.00	21.70	15.30	−56

Source: Department of Agriculture, Ioannina Office.

TABLE 15

Ktismata and Katarraktis Changes in Land Use, 1961–1991 (in 1,000s of stremmata)

	1961	1971	1981	1991
Ktismata (Arnista)				
Cultivated and fallow land	1.8	1.8	0.9	1.0
Grazing land, total	5.7	4.1	5.1	5.1
Community grazing land	5.6	3.9	3.8	3.8
Private grazing land	0.1	0.2	1.3	1.3
Forest	1.3	2.5	2.9	2.9
Area under water	0.1	0.1	0.2	0.1
Public residential areas (roads, squares, etc.)	0.5	0.6	0.4	0.4
Other areas	n/a	0.0	0.1	0.1
Total land	9.5	9.0	9.5	9.5
Katarraktis (Gliziani)				
Cultivated and fallow land	0.7	0.7	0.7	0.4
Grazing land, total	2.5	2.6	2.5	2.8
Community grazing land	2.5	2.6	2.2	2.2
Private grazing land	0.0	0.0	0.3	0.6
Forest	0.0	0.0	0.2	0.2
Area under water	0.1	0.1	0.1	0.1
Public residential areas (roads, squares, etc.)	0.6	0.6	0.1	0.1
Other areas	n/a	0.0	0.3	0.3
Total land	3.9	4.0	3.8	3.8

Source: Department of Agriculture, Ioannina Office.

TABLE 16
Eastern Kasidiaris Communes Land Redistribution Programs

	Date Work Started	Date Completed	Number of Stremmata (1000m²) Before	Number of Stremmata After	Number of Holdings
Areti	1979	1981	828	665	84
Vrontismeni	1991	1993	567	490	80
Doliana	1968	1976	2,582	2,368	229
Doliana, Parakalamos, Sitaria	1982	1985	1,941	1,638	324
Koukli	1979	1981	2,540	2,231	301
Mazaraki	1979	1981	1,532	1,311	152
Parakalamos	1970	1976	2,791	2,279	302
Repetisti	1969	1976	1,438	1,216	133

Sources: Department of Agricultural Improvement and Department of Environment and Land Planning, Ioannina.

TABLES ON CROP CULTIVATION AND ANIMALS (LIVESTOCK)

Crops

TABLE 17
Selected Crop Cultivation 1961–1992, Eastern and Western Kasidiaris (in stremmata cultivated, 1000s m²)

	1961	1971	1975	1980	1985	1992
Eastern Kasidiaris	19,394	17,201	17,877	17,178	20,089	21,835
Western Kasidiaris	17,459	5,561	5,328	5,095	5,360	4,843
Selected villages						
Doliana	3,912	4,280	4,338	3,322	4,681	3,680
Parakalamos	3,944	4,391	4,385	3,520	3,813	5,130
Katarraktis	610	407	331	407	94	568
Ktismata	1,737	507	395	340	390	420

Note: Only selected crops have been used in these tables: the total crop production was surveyed, and the most significant crops being cultivated were selected. Crops included are soft wheat, barley, oats, rye, corn, grain fodder, hay fodder, alfalfa, clover, cut pasture, and summer potatoes.

TABLE 18
Animal Fodder Cultivation (Alfalfa, Clover, and Corn), 1961–1992, Eastern and Western Kasidiaris (in stremmata cultivated, 1000s m²)

	1961	1971	1975	1980	1985	1992
Eastern Kasidiaris						
Alfalfa	2,215	4,465	5,619	5,247	6,260	7,536
Clover	109	531	537	244	1,039	0
Corn	5,978	4,333	2,840	2,208	6,438	8,344
Western Kasidiaris						
Alfalfa	923	1,861	2,132	2,404	1,884	1,315
Clover	6	0	110	0	0	0
Corn	2,922	463	312	197	301	450
Selected villages						
Doliana						
Alfalfa	340	920	1,037	468	478	450
Clover	4	30	35	74	1,039	0
Corn	803	1,500	285	138	971	1,050
Parakalamos						
Alfalfa	600	1,200	1,600	1,100	1,300	1,935
Clover	50	300	400	100	0	0
Corn	1,280	820	760	760	930	2,310
Katarraktis						
Alfalfa	65	90	62	96	50	350
Clover	0	6	6	0	0	0
Corn	240	115	60	65	42	5
Ktismata						
Alfalfa	160	230	170	200	60	20
Clover	2	0	0	0	0	0
Corn	620	150	100	20	150	130

Animal Statistics

TABLE 19
Animal Numbers, 1940–1995, Eastern and Western Kasidiaris

	Sheep		Goats		Cattle		Pigs		Chickens	
	Eastern Kasidiaris	Western Kasidiaris	Eastern Kasidiaris	Western Kasidiaris	Eastern Kasidiaris	Western Kasidiaris	Eastern Kasidiaris	Western Kasidiaris	Eastern Kasidiaris	Western Kasidiaris
1940	12,125	29,677	7,299	12,296	1,902	1,495	53	38	11,150	7520
1941	11,670	21,930	6,270	8,060	1,536	1,242	55	22	9,800	4,900
1952	13,583	22,685	6,719	17,027	1,431	1,820	11	160	17,220	14,900
1955	24,500	26,200	13,725	13,800	1,778	1,740	32	92	23,900	13,900
1961	18,151	27,400	8,220	12,300	2,739	1,143	54	12	24,580	13,600
1965	15,371	17,590	4,876	4,991	1,059	585	431	0	13,850	9,350
1971	17,640	13,185	5,370	5,140	751	268	464	4	84,050	321,000
1975	16,237	17,268	6,903	5,449	943	471	2,208	0	68,690	45,000
1980	22,039	12,339	7,237	5,640	519	70	4,775	255	35,000	45,000
1985	21,712	9,714	7,486	3,738	300	35	4,375	0	113,805	6,477
1991	21,307	8,253	6,059	3,540	440	122	7,620	0	113,260	4,915
1995	19,931	9,110	5,366	3,502	652	137	5,955	0	152,123	3,930

Source: Department of Agriculture, Ioannina Office, handwritten records.

Note: Eastern Kasidiaris Villages: Areti (Grimpiani), Vasilopoulo (Brigianista), Vrontismeni, Doliana, Ieromnimi, Kalpaki, Katarraktis (Glizi-ani), Koukli, Limni (Zaravina), Lithino, Mazaraki, Mavronoros, Parakalamos (Pogthoriani), Repetista, Riachovo, and Sitaria (Mosiori). Western Kasidiaris Villages: Delvinaki, Agia Marina (Kousovitsa), Argyrohori, Dimokorio, Kastani, Kerasovo, Kefalovriso (Metzities), Krismata (Arnista), Lavdani, Mavropoulo, Peristeri, Stratinista, and Haravgi (Valtista).

TABLE 20
Ktismata and Katarraktis Animal Numbers, 1940–1995

	Sheep	Goats	Cattle	Pigs	Chickens
Katarraktis					
1940	800	400	59	0	400
1941	800	400	59	0	400
1952	700	200	55	1	500
1955	1,500	800	65	0	800
1961	1,160	510	51	0	850
1965	700	151	9	0	200
1971	1,150	165	1	0	0
1975	1,213	185	0	0	0
1980	760	100	0	0	0
1985	675	175	0	0	320
1991	590	135	0	0	320
1995	478	80	0	0	381
Ktismata					
1940	600	300	165	12	100
1941	500	350	155	5	250
1952	1,200	800	246	18	1,500
1955	1,300	600	247	5	1,200
1961	1,200	550	137	3	1,400
1965	900	400	83	0	1,000
1971	660	290	19	0	0
1975	780	210	6	0	0
1980	540	180	4	0	0
1985	450	245	0	0	720
1991	420	395	0	0	830
1995	438	410	0	0	880

Source: Department of Agriculture, Ioannina Office, handwritten records.

Notes

1. Of course in Strathern's terms everything is partially connected, once it is recognized that multiple perspectives are possible, and therefore there are no stable centers (Strathern 1991: xx). That is discussed in chapter 4. My concern here is more what marginality is imagined to be; and one of those imaginings is that in being peripheral, it is difficult to get to and to see clearly, in both physical and perceptual senses.

2. Stephen Nugent argues that the Caboclos of Amazonia constitute such a group, and have as a result been relatively ignored both in anthropology and by "the politics of cultural identity," as he puts it (Nugent 1999: 183).

3. A general example of a political economy approach to marginalization is Eric Wolf's *Europe and the People without History* (Wolf 1982), and examples of more culturalist approaches include Ann Stoler's *Race and the Education of Desire* (Stoler 1999) and, in a different way, Rosalind Coward's *Patriarchal Precedents* (Coward 1983). In addition to these more historical accounts, there have been a couple of decades of debate on what to do about it: for example, issues surrounding "identity politics," which was later dubbed "political correctness" (e.g., Sawicki 1988; University of Birmingham Centre for Contemporary Cultural Studies 1982; Alcoff 1988; and Hall and du Gay 1996); ongoing battles over indigenous rights (e.g., Conklin 1997; Conklin and Graham 1995; Turner 1992; Weiner 1999; Corrigan and Sawchuk 1996; Larbalestier 1990; and Howard 1982); and the continual debates about indigenous peoples and the environment in relation to development (e.g., Brosius 1999; Milton 1993; Milton 1996; Descola and Pálsson 1996; and Hobart 1993).

4. This is also frequently said of the Balkans more generally (Todorova 1997: 15–16).

5. See, for example, Tsing (1993), Day, Papataxiarchis, and Stewart (1999), Coutin and Hirsch (1998); for a critique of this trend, see Nugent (1999).

6. See in particular "The New Modernities," in Strathern (1999).

7. Latour (1993), Law and Hassard (1999).

8. Butler (1993; 1990), Sedgwick (1990), Kulick (1998).

9. I tend to agree with Žižek that most postmodernity is still a form of modernity, in that it is based upon deconstructing things to understand them—separating things out to see "underneath" them (Žižek, Wright, and Wright 1999: 39–52).

10. It is interesting to note that queer theory is predicated on precisely this idea of utilizing a refusal to be "identitied" as the main hope for the radical effects of certain practices and performances in social life, particularly relating to gendered and sexual practices. That idea is explored to its limits, perhaps, by Judith Butler

(1990; 1993), but also notably by Sedgwick (1990). There have been two major critiques of the "queer" approach. First, the suggestion that queer theory, being substantially concerned with representation, takes little or no account of political economy and is "ahistorical," which disguises a perhaps unconscious reproduction of bourgeois individualism, this time focusing on consumption and the key position "identification" (one could call it "branding") has within late capitalism (Fraser 1997; Hennessy 1993; Hennessy 1995). This is similar to Strathern's critique of Appadurai's approach to exchange (Strathern 1992b). Second, and connected with the first point, that queer theory assumes "visibility" is self-generated, and that individuals have the capacity to constitute an identity in the appropriate form, and to have this be "recognized" (Adkins 2002).

11. See Herzfeld for a detailed analysis of the use of folklore in modern Greek discourse (Herzfeld 1986), esp. Appendix A, "Politis' Folklore Taxonomy," pp. 145–48.

12. Nitsiakos and Mantzos (2003: 197).

13. See Pettifer (1994), Hart and Budina (1995), and Peckham (1992) for brief details of the claims that Northern Epirus is Greek. See, for example, Jacques (1995) and Pollo and Puto (1981) for the opposing view, that it is Albanian.

14. It has been argued that this was the case for most peoples living in Balkan areas during conflicts over territory in the Balkan region, owing in part to the considerable involvement of states outside the region (e.g., Gallagher 2001: 1–6).

15. I am not alone in initially drawing this conclusion. In particular, those working on issues of class and representation in Euro-American contexts have noted the incapacity of certain peoples to become "visible" or "recognized" in the appropriate manner (Adkins 2002; Adkins and Lury 1999; Skeggs 1997).

16. Theodosiou (2003); Nitsiakos and Mantzos (2003) note that polyphonic singing has become one of those traditions that is argued about by nationalist folklorists on both sides of the border, so that it is unclear, in the end, whether it is "Greek" or "Albanian."

17. Fraser (1989), Taylor (1994).

18. Herzfeld (1992) focuses on the particular and somewhat brutal form of bureaucratic indifference toward people's particularities embedded within ideologies of bureaucratic "objectivity." This objectivity, Herzfeld suggests, turns out to be "objectively" promoting certain types of national identity at the expense of other possibilities. This is an active and deliberate practice of producing indifference. As Herzfeld describes it, "The association of blood, war and intellect . . . accounts for the ease with which Nazi leaders could harmonize mass murder with a view of themselves as decent family men—an emphasis that once again highlights the importance of familial metaphors for systematic indifference to those who are different" (Herzfeld 1992: 28–29). My interest in indifference includes these kinds of active forms, but it also encompasses the more passive kinds, where indifference is the outcome of having no reason to be interested. This will become clearer later.

19. The first part of this phrase echoes a line in the 1971 song "Μπάλλος/ "Ballos," by Dionysis Savvopoulos: "Εδώ είναι Βαλκάνια, δεν είναι παίξε-γέλασε"—"This is the Balkans, it is not fun and games." The line is well known everywhere in Greece, and it is likely that people in Epirus were borrowing from

it, though I never asked. Note, however, that Epirots' replacement of the second part of Savvopoulos's phrase with "what do you expect?" changes its implication rather radically. Savvopoulos's lyric draws attention to the serious consequences of a place's being designated as "Balkan" (it is not just a name/game), rather than to its incomprehensibility. In fact, "what do you expect?" was often uttered by people in Epirus with a wry smile and an edge of cynical humor, which evoked both the sense of "game" and the seriousness of such a "game." Over time, I had the sense that people used the phrase as a polite way to avoid answering my questions, to avoid discussing issues that they found troublesome in some way. In any event, the complexities of the relationships and separations between notions of Greece and Greekness, of "Balkan," and the way different parts of Greece become diversely entangled in that is part of what I explore in this book.

20. I am not alone in this experience. See, for example, Karakasidou (1993; 1997: xv–xvii), which is an example from another part of northern Greece, Macedonia.

21. As Misha Glenny puts it, "The fog that shrouds these lands lifts from time to time, revealing unexpected features, before it descends again to create a new and complex landscape. . . . But a consensus has never been found, nor could it be" (Glenny 1999: xxii).

22. Indeed, there are "ordinary Greeks" everywhere in Greece. For example, see Herzfeld's study of artisans in Crete (Herzfeld 2004).

23. See, for example, Konstandinou (1995), and Nitsiakos and Mantzos (2003) for an example of how this was used in nationalist rhetoric.

24. This is the main reason I avoid using the term "local" in this book and restrict my use of the term "global"; the interweaving of here and elsewhere, both perceptually and in practice, made the term "local" unhelpful. This topic is obviously one of considerable debate within anthropology, and I will return to it (Appadurai 1995; 1996a; Friedman 2002; Gupta and Ferguson 1999b; Kearney 1995; Lovell 1998; Wilk 1995).

25. See Nitsiakos and Mantzos (2003), Hart (1999), and Seremetakis (1996) for discussions on the more recent debates concerning Northern Epirots since the border was reopened.

26. This is different from Appadurai's plea for the removal of the hyphen (Appadurai 1996b: 19, 39–40, 159), and from Turner's opposite view, that the significance of nationalities has been removed by global capital (Turner 2003: 50–52). I mean it more in the terms of Gourgouris, who suggests that the state in Greece requires the idea of nation as a fantasy, to legitimate its right to exist (Gourgouris 1996: 14). See also Donnan and Wilson for a discussion on the complexity of the hyphen in locations around state borders (Donnan and Wilson 1999: 1–17), and see Veremis (2003: 60) for one discussion (among many) on Greeks' separation of their sense of "nation" from their deep suspicion of their "state."

27. This makes the "ordinariness" of the "just Greek" peoples rather different from the kind of "ordinariness" claimed by people who feel they constitute the hegemonic "norm" (see, for example Savage, Bagnall, and Longhurst 2001). This will become clearer in the following chapters.

28. See Hart (1999) and Mikalopoulou (1993) for discussions on the Tsamides issue. See Ladas for a description of the debates in the League of Nations about what to do about these people (1932: 384–90). See Hirschon (2003) for a detailed exploration of the wider experience and implications of these exchanges.

29. Another spelling of this city's name is "Yannina": both spellings also exist in Greek script versions (Ιωάννινα and Γιάννινα). I am aware that the different spellings relate to debates about the Greek language (see Herzfeld 1986). I am using "Ioannina" solely because it is the more common spelling.

30. As part of the EC-funded Archaeomedes I research program, which was titled Archaeology and Desertification in the Mediterranean Basin (Green 1995a).

31. Green (1997b; 2002; 2003; 1991).

32. I seemed to associate myself continually with places that friends and colleagues in other parts of Greece thought had peculiar names. "Kasidiaris" in Greek means "scurfy" (scurf is a condition of flaky scaling that afflicts the heads of some balding people). Friends in Athens thought this was strange enough; but when I gave them my address, the response was genuine bemusement.

33. The epicenter of the quake was 39.5 degrees latitude and 21.2 degrees longitude, just south of the Mitsikeli mountain (map 3); its magnitude was 5.9 on the Richter scale.

34. See, for example, Appadurai (1996b), Ong (1999), Clifford (1997), Kaplan (1996), and, for a useful overview, Low and Lawrence-Zuñiga (2003).

35. This is making a different point from the one asserted by Clifford in *Routes* (1997). Clifford's focus on the cultural connections involved in traveling ("a view of human location as constituted by displacement as much as by stasis" [2]; "Intercultural connection is, and has long been, the norm" [5]) attends to the cultural outcomes of contacting and communicating with others, but does not make a distinction between traveling as a practice and movement as a conceptual starting point. Seen as a starting point, travel need not involve "displacement," though it can do so; moreover, Clifford's approach does not provide an opportunity to consider what happens when movement stops, changes, or stalls.

36. This project was funded by DGXII of the European Commission of the European Union: contract number EV5V-0021 (Archaeomedes I); subsequent projects included EV5V-CT94-0486 (Environmental Perception and Policy Making); and ENV 4-CT95-0159 (Archaeomedes II), also funded by the same source.

37. See King, Sturdy, and Whitney (1993).

38. Although this might sound like Evans-Pritchard's account of how the Nuer always ended up discussing cattle whatever he discussed with them (Evans-Pritchard 1978), I sincerely hope no parallels will be drawn between Evans-Pritchard and my approach to ethnography. My reason for including this encounter is to draw out the circumstances that led me to be interested in the "whereness" of places. Such encounters were crucial in enabling me to understand how "erosion," in the Epirot context, did not (and could not) mean what the research program assumed it meant, and that this had a great deal to do with the historical, political, economic, and social constitution of the "whereness" of this place. The fact that these constructions of "whereness" contrasted with geomorphological accounts led me to explore the "gaps" and contradictions, as well as the relations, between different "Western" discourses. It led me to understand that such gaps exist not

only *between* "Western" and whatever might count as "non-Western" understandings of the world but within "Western" understandings as well.

39. Just two examples will suffice here: Vacalopoulos's *The History of Hellenism: Epirus* and Archbishop Sevastianos's *The Crucified Northern Epirus* (Vacalopoulou 1995; Sevastianos 1989). Both are explicitly about Greek nationalism and its relation to territory, as is the case for most such books.

40. A few examples chosen at random are Glenny (1999), Mazower (2001), Gallagher (2001), and Stavrianos (2000).

41. Ktismata and Katarraktis; see chapter 6.

42. Herzfeld also records being accused of being a "spy" while carrying out ethnography in Greece. And as in my case, he saw this as suspicion "against those who appear to represent an encompassing and potentially dangerous source of powerful intervention" (Herzfeld 2004: 15).

CHAPTER 2
TRAVELS

1. Selecting some accounts over others caused me considerable anxiety, an acute awareness of my own complicity in making things, places, and people appear and disappear. I have tried as far as possible to put pressure on my own tendencies toward choosing one over another encounter, and to include encounters that I had initially dismissed because they did not seem "appropriate."

2. See Bailey (1997) and van der Leeuw (1998).

3. I should perhaps explain that I grew up in Greece, and therefore I have no "foreign accent" when speaking Greek. It was therefore quite possible for the visitor to think that I was a local journalist on this first acquaintance.

4. This is a distinction that Ioannis Lambridis also made in 1889. He called the two sides "northern or main Pogoni, and southern or Old Pogoni" (Lambridis 1993 [1889]: 7). His distinctions were much more detailed than those given by people I spoke with, and while he mentioned the main Argyrokastro road, he mostly used mountains and rivers to divide the two sides.

5. While one *could* argue that the ideal was patrilocality, in practice uxorilocality and neolocality were so common that most people did not really clearly state that patrilocality was the "norm" or even the ideal.

6. EDES (Ελληνικός Δημοκρατικός Εθνικός Στρατός—Greek Democratic National Army), at first a fairly liberal and antimonarchist resistance group founded by General Napoleon Zervas in Epirus during World War II. In the beginning, EDES cooperated with ELAS (Εθνικός Λαϊκός Απελευθερωτικός Στρατός—National Popular Liberation Army), the communist-sponsored resistance group, in campaigns against the Italian and German invasions of Greece, but EDES rapidly took a political turn to the right and, between October 1943 and February 1944, had battles with ELAS, an early sign of the civil war to come (Clogg 1992: 125–29 ff). ELAS was the military arm of EAM (Εθνικών ΑπελευθερωτικώνΜετωπών—National Liberation Front). EAM was formed in September of 1941; ELAS, as an active armed resistance force, was formed in December 1942 (ibid.: 125–29).

7. Killick (1997), Hogan (1987).

8. In the Astoria district; most Pogoni peoples living in New York live in this district.

9. These descriptions do not strike me as the equivalent of saying that people maintained a sense of "community" even when they moved away, and that somehow this sense was linked to the place. The papers collected in Dimen and Friedl are fairly "classic" examples in Greek ethnography of how the sense of "community" is linked via regions and kinship in this way (Dimen and Friedl 1976). The difference here, I think, is the focus on movement as the trope through which place and relations were discussed and constituted.

10. See Green (1997a) for a more detailed analysis.

11. Many historians writing about the area have tried to estimate how many people in Northern Epirus in the past were Greek, but the way this designation was gauged was somewhat vague at times. For example, Konstandinos Vacalopoulos states that at the beginning of the twentieth century, there were "20,000 Greeks (18,000 Greek-speaking, 2,000 Albanian-speaking) and 20,000 Albanians in the administrative district of Argyrokastro" (Vacalopoulou 1995: 483, my translation). Vacalopoulos took his figures from a statistical study carried out in 1905 by Christos Christovasili (ibid.); and although he does not say how "Albanian-speaking Greeks" were distinguished from "Albanians" (let alone how he calculated the total population), the usual method used in Greece was on religious grounds: Orthodox peoples were Greeks, and Muslims and Catholics were Albanian.

12. There is no direct translation for "ethnicity" in Greek; the word εθνικισμός—ethnikismos—is usually understood to mean "nationalism." Michalis, by combining "race" and "culture" seemed to be attempting to avoid discussing nationality directly; he was not alone in this habit among people living around the border area.

13. Sevastianos also published books advancing his views; the title of one of the better known among them was *The Crucifed Northern Epirus* (Η Εσταυρωμένη Βόρειος 'Ηπειρος); the cover has a drawing of a hand with an iron manacle and chain around the wrist nailed to a piece of wood (Sevastianos 1989). A map of the region (ibid.: 10) shows Epirus covering not only the current territory of the region in Greece but also the entirety of Albania; Northern Epirus, somewhat confusingly, is labeled as being located in the center of this region.

14. This is something that Campbell has of course studied in considerable detail (Campbell 1964).

15. See, for example, the work of Vasilis Nitsiakos (1985; 1986; 1995) and Koukoudis (2003), as well as the more classic study carried out by Wace and Thompson (1972).

16. Nitsiakos argues that this was made possible by the system of Ottoman land management, much of which depended on the use of lands by pastoralist peoples (Nitsiakos 1986).

17. I am using the term used by people on the Greek side of the border; these people are elsewhere also variously known as Chams, Cams, and Tchams, particularly in Albania. See Hart (1999: 202 and 206–9).

18. Arvanitika is spoken by peoples referred to as Arvanites; there is disagreement concerning whether this is a separate language or an argot based on Albanian. See Tsitsipis (1998) for a detailed analysis of the relationship between Greek and Arvanitika. The elision between Arvanites and Tsamides deeply irritates some political commentators, usually on the grounds that the "ethnic origins" of these two groups are asserted to be entirely different.

19. See, for example, Papadopoulos (1992). The text states bluntly, "Σήμερα στη Θεσπρωτία δεν ζει κανένας Αλβανός Τσάμης" ("No Albanian Tsamis lives in Thesprotia today") (Papadopoulos 1992: 117). Papadopoulos asserted that there was a difference between "Albanian" Tsamides and "Greek" ones; others have denied this as a distinction. One of the better sources on the experience of these people in terms of international disputes and negotiations about nation-state borders is Mikalopoulou (1993). See also Hart (1999: 202 and 206–9), for some details in English.

20. *Armatoloi* were often depicted in pre-Independence Greece as having been "heroic" Greek irregular militias, somewhat in the style described by Hobsbawm (1985). However, as noted by Koliopoulos, their reputation became somewhat tarnished after Independence, when they were recast as "brigands" (Koliopoulos 1990). In Epirus, *armatoloi* was a term used both for Greek fighters for independence and to refer to irregular militias used by Ottoman administrators in Epirus to collect taxes and maintain order in outlying areas during the Ottoman period. It was the latter meaning that this man was referring to. These unsalaried irregular militias collected what they could, generally using violent means, from the Ottoman subjects from whom they took taxes. Moreover, these peoples were known to be animal rustlers and thieves when they were not acting on behalf of the Ottoman Porte.

21. A white spirit made from grapes that is somewhat like raki and ouzo, except there is no aniseed added.

22. The Athens News Agency, on December 12, 1997, reported, "Foreign Undersecretary Yiannos Kranidiotis told Parliament late last night that the Greek government did not recognize any issue concerning the property of 'Tsamides' "; similar reports were carried by Greek newspapers from 1994 onward.

23. Obviously, I have not focused on the analysis of narrative accounts in this chapter, let alone the way I have patched them together; had I done so, the chapter would have taken up the entirety of this book. However, I have been mindful of some of the issues involved, gleaned from an appreciation of the work of the following, among others: Steedly (1993), Munro (2001), Pratt (1992), and Stewart (1996).

24. My thanks to Ilana Gershon for drawing my attention to this reference.

25. Herzfeld suggests that the word *Greki* (with emphasis on the final syllable) is "Ionian dialect"; he quotes a nineteenth-century anti-Hellenist writer, Manousis, as using it instead of *Romios* (Herzfeld 1986: 38). The most comprehensive etymology I have seen appears in Babiniotis (1998: 443 and 596).

26. For a discussion on the relevance of the word "hellene" as opposed to "romios," see Herzfeld (1987, esp. 45–46 and 101–3) and Faubion (1993: 58).

27. Anastasia Karakasidou, who has worked in the Greek region of Macedonia to the east of Epirus, indicated in a personal communication that *Greki* is also

used there, and she confirmed that so far as she is aware, it is not used in southern Greece. And in another personal communication, Asterios Koukoudis, who has carried out a wide-ranging study of Vlachoi in the northern Greek region, suggested that Babiniotis "might not know that the term is still in use in *some* parts of Greece, not as 'Τραικός' with a 'gamma' but as 'Γκρέκος' with 'gamma' and 'kappa' at the beginning" (email, June 27, 2002; emphasis added).

28. How "Balkan" other parts of Greece, or even the whole of Greece, is taken to be is a matter of debate; I return to this issue in chapters 4 and 7. My point here is that the greater or lesser "Balkanness" of different regions remained unnamed in wider debates about Greece and Greekness; it was a distinction that constituted a nondistinction in nationalist terms.

29. My thanks to Nikoleta Katsakiori for drawing my attention to Koukoudis's work.

30. Except to argue that Greeks provided the Balkans with their most powerful intellectual resources (Kitromilides 1994; 1990); see chapter 4.

31. While many islands were similarly not included in contemporary Greece until 1913 (Crete and Lesbos, for example), I am concerned here with a *combination* of elements in the mainland that together render Epirus somewhat peripheral to the main story told about Greece.

32. The exceptions in Epirus were the southern coastal towns of Preveza and Parga. These were mainland dependencies of the seven Ionian islands, which included Corfu (Fleming 1999: 70–77).

33. It is worth noting here that during the early nineteenth century, there was a political division in Greece between those Veremis calls "autochthons" and those he calls "heterochthons": the former, who were defined as people born within the boundaries of the 1830s Greek state, "refused to acknowledge" the Orthodox Christians living outside those boundaries, which of course included Epirots (Veremis 1990: 11). This was on the grounds that only those born within those boundaries counted as the "true heirs" to the classical Hellenic world that was the "origin of Western civilization." In later years, of course, the irredentist movement, which argued that all those territories containing Orthodox Christians were part of the Greek nation, gained the upper hand. Yet the sense of a distinction between the northern and southern halves of the mainland endured and still held some purchase in Epirus in the 1990s, even if this distinction was not explicitly acknowledged or named.

34. So long as they were referred to as Sarakatsani; *Gréki* can denote any unnamed or apparently undistinguished Greeks associated with the Epirot (or other "Balkan") region; assertions of being Sarakatsani, like assertions of "pure" Greekness, resists that possibility.

CHAPTER 3
MOVING MOUNTAINS

1. See, for example, Low and Lawrence-Zuñiga (2003) for an overview of these arguments, but also Olwig and Hastrup (1997), Lovell (1998), Gupta and Fergu-

son (1997), Bender (1993), Augé (1995), Malkki (1992), Stoller (1996), Gray (1999), Kearney (1995), Appadurai (1996a), and Fortier (1999).

2. The phenomenological approach with which I experimented made use particularly of the work of Tim Ingold (2000b), Michael Jackson (1989), Christopher Tilley (1994), and even Thomas Csordas (1990; 1994). As will be obvious, their work has influenced my approach in a number of ways, particularly in its combination of the embodied experiences of moving through and using places with narrative accounts of them.

3. Lambridis (1993 [1889]: 12).

4. Going *through* it is of course another option, but one never used, to my knowledge.

5. See King, Sturdy, and Bailey (1997).

6. One of the more notable sources in English about the Smolikas is the novel *Captain Corelli's Mandolin* (De Bernières 1995: 101); on the Mourgana, see Tsantinis (1988). For a Web site listing most of these mountains, see http://www.nature .ariadne-t.gr/mountains/mountains.html.

7. All the maps I have reproduced that include topography and other details of the Albanian side of the border were produced since the border opened and in any case did not depend on physical visits to the place, as did the tectonic and geological maps.

8. Although developments in satellite technology have now made it possible to generate much more detailed images of all parts of the earth's surface than was possible in the early 1980s, my point remains the same: what becomes visible and invisible is still politically mediated.

9. Agelopoulos (2000), Brown (2003), Cowan (1997; 2000), Danforth (2000), Karakasidou (1993; 2002), Mackridge and Yannakakis (1997), Peckham (2001: 137–46), Wilkinson (1951).

10. Most "Western" observers gave Ali Pasha the nickname "Lion of Ioannina" rather than "diamond" (McNeill 1992: 267; *Encyclopaedia Britannica* (online), s.v. "Ali Pasa Tepelenë").

11. Others suggest that it was the Greek national forces that used the napalm against the communists (McNeill 1992: 268). At the time, an alliance had been forged between the United States and the more right-wing side in an attempt to defeat the communists, so the point is moot.

12. See King, Sturdy, and Bailey (1997) and Bailey, King, and Sturdy (1993).

13. This contributes an additional interesting example to the debate Herzfeld discusses about the "evil eye" as a symbol of a "Mediterranean culture area" (Herzfeld 1984).

14. Indeed, Holmes suggests that the European Union particularly developed this form of modernity, using almost entirely bureaucratic means (Holmes 2000: chap. 2).

15. Herzfeld (1997: 29).

16. The harsh effects of the "teeth" of poetics, their hegemonic qualities, are explored more fully by Herzfeld in *The Social Production of Indifference* (Herzfeld 1992) and in his much more recent study of the almost impossible position in which artisans in Crete find themselves in the context of neoliberalist "global hierarchies of value" (Herzfeld 2004).

CHAPTER 4
THE BALKAN FRACTAL

1. Todorova (1997: 59), Scopetea (2003), (Karakasidou 2002: 585).

2. This understanding of hegemony is similar to its use by Jane Cowan (Cowan 1990: 12–14); my reliance on Crehan's interpretation is based on the way Crehan explicitly emphasizes the interplay between how things seem and how things are, whereas in Cowan's usage, this remains implicit.

3. A very similar notion of this particular way parts relate to wholes is conveyed by Strathern's use of the term "merographic" (Strathern 1992a: 72–81).

4. See Cowan (2000: xv) for a current example involving the region of Macedonia in northern Greece and the former Yugoslav Republic of Macedonia.

5. See also Gal and Irvine (1995), Gal (1991; 2002).

6. Roessel notes how British philhellenes also attempted to define Greece as standing outside the Balkans (Roessel 2002: 143–45).

7. A notable exception to this widespread rejection of the term "Balkan" can be seen in the work of a loose circle of intellectuals, mostly based in Belgrade, who use broadly postmodernist approaches in their effort to reclaim "Balkanism" as a radical challenge to the (Western, neoliberal) forces of "globalization." See Bjelić and Savić (2002) for an overview of the somewhat eclectic range of approaches that characterizes this circle.

8. But see, anyway, Gligorov (1992), Todorova (1997: 119), Goldsworthy (1998: 5), Glenny (1999: xxiii–xxiv), Mazower (2001: 4), Gallagher (2001: 2, 10), and Norris (1999: 10–12).

9. For a detailed exploration of the way fractals have been used in theoretical debates, see Abbott (2001).

10. For a particularly extreme example of this kind of accusation, see Glynn (1993); but see also Ellis and Wright (1998), Gligorov (1992), Harris (1998), Kovach (1995), Lazarova (1999), and Turner's defense against the accusation that "critical multiculturalism" is "balkanizing" (Turner 1993: 418). I should note, however, that some scholars, notably a loose circle of "radical intellectuals" based in Belgrade, quite enjoy this type of accusation and even advocate it as a means to undermine the hegemonic power of globalization. For example, Bjelić, in his introduction to *Balkan as Metaphor*, suggests that "*Balkanism* . . . allows Balkan scholars to mount resistance to the imperial culture of globalization" (Bjelić 2002: 14, emphases aded).

11. There are many examples; the following are just a selection: Jelavich and Jelavich (1986), Gallagher (2001), Glenny (1999), Hosch (1972), Mazower (2001), Stavrianos (2000).

12. J. R. McNeill has also carried out one of most detailed studies of this kind, in which he explores the interrelationship of historical, political, social, and environmental conditions in five mountain ranges around what he calls the "Mediterranean region," including the Pindos (McNeill 1992). His focus was upon the physical environment itself and how it was "shaped."

13. I am deliberately not engaging with Žižek's concept of the "Real" as against the "real," based on his reading of Lacan. To do so would extend this chapter far beyond its intended scope.

14. This is not the same as the "fractal recursivity" that Irvine and Gal suggest nineteenth- and early twentieth-century sociolinguists were using to classify and categorize peoples, territories, and practices (Irvine and Gal 2000). Those linguists were attempting to draw diversity into a homogenous (modernist) paradigm, to reduce diversity and difference to a single scale of evaluation. In contrast, my approach is to keep the existence of different scales of evaluation visible (different disciplinary approaches, different techniques and technologies, different accounts of how things seem, different experiences and ways of doing things), but to explore how they become entangled with one another—how they interweave both separation and relation.

15. My thanks to Karen Sykes for providing me with this metaphor in a personal communication.

16. For an example of how this worked in the Macedonian region, see Brown (2003: chap. 2).

17. See Navaro-Yashin (2002: 141) for an account of such arguments.

18. See also Agelopoulos (2000).

19. This is one of the many reasons I am particularly disinclined to use the word "ethnicity" in this book. It does not capture the kinds of distinctions (or lack thereof) that I am exploring here.

20. For that reason among others, I agree with Fleming that the theory that millets formed the "natural" basis of nations within the Ottoman empire is singularly unconvincing (Fleming 1999: 58–59). See also Veremis (1990) and Kitromilides (1990) for the same argument.

21. Ethnographic studies of how this has been experienced in practice demonstrate the sheer diversity of people's engagements with this particular issue. See, for example, Karakasidou (1997), Jansen (2003), Bringa (1995), Voutira (2003), and Ballinger (2003). See also Irvine and Gal (2000: 60–72) for an account of the way the language issue became embroiled in this process, and Hayden (1996) for a discussion of the more recent version of it (called "ethnic cleansing") in former Yugoslavia.

22. A similar point is made by Irvine and Gal, who refer to this process as "erasure" (Irvine and Gal 2000: 69–71).

23. On modernity and Enlightenment in relation to the Balkans (or parts of them), see Gourgouris (1996), Tziovas (2003), Pippidi (1999), Todorova (1997), Wolff (1994), Goldsworthy (1999), and Kitromilides (1994; 1996).

24. This asserted ambiguity as being deeply problematic in perceptions of the region has been widely noted. See, for example, Cowan (2000), Bracewell and Drace-Francis (1999), Danforth (2000), Ballinger (1999), and Pippidi (1999). Scopetea wryly comments, "What could not be predicted, was that the ambiguity would prove so time resistant; . . . a 'Western identity' can still be granted or withheld from the Balkans or from selected parts of it" (Scopetea 2003: 175). See also Močnik (2002) for a critique of Todorova's perspective.

25. A similar point, but reflecting a different perspective, is made by Bjelić, using Foucault: "According to Foucault's notion of power and domination, knowledge of certain places, bodies, and histories is concealed and subjugated because such entities resist the discourse of universal rationality—indeed, their incorporation into that discourse would rupture it" (Bjelić 2002: 7). Bjelić's impli-

cation is that the Balkans are successfully maintained as the "other," as the opposite and outside of "Western modernity," because of the threat the region poses to the logic of this form of modernity. My argument is rather that the Balkans have been continuously in the process of being incorporated ever since they were named as such; the "threat" has been the apparent endlessness of the process.

26. This is perhaps one of the most extraordinary claims about the Balkans to date. See Kaplan (1994: xxiii). For critiques of Kaplan's argument, see Todorova (1997: 119), Goldsworthy (1999), Karakasidou (2002), and Bracewell and Drace-Francis (1999).

27. See, for example, "The War in Bosnia" (1995), Gligorov (1992), Hickey, Maier, and Paige (1999), Husarska (1999), Magas (1989), and Mestrovic (1996).

28. I owe a considerable debt to Marilyn Strathern in the following argument, both for her chapter "The New Modernities" in *Property, Substance and Effect* (1999), and for her comments as I was working through these ideas. Of course, all the errors and oversimplifications are my own.

29. I am grateful to Marilyn Strathern for putting this so succinctly in a personal communication (April 2003).

30. A similar point is made by Pamela Ballinger, when she asks whether the failure of postmodern theorists to look at the "hybridity" of Balkan borders might be related to the fact that it is an "embarrassing example," showing that hybridities do not always avoid "essentialized identities" (Ballinger 2003: 262).

31. Whether "critical" or "difference" versions of multiculturalism in Turner's terms, and I agree with Strathern that they fold into one another (Strathern 1999: 278 n. 11).

32. In Douglas Holmes's terms, these Balkan politicians are cast as "integralist": an essentialist version of a "commitment to traditional cultural forms" (Holmes 2000: 3) that contemporary European political elites indelibly link with the extreme right. Holmes's study of Western European "integralist" groups, whom he describes as drawing upon a long-standing political philosophy that is decidedly "Counter-Enlightenment" in character (ibid.: 6–9), also demonstrates the existence of "alternative modernities" *within* the "West" as well as "outside" of it. The frequent assumption that "Western" forms of modernity and modernization are internally homogeneous and coherent—an assumption that scholars make in order to contrast them with "alternative" forms existent "outside" the "West" (e.g., Ong 1996; Ong and Nonini 1997: 15–16)—tends to miss the multiple, and often self-contradictory, modernities that exist in "Western" terms.

33. An interesting example of that is the current process of expansion of the European Union to include a number of new member states, which requires that each state meet a series of conditions to qualify. In May 2004, ten new states were granted membership (Cyprus, the Czech Republic, Estonia, Hungary, Latvia, Lithuania, Malta, Poland, Slovakia, and Slovenia). Only a single state regularly labeled "Balkan," Slovenia, was included in this group; applications for membership from others thus labeled have been rejected on the grounds that they have not yet met the necessary conditions (*Independent*, April 17, 2003: 4; *Guardian*, April 17, 2003: 17; *Times*, April 17, 2003: 4).

34. An even more interesting example is that of a political movement in Istria (in the Julian March, on the Italian-Croatian border), described by Ballinger as an attempt to establish "authentic hybridity" (Ballinger 2003: 248–57). Partly

on the basis of the European Union's policies of "European integration," some politicians argued that the Istrians possessed a "unique Latin-Slav cultural and ethnic mix" (ibid.: 250). This raises two interesting points: that "hybridity" easily lends itself to essentialist forms; and that the political movement of the Istrian region was encouraged to generate such an essentialist approach by the European Union's "integration" policy, which is strongly informed by an idea of "difference multiculturalism" (ibid.: 259–60; see also Holmes 2000: 19–36; Shore 1993).

35. This is a point also made by Wilk (1995), Nugent (1998), and Nugent 1999.

36. See also chapter 1, n. 19.

CHAPTER 5
COUNTING

1. Just two of the more interesting explorations of this are Goldman (1991), who provides a fascinating analysis of the development of the relationship between the nascent "statistical movement" and government policy-making in Britain, and Holt (2000), who is a contemporary advocate of such a relationship.

2. I could call these "facts-in-the-world" in Dumit's terms (Dumit 1997: 86). Like Dumit, I am interested in the process by which some kinds of information (in this case, numbers), given the appropriate authoritative backing and people's own ideas about "objectivity," become "objects" that can materially alter the world. However, Dumit was using the phrase in a context where the "facts" in question (produced by PET scanning, which some argue can reveal the functions of the brain while it is actually working) had an effect of altering the conception of self ("objective self-fashioning," as Dumit calls it). I do not wish to imply this in my use of the term "facts" here. Many anthropological studies of official statistics are aimed precisely at understanding the process by which such "facts" can have an effect on people's conception of themselves (e.g., Appadurai 1996c), but I am avoiding Dumit's otherwise very useful conception.

3. Holt puts it bluntly: "In a nutshell, the challenge for Official Statisticians is: Get them right, Get them trusted and Get them used" (Holt 2000: 1011). Strathern, using Michael Power's work on "the audit society" (Power 1997; 1994), is rather more circumspect in discussing motivations for carrying out audits: "Power quickly followed his citation about checking being necessary in situations of mistrust . . . by the well-established point that checking itself requires trust—trust in measures used, trust in sources of information—since it simply would not be humanly possible to check everything" (Strathern 2000: 7).

4. Much of this information is incomplete or incompatible, and most of it is relatively out-of-date, especially data dependent upon decennial censuses. My intention is to attempt to take a small slice through the generation of various types of accounting through counting about this place, so as to give one small indication of the combinations of abstractions, "interests," and negotiations involved across various scales.

5. Indeed, as Goldman notes, this is the most common reason given for the massive development of statistical techniques during the nineteenth century in northern and western Europe: there was a perceived need to "see" things that had become "obscure" as a result of the increasing complexity of industrial societies

(Goldman 1991: 433). Goldman also notes, however, that the "statists" involved in developing the "science of statistics" were also strongly influenced by the idea that statistics could provide a "science of society" that would generate "social laws" that were analogous to "natural laws," and that these could be used to both predict and "engineer" social change. See also Hacking (1981).

6. The word Spiros literally used was "zucchini" (κολοκύθια), but that doesn't have the same connotations in English as it does in Greek.

7. This is not limited to Greeks, of course. Shryock, for example, who studied the Bedouin peoples of Jordan, was also continually advised that people would lie to him, and he notes that Favret-Saada had similar experiences in France (Shryock 1997: 16). Interestingly, Shryock notes that the pervasive assumption of "multiple truths" among many peoples in the region has been one means of "orientalising" them from a "Western" perspective. He argues that "multiple truths" is a form of sociality that does not sit well with a nationalistic logic that expects a coherent story from people who are all supposed to be part of the "same culture" (ibid.: 314–16).

8. Herzfeld analyzes the issue of lying as deeply associated with the Greek notion of Original Sin as developed within Orthodox teachings during the nineteenth and twentieth centuries, and which subsequently became a part of everyday social life and practice (Herzfeld 1987: 35–36; 2004: 46). While this may be the case, the underlying cause or meaning of "pervasive lying" was not the focus of people who spoke to me about it. It was discussed more as an aspect of sociality; people were making a commentary about the character of social relations, rather than reflecting upon those relations.

9. See Library of Congress, Federal Research Division, *Country Studies, Area Handbook Series, Albania*: http://lcweb2.loc.gov/frd/cs/altoc.html#al0049; and Keefe et al. (1971).

10. This echoes the point made by Charles Stewart in his rejection of the notion that belief in "exotica"—devils and such—in Naxos is a "left-over" from the past. In Stewart's view, it is entirely a part and construction of the present (Stewart 1991: 5–6).

11. There are, of course, a range of other studies of the idea and politics of number in general. Among the more intriguing are Annelise Riles's work in Fiji (Riles 1998; 2000), and the work done by Marilyn Strathern and others on auditing practices, which is an excellent source for consideration of the process of classification and categorization as a standardizing technology. See, for example, the edited collection *Audit Cultures* (Strathern 2000) and Strathern (1997). See also one of the foremost economic analysts of audit, Michael Power (Power 1994; 1997), and Daniel Miller's treatment of the subject (Miller 1998, esp. 201–5).

CHAPTER 6
EMBODIED RECOUNTING

1. Of course statistics also, and very importantly, appear in graphical form as pie charts, flow charts, bar charts, and so on. These have been omitted from the manuscript owing to the practical limitations on how much artwork can be pub-

lished in an academic book before it becomes prohibitively expensive. Detailed statistical charts can be found in Green (1995b).

2. The reason for this level of control over forests was that Epirus had experienced several bouts of severe deforestation within the nineteenth and twentieth centuries, owing to heavy reliance on firewood and charcoal as household fuel and as a commodity, as well as to a range of wars, in which forests were regularly burned down to rout out enemies (McNeill 1992: 292–300). See Scott for a more detailed account of the development of "scientific forestry" (Scott 1998: 11–22).

3. Parenthetically, it would seem the social groups with whom James Faubion spent time in Athens were quintessentially "city people" (Faubion 1993).

4. This kind of mixed sense of belonging has of course been noted in many other parts of the world. See, for example, Olwig (1997), Brah (1997), Danforth (1995), and Stoller (1996).

5. A brief but interesting outline is given by William McNeill, who was himself an American participant in these interventions (McNeill 1978: 79–91).

6. See Amin (1995) and Doray (1988) for discussions of Fordism.

7. There are various sources describing the junta, including Legg and Roberts (1997), McNeill (1978), Andrews (1980), Murtagh (1994), and Theodoracopulos (1976). An interesting collection is Clogg and Yannopoulos (1972), as it was written during the junta. Surprisingly, I could find no detailed anthropological treatment of this period.

8. The census in Greece had begun in 1913, but I could not find any figures before 1920.

9. That is not a reasonable assumption for the Epirus area (Green and King 1996). See also McNeill (1992) for details of the changing policies toward the environment in Epirus.

10. In contrast to the Sarakatsani, Vlachoi were often "semitranshumant" rather than fully transhumant; this meant it was possible for them to register as village residents before the 1938 change in the law.

11. McNeill provides a detailed analysis of the process of deforestation of Epirus in the course of his discussion on the Pindos mountain range. He suggests that this earlier bareness of the landscape that people recalled was relatively recent and was the result of sustained overexploitation during the previous 150 years (McNeill 1992: 292–300).

12. More details of the Aristi story can be found in Voula Papapetrou's contribution to Green et al. (1999).

13. This is a fairly vague Turkish term meaning "master" and person of high rank or social status, usually ascribed by their official position within some part of the Ottoman administration. Occasionally, this person was also referred to as a *bey* in Epirus; the term *agas* has been retained because *bey* was also used to refer to a landowner (also called a *tsiflikas*), as opposed to a land manager.

14. This kind of selling up on the part of Ottoman landowners occurred in many communes across Epirus between 1908 and 1913, and was probably precipitated by the "Young Turk" revolution in Constantinople. The new administration began to espouse nationalist ideals, increasingly seeing the millets as containing dangerous minorities and as having led to insurrections against the empire; the "Young Turks" made enormous changes to the way Ottoman territories were to

be administered, and began to push for more "Turkification" of the remaining Ottoman territories (Peckham 2001: 138; Palmer 1992: 200–11; Ladas 1932: 10–21). The period was described by people in Epirus as one of serious instability, during which many predicted that it would not be long before the Ottoman Empire would lose Epirus to an expanded Greek state. As a result, many Ottoman landowners sold up and left.

15. These were included in the original territorial survey drawings; they have been omitted here because of the reproduction size of the map in this volume: the houses appear as almost invisible specks at this scale.

16. Bakalaki argues that this construction of Albanians was particularly attractive to Greeks: the assertion of the "wildness" and "disheveled" character of Albanians entering Greece functioned to convey the idea that Greeks themselves were more "modern" than (Balkan) Albanians (Bakalaki 2003). See also Karydis (1996) for an extended account of the way Albanians have been represented in Greece. See also Green (1998a; 1998c) for further discussion of the situation on the Greek-Albanian border itself.

CHAPTER 7
DEVELOPMENTS

1. As Keith Brown reminded me in his preface to *The Past in Question*, the phrase "There is no there there" was coined by Gertrude Stein (Brown 2003: xv). She was referring to Oakland, California, where she spent some of her childhood years (Stein 1937: chap. 4). Insofar as Stein was a key member of the early twentieth-century Left Bank group of artists and writers in Paris that was experimenting with the way modernism could make certainties uncertain, she is a fortuitously appropriate source for such a phrase in this context.

2. This was a reference to the fact that Albania had close relations with China between 1960 and 1978, having broken its previous relations with Moscow (Jacques 1995).

3. See Pettifer (1994) and Hart and Budina (1995) for an outline of this history.

4. In her study of the recent rise of "Islamism" in Turkey, Navaro-Yashin, among many others, notes how this elision between "Westernization," "modernization," and "capitalism," while extremely common, often masks a much more diverse and complex set of relations (Navaro-Yashin 2002: chap. 3).

5. See, for example, Bakalaki (1994) and Herzfeld (1986; 1987).

6. εκσυγχρονισμός /*eksynchronismos*.

7. νεωτερισμός/*neoterismos* or μοντερνισμός/*modernismos*.

8. By "Northern Epirot," Latsis meant Albanian citizens "of Greek descent"; I have already discussed how ambiguous such a classification can be (see chapter 2). In practical terms, people such as Kostas and Maria had to name themselves and be accepted as Northern Epirots in order to qualify for the benefits that Latsis was offering. Once again, as in the case of the three men challenged by the border soldiers at the bus stop, these continual assertions (or, rather, requirements) of unambiguous distinction had the effect of both constituting them as such and also highlighting their contestability.

9. A detailed study of this can be found in Theodosiou (2003).

10. Of course, this kind of experience was occurring in the much wider context of the spread of what Herzfeld refers to as the "global hierarchy of value" (Herzfeld 2004), what Wilk refers to as "global systems of common difference" (Wilk 1995), and what Holmes refers to as "fast-track capitalism" (Holmes 2000). Herzfeld focuses on the impossible position in which Cretan artisans find themselves within that hierarchy: they are defined as "authentic" representatives of "tradition," but because of that, they are denied the symbolic capital to have a "proper" place within the hierarchy. The "global hierarchy of value," Herzfeld argues, imposes a division between the means to evaluate what is and is not "traditional" and "authentic" and the peoples and activities thus evaluated. If people come to be defined as *embodying* "tradition," that effectively marginalizes them: they are not the ones who define "tradition"; they *are* "tradition" (Herzfeld 2004: 199). While there are clearly similar processes at work in the contradictory ways in which people from Albania were assessed in Epirus, there was something else as well: the ambiguity of the peoples from Albania meant that they sometimes could, and sometimes could not, "embody tradition." What emerged out of that was a clear sense of the current power of the "neoliberal" form of modernization; but not such a clear sense of its inevitability as appears to have been the case in Crete.

11. I am using the word "sanctuary" as a loose translation of εκτροφείο/ *ektrofeio*; the word is more often translated as "breeding ground."

12. I am grateful to Chris Fuller for asking me, at a seminar I gave at the London School of Economics in May 2004, why I assumed the mayor was talking about modernity. Prior to his question, I had taken it for granted that the hamburger was self-evidently iconic of a particular form of modernization; the additional point, that hamburgers "do not necessarily mean the same thing to everyone everywhere" (Herzfeld 2004: 212) needed clarifying.

13. See Ray (2001) and Kovach (2000) for further details on the notion of "culture" being used, and how "culture" was to be embedded in these projects. See also Holmes (2000: chap. 2), who outlines quite how ambivalent and self-contradictory European policies on "culture" have been. Once again, this is an example of how any idea that the "West" constitutes a homogenous and coherent account of the way things are is highly questionable.

14. This woman subsequently became one of my Ph.D. students at the Department of Social Anthropology at Manchester.

15. Escobar, among many others, has carried out an effective critique of the idea that it is possible to turn the "environment" into a marketable commodity while simultaneously "conserving" or "sustaining" it (Escobar 1996); similarly, Conklin has questioned the possibility of packaging and marketing "culture" in this way (Conklin 1997).

Bibliography

Abbott, Andrew Delano. 2001. *Chaos of Disciplines*. Chicago: University of Chicago Press.

Adkins, L. 2002. "Sexuality and Economy: Historicisation vs Deconstruction." *Australian Feminist Studies* 17 (37):31–41.

Adkins, Lisa, and Celia Lury. 1999. "The Labour of Identity: Performing Identities, Performing Economies." *Economy and Society* 28 (4):598–614.

Agelopoulos, Georgios. 2000. "Political Practices and Multi-Culturalism: The Case of Salonica." In *Macedonia: The Politics of Identity and Difference*, edited by J. K. Cowan, 140–55. London: Pluto Press.

Alcoff, Linda. 1988. "Cultural Feminism versus Post-Structuralism: The Identity Crisis in Feminist Theory." *Signs* 13 (3):405–36.

Amin, Ash, ed. 1995. *Post-Fordism: A Reader*. Oxford: Blackwell.

Anderson, Benedict. 1983. *Imagined Communities: Reflections on the Origin and Spread of Nationalism*. London: Verso.

Andrews, Kevin. 1980. *Greece in the Dark: 1967–1974*. Amsterdam: Adolf M. Hakkert.

Appadurai, Arjun. 1995. "The Production of Locality." In *Counterworks: Managing the Diversity of Knowledge*, edited by R. Fardon, 204–25. London: Routledge.

———. 1996a. "Global Ethnoscapes: Notes and Queries for a Transnational Anthropology." In *Modernity at Large: Cultural Dimensions of Globalization*, 48–65. Minneapolis: University of Minnesota Press.

———. 1996b. *Modernity at Large: Cultural Dimensions of Globalization*. Minneapolis: University of Minnesota Press.

———. 1996c. "Number in the Colonial Imagination." In *Modernity at Large: Cultural Dimensions of Globalization*, 114–35. Minneapolis: University of Minnesota Press.

Augé, Marc. 1995. *Non-Places: Introduction to an Anthropology of Supermodernity*. Translated by J. Howe. London: Verso.

Babiniotis, Georgios. 1998. *Lexiko Tis Neas Ellinikis Glossas (Dictionary of the Modern Greek Language)*. Athens: Kentro Lexikologias E.P.E.

Bailey, Geoff, ed. 1997. *Klithi: Palaeolithic Settlement and Quaternary Landscapes in Northwest Greece*. Cambridge, UK: McDonald Institute for Archaeological Research.

Bailey, G., G. King, and D. Sturdy. 1993. "Active Tectonics and Land-Use Strategies: A Palaeolithic Example from Northwest Greece." *Antiquity* 67 (255): 202–24.

Bakalaki, Alexandra. 1994. "Gender-Related Discourses and Representations of Cultural Specificity in Nineteenth-Century and Twentieth-Century Greece." *Journal of Modern Greek Studies* 12:75–112.

Bakalaki, Alexandra. 2003. "Locked into Security, Keyed into Modernity: The Selection of Burglaries as Source of Risk in Greece." *Ethnos* 68 (2):209–29.

Baker, Susan, ed. 1997. *The Politics of Sustainable Development: Theory, Policy and Practice within the European Union*. London: Routledge.

Bakić-Hayden, Milica. 1992. "Orientalist Variations on the Theme 'Balkans': Symbolic Geography in Recent Yugoslav Cultural Politics." *Slavic Review* 51 (1):1–15.

———. 1995. "Nesting Orientalisms: The Case of Former Yugoslavia." *Slavic Review* 54 (4):917–31.

Ballinger, Pamela. 1999. "Definitional Dilemmas: Southeastern Europe as 'Culture Area'?" *Balkanologie* 3 (2):73–91.

———. 2003. *History in Exile: Memory and Identity at the Borders of the Balkans*. Princeton: Princeton University Press.

Barnes, J. A. 1994. *A Pack of Lies: Towards a Sociology of Lying*. Cambridge: Cambridge University Press.

Barrier, G. N., ed. 1981. *The Census in British India: New Perspectives*. Boston: Little, Brown.

Basso, Keith H. 1996. "Wisdom Sits in Places: Notes on a Western Apache Landscape." In *Senses of Place*, edited by S. Feld and K. H. Basso, 53–90. Santa Fe, N.M.: School of American Research Press.

Bellier, Irene. 2000. "The European Union, Identity Politics and the Logic of Interests' Representation." In *An Anthropology of the European Union*, edited by I. Bellier and T. Wilson, 53–73. Oxford: Berg.

Bender, Barbara. 1993. "Landscape—Meaning in Action." In *Landscape: Politics and Perspectives*, edited by B. Bender, 1–18. Oxford: Berg.

———. 1999. "Subverting the Western Gaze: Mapping Alternative Worlds." In *The Archaeology and Anthropology of Landscape: Shaping Your Landscape*, edited by P. Ucko and R. Layton, 31–45. London: Routledge.

Benjamin, Walter. 1999. *The Arcades Project*. Translated by R. Tiedemann. Cambridge: Harvard University Press, Belknap Press.

Biberaj, Elez. 1990. *Albania: A Socialist Maverick*. Boulder, Colo.: Westview Press.

Bjelić, Dušan I. 2002. "Introduction: Blowing Up the 'Bridge.' " In *Balkan as Metaphor: Between Globalization and Fragmentation*, edited by Dušan I. Bjelić and Obrad Savić, 1–22. Cambridge: MIT Press.

Bjelić, Dušan I., and Obrad Savić, eds. 2002. *Balkan as Metaphor: Between Globalization and Fragmentation*. Cambridge: MIT Press.

Boon, James A. 1999. *Verging on Extra-Vagance: Anthropology, History, Religion, Literature, Arts . . . Showbiz*. Princeton: Princeton University Press.

Bracewell, Wendy, and Alex Drace-Francis. 1999. "South-Eastern Europe: History, Concepts, Boundaries." *Balkanologie* 3 (2):47–66.

Brah, Avtar. 1997. *Cartographies of Diaspora: Contesting Identities*. London: Routledge.

Braudel, Fernand. 2001. *The Mediterranean in the Ancient World*. London: Allen Lane.

Bringa, Tone. 1995. *Being Muslim the Bosnian Way: Identity and Community in a Central Bosnian Village*. Princeton: Princeton University Press.

Brosius, J. P. 1999. "Green Dots, Pink Hearts: Displacing Politics from the Malaysian Rain Forest." *American Anthropologist* 101 (1):36–57.

Brown, David. 2002. "Yugoslavia: Death of a Federation." *Guardian* (on-line edition), February 12.

Brown, Keith. 2003. *The Past in Question: Modern Macedonia and the Uncertainties of Nation*. Princeton: Princeton University Press.

Butler, Judith. 1990. *Gender Trouble: Feminism and the Subversion of Identity*. New York: Routledge.

———. 1993. *Bodies That Matter: On the Discursive Limits of "Sex."* London: Routledge.

Campbell, John K. 1964. *Honour, Family and Patronage: A Study of Institutions and Moral Values in a Greek Mountain Community*. Oxford: Clarendon Press.

Clifford, James. 1997. *Routes: Travel and Translation in the Late Twentieth Century*. Cambridge: Harvard University Press.

Clogg, Richard. 1992. *A Concise History of Greece*. Cambridge: Cambridge University Press.

Clogg, Richard, and George Nicolas Yannopoulos, eds. 1972. *Greece under Military Rule*. London: Secker & Warburg.

Cohen, Roger. 1995. "A Balkan Gyre of War, Spinning onto Film." *New York Times*, March 12, 24.

Cohn, Bernard S. 1990. "The Census, Social Structure and Objectification in South Asia." In *An Anthropologist among the Historians and Other Essays*, 224–54. Delhi: Oxford University Press.

Collard, Anna. 1989. "Investigating Social Memory in a Greek Context." In *History and Ethnicity*, edited by E. Tonkin, M. McDonald, and M. Chapman, 89–103. London: Routledge.

Conklin, B. A. 1997. "Body Paint, Feathers, and VCRs: Aesthetics and Authenticity in Amazonian Activism." *American Ethnologist* 24 (4):711–37.

Conklin, B. A., and L. R. Graham. 1995. "The Shifting Middle Ground—Amazonian Indians and Eco-Politics." *American Anthropologist* 97 (4):695–719.

Connerton, Paul. 1989. *How Societies Remember*. Cambridge: Cambridge University Press.

Corrigan, S. W., and J. Sawchuk. 1996. *The Recognition of Aboriginal Rights*. Brandon: Bearpaw Pub.

Cosgrove, Denis E. 1996. *Geography and Vision: An Inaugural Lecture*. Egham: Royal Holloway University of London.

———, ed. 1999. *Mappings*. London: Reaktion.

Coutin, S. B., and S. F. Hirsch. 1998. "Naming Resistance: Ethnographers, Dissidents, and States." *Anthropological Quarterly* 71 (1):1–17.

Cowan, Jane K. 1990. *Dance and the Body Politic in Northern Greece*. Princeton: Princeton University Press.

———. 1997. "Idioms of Belonging: Polyglot Articulations of Local Identity in a Greek Macedonian Town." In *Ourselves and Others: The Development of a Greek Macedonian Cultural Identity since 1912*, edited by P. A. Mackridge and E. Yannakakis, 153–71. Oxford: Berg.

———, ed. 2000. *Macedonia: The Politics of Identity and Difference*. London: Pluto Press.

Cowan, Jane K., and Keith Brown. 2000. "Introduction: Macedonian Inflections." In *Macedonia: The Politics of Identity and Difference*, edited by J. K. Cowan, 1–27. London: Pluto Press.

Cowan, Jane K., Marie Dembour, and Richard Wilson, eds. 2001. *Culture and Rights: Anthropological Perspectives*. Cambridge: Cambridge University Press.

Coward, Rosalind. 1983. *Patriarchal Precedents: Sexuality and Social Relations*. London: Routledge & Kegan Paul.

Crehan, Kate. 2002. *Gramsci, Culture and Anthropology*. London: Pluto Press.

Csordas, Thomas J. 1990. "Embodiment as a Paradigm for Anthropology." *Ethos* 18 (1):5–47.

———, ed. 1994. *Embodiment and Experience: The Existential Ground of Culture and Self*. Cambridge: Cambridge University Press.

Danforth, Loring. 1995. *The Macedonian Conflict: Ethnic Nationalism in a Transnational World*. Princeton: Princeton University Press.

———. 2000. " 'How Can a Woman Give Birth to One Greek and One Macedonian?' The Construction of National Identity among Immigrants to Australia from Northern Greece." In *Macedonia: The Politics of Identity and Difference*, edited by J. K. Cowan, 85–103. London: Pluto Press.

Das, Vina. 1985. "Anthropological Knowledge and Collective Violence: The Riots in Delhi, November 1984." *Anthropology Today* 1 (3):4–6.

Day, Ronald E. 2001. *The Modern Invention of Information: Discourse, History, and Power*. Carbondale: Southern Illinois University Press.

Day, Sophie, Evthymios Papataxiarchis, and Michael Stewart, eds. 1999. *Lilies of the Field: Marginal People Who Live for the Moment*. Boulder, Colo.: Westview Press.

De Bernières, Louis. 1995. *Captain Corelli's Mandolin*. London: Minerva.

de Certeau, Michel. 1988. *The Practice of Everyday Life*. Berkeley and Los Angeles: University of California Press.

P. Descola and G. Pálsson, eds. 1996. *Nature and Society: Anthropological Perspectives*. London: Routledge.

Dimen, Muriel, and Ernestine Friedl, eds. 1976. *Regional Variation in Modern Greece and Cyprus: Toward a Perspective on the Ethnography of Greece*. New York: New York Academy of Sciences.

Donnan, Hastings, and Thomas M. Wilson. 1999. *Borders: Frontiers of Identity, Nation and State*. Oxford: Berg.

Doray, Bernard. 1988. *From Taylorism to Fordism: A Rational Madness*. London: Free Association.

Douglas, Mary. 1966. *Purity and Danger: An Analysis of Concepts of Pollution and Taboo*. London: Routledge & Kegan Paul.

du Boulay, Juliet. 1974. *Portrait of a Greek Mountain Village*. Oxford: Clarendon Press.

———. 1976. "Lies, Mockery and Family Integrity". In *Mediterranean Family Structures*, edited by J. G. Peristiany, 389–406. Cambridge: Cambridge University Press.

Dumit, Joseph. 1997. "A Digital Image of the Category of the Person: Pet Scanning and Objective Self-Fashioning". In *Cyborgs and Citadels: Anthropological*

Interventions in Emerging Sciences and Technologies, edited by G. L. Downey and J. Dumit, 83–102. Santa Fe, N.M.: School of American Research Press.

Ellis, M., and R. Wright. 1998. "The Balkanization Metaphor in the Analysis of US Immigration." *Annals of the Association of American Geographers* 88 (4):686–98.

Escobar, Arturo. 1996. "Constructing Nature: Elements for a Poststructural Political Ecology." In *Liberation Ecologies: Environment, Development, Social Movements*, edited by R. Peet and M. J. Watts. London: Routledge.

Evans-Pritchard, E. E. 1978. *The Nuer: A Description of the Modes of Livelihood and Political Institutions of a Nilotic People*. Oxford: Oxford University Press.

Faubion, James D. 1993. *Modern Greek Lessons: A Primer in Historical Constructivism*. Princeton: Princeton University Press.

Ferme, Marianne. 1998. "The Violence of Numbers: Consensus, Competition, and the Negotiation of Disputes in Sierra Leone." *Cahiers d'Études africaines* 150–52 (XXXVIII-2–4):555–80.

Fleming, K. E. 1999. *The Muslim Bonaparte: Diplomacy and Orientalism in Ali Pasha's Greece*. Princeton: Princeton University Press.

Fortier, A. M. 1999. "Re-Membering Places and the Performance of Belonging(s)." *Theory, Culture and Society* 16 (2):41–64.

Foss, A. 1978. *Epirus*. London: Faber.

Fraser, Nancy. 1989. *Unruly Practices: Power, Discourse and Gender in Contemporary Social Theory*. Minneapolis: University of Minnesota Press.

———. 1997. *Justice Interruptus: Critical Reflections on the 'Postsocialist' Condition*. New York: Routledge.

Frazee, Charles A. 1969. *The Orthodox Church and Independent Greece, 1821–1852*. Cambridge: Cambridge University Press.

Friedl, Ernestine. 1962. *Vasilika: A Village in Modern Greece*. New York: Holt Rinehart and Winston.

Friedman, Jonathan. 2002. "Transnationalism, Socio-Political Disorder, and Ethnification as Expressions of Declining Global Hegemony." In *The Anthropology of Politics: A Reader in Ethnography, Theory and Critique*, edited by J. Vincent, 285–300. Oxford: Blackwell.

Friedman, Victor A. 1996. "Observing the Observers: Language, Ethnicity and Power in the 1994 Macedonian Census and Beyond." In *Toward Comprehensive Peace in Southeastern Europe*, edited by B. R. Rubin, 81–128. New York: Twentieth Century Fund Press.

Gal, Susan. 1991. "Bartok's Funeral—Representations of Europe in Hungarian Political Rhetoric." *American Ethnologist* 18 (3):440–58.

———. 2002. "A Semiotics of the Public/Private Distinction." *differences: A Journal of Feminist Cultural Studies* 13 (1):77–95.

Gal, S., and J. T. Irvine. 1995. "The Boundaries of Languages and Disciplines: How Ideologies Construct Difference." *Social Research* 62 (4):967–1001.

Gallagher, Tom. 2001. *Outcast Europe. The Balkans, 1789–1989: From the Ottomans to Milošević*. London: Routledge.

Gleick, James. 1996. *Chaos: Making a New Science*. London: Minerva.

Glenny, Misha. 1993. *The Fall of Yugoslavia: The Third Balkan War*. London: Penguin.

Glenny, Misha. 1999. *The Balkans, 1804–1999: Nationalism, War and the Great Powers*. London: Granta Books.

Gligorov, V. 1992. "Balkanization—a Theory of Constitution Failure." *East European Politics and Societies* 6 (3):283–302.

Glynn, P. 1993. "The Age of Balkanization." *Commentary* 96 (1):21–24.

Goldman, L. 1991. "Statistics and the Science of Society in Early Victorian Britain: An Intellectual Context for the General Register Office." *Social History of Medicine* 4 (3):415–34.

Goldsworthy, Vesna. 1998. *Inventing Ruritania: The Imperialism of the Imagination*. New Haven: Yale University Press.

———. 1999. "The Last Stop on the Orient Express: The Balkans and the Politics of British In(ter)Vention." *Balkanologie* 3 (2):107–15.

Gourgouris, Stathis. 1996. *Dream Nation: Enlightenment, Colonization, and the Institution of Modern Greece*. Stanford: Stanford University Press.

Gray, J. 1999. "Open Spaces and Dwelling Places: Being at Home on Hill Farms in the Scottish Borders." *American Ethnologist* 26 (2):440–60.

Green, Sarah. 1991. "Marking Transgressions: The Use of Style in a Women-Only Community." *Cambridge Anthropology* 15 (2):71–87.

———. 1995a. "Contemporary Change in Use and Perception of the Landscape in Epirus: An Ethnographic Study." In *Understanding the Natural and Anthropogenic Causes of Soil Degradation and Desertification in the Mediterranean Basin*, vol. 1, *Land Degradation in Epirus*, edited by S. E. van der Leeuw, 171–324. Brussels: Directorate General XII of the Commission of the European Union.

———. 1995b. "The Perception and Use of Natural and Cultural Environments in Epirus: Part II." In *Environmental Perception and Policy Making: Cultural and Natural Heritage and the Preservation of Degradation-Sensitive Environments in Southern Europe*, edited by N. Winder and S. E. van der Leeuw, 38–66. Brussels: DG XII of the Commission of the European Union.

———. 1997a. "Post-Communist Neighbours: Relocating Gender in a Greek-Albanian Border Community." In *Surviving Post-Socialism: Local Strategies and Regional Responses in Eastern Europe and the Former Soviet Union*, edited by S. Bridger and F. Pine, 80–105. London: Routledge.

———. 1997b. *Urban Amazons: Lesbian Feminism and Beyond in the Gender, Sexuality and Identity Battles of London*. London: Macmillan.

———. 1998a. "A Proposito Della Dimensione Corporea Del Conflitto Sul Confine Greco-Albanese." *Etnosistemi: Processi e dinamiche culturali* 5:121–35.

———. 1998b. "Interweaving Landscapes: The Relevance of Ethnographic Data on Rural Groups in Epirus for Palaeolithic Research." In *Klithi: Palaeolithic Settlement and Quaternary Landscapes in Northwestern Greece*, edited by G. Bailey, 637–52. Cambridge, UK: McDonald Institute Monographs.

———. 1998c. "Relocating Persons and Places on the Greek-Albanian Border." In *Incontri Di Etnologia Europea/European Ethnology Meetings*, edited by G.P.C. Papa and F. M. Zerelli, 259–81. Perugia: Edizioni Scientiche Italiane.

———. 2002. "Culture in a Network: Dykes, Webs and Women in London and Manchester." In *British Subjects: An Anthropology of Britain*, edited by N. Rapport. Oxford: Berg.

———. 2003. "Digital Ditches: Working in the Virtual Grassroots." In *New Technologies at Work: People, Screens and Social Virtuality*, edited by C. Garsten and H. Wulff, 45–68. Oxford: Berg.

———. Forthcoming. "Abandoned Backwater, Ruggedly Hostile Balkan Borderland and/or Natural Wilderness: On Negotiating a Relocation of 'Nature' in Epirus, Northwestern Greece." In *Replacing Nature: Ethnographies of Connection and Administrations of Distance*, edited by B. Campbell.

Green, Sarah, and Geoffrey King. 1996. "The Importance of Goats to a Natural Environment: A Case Study from Epirus (Greece) and Southern Albania." *Terra Nova* 8:655–58.

———. 2001. "Seeing What You Know: Changing Constructions and Perceptions of Landscape in Epirus, Northwestern Greece, 1945 and 1990." *History and Anthropology* 12 (3):255–88.

Green, Sarah, Sylvie Servain, Voula Papapetrou, Vasilis Nitsiakos, and Geoffrey King. 1999. *Negotiating Perceptions of Fragile Environments in Epirus, Northwestern Greece (Archaeomedes II Programme: Final Report)*. Directorate General XII of the Commission of the European Union, (ENV 4-CT95-0159).

Gunther, John. 1940. *Inside Europe*. New York: Harper & Brothers.

Gupta, Akhil, and James Ferguson, eds. 1997. *Anthropological Locations: Boundaries and Grounds of a Field Science*. Berkeley and Los Angeles: University of California Press.

———. 1999a. "Culture, Power, Place: Ethnography at the End of an Era." In *Culture, Power, Place: Explorations in Critical Anthropology*, edited by A. Gupta and J. Ferguson, 1–29. Durham, N.C.: Duke University Press.

———, eds. 1999b. *Culture, Power, Place: Explorations in Critical Anthropology*. Durham, N.C.: Duke University Press.

Hacking, I. 1981. "How Should We Do the History of Statistics." *I & C* (8): 15–26.

Hall, Stuart, and Paul du Gay, eds. 1996. *Questions of Cultural Identity*. London: Sage.

Hammond, N.G.L. 1983. "Travels in Epirus and South Albania before World-War-2." *Ancient World* 8 (1–2):13–46.

Harris, Robin. 1998. "The Rise of English Nationalism and the Balkanization of Britain." *The National Interest* 54 (Winter):40–41.

Hart, L. K. 1999. "Culture, Civilization, and Demarcation at the Northwest Borders of Greece." *American Ethnologist* 26 (1):196–220.

Hart, Laurie Kain, and Kestrina Budina. 1995. "Northern Epiros: The Greek Minority in Southern Albania." *Cultural Survival Quarterly* 19 (2):54–63.

Harvey, David. 1990. *The Condition of Postmodernity: An Enquiry into the Origins of Cultural Change*. Oxford: Blackwell.

Harvie, Christopher. 1994. *The Rise of Regional Europe*. London: Routledge.

Hayden, R. M. 1996. "Imagined Communities and Real Victims: Self-Determination and Ethnic Cleansing in Yugoslavia." *American Ethnologist* 23 (4):783–801.

Helman, Cecil. 1991. *Body Myths*. London: Chatto & Windus.

Hennessy, R. 1993. "Queer Theory—a Review of the 'Differences' Special Issue and Wittig's 'The Straight Mind.' " *Signs* 18 (4):964–73.

Hennessy, R. 1995. "Queer Visibility in Commodity Culture." In *Social Postmodernism: Beyond Identity Politics*, edited by L. J. Nicholson and S. Seidman. Cambridge: Cambridge University Press.

Herzfeld, Michael. 1984. "The Horns of the Mediterraneanist Dilemma." *American Ethnologist* 11 (3):439–54.

———. 1985. "Stealing to Befriend." In *The Poetics of Manhood: Contest and Identity in a Cretan Mountain Village*, 163–205. Princeton: Princeton University Press.

———. 1986. *Ours Once More: Folklore, Ideology, and the Making of Modern Greece*. New York: Pella Publishing.

———. 1987. *Anthropology through the Looking Glass: Critical Ethnography in the Margins of Europe*. Cambridge: Cambridge University Press.

———. 1990. "Pride and Perjury—Time and the Oath in the Mountain Villages of Crete." *Man* 25 (2):305–22.

———. 1992. *The Social Production of Indifference: Exploring the Symbolic Roots of Western Bureaucracy*. Oxford: Berg.

———. 1997. *Cultural Intimacy: Social Poetics in the Nation-State*. London: Routledge.

———. 2004. *The Body Impolitic: Artisans and Artifice in the Global Hierarchy of Value*. Chicago: University of Chicago Press.

Hickey, Jennifer G., Timothy W. Maier, and Sean Paige. 1999. "Balkanization. (U.S.-Led Bombing in Yugoslavia)." *Insight on the News* 15 (15):12–13.

Hirsch, Eric. 1995. "Landscape: Between Place and Space." In *The Anthropology of Landscape: Perspectives on Place and Space*, edited by E. Hirsch and M. O'Hanlon, 1–30. Oxford: Oxford University Press.

Hirschon, Renée. 1989. *Heirs of the Greek Catastrophe: The Social Life of Asia Minor Refugees in Piraeus*. Oxford: Clarendon Press.

Hirschon, Renée, ed. 2003. *Crossing the Aegean: An Appraisal of the 1923 Compulsory Population Exchange between Greece and Turkey*. New York: Berghahn Books.

Hobart, Mark, ed. 1993. *An Anthropological Critique of Development: The Growth of Ignorance*. London: Routledge.

Hobsbawm, E. J. 1985. *Bandits*. Harmondsworth: Penguin.

Hogan, Michael J. 1987. *The Marshall Plan: America, Britain, and the Reconstruction of Western Europe, 1947–1952*. Cambridge: Cambridge University Press.

Holmes, Douglas, R. 2000. *Integral Europe: Fast-Capitalism, Multiculturalism, Neofascism*. Princeton: Princeton University Press.

Holt, T. 2000. "The Blackett Memorial Lecture: 30th November 1999—the Future for Official Statistics." *Journal of the Operational Research Society* 51 (9):1010–19.

Hosch, Edgar. 1972. *The Balkans: A Short History from Greek Times to the Present Day*. Translated by T. Alexander. London: Faber and Faber.

Howard, M. C. 1982. "Australian Aboriginal Politics and the Perpetuation of Inequality." *Oceania* 53 (1):82–101.

Husarska, Anna. 1999. "Balkanization? You Just Wait . . . : As Part of Montenegro Races Back to the Past, the Return of Clan Gatherings. This Isn't Funny." *Newsweek International* November 8:2.

Ingold, Tim. 1995. "Building, Dwelling, Living: How Animals and People Make Themselves at Home in the World." In *Shifting Contexts: Transformations in Anthropological Knowledge*, edited by M. Strathern, 57–80. London: Routledge.

———. 2000a. "Globes and Spheres: The Topology of Environmentalism." In *The Perception of the Environment*, 209–18. London: Routledge.

———. 2000b. *The Perception of the Environment: Essays on Livelihood, Dwelling and Skill.* London: Routledge.

———. 2000c. "To Journey along a Way of Life: Maps, Wayfinding and Navigation." In *The Perception of the Environment: Essays on Livelihood, Dwelling and Skill*, edited by T. Ingold, 219–42. London: Routledge.

Irvine, Judith T., and Susan Gal. 2000. "Language Ideology and Linguistic Differentiation." In *Regimes of Language: Ideologies, Polities, and Identities*, edited by P. V. Kroskrity, 35–83. Santa Fe, N.M.: School of American Research Press; Oxford: James Currey.

Jackson, Michael. 1989. *Paths toward a Clearing: Radical Empiricism and Ethnographic Inquiry.* Bloomington: Indiana University Press.

Jacques, Edwin E. 1995. *The Albanians: An Ethnic History from Prehistoric Times to the Present.* Jefferson, N.C.: McFarland and Company.

Jansen, Stef. 2003. "'Why Do They Hate Us?' Everyday Serbian Nationalist Knowledge of Muslim Hatred." *Journal of Mediterranean Studies* 13 (2):215–37.

Jelavich, Charles, and Barbara Jelavich. 1986. *The Establishment of the Balkan National States, 1804–1920.* Seattle: University of Washington Press.

Jenkins, T. N. 2000. "Putting Postmodernity into Practice: Endogenous Development and the Role of Traditional Cultures in the Rural Development of Marginal Regions." *Ecological Economics* 34 (3):301–14.

Jones, Howard. 1989. *"A New Kind of War": America's Global Strategy and the Truman Doctrine in Greece.* New York: Oxford University Press.

Kalliatake, Mertikopoulou Kallia, Eleuterios Prevelakes, and William Meyer. 1996. *I Ipeiros, O Ali Pasas Kai I Elliniki Epanastasi: Proxenikes Ektheseis Tou "William Meyer" Apo Tin Preveza.* Athens: Akadimia Athinon.

Kaplan, Caren. 1996. *Questions of Travel: Postmodern Discourses of Displacement.* Durham, N.C.: Duke University Press.

Kaplan, Robert D. 1994. *Balkan Ghosts: A Journey through History.* New York: Vintage.

Karakasidou, Anastasia. 1993. "Politicizing Culture: Negating Ethnic Identity in Greek Macedonia." *Journal of Modern Greek Studies* 11:1–28.

———. 1997. *Fields of Wheat, Hills of Blood: Passages to Nationhood in Greek Macedonia, 1870–1990.* Chicago: University of Chicago Press.

———. 2002. "The Burden of the Balkans." *Anthropological Quarterly* 75 (3):575–89.

Karydis, Vasilis. 1996. *I Eglimatikotita Ton Metanaston Stin Ellada. Zitimata Theorias Kai Antieglimatikis Politikis.* Athens: Papazisis.

Kearney, M. 1995. "The Local and the Global—the Anthropology of Globalization and Transnationalism." *Annual Review of Anthropology* 24:547–65.

Keefe, Eugene K., Sarah Jane Elpern, William Giloane, James M. Moore Jr., Stephen Peters, and Eston T. White. 1971. *Area Handbook for Albania.* Washington, D.C.: The American University.

Kertzer, David, and Dominique Arel, eds. 2002a. *Census and Identity: The Politics of Race, Ethnicity, and Language in National Censuses.* Cambridge: Cambridge University Press.

———. 2002b. "Censuses, Identity Formation, and the Struggle for Political Power." In *Census and Identity: The Politics of Race, Ethnicity, and Language in National Censuses,* edited by D. Kertzer and D. Arel, 1–42. Cambridge: Cambridge University Press.

Killick, J. R. 1997. *The United States and European Reconstruction, 1945–1960.* Edinburgh: Keele University Press.

King, Geoff, Derek Sturdy, and Geoff Bailey. 1997. "The Tectonic Background to the Epirus Landscape." In *Klithi: Palaeolithis Settlement and Quaternary Landscapes in Northwest Greece,* edited by G. Bailey, 541–58. Cambridge, UK: McDonald Institute for Archaeological Research.

King, Geoffrey, Derek Sturdy, and John Whitney. 1993. "The Landscape Geometry and Active Tectonics of Northwest Greece." *Geological Society of America Bulletin* 105:137–61.

Kitromilides, Paschalis M. 1990. " 'Imagined Communities' and the Origins of the National Question in the Balkans." In *Modern Greece: Nationalism and Nationality,* edited by M. Blinkhorn and T. Veremis, 23–66. London: Sage; Athens: ELIAMEP.

———. 1994. *Enlightenment, Nationalism, Orthodoxy: Studies in the Culture and Political Thought of South-Eastern Europe.* Aldershot: Variorum.

———. 1996. " 'Balkan Mentality': History, Legend, Imagination." *Nations and Nationalism* 2 (2):163–91.

Koliopoulos, John S. 1990. "Brigandage and Irredentism in Nineteenth-Century Greece." In *Modern Greece: Nationalism and Nationality,* edited by M. Blinkhorn and T. Veremis, 67–102. London: Sage; Athens: ELIAMEP.

Konstandinou, Kostoula. 1995. *Pogoniaka Chronika.* Ioannina: Pogonisia Vivliothiki 4.

Koukoudis, Asterios. 2003. *The Vlachs: Metropolis and Diaspora.* Translated by D. Whitehouse. Thessaloniki: Zitros Publications.

Kovach, I. 2000. "LEADER, a New Social Order, and the Central- and East-European Countries." *Sociologia Ruralis* 40 (2):181–89.

Kovach, Y. 1995. "*The Balkanization of the West: The Confluence of Postmodernism and Postcommunism* by Stjepan G Mestrovic." *South Slav Journal* 16 (1/2):103.

Kulick, Don. 1998. *Travesti: Sex, Gender, and Culture among Brazilian Transgendered Prostitutes.* Chicago: University of Chicago Press.

Ladas, Stephen P. 1932. *The Exchange of Minorities: Bulgaria, Greece and Turkey.* New York: Macmillan.

Lambridis, I. 1993 (1889). *Ipeirotika Meletimata: Pogoniaka.* Ioannina: Institute of Epirot Studies.

Lambropoulos, Vassilis. 2003. "Must We Keep Talking about "the Balkans"?" In *Greece and the Balkans: Identities, Perceptions and Cultural Encounters since the Enlightenment*, edited by D. Tziovas, 265–70. London: Ashgate.

Larbalestier, J. 1990. "The Politics of Representation—Australian Aboriginal Women and Feminism." *Anthropological Forum* 1 (2):143–57.

Latour, Bruno. 1993. *We Have Never Been Modern*. New York: Harvester Wheatsheaf.

Law, John, and John Hassard, eds. 1999. *Actor Network Theory and After*. Oxford: Blackwell.

Lazarova, E. 1999. "Europeization as De-Balkanization." *Etudes Balkaniques* 35 (1/2):143–48.

Legg, Keith R., and John M. Roberts. 1997. *Modern Greece: A Civilization on the Periphery*. Boulder, Colo.: Westview Press.

Lévi-Strauss. 1963. "The Structural Study of Myth." In *Structural Anthropology*, 206–31. New York: Basic Books.

Lovell, Nadia, ed. 1998. *Locality and Belonging*. London: Routledge.

Low, Setha M., and Denise Lawrence-Zuñiga. 2003. "Locating Culture." In *The Anthropology of Space and Place: Locating Culture*, edited by S. M. Low and D. Lawrence-Zuñiga, 1–47. Malden, Mass.: Blackwell.

Lury, C. 1998. *Prosthetic Culture: Photography, Memory and Identity*. London: Routledge.

Mackridge, Peter A., and Eleni Yannakakis, eds. 1997. *Ourselves and Others: The Development of a Greek Macedonian Cultural Identity since 1912*. Oxford: Berg.

Magas, B. 1989. "Yugoslavia—the Specter of Balkanization." *New Left Review* (174):3–31.

Makris, E. P. 1992. *Zoi Kai Paradosi Ton Sarakatsanaion*. Ioannina: E. P. Makris.

Malkki, Liisa. 1992. "National Geographic: The Rooting of Peoples and the Territorialization of National Identity among Scholars and Refugees." *Cultural Anthropology* 7 (1):24–44.

Martin, Emily. 1989. "The Cultural Construction of Gendered Bodies: Biology and Metaphors of Production and Destruction." *Ethnos* 54 (3/4):143–60.

Mazower, Mark. 2001. *The Balkans*. London: Phoenix.

McDonald, M. 1996. " 'Unity in Diversity': Some Tensions in the Construction of Europe." *Social Anthropology* 4 (1):47–60.

McNeill, J. R. 1992. *The Mountains of the Mediterranean World: An Environmental History*. Cambridge: Cambridge University Press.

McNeill, William Hardy. 1964. *Europe's Steppe Frontier, 1500–1800*. Chicago: University of Chicago Press.

———. 1978. *The Metamorphosis of Greece since World War II*. Oxford: Blackwell.

Mestrovic, S. G. 1996. "The Balkanization of the Balkans." *Society* 34 (1):70–80.

Mikalopoulou, D. 1993. *Tsamides*. Athens: Arsenidi.

Miller, Daniel. 1998. "Conclusion: A Theory of Virtualism." In *Virtualism: A New Political Economy*, edited by J. G. Carrier and D. Miller, 187–215. Oxford: Berg.

Milton, Kay, ed. 1993. *Environmentalism: The View from Anthropology.* London: Routledge.

———. 1996. *Environmentalism and Cultural Theory: Exploring the Role of Anthropology in Environmental Discourse.* London: Routledge.

Mimica, Jadran. 1988. *Intimations of Infinity: The Mythopoeia of the Iqwaye Counting System and Number.* Oxford: Berg.

Močnik, Rasto. 2002. "The Balkans as an Element in Ideological Mechanisms." In *Balkan as Metaphor: Between Globalization and Fragmentation*, edited by Dušan I. Bjelić and Obrad Savić, 79–116. Cambridge: MIT Press.

Mongia, R. V. 1999. "Race, Nationality, Mobility: A History of the Passport." *Public Culture* 11 (3):527–55.

Munro, R. 2001. "Calling for Accounts: Numbers, Monsters and Membership." *Sociological Review* 49 (4):473–93.

Murtagh, Peter. 1994. *The Rape of Greece: The King, the Colonels and the Resistance.* London: Simon & Schuster.

Navaro-Yashin, Yael. 2002. *Faces of the State: Secularism and Public Life in Turkey.* Princeton: Princeton University Press.

———. 2003. "Legal/Illegal Counterpoints: Subjecthood and Subjectivity in an Unrecognized State." In *Global Perspectives on Human Rights*, edited by J. Mitchell and R. Wilson. London: Routledge.

Nitsiakos, Vasilis. 1985. "I Imi-Nomadiki Ktinotrofiki Koinotita Stin Ipeiro: Scheseis Paragogis Kai Koinoniki Sygrotisi." *Epirus: Society-Economy Fifteenth–Twentieth Centuries*, 277–88.

———. 1995. *Oi Oreines Koinotites Tis Voreias Pindou Ston Apoiho Tis Makras Diarkeias.* Athens: Plethron.

Nitsiakos, Vasilis, and Constantinos Mantzos. 2003. "Negotiating Culture: Political Uses of Polyphonic Folk Songs in Greece and Albania." In *Greece and the Balkans: Identities, Perceptions and Cultural Encounters since the Enlightenment*, edited by D. Tziovas, 192–207. London: Ashgate.

———. 1986. "I Exeliksi Tis Iminomadikis Ktinotrofikis Koinotitas Sta Plaisia Ton Ethnikon Agrotikon Scheseon. Anafora Sto Paradeigma Tis Aetomilitsas." *Epirot Chronicles (Ipeirotika Chronika)*, 261–84.

Norris, David A. 1999. *In the Wake of the Balkan Myth: Questions of Identity and Modernity.* Basingstoke, UK: St. Martin's Press.

Nugent, D. 1998. "The Morality of Modernity and the Travails of Tradition: Nationhood and the Subaltern in Northern Peru." *Critique of Anthropology* 18 (1):7–33.

Nugent, Stephen. 1999. "Verging on the Marginal: Modern Amazonian Peasantries." In *Lilies of the Field: Marginal People Who Live for the Moment*, edited by S. Day, E. Papataxiarchis, and M. Stewart, 179–95. Boulder, Colo.: Westview Press.

Olwig, Karen Fog. 1997. "Cultural Sites: Sustaining a Home in a Deterritorialized World." In *Siting Culture: The Shifting Anthropological Object*, edited by K. F. Olwig and K. Hastrup, 17–38. London: Routledge.

Olwig, Karen Fog, and Kirsten Hastrup, eds. 1997. *Siting Culture: The Shifting Anthropological Object.* London: Routledge.

Ong, Aihwa. 1996. "Anthropology, China and Modernities: The Geopolitics of Cultural Knowledge." In *The Future of Anthropological Knowledge*, edited by H. L. Moore, 60–92. London: Routledge.

———. 1999. *Flexible Citizenship: The Cultural Logics of Transnationality.* Durham, N.C.: Duke University Press.

Ong, Aihwa, and Donald M. Nonini, eds. 1997. *Undergrounded Empires: The Cultural Politics of Modern Chinese Transnationalism.* New York: Routledge.

Palmer, Alan Warwick. 1992. *The Decline and Fall of the Ottoman Empire.* London: Murray.

Pálsson, Gísli. 1996. "Human-Environmental Relations: Orientalism, Paternalism and Communalism." In *Nature and Society: Anthropological Perspectives*, edited by P. Descola and G. Pálsson, 63–81. London: Routledge.

Papadopoulos, Alexandros K. 1992. *O Alvanikos Ethnikismos Kai O Oikoumenikos Ellinismos: 'Apeiros' Hora.* Athens: 'Nea Synora' Publishers—A.A. Livani.

Papataxiarchis, Evthymios. 1999. "A Contest with Money: Gambling and the Politics of Disinterested Sociality in Aegean Greece." In *Lilies of the Field: Marginal People Who Live for the Moment*, edited by S. Day, E. Papataxiarchis, and M. Stewart, 158–75. Boulder, Colo.: Westview Press.

Peckham, J.R.S. 1992. "Albanians in Greek Clothing." *World Today* 48:58–59.

Peckham, Robert Shannan. 2001. *National Histories, Natural States: Nationalism and the Politics of Place in Greece.* London: I. B. Tauris.

Pettifer, James. 1993. *The Greeks: The Land and People since the War.* London: Viking.

———. 1994. "Albania, Greece and the Vorio Epirus Question." *World Today* 50:147–49.

Pippidi, Andrei. 1999. "Changes of Emphasis: Greek Christendom, Westernization, South-Eastern Europe and Neo-Mitteleuropa." *Balkanologie* 3 (2):93–106.

Plomer, William. 1970 (1936). *The Diamond of Jannina: Ali Pasha, 1741–1822.* London: Cape.

Pollo, Stefanaq, and Arben Puto. 1981. *The History of Albania from Its Origins to the Present Day.* London: Routledge & Kegan Paul.

Poovey, Mary. 1995. *Making a Social Body: British Cultural Formation, 1830–1864.* Chicago: University of Chicago Press.

Porter, Theodore M. 1995. *Trust in Numbers: The Pursuit of Objectivity in Science and Public Life.* Princeton: Princeton University Press.

Power, Michael. 1994. *The Audit Explosion.* London: Demos.

———. 1997. *The Audit Society: Rituals of Verification.* Oxford: Oxford University Press.

Pratt, Mary Louise. 1992. *Imperial Eyes: Travel Writing and Transculturation.* London: Routledge.

Ray, Christopher. 2000. "The EU LEADER Programme: Rural Development Laboratory." *Sociologia Ruralis* 40 (2):163–71.

———. 2001. *Culture Economies: A Perspective on Local Rural Development in Europe.* Newcastle upon Tyne: CRE Press.

Riles, Annelise. 1998. "Division within the Boundaries." *JRAI* 4 (3):409–24.

Riles, Annelise. 2000. *The Network Inside Out*. Ann Arbor: University of Michigan Press.

Roessel, David E. 2002. *In Byron's Shadow: Modern Greece in the English and American Imagination*. Oxford: Oxford University Press.

Sakellariou, Michael V., ed. 1997. *Epirus: Four Thousand Years of Greek History and Civilization*. Athens: Ekdotike Athenon.

Salmon, Tim. 1995. *The Unwritten Places*. Athens: Lycabettus Press.

Savage, M., G. Bagnall, and B. Longhurst. 2001. "Ordinary, Ambivalent and Defensive: Class Identities in the Northwest of England." *Sociology—the Journal of the British Sociological Association* 35 (4):875–92.

Sawicki, Jana. 1988. "Identity Politics and Sexual Freedom: Foucault and Feminism." In *Feminism and Foucault: Reflections on Resistance*, edited by I. Diamond and L. Quinby, 177–91. Boston: Northeastern University Press.

Scopetea, Ellie. 2003. "The Balkans and the Notion of the 'Crossroads between East and West.'" In *Greece and the Balkans: Identities, Perceptions and Cultural Encounters since the Enlightenment*, edited by D. Tziovas, 171–76. London: Ashgate.

Scott, James C. 1998. *Seeing Like a State: How Certain Schemes to Improve the Human Condition Have Failed*. New Haven: Yale University Press.

Sedgwick, Eve Kosofsky. 1990. *Epistemology of the Closet*. Berkeley and Los Angeles: University of California Press.

Seremetakis, C. Nadia. 1991. *The Last Word: Women, Death, and Divination in Inner Mani*. Chicago: University of Chicago Press.

———. 1996. "In Search of the Barbarians: Borders in Pain." *American Anthropologist* 98 (3):489–91.

Sevastianos, Metropolitan of Drinopolis. 1989. *I Estavromeni Voreios Ipeiros*. Athens: Georgios L. Kafouros.

Shore, C. 1993. "Inventing the 'People's Europe'—Critical Approaches to European-Community 'Cultural Policy.'" *Man* 28 (4):779–800.

———. 2000. *Building Europe: The Cultural Politics of European Integration*. London: Routledge.

Shryock, Andrew. 1997. *Nationalism and the Genealogical Imagination: Oral History and Textual Authority in Tribal Jordan*. Berkeley and Los Angeles: University of California Press.

Skeggs, Beverley. 1997. *Formations of Class and Gender: Becoming Respectable*. London: Sage.

Stam, Robert, and Ella Shohat. n.d. "Unthinking Eurocentrism: Multi-Culturalism, Film and the Media." Teachers for a Democratic Culture. [A revised version was published as Shohat, E., and R. Stam. 1994. *Unthinking Eurocentrism: Multiculturalism and the Media*. London: Routledge.]

Stavrianos, L. S. 2000. *The Balkans since 1453*. London: C. Hurst.

Steedly, Mary Margaret. 1993. *Hanging without a Rope: Narrative Experience in Colonial and Postcolonial Karoland*. Princeton: Princeton University Press.

Stein, Gertrude. 1937. *Everybody's Autobiography*. New York: Random House.

Stewart, Charles. 1991. *Demons and the Devil: Moral Imagination in Modern Greek Culture*. Princeton: Princeton University Press.

Stewart, Kathleen. 1996. *A Space on the Side of the Road: Cultural Poetics in an "Other" America*. Princeton: Princeton University Press.

Stolcke, Verena. 1995. "Talking Culture—New Boundaries, New Rhetorics of Exclusion in Europe." *Current Anthropology* 36 (1):1–24.

———. 1999. "New Rhetorics of Exclusion in Europe." *International Social Science Journal* 51 (1):25–35.

Stoler, Ann Laura. 1999. *Race and the Education of Desire: Foucault's History of Sexuality and the Colonial Order of Things*. Durham, N.C.: Duke University Press.

Stoller, Paul. 1996. "Spaces, Places, and Fields: The Politics of West African Trading in New York's Informal Economy." *American Anthropologist* 98 (4):776–88.

Strathern, Marilyn. 1991. *Partial Connections*. Savage, Md.: Rowman & Littlefield.

———. 1992a. *After Nature: English Kinship in the Late Twentieth Century*. Cambridge: Cambridge University Press.

———. 1992b. "Qualified Value: The Perspective of Gift Exchange." In *Barter, Exchange and Value: An Anthropological Approach*, edited by C. Humphrey and S. Hugh-Jones, 169–91. Cambridge: Cambridge University Press.

———. 1995. "The Nice Thing about Culture Is That Everyone Has It." In *Shifting Contexts: Transformations in Anthropological Knowledge*, edited by M. Strathern, 153–76. London: Routledge.

———. 1996. "Cutting the Network." *Journal of the Royal Anthropological Institute* 2 (3):517–35.

———. 1997. " 'Improving Ratings': Audit in the British University System." *European Review* 5:305–21.

———. 1999. *Property, Substance and Effect: Anthropological Essays on Persons and Things*. London: Athlone Press.

———, ed. 2000. *Audit Cultures*. London: Routledge.

Sturdy, Derek, and D. Webley. 1988. "Palaeolithic Geography: Or, Where Are the Deer?" *World Archaeology* 19:262–68.

Sturdy, D., D. Webley, and G. N. Bailey. 1994. "Prehistoric Land Use." In *Understanding the Natural and Anthropogenic Causes of Land Degradation in the Mediterranean Basin*, vol. 1, *Land Degradation in Epirus*, edited by S. E. van der Leeuw, 81–170. Brussels: Directorate General XII of the Commission of the European Union.

Sykes, K. 2003. "My Aim Is True: Postnostalgic Reflections on the Future of Anthropological Science." *American Ethnologist* 30 (1):156–68.

Taylor, Charles. 1994. "The Politics of Recognition." In *Multiculturalism: A Critical Reader*, edited by D. T. Goldberg, 75–106. Oxford: Blackwell.

Theodoracopulos, Taki. 1976. *The Greek Upheaval: Kings, Demagogues and Bayonets*. London: Stacey International.

Theodosiou, Aspasia. 2003. "Authentic Performances and Ambiguous Identities: Gypsy Musicians on the Greek-Albanian Border." Ph.D. diss.: University of Manchester.

Tilley, Christopher Y. 1994. *A Phenomenology of Landscape: Places, Paths and Monuments*. Oxford: Berg.

Todorova, Maria Nikolaeva. 1997. *Imagining the Balkans.* New York: Oxford University Press.

Torpey, John C. 2000. *The Invention of the Passport: Surveillance, Citizenship and the State.* Cambridge: Cambridge University Press.

Trotsky, Leon. 1980. *The Balkan Wars, 1912–1913.* New York: Monard Press.

Tsantinis, Kostas. 1988. *Mourgana: Enas Defteros Grammos.* Athens: Pataki Publishers.

Tsing, Anna L. 1993. *In the Realm of the Diamond Queen: Marginality in an Out-of-the-Way Place.* Princeton: Princeton University Press.

Tsitsipis, Lukas D. 1998. *A Linguistic Anthropology of Praxis and Language Shift: Arvanitika (Albanian) and Greek in Contact.* Oxford: Clarendon Press; New York: Oxford University Press.

Turner, Terence. 1992. "Defiant Images: The Kayapo Appropriation of Video." *Anthropology Today* 8 (6):5–16.

———. 1993. "Anthropology and Multiculturalism—What Is Anthropology That Multiculturalists Should Be Mindful of It?" *Cultural Anthropology* 8 (4):411–29.

———. 2003. "Class Projects, Social Consciousness, and the Contradictions of 'Globalization.' " In *Globalization, the State, and Violence*, edited by J. Friedman, 35–66. Walnut Creek, Calif.: AltaMira Press.

Tziovas, Dimitris, ed. 2003. *Greece and the Balkans: Identities, Perceptions and Cultural Encounters since the Enlightenment.* London: Ashgate.

University of Birmingham Centre for Contemporary Cultural Studies. 1982. *The Empire Strikes Back: Race and Racism in 70s Britain.* London: Routledge in association with the Centre for Contemporary Cultural Studies, University of Birmingham.

Urla, J. 1993. "Cultural Politics in an Age of Statistics—Numbers, Nations, and the Making of Basque Identity." *American Ethnologist* 20 (4):818–43.

Vacalopoulou, Konstandinos A. 1995. *Istoria Tou Voreiou Ellinismou: Ipeiros.* Thessaloniki: Kiriakidi Brothers Publishing House.

van der Leeuw, Sander E., ed. 1998. *The Archaeomedes Project: Understanding the Natural and Anthropogenic Causes of Land Degradation and Desertification in the Mediterranean Basin.* Luxembourg: Office for Official Publications of the European Communities.

van der Veer, P. 1997. "The Victim's Tale: Memory and Forgetting in the Story of Violence." In *Violence, Identity and Self-Determination*, edited by H. de Vries and S. Weber, 186–200. Stanford: Stanford University Press.

Verdery, Katherine. 1999. *The Political Lives of Dead Bodies: Reburial and Postsocialist Change.* New York: Columbia University Press.

Veremis, Thanos. 1990. "From the National State to the Stateless Nation, 1821–1910." In *Modern Greece: Nationalism and Nationality*, edited by M. Blinkhorn and T. Veremis, 9–22. London: Sage; Athens: ELIAMEP.

———. 2003. "1922: Political Continuations and Realignments in the Greek State." In *Crossing the Aegean: An Appraisal of the 1923 Compulsory Population Exchange between Greece and Turkey*, edited by R. Hirschon, 53–62. New York: Berghahn Books.

Verran, Helen. 2001. *Science and an African Logic*. Chicago: University of Chicago Press.

Voutira, Eftihia. 2003. "When Greeks Meet Other Greeks: Settlement Policy Issues in the Contemporary Greek Context." In *Crossing the Aegean: An Appraisal of the 1923 Compulsory Population Exchange between Greece and Turkey*, edited by R. Hirschon, 145–62. New York: Berghahn Books.

Wace, A.J.B., and Maurice Scott Thompson. 1972. *The Nomads of the Balkans: An Account of Life and Customs among the Vlachs of Northern Pindus*. London: Methuen & Co.

Wagner, Roy. 1991. "The Fractal Person." In *Big Men and Great Men: Personifications of Power in Melanesia*, edited by M. Strathern and M. Godelier, 159–73. Cambridge: Cambridge University Press.

"The War in Bosnia: Can the Balkans Be Saved from Balkanisation?" 1995. *World Today* 51 (8/9):155.

Watson, James L. 1997. *Golden Arches East: McDonald's in East Asia*. Stanford: Stanford University Press.

Weiner, J. F. 1999. "Culture in a Sealed Envelope: The Concealment of Australian Aboriginal Heritage and Tradition in the Hindmarsh Island Bridge Affair." *Journal of the Royal Anthropological Institute* 5 (2):193–210.

Wilk, R. 1995. "Learning to Be Local in Belize: Global Systems of Common Difference." In *Worlds Apart: Modernity through the Prism of the Local*, edited by D. Miller, 110–33. London: Routledge.

Wilkinson, Henry Robert. 1951. *Maps and Politics: A Review of the Ethnographic Cartography of Macedonia*. Liverpool: Liverpool University Press.

Winchester, S. 1999. *The Fracture Zone: A Return to the Balkans*. London: Viking.

Wolf, Eric R. 1982. *Europe and the People without History*. Berkeley and Los Angeles: University of California Press.

Wolff, Larry. 1994. *Inventing Eastern Europe: The Map of Civilization on the Mind of the Enlightenment*. Stanford: Stanford University Press.

Žižek, Slavoj. 1997. *The Plague of Fantasies*. London: Verso.

———. 2002 (1989). *The Sublime Object of Ideology*. London: Verso.

Žižek, Slavoj, Elizabeth Wright, and Edmond Wright. 1999. *The Žižek Reader*. Oxford: Blackwell.

Index

abandoned land, 7–8; classification of, 173, 176, 181–82; and grazing/cultivated areas, 28, 119, 120, 121, 123; in Katarraktis, 213; in Ktismata, 209; as "land degradation," 33, 179; as "nature," 34; and place, 7–8, 53; 120. *See also* land degradation

Abbott, Andrew, 270n.9

accounts: and counting, 273n.4; diversity of, 36–37, 96, 104, 112–13, 193; gaps in, 160; geomorphological, 91, 107, 111; and hegemony, 129–30; and indifference, 173; and interests, 166; interweaving of, 89–90, 93–94, 97, 113–14, 141–42, 172, 174; narrative, 162, 267n.23; as negotiations, 161, 162–63; partiality of, 164, 177; of Pogoni peoples, 40, 73–74, 79, 192; and statistics, 170, 177, 183; and stereotyping, 100, 102; techniques of generating, 9–10, 30, 159–60. *See also* scales

actor network theory, 5, 113–14, 130, 136

aerial photographs, 30, 180

agas, 207, 208

Agelopoulos, Georgios, 148

agriculture. *See* cultivation; pastoralism

Agriculture, Ioannina Department of, 161, 181, 195, 202, 203

Albania: border villages in, 56; and China, 6, 227, 276n.2; communist revolution in, 28, 57, 189; "disappearance" of, 49, 64; and infrastructure, 228; as "Inside," 41, 202; and land redistribution programs, 226; and mapping practices, 96–98, 108; and modernization, 228–29; and Pogoni/Kasidiaris regions, 122; postsocialist period of, 7, 46, 153; and relations with Greece, 222; during Second World War, 48; socialist period of, 59, 97, 229–30; and statistics, 169; and transhumant pastoralism, 65, 235. *See also* Albania, Southern; Albanian government; Albanians; Northern Epirus

Albania, Southern, 12, 15, 224, 262n.13; Greek claims to (pre-1970s), 49; and

movement and travel, 170; and Pogoni region, 15; socialist period of, 229–30. *See also* Northern Epirus

Albanian government, 62, 110, 170, 229; and Greek Orthodox Church, 109; and Tsamides, 15, 16, 77

Albanians, 12, 44, 131, 182, 219; ambiguity of, 58–59, 242; crossing Greek-Albanian border, 28, 64, 101, 108, 194, 212, 222; and Delvinaki, 66, 236; diverse attitudes toward in Epirus, 42–43, 46, 227, 231, 233; fear of, 35, 41, 61; and gaps, 220; and Greece, 62, 109, 194, 222, 223, 224, 231, 276n.16; and modernity, 231; and movement and travel, 233–34; and Northern Epirots, 228; and pastoralism, 202; Southern, 15; and Tsamides, 75, 76. *See also* Northern Epirots

Ali Pasha, 85–86, 100, 101, 269n.10

Althusser, Louis, 221

ambiguity, 10–12, 17, 78, 159; and the Balkans, 151, 152, 263n.21, 271n.24; of being "Balkan," 87; of borders and boundaries, 44–45, 135–36, 188; and clarity, 12, 13, 36, 64, 132; and classification, 169–70, 182; and connections, 129; and cultural heritage, 39; and difference, 173; of forest, 181; and fractals, 157; and gaps, 140; and Greek-Albanian border, 16, 56, 221, 224, 226–27; of *Gréki*, 81, 83–84; and interrelations, 139; of Kasidiaris region, 17, 88; and location, 17–19, 93; of maps, 31–36; of marginality, 4; and modernity, 247; and nations/nationality, 15, 223, 262n.16; and Northern Epirots, 42, 58–59; and ordinariness, 72–73, 217, 218–19, 236; and "sameness," 14; and statistics, 182; and Tsamides, 15–16, 75–77, 77–78; and visibility, 80

Amelia, of Ktismata, 56–60, 61, 210

andartes. See resistance groups

Anderson, Benedict, 188

Andrić, Ivo, 144

animal rustlers, 23, 25

animals, 40, 65; commercially farmed, 71, 72, 203–4; donkeys, 215–16; horses, 26; and Katarraktis, 215; and land degradation, 91; as pests, 49; snakes, 53; statistical accounts of, 170, 195, 202–4; theft of, 46, 74; and wild boar, 237, 239, 240. *See also* cattle; goats; sheep; sheepdogs; wild boar
anthropology: and analysis of statistics, 173–74, 274n.11; and concepts of place, 90; and fractals, 135; and marginality, 1–3
Appadurai, Arjun, 163, 174, 212, 263n.26, 273n.2
Archaeomedes research program, 264nn.30 and 36
Arel, Dominique, 163, 169
Areti, 58, 64, 72, 205, 257
Argyrohori, 40, 43–44, 45, 52, 61, 62, 126, 225–26; population statistics of, 196, 198, 252, 253; and reforestation, 179; shifting location of, 58
Argyrokastro (Gjirokastër), 46, 57, 67, 73
Aristi, 19, 26, 42, 200, 201
armatoloi, 76, 267n.20. *See also* resistance groups
Arnista, 193
Arta, 100, 103; statistical data on, 249, 251
Astoria, 266n.8
Athenians, 50–51, 86, 101, 102, 122. *See also* Athens
Athens, 23, 54, 99; coming and going from, 22, 47, 48, 50–51, 56, 58, 60, 61, 186; and relations with Epirus, 83, 121, 178; as location of idealized Europe, 87, 89; and population statistics, 184, 187–88
Australia, 52, 54, 68, 199
Austria, 151, 152
Austro-Hungarian empire. *See* Hapsburg Empire

Babiniotis, Georgios, 81–82
Bailey, Geoff, 112
Bakalaki, Alexandra, 216, 224, 225, 230, 276n.16
Baker, Susan, 219
Bakić-Hayden, Milica, 133
Balkan Wars (1912–13), 92, 145
Balkanism, 139, 151, 270nn. 7 and 10. *See also* Balkanization; Balkans, the

Balkanization, 130, 134, 140, 152, 158; of analysis, 139; and Balkanism, 270n.10; and culture, 155; as a metaphor, 136, 153–54. *See also* Balkanism; Balkans, the
Balkans, the, 2, 128–29, 131, 137–41, 151–53; and ambiguity, 12, 263n.21, 271n.24; appearance and disappearance of, 14, 133, 151–53, 156, 157, 158; as bridge/crossroads, 129, 143, 154, 261n.4; and Britain, 144; as "chaos," 131–32, 213; and contested boundaries, 136; diverse explanations of, 137–41; emergence of concept of, 14, 138, 145, 146; as a fantasy, 137–38; and fractals, 14, 17, 130–31, 133, 134, 149, 150; as a gap, 88, 159; and Greece, 99; and Greek-Albanian border, 224; and Hapsburgs, 144; hegemonic concept of, 101, 129–30, 131, 140–41, 157; and maps, 30, 33, 149; as meaningless, 139–40, 142; and Mediterranean, 92–93; and modernity, 131–32, 133, 136, 156, 219, 271n.25; as "monstrous," 131, 145, 150; as mosaic/Macedonian Salad, 145; and mountains, 100; and multilingualism, 83; and Ottomans, 144; and "pet nations," 145–46; as political fault line, 130, 143, 144; proliferation of, 157; relational character of, 126, 127, 129, 138–39, 155; and Russia, 144; and safety, 225; and statistics, 169; as a "tinderbox," 109; and Tsamides, 21; as virus/toxin, 2, 131, 137; and Vlachoi, 71; and "West," 132, 138; what to expect of, 11–12, 17, 34, 59, 142, 196, 262n.19; "whereness" of, 90, 143. *See also* Balkanism; Balkanization
Ballinger, Pamela, 143, 272n.34; and hybridity, 155, 272n.30; and invention of the Balkans, 138
Barnes, J. A., 166
Barrier, G. N., 174
Basso, Keith, 89, 176
Belgrade, 270n.7
Bellier, Irene, 219
Bender, Barbara, 30
Benjamin, Walter, 5
Berati, 100
Berisha, Sali, 46, 110
Biberaj, Elez, 216, 228

Lightning Source UK Ltd.
Milton Keynes UK
UKOW02f1218120116

266260UK00001B/18/P